Legal Aspects of Marketing

JOHN LIVERMORE

LL.B., Diploma in Social Studies
Senior Lecturer in Commercial Law, Faculty of Economics & Commerce,
University of Tasmania

Published on behalf of
THE INSTITUTE OF MARKETING
and **THE CAM FOUNDATION**

FOURTH EDITION

HEINEMANN : LONDON

William Heinemann Ltd
10 Upper Grosvenor Street, London W1X 9PA

LONDON   MELBOURNE   TORONTO
JOHANNESBURG   AUCKLAND

434 91143 7 ✓

Made and printed in Great Britain by
Butler and Tanner Ltd, Frome and London

In memory of my father,
Frank Livermore

Foreword

It is a privilege to welcome and to recommend a book in which the broad scope of the subject, the depth of expert knowledge, and the clarity of style must make it a particularly valuable work not only for the marketing student but also for the experienced, practising marketing man and woman.

Increasingly, the influence of legislation is making itself felt in our everyday conduct of business affairs and it is imperative that the marketing executive—with a growing responsibility in company planning and operations—should understand the legal implications of his recommendations and decisions.

This book forms an integral part of the new series of publications designed to support the Institute of Marketing's new examinations. Our thanks are due to John Livermore for providing us with a work which is both comprehensive and practical.

PETER B. BLOOD
Director-General,
Institute of Marketing

Preface

This book is intended mainly for students taking the Part II examination of the Institute of Marketing in commercial law and has been written to cover the Institute's syllabus. In addition, students of the Institute of Purchasing and Supply taking the Legal Aspects of Purchasing and Supply paper will find that their syllabus has been taken into account. The text will prove useful also to Business Education Council students taking Marketing or Purchasing options.

Students of the Institute of Cost and Management Accountants, the Association of Certified Accountants, the Institute of Chartered Accountants in England and Wales, the Institute of Chartered Secretaries and Administrators, and the Institute of Bankers will discover useful material covering parts of their commercial law syllabuses. Lastly, but by no means least, this book is intended to serve as a basic reference work for practitioners in marketing, purchasing, and distribution.

One writer in the field once observed that writing a text on commercial law was like trying to paint the Clapham omnibus as it roared past. In the light of continued rapid change in this area, which affects Australasia as much as the United Kingdom, the experience as I see it is more akin to lying in the track of Concorde in the hope of seeing one of the hostesses. Legislation which is dealt with in this edition includes the Employment Act 1980, the Companies Act 1981, the Supply of Goods and Services Act 1982, the Civil Aviation Act 1980, the Carriage by Air and Road Act 1979, the Insurance Brokers (Registration) Act 1979, and the Insurance Companies Act 1974. Main changes are concerned with the removal of comment on the Unfair Contract Terms Act 1977 to Chapter 1 and the insertion of a new section in Chapter 8 dealing with copyright. In Chapter 12 recent cases on documentary credits have been given prominence including *Trendtex Trading Corporation v. Credit Suisse*, a case that Nigerian readers in particular (who judging from their number, have been assisted by this work) may find of interest.

Other new cases which are of special interest include *Pao On v. Lan Yin* and *North Ocean Shipping Co. Ltd. v. Hyundai* which explore the ambit of economic duress. The *Belgian Tobacco* case (FEDTAB) and the *Distillers* case (1980) concerning Article 85 are noted in Chapter 2. *Leyland Vehicles v. Jones* and *Marley Tile v. Shaw* in Chapter 3 illustrate the prominence in industrial cases of the issues of the closed shop and trade union rights and activities. Complexities in the chain of liability between manufacturer and ultimate consumer are explored in *Lambert v. Lewis* and *Lexmead (Basingstoke) Ltd. v. Lewis* in Chapter 4. The Supply of Goods and Services Act 1982 is also noted in this chapter.

The issue of the agent's commission is illustrated by a recent case *Alpha*

Trading v. Dunnshaw in Chapter 6. In Chapter 8 the topical problem of video pirating is exemplified in *Rank Film Distributors v. Video Information Centre.* Important passing off cases noted include *Erven Warnink BV, Hexagon Property v. ABC, Cadbury Schweppes Pty. v. Pub Squash Co. Ltd.*, and an Australian 'champagne' case, *Comite Interprofessionel du Vin de Champagne v. N.L. Burton Pty. Ltd.* Proposals for an E.E.C. trademark are also covered. Chapter 9 has been updated by the inclusion of two key trade description cases, *R v. Thompson Holidays* and *DPP v. Taylor.* As stated Chapter 10 includes an outline of the Companies Act 1981; overdue consolidation of company statute law is promised. Chapter 12 has been expanded to include a case clarifying the legal position concerning the use of a credit card, *R v. Lambie* and recent documentary credit cases have been noted.

The bibliography has been revised and new references added.

The law as stated is that prevailing on 1 January 1984.

JOHN LIVERMORE, LLB, Diploma in
Social Studies,
Senior Lecturer in Commercial Law,
Department of Accounting and Finance,
University of Tasmania

Acknowledgements

Acknowledgements are gratefully given to the following professional bodies for permission to reproduce questions in the text from their examination papers: the Institute of Marketing, the Institute of Purchasing and Supply, the Institute of Cost and Management Accountants, the Institute of Certified Accountants, the Institute of Chartered Accountants in England and Wales, the Institute of Chartered Secretaries and Administrators and the Institute of Bankers.

An extract from Mr. Blanco-White's authoritative work *Patents for Invention* (Stevens, 1962) is reproduced by kind permission of the publishers, Sweet and Maxwell.

I am grateful to Ms Susan Palmer-Jones of Heinemann for her continued help both with this edition and with my enquiries. I would like to express my thanks to the compiler of the table of cases and statutes and the index, Mrs Audrey Bamber, and I would also like to express my appreciation to Mr. George Atkinson, Regional Director of Forward Trust in Bristol, for copies of the guidelines issued to the company in dealing with consumer credit transactions under the 1974 Act.

Friends and colleagues who have encouraged me in my research generally, though not specifically for this work, include Dr. Bruce Felmingham, Senior Lecturer in Economics at the University of Tasmania, who has patiently explained areas of economic policy which would otherwise have remained a blank as well as demonstrating that academics need not be dull and staid. I would also like to thank Frank Bates, Reader in Law in the Faculty of Law at this University, who has always had time to criticize constructively and encourage my academic endeavours, and to Derek Roebuck, Associate Professor of Law at the University of Papua New Guinea and one-time Professor of Law here, who, with the other two worthy gentlemen, belong to a species I sometimes feel require urgent protection, namely *homines excellentissime*.

Contents

1. *Contract*

DEFINITION

A contract has been defined as 'an agreement between two or more persons which is intended by them to have legal consequence'. Not all agreements are contracts, however. In *Jones v. Vernon's Pools Ltd.*, 1938, a clause 'binding in honour only' in a football pools coupon was held to exclude legal relations. By contrast the court in another case decided that three participants had created a legal relationship by sharing the entry costs so that all were entitled to a share of the prize money (*Simpkins v. Pays*, 1955). An agreement between a husband and wife who had separated was held to have been made with the intention of creating legal relations (*Merritt v. Merritt*, 1970).

CLASSIFICATION

There are three main divisions:

(*a*) simple contracts;
(*b*) speciality contracts;
(*c*) contracts of record.

(*a*) *Simple contracts* (the most important type of contract) must possess the following essentials:

1. an offer and an unqualified acceptance;
2. valuable consideration;
3. an intention to create legal relations;
4. genuineness of consent;
5. contractual capacity of the parties to the contract;
6. legality of objects;
7. possibility of performance;
8. certainty of terms.

(*b*) *Contracts by deed* (also termed speciality contracts) are promises written on paper, signed, sealed, and delivered. Speciality contracts do not require consideration as do simple contracts, except when they are of a restrictive nature. A party to a speciality contract cannot deny the truth of the writing in the absence of fraud, mistake, misrepresentation, and other vitiating elements to be later dealt with. Additionally, an action on a speciality contract must be brought within twelve years as opposed to six for a simple contract (Limitation Act 1939).

(*c*) *Contracts of record* are not true contracts but obligations imposed by a Court of Record—e.g. a County Court or Queen's Bench Division. This type of contract is not important in the general law of contract.

1:1 OFFER AND ACCEPTANCE

(i) RULES AS TO OFFER

(a) Offer defined

1. An offer may be made orally, in writing, or implied by the conduct of the parties. All offers must be communicated to the person they are made to (the offeree) before they can be accepted. For example, a person finding an object or giving information for which a reward is offered must have notice of that offer, otherwise he has no legal claim to the reward (*Williams v. Carwardine*, 1833).

An offer may be made to:

(*a*) A specific person, when only that person may accept.
(*b*) A specific group of persons, when any person from that group may accept.
(*c*) The world at large, when anyone may accept.

Example

A woman purchased an influenza preventive from a patent medicine company. The company offered to pay £100 to anyone who contracted influenza after using their product in a specified manner after a specific period. When the company failed to pay a dissatisfied customer they were successfully sued on the grounds that the offer had been accepted by the carrying out of the conditions of use and that a £1,000 deposit with the company's bankers was a sufficient consideration to back the advertised promise.

(*Carlill v. Carbolic Smoke Ball Co. Ltd.*, 1893)

2. Invitation to treat or an invitation to make an offer must be distinguished from an offer. Commonplace examples of these are the display of goods in a shop window or in a self-service store or an auctioneer's request for bids.

Example

Goods, wrapped and priced, were displayed in a self-service shop. These were on the Poisons List and could legally be sold only under the supervision of a qualified pharmacist. In the shop such a person was in attendance at the checkout point with the cashier.

Held: When the customer took the goods from the shelves, his action amounted to an offer to buy which was accepted when payment was received by the cashier. Display of the goods did not constitute an offer by the shopkeeper to sell at the marked price.

(*Pharmaceutical Society of Great Britain v. Boots Cash Chemists (Southern) Ltd.*, 1953)

Example

A shopkeeper displayed a flick knife in his shop window with a price ticket. He was charged with offering a flick knife for sale contrary to the Restriction of Offensive Weapons Act, 1959.

Held: No offence was committed as display of goods in a shop window was not an offer for sale.

(*Fisher v. Bell*, 1961)

Example

A member of a firm of auctioneers auctioned a car. At the time of the auction the steering gear and a tyre were defective. The auctioneers were convicted of 'offering to sell' a motor vehicle for delivery in such a condition that its use on the road in that condition would be unlawful under s. 68 (1) of the Road Traffic Act 1960.

Held: An auctioneer, in carrying out his duties as an auctioneer, did not, when he stood on the rostrum, make an offer to sell the particular goods displayed. He merely invited those present at the auction to make offers to buy them. The offers came from the bidders and the auctioneer's acceptance of the final offer was communicated by the fall of his hammer. The auctioneers, therefore, were not guilty of an offence under the 1960 Act.

(*British Car Auctions v. Wright*, 1972, applying *Fisher v. Bell* and *Payne v. Cave*, 1789)

Example

A council house tenant under a local authority scheme to sell such houses applied to Manchester City Council on a printed form provided by the Council for details of the price of the house and mortgage terms available from the Council. On 10 February 1971 the City Treasurer wrote to the tenant stating that the Council '*may be prepared to sell the house* [italics provided] to you at the purchase price of £2,725 less 20% = £2,180 (freehold).' The letter gave details of the mortgage likely to be made available to the tenant and invited formal application to buy the house on an enclosed application form. The form was headed 'Application to buy a council house' and ended with the statement 'I ... now wish to purchase my council house. The above answers are correct and I agree that they shall be the basis of the arrangement regarding the purchase.' The tenant completed the form except for the purchase price and returned it to the Council on 5 March. On 18 March the tenant wrote to the Council: 'I would be obliged if you will carry on with the purchase per my application already in your possession.'

Before contracts were prepared and exchanged there was a change in control of the Council following local government elections in May 1971. On 7 July 1971 the Council resolved immediately to discontinue the scheme for the sale of council houses and proceed with sales only where there had been an exchange of contracts. On 27 July the Council wrote to the tenant to advise him that the Council could not proceed with his application to purchase.

The tenant brought an action claiming specific performance of the contract alleging that there was a binding contract for the sale of the house constituted by an offer contained in the City Treasurer's letter of 10 February and the tenant's acceptance of it by the return of the application form on 5 March and his letter of 18 March. At the court of first instance and on appeal by the Council to the Court of Appeal it was held there was a binding contract for sale. On appeal to the House of Lords:

Held: The Council and the tenant had not concluded a binding contract because the Council had never made an offer capable of acceptance, since the statements in the City Treasurer's letter of 10 February that the Council 'may be prepared to sell' and inviting the tenant to make formal application to buy were not an offer to sell but merely an invitation to treat. Accordingly the tenant was not entitled to specific performance and the Council's appeal was allowed.

(Gibson v. Manchester City Council, 1979)

3. Statement of intention distinguished.

Example

An auctioneer advertised that goods, including office furniture, would be sold at a certain place on a particular day. The plaintiff went to the sale, but the office furniture lots in which he was interested were withdrawn. He sued the auctioneer to recover damages for his loss of time and expenses.

Held: The advertising of the sale was a mere statement of an intention to hold a sale and not an offer which could be accepted to form a binding contract.

(Harris v. Nickerson, 1873)

A communication of information in the course of negotiations.

Example

An enquiry about an area of land in Jamaica was sent by telegraph which ran 'Will you sell us Bumper Hall Pen. Telegraph lowest cash price.' The land owners replied 'Lowest price for Bumper Hall Pen—£900.' The enquirers then telegraphed 'We agree to buy Bumper Hall Pen for £900 asked by you.' No reply was forthcoming, so an action to enforce the alleged contract was brought.

Held: The statement as to lowest price by the owners was a statement of the minimum price *if* the land was to be sold and *not* an offer to sell.

(Harvey v. Facey, 1893)

1:2 RULES GOVERNING ACCEPTANCE

(i) WHO MAY ACCEPT

Acceptance may be oral, written, or implied by conduct. In some circumstances it may be difficult to discover a clear acceptance in a business deal.

(ii) ACCEPTANCE MUST BE UNQUALIFIED AND UNCONDITIONAL

Acceptance must be absolute and unqualified and once acceptance is complete the offer cannot be revoked.

(a) Counter offer

A counter offer or conditional acceptance automatically rejects the original offer and the original offer cannot be revived by a purported subsequent acceptance.

Example

A farm was offered for sale at £1,000. A counter offer was made by the plaintiff for £950, but two days later he agreed to pay £1,000. On being refused completion of the sale he brought an action for specific performance.

Held: There was no binding contract between the parties as the counter offer had destroyed the original offer which could not be revived by the second offer to buy at £1,000.

(Hyde v. Wrench, 1840)

(b) Mere enquiry not a counter offer

Example

A company offered to sell iron at £2.00 a ton, offer 'open till Monday'. The firm to whom the goods were offered telegraphed 'Please wire whether you would accept forty (shillings) for delivery over two months, or if not, longest limit you could give.' No reply being received, the same firm sent a telegram early on Monday accepting the original offer and sued for breach when the iron had been sold elsewhere.

Held: The first telegram was an enquiry and not a counter offer.

(Stevenson, Jacques & Co. v. McLean, 1880)

(c) Where parties contract on each others' standard terms it will be a matter for construction by the courts as to whether one party's conditions amount to a counter offer

Example

In response to an enquiry by the buyers, the sellers sent a quotation on 23 May 1969 offering to sell a machine tool to the buyers for £75,535, to be delivered within ten months. The offer was stated to be subject to certain terms and conditions which 'shall prevail over any terms and conditions in the buyer's order'. The conditions included a price variation clause providing for the goods to be charged at the price in force on the date of delivery and provision that cancellation by the buyer for late delivery would not be accepted. The buyers placed an order for the machine on 27 May. Their order stated to be subject to certain terms and conditions which were materially different from those in the sellers' quotation. The buyers' order in particular gave them the right to cancel for late delivery and did not provide for price variation. At the bottom of the buyers' order there was a tear-off acknowledgement of receipt of order which stated 'We accept your order on the terms and conditions stated thereon'. On 5 June the sellers completed and signed the acknowledgement and returned it to the buyers with a letter stating that the buyers' order was being accepted on the *sellers'* quotation of 23 May.

The sellers, on delivering the machine, claimed the price had increased by £2,892. The buyers refused to pay this and the sellers brought an action claiming that they were entitled to increase the price under the price variation clause in their offer. The buyers argued that the contract had been concluded on their terms and not those of the sellers. In the Queen's Bench Division the sellers' claim was upheld on the basis that the sellers' terms were to prevail since they had stated this in their initial offer and all later negotiations had been subject to that. The buyers appealed.

Held: The Court of Appeal held that the buyers' order of 27 May was a counter offer which destroyed the offer made by the sellers. However, the sellers, by completing and returning the acknowledgement slip, had accepted the counter offer on the buyers' terms. Therefore the sellers could not increase the price under the price variation clause contained in their own offer.

(Butler Machine Tool Co. Ltd. v. Ex-Cell-O Corporation (England) Ltd., 1979)

It is interesting to note that Lord Denning, in the above case, felt that in a situation where there was a concluded contract but the terms varied then these had to be construed together by the court. Although the majority of the court in the *Butler* case reached their decision by strictly analysing each document, Lord Denning observed:

'... in many of our cases our traditional analysis of offer, counter offer, rejection and so forth is out of date. The better way is to look at all the documents passing between the parties and glean from them, or from the conduct of the parties, whether they have reached agreement on all material terms, even though there may be differences between the forms and conditions printed on the back of them.'

(iii) MUST BE COMMUNICATED
The offeree must positively accept; silence does not imply consent.

Example

An uncle wrote to his nephew offering to buy a horse from him, stating that 'If I hear no more about him, I consider the horse mine at £30 15*s*.' The nephew sent no reply, but told an auctioneer not to sell the horse. By mistake the horse was sold at an auction and the uncle sued the auctioneer.
Held: The uncle's offer had not been accepted as the nephew's silence did not amount to a valid acceptance.

(Felthouse v. Bindley, 1862)

(iv) MAY BE IMPLIED
If acceptance is not communicated there is no valid acceptance unless the offeror has waived communication either expressly or impliedly.

Example

A railway company was supplied with coal by a contractor and after a number of years he suggested a formal contract be drawn up between them. The draft form of agreement was accepted by the contractor who added the name of an arbitrator in a space left blank for the purpose, signed the draft and then returned it.
Held: Although mental agreement by the company to the terms of the draft as completed by the contractor was not enough, a valid contract existed from the time when the company ordered coal after receiving the draft or, at the latest, when coal was delivered.

(Brogden v. Metropolitan Railway Co., 1877)

(v) MUST REACH OFFEROR OR HIS AGENT

1:3 LAPSE OF OFFER

(i) AN OFFER WILL LAPSE IN THE FOLLOWING CIRCUMSTANCES:

(*a*) If the offeree dies before acceptance.
(*b*) If the offeror dies and the death is known to the offeree before he accepts. If the contract is not one for personal services and the offeree does not know of the death when he accepts then there is a valid agreement.
(*c*) If the offer is not accepted within the time laid down or within a reasonable time.

Example

A person offered to buy shares in a company in June and this offer was accepted in November.
Held: There had been an unreasonable delay and the offer had lapsed.
(*Ramsgate Victoria Hotel Co. v. Montefoire*, 1866)

(*d*) If the offeree does not make a valid acceptance, or makes a counter offer.

Example

An offer was made for the sale of iron by letter 'awaiting your reply by return'. The offer was not accepted by return.
Held: As the condition regarding acceptance had not been complied with there was no contract.
(*Tinn v. Hoffman*, 1873)

(ii) AN OFFER WILL BE REVOKED IN THE FOLLOWING
     CIRCUMSTANCES:

(*a*) An offer may be revoked at any time before acceptance, but to be effective the revocation must be communicated before acceptance. A revocation can be effective if the offeree learns of the revocation indirectly from a reliable source.

Example

An agreement was made to sell property, the 'offer to be left over until Friday'. On Thursday afternoon the prospective buyer learnt that the seller had contracted to sell the property to another party. On Thursday, the prospective buyer delivered an acceptance at the seller's house. When the seller went ahead with the earlier sale the plaintiff sought a decree of specific performance.
Held: The retraction of the offer was implied by the sale of the property to the third party when the offeree became aware of it.
(*Dickinson v. Dodds*, 1876)

(*b*) It should be noted that an offeror is not bound to keep an offer open for a specified period of time unless the offeree has given some consideration to keep the offer open. If an option has been purchased in this way, the offeror will be in breach of contract if he makes a sale in such circumstances.

1:4 POST RULES

Where contracts are made by letter, telegram or cable, special rules apply.

(i) An offer is effective only when it reaches the offeree, so that if the offer is incorrectly addressed it will not come into effect until received by the offeree. (ii) An acceptance is effective as soon as it is posted even though it never reaches the offeror, provided that it is correctly addressed.

Example

Shares were allotted by letter to the defendant but this never reached him.
Held: He became a member of the company when the allotment letter was posted.

(Household Fire Insurance v. Grant, 1879)

(iii) Revocation is effective when it reaches the offeree, but it must reach him before he posts his acceptance.

Example

A Cardiff businessman wrote to the plaintiff at his New York office offering to sell tin plate. On the day of receipt, the plaintiff telegraphed acceptance. Three days before this the offeror had posted a letter of revocation, which arrived after dispatch of the acceptance telegram.
Held: Offeror bound by his contract.

(Byrne v. L. Van Tienhoven, 1880)

(iv) If the express terms of an offer state that a postal acceptance must be received, an acceptance to be valid, has to conform to those terms.

Example

The defendant gave the plaintiffs an option to purchase a house, the option to be exercised within six months by notice in writing to the defendant. The plaintiffs posted a letter exercising the option and sent it by ordinary post but the letter was never received by the defendants.
Held: As the express terms laid down that acceptance should reach the offeror and this had not happened the option had not been validly exercised.

(Holwell Securities v. Hughes, 1974)

(v) If the method of acceptance has been laid down, but not in terms insisting that only that method is binding, any other method communicated to the offeror which is no less disadvantageous to him will create a binding contract.

Example

The conditions of sale of a school by tender included one condition that provided that the person whose offer was accepted should be notified by letter sent to him by post at the address given in his tender. Every letter would be 'deemed to have been received in due course of post'. On 26 August 1964 the defendant posted a tender offering £28,500. On 15 September the seller's surveyor wrote to the defendant's surveyors stating that the seller had accepted the defendant's offer. After Ministerial approval for the sale had been obtained the seller's solicitors informed the defendant's solicitors of this and asked them to confirm that there was a binding contract. On 5 January the defendant's solicitors replied that they were unable to confirm there was a binding contract. The plaintiff's solicitors then, on 7 January 1965, sent a formal letter of acceptance to the defendant at the address given in the tender. On the same day the defendant wrote purporting to withdraw the offer. The plaintiff sought a declaration, specific performance, and damages in that a binding contract existed by the tender on the letters of 15 September or 7 January.

Held: Where an offer lays down a specific mode of acceptance, but does not stipulate that only acceptance in that mode shall be binding, acceptance in any other mode not less advantageous to the offeror will create a binding contract. The letter of 15 September constituted sufficient communication of acceptance.

(*Manchester Diocesan Council for Education v. Commercial & General Investments Ltd.*, 1970)

(iv) ACCEPTANCE SUBJECT TO CONTRACT

This is a conditional acceptance and indicates that the parties are not prepared to be bound until a formal contract is prepared and signed by them. In *Eccles v. Bryant and Pollock*, 1948, a sale of a house on the terms 'subject to contract' was not a contract. The courts have accepted the words 'subject to contract' as indicating that there is still something to be agreed to by the parties and until that has been finally agreed there will be no legally binding agreement between the parties. Where in a written agreement the words 'provisional agreement' are used the courts are likely to construe this as being an agreement binding on the parties, though subsequently to be replaced by a formal contract.

(v) TENDERS

A tender is an offer for the supply of goods and services and is usually made in response to a request for tenders. Tenders take the following forms:

(a) Single tender

Acceptance of such a tender results in a contract—as in the case of the supply of a certain number of articles in one consignment.

(b) Standing offer

There are two possible cases. If the tender is in response to an invitation to supply goods '*if* and when required', so-called 'acceptance' of the tender does not convert it into a binding agreement and the tenderer cannot insist upon orders being placed. Each order placed is an individual act of acceptance which creates a separate contract. But if the tender is in response to an invitation for the definite supply of a stated quantity of goods to be delivered '*as* and when required', acceptance of the tender creates a binding contract and the tenderer is obliged to supply in those terms.

Example

A firm submitted a tender to the L.C.C. for supply of goods 'in such quantities and at such times and in such manner as the Committee shall from time to time determine'. The tender was accepted but no orders were placed. The firm sued for breach of contract.

Held: As the terms of the tender were not certain, no contract was formed on the acceptance of the tender. The tender was a standing offer that only became a contract on the placing of a specific order.

(Percival v. L.C.C., 1918)

(c) Sole supplier

The person requesting the tender agrees to take all his requirements in certain goods if he should need them. This does not mean any orders must be placed, but if any goods are required they must be purchased from the tenderer.

1:5 STANDARD FORM CONTRACTS

Where a document is used as a contractual document the offeree is held to be bound by all the conditions contained in the document even though he has not read them.

Example

A customer ordered an automatic slot machine by signing a form which contained the following terms in small print—'Any express or implied condition, statement or warranty . . . is hereby excluded'. The customer claimed damages when the machine, after delivery, failed to work satisfactorily.
Held: Since there had been no misrepresentation and the customer had signed the agreement the terms were binding on her.

(L'Estrange v. F. Graucob Ltd., 1934)

(i) EXEMPTION CLAUSES

(a) Notice of the conditions must be available at the time of making the contract

Example

A couple booked a room in a hotel at the reception desk. In the bedroom a notice excluded liability for the theft of valuables. The wife had her furs stolen.
Held: The contract took place at reception and there had been insufficient notice of the exclusion notice.

(Olley v. Marlborough Court Ltd., 1949)

(b) The offeree must have had reasonable notice of the conditions

Example

An illiterate woman asked a relative to buy a rail excursion ticket for her. On the face of the ticket were the words 'Excursion. For conditions see back.' On the back it stated the ticket was issued subject to conditions in the company's timetables. These excluded liability for personal injury. The woman was injured.
Held: Her illiteracy made no difference to the legal position. She was bound by the contract which had incorporated the exclusion clause by reference to the timetables.

(Thompson v. L.M.S. Railway Ltd., 1930)

(c) The document must be a contractual one and not a mere receipt

Example

A man hired a deck chair. A notice near the stack stated 'Hire of Chairs—2*d*. [1p] per session of 3 hours'. He hired two chairs, paid his money, and received a ticket which he did not read. The reverse of the ticket contained a clause excluding liability for any damage or injury caused by a chair being defective. The chair broke and the hirer injured his back.

Held: The exclusion clause had no effect as it was not part of a contractual document—the ticket was a mere receipt.

(Chapelton v. Barry Urban District Council, 1940)

(d) Terms of the contract containing the exemption clause strictly construed against the parties in whose favour it is drawn

Example

The plaintiff hired a tradesman's cycle to deliver newspapers on terms that provided 'Nothing in this agreement shall render the owners liable for any personal injuries to the riders of the machine hired'. The defendants on their part contracted 'to maintain the machine in working order'.

Held: The clause would protect the defendants from breach of contractual obligation to maintain the cycle, but would not exclude liability in tort if negligence could be established.

(White v. John Warwick & Co. Ltd., 1953)

Example

The plaintiff drove his car to an automatic car park. A notice outside included the words 'All cars parked at owner's risk'. A machine delivered a ticket which stated it was issued subject to conditions displayed on the premises. Conditions displayed only inside the garage stated that the company were excluded from liability for damage to cars *and* injury caused to a customer while his car was in the park. On returning to his car the plaintiff was injured by the negligence of the defendants.

Held: The offer was displayed on the machine and accepted by the customer driving into the entrance and taking the ticket from the machine. The words printed on the ticket could not alter the contract, the terms of which were restricted to those on the outside notice relating to damage to cars.

(Thornton v. Shoe Lane Parking Co. Ltd., 1971)

(But now see the Unfair Contract Terms Act 1977 s. 2; 1:6.)

(e) Agents' or employees' representations

Where an agent or employee of a firm makes a representation about the effect of the exemption clause this can over-ride the effect of the clause itself.

Example

A dress was taken to a dry cleaners for cleaning. The receipt contained words excluding liability for damage. The customer asked what this meant, was told that it only related to beads and sequins on the dress. She then signed the receipt. The dress came back badly stained.

Held: The exclusion clause did not protect the firm as they had misrepresented its effect in persuading the customer to sign.

(*Curtis v. Chemical Cleaning & Dyeing Co. Ltd.,* 1951)

(ii) FUNDAMENTAL BREACH

(*a*) *No reliance on exclusion clause*

It is important to note that an offeror may not be able to rely on an exclusion clause if he is in fundamental breach of the contract.

Example

A customer entered into a hire purchase agreement for the purchase of a second-hand car which at the time of inspection was in working order. The contract contained a clause exempting all conditions and warranties as to roadworthiness of the vehicle. At night the car was left at the customer's house and he found the car so defective that it could not be driven.

Held: There was a fundamental breach of the contract and the customer was not liable on the agreement, for the company could not rely on the exemption clause. 'A car that will not go is no car at all.'

(*Karsales (Harrow) Ltd. v. Wallis,* 1956)

(*b*) *Question of construction*

It is a question of construction in each case as to whether a clause will exempt or limit liability for fundamental breach.

Example

A ship was chartered from a company to carry cargo from America to Europe. The charter party (marine contract) contained a demurrage clause (allowing for delay time) which laid down that $1,000 a day would be paid for demurrage. The chartering company delayed in loading and discharge of the cargo and after dispute the charter party was reaffirmed. When the agreement terminated the owners sued the chartering company for damages in excess of the demurrage clause provision, claiming that the clause did not apply as there had been a fundamental breach.

Held: The owners having affirmed the charter party were bound by its terms, including demurrage provisions, which were for payment of agreed damages. The delays were not a breach of a fundamental term of the contract.

A fundamental term was either:

1. A breach of contract more serious than one entitling the other party to damages only.
2. A performance totally different from that contemplated by the contract.

(*The Suisse Atlantique,* 1966)

It is now clearly established by a recent House of Lords decision, *Photo Production Ltd. v. Securicor Transport Ltd.,* that there is no rule of law by which exemption clauses are eliminated, or deprived of their effect, regardless of their terms. This decision firmly rejected the argument, mainly advanced by Lord Denning in previous cases, that fundamental breach is a rule of law. The House of Lords in the *Photo Production* case overturned the earlier decision of the Court of Appeal and expressly overruled *Harbutt's Plasticine Ltd. v. Wayne Tank and Pump Co. Ltd.*, 1970 and *Wathes (Western) Ltd. v. Austin (Menswear) Ltd.* 1976. In doing so their Lordships approached the question of whether an exemption clause applied when there was fundamental breach as turning on the construction of the whole contract.

Example

The plaintiffs owned a factory and contracted with Securicor to provide security at the factory, including night patrols. While carrying out a night patrol at the factory a Securicor patrolman deliberately lit a fire which got out of control and completely destroyed the factory and the stock valued at £615,000. Securicor were sued for damages by the plaintiffs on the ground that they were liable for the act of their employee. Securicor pleaded, amongst other defences, that an exemption clause in the contract absolved them from any liability for any injurious act or default by any employee unless such act or default could have been foreseen or avoided by due care on the part of Securicor. Securicor, under this clause, disclaimed liability for any loss suffered by the plaintiffs through fire or any other cause except where this was attributable to negligence of Securicor's employees acting in the course of their employment.

Securicor were held not to have been negligent in employing the patrolman and the trial judge held that Securicor could rely on the exemption clause. On appeal by the factory owners the Court of Appeal reversed the lower court's decision, holding that Securicor were in fundamental breach of the contract which prevented them from relying on the exemption clause. The factory owners then appealed to the House of Lords.

Held: (i) There was no rule of law by which an exemption clause in a contract could be removed from a consideration of the parties' position when there was a breach of contract (whether fundamental or not) or by which an exemption clause could be deprived of effect regardless of the contract's terms. This was so because the parties were free to choose to exclude or modify their contractual obligations. Whether an exemption clause applied when there was a fundamental breach, breach of a fundamental term, or any other breach, turned on the construction of the whole contract, including any exemption clause.

(ii) Although Securicor were in breach of their implied obligation to operate their service with due and proper regard to the safety and security of the plaintiff's factory and premises, Securicor were protected from liability by a clear and unambiguous exemption clause.

The House of Lords expressed the view that in commercial matters generally, when parties were not of unequal bargaining power and risks were normally covered by insurance, the parties should be left to apportion risks as they saw fit.

Per Lord Wilberforce: 'In commercial contracts negotiated between businessmen capable of looking after their own interests and deciding how risks inherent in the performance of various kinds of contract can be most economically borne (generally by insurance) it is, in my view, wrong to place a strained construction on words in an exclusion clause which are clear and fairly susceptible of one meaning only even after due allowance has been made for the presumption in favour of the implied primary and secondary obligations.'

(*Photo Productions Ltd. v. Securicor Transport Ltd.*, 1980)

However and exemption clause does not, of itself, defend a party who has committed a fundamental breach:

Example

Farmers agreed to buy cabbage seed from merchants with whom they had dealt for some years. The sale was subject to the merchants' standard terms and conditions. One of these stated: 'In the event of any seeds sold by us not complying with the express terms of the contract of sale or any seeds proving defective in varietal purity we will refund all payments made to us by the buyer in respect of the seeds and this shall be the limit of our obligation. We hereby exclude all liability for any loss or damage arising from the use of any seeds supplied by us and for any consequential loss or damage arising out of such use or of any defects in any seeds supplied by us or from any other loss or damage whatsoever save for refund as aforesaid.' Both parties knew that the seeds sold were for winter white cabbage and the merchants knew the farmers normally sowed the cabbage in seed beds in March and transplanted in June and July. The merchants also knew that the cabbage was for human consumption. The farmers planted about sixty acres and the seeds germinated. In September it was noticed that the cabbages were of lush growth with loose fluffy hearts. The merchants agreed, after discussions with the farmers, that what had been grown was not suitable for either human or animal consumption and that they, the merchants, had sold seed wholly different in kind by description and commercially. In response to a claim by the farmers for damages the merchants held that they were protected by the exemption clause and liable only for £200, the cost of the seeds.

Held: On the facts the seed supplied was in no sense vegetable seed at all and the clause could not be construed to cover that situation. Delivery was of something wholly different in kind from that which was ordered and which the merchant had agreed to supply. It was making commercial nonsense of the contract to suggest that either party could have intended that the clause was to operate in the circumstances of the case. In looking at a commercial contract the terms had to be construed in a commercial sense. What was delivered was not vegetable seed at all and the merchants could not rely on their conditions.

(*George Mitchell (Chesterhall) Ltd v. Finney Lock Seeds Ltd*, affirmed by the House of Lords, 1983)

An exemption clause may become incorporated in a contract where the parties usually expect such terms to be included and they are, as may be in the case of two businesses, of equal bargaining power.

Example

A dragline crane was hired by the plaintiff to the defendants, who had had two previous dealings with the plaintiff in the same year on terms that included the following condition: 'The hirer shall be responsible for and indemnify the former owner against ... all expenses in connection with or arising out of the use of the plant.' The agreement in question had been arranged by telephone. After delivery of the crane a printed form was sent by the plaintiff, which contained the conditions of hire including the condition quoted, which the defendants neither signed nor returned to the plaintiff. The crane sank in marsh near Ipswich while being operated and was extracted at great expense. The question of liability for meeting this cost fell to be decided.

Held: The defendants were liable for the cost of retrieving the crane as the term had been incorporated by a previous course of dealings. As each party were plant hirers they knew that conditions of hire similar to those in the agreement at issue were customarily laid down.

(*British Crane Hire Corporation v. Ipswich Plant Hire Ltd.*, 1974)

Note: It is no longer possible to exclude fundamental breach of contract in standard written business transactions with a consumer under s. 3 (1) of the Unfair Contract Terms Act 1977. This statutory reform significantly cuts down the importance of the fundamental breach doctrine (*see* 1 : 6).

(iii) INDEMNITY CLAUSES

Indemnity clauses effectively operate as provisions restricting a right or a remedy. Therefore they fall within the definition of an exemption clause, that is, any term in a contract excluding, restricting or modifying a remedy or liability arising out of a breach of a contractual obligation.

A contracting party, *A*, may attempt to avoid the consequences of liability by making the person with whom he contracts, *B*, bear the loss resulting from his, *A*'s, own breach of duty. For example, a car ferry operator may contract with a car owner on terms that the latter will indemnify the operator against third party claims arising from damage caused to other cars or their occupants on the ferry by the negligent positioning of the car by the operator's employees. A clause may exceptionally require *A* to indemnify *B* against liability *B* incurs to *A*, so that if *A* sues *B*, *A* has to pay back to *B* what he recovers from *B*: in effect 'a boomerang clause'. (But see 1 : 6 for the effect on such a clause in a *consumer* contract of the *Unfair Contract Terms Act* 1977, ss. 4 & 13.) The effect of a 'boomerang' clause was considered by the House of Lords in a standard form commercial contract.

Example

Chrysler (Scotland) Ltd contracted with the defendants on the basis of Chrysler's standard form general conditions of contract. The contract included the following clause: 'In the event of the order involving the carrying out of work by the supplier and its subcontractors on land and/or premises of the purchaser, the supplier will keep the purchaser indemnified against: (a) All losses and costs incurred by reason of the supplier's breach of any statute, bye-law or regulation;

(b) Any liability, loss, claim or proceedings whatsoever under statute or common law (i) in respect of personal injury to, or death of any person whomsoever, (ii) in respect of any injury or damage whatsoever to any property, real or personal, arising out of this or in the course of or caused by the execution of this order. The supplier will insure against and cause all subcontractors to insure against their liability hereunder.'

In carrying out the work at Chrysler's premises an employee of South Wales Switchgear suffered injury due to an accident caused by negligence and breach of statutory duty by Chrysler. Chrysler claimed to be indemnified in respect of the liability by virtue of the indemnity clause quoted above.

Held: In allowing the appeal by the supplier, the House of Lords held that the clause, on its true construction, was to be determined on the basis of tests laid down in *Canada Steamship Co. Ltd. v. The King* that applied equally to exemption and indemnity clauses. On this basis the clause did not provide indemnity against Chrysler's own negligence. This was so because (i) no such express provision was made for such an indemnity; (ii) the words 'any liability ... whatsoever ... under common law ... in respect of personal injury' although wide enough to cover Chrysler's own negligence, did so only in respect of its liability for the acts and omissions of South Wales Switchgear's employees and not for Chrysler's liability for their own employees; (iii) the head of damages under common law liability for personal injury might be based on a ground other than Chrysler's own negligence.

(Smith v. South Wales Switchgear Co. Ltd., 1978)

(iv) LEGISLATION ON EXEMPTION CLAUSES

The Law Commission has reported on exemption clauses and their specific recommendations that these should be invalid in sale of goods contracts with consumers have been incorporated in the Supply of Goods (Implied Terms) Act 1973 (*see* Chapter 2).

1:6 UNFAIR CONTRACT TERMS ACT 1977

This Act, which came into effect on 1 February 1978, is based upon the recommendations of the 1975 Law Commission Second Report on Exception Clauses and seeks to impose further limits on the extent to which civil liability is incurred for breach of contract, or for negligence, or other causes. Under the Act it is no longer possible to exclude liability for death or personal injury in any contract or notice. Similarly, exclusion of liability for loss or damage caused by negligence (other than death or injury) will not be possible unless it passes a reasonableness test laid down by the Act and interpreted by the courts. All business dealings which use standard form contracts, subject to exceptions, and all trade contracts with consumers, must also pass this statutory reasonableness test where the contract purports to avoid liability for breach of contract as well as fundamental breach. The Act specifically excludes certain contracts from its provisions, including those of insurance and travel by sea and scheduled air services.

Exemption clauses in contracts in general are affected by the Unfair Contract Terms Act which came into force on 1 February 1978- Part I, which affects the law in England, Wales and Northern Ireland, makes changes in contracts that contain exemption clauses relating to negligence and deals with guarantees in consumer sale of goods contracts. Such exemption clauses as well as those in hire purchase and sale of goods contracts are subjected to a 'reasonableness' test. The legislation does not apply to insurance and certain international contracts (such as travel by sea and scheduled airlines) or to sales by auction or competitive tender (s. 12 (2)).

(i) NEGLIGENCE

In the case of exemption for negligence this is defined as the breach of any obligation, arising from the express or implied terms of a contract, to take reasonable care or exercise reasonable skill in the performance of the contract or of any common law duty to take reasonable care or exercise reasonable skill or of the common duty of care (s. 1 (1)) imposed by the Occupiers' Liability Act 1957. Liability under the Act for breach of obligations or duties arises only from things done or to be done in the course of business (whether a person's own business or another's; business as defined includes professional, local government and public authority activities (s. 14), or from occupation of premises used for the business purposes of the occupier (s. 1 (3)).

For the purposes of the Act it is immaterial whether the breach is inadvertent or intentional, or whether liability arises directly or vicariously (*see* 3 : 5). A person cannot exclude or restrict his liability for death or personal injury resulting from negligence by reference to any contract term or notice given to persons (s. 2 (1)). In the case of other loss or damage, a person cannot exclude or restrict his liability for death or personal injury except so far as the term or notice satisfies the requirement of reasonableness (s. 2 (2)) (*see* below). A person's agreement to, or awareness of, a contract or notice (written or oral; s. 14) purporting to exclude or restrict liability for negligence is not taken as indicating his voluntary acceptance of any risk (s. 2 (3)). The effect of s. 2 renders ineffective car park notices of the type in *Thornton's* case (*see* 1 : 5), exempting liability for injury. In the case of loss or damage to a car, in such an example, the exemption term is subject to a reasonableness test (*see* vii). Importantly, s. 2 (3) nullified the effect of extensive case law dealing with the question of notice of such terms (*see* Chapter 1). Notice no longer, under the legislation, constitutes acceptance of the exemption term.

(ii) LIABILITY IN CONTRACT

Where parties contract with each other, one as a consumer on the other's written standard terms of business the latter cannot exclude or restrict his liability for breach of contract, when in breach, or claim to be entitled to render either a substantially different contractual performance from that reasonably expected of him or to render no performance at all in relation to part or all the contract (s. 3 (1)). Effectively this provision means that it is no longer possible to exclude fundamental breach of contract in a standard written business transaction (*see* 1 : 5).

(iii) LIABILITY FOR LOSS ARISING FROM SALE OR SUPPLY OF GOODS

Liability for loss or damage cannot be excluded or restricted by reference to any contract term or notice contained in or operating by reference to a guarantee of goods. Such goods are limited by definition to those of a type ordinarily supplied for private use and consumption; the loss or damage must arise from the goods proving defective while in consumer use, and result from the negligence of a person concerned in the manufacture or distribution of the goods (s. 5(1)). Goods are regarded 'as in consumer use' when a person has use or possession of them other than for exclusive business purposes. A guarantee includes anything in writing which contains or purports to contain a promise or assurance, irrespective of wording and presentation, the defects will be completely or partly replaced, repaired or compensated monetarily (s. 5(2)). Section 5 does not apply between parties where possession or ownership of the goods has passed (*see* 4:4). The problems of distinguishing consumer from business use which arise from interpreting this section are similar to those already discussed above (*see* 4:7). Dealing as a consumer is defined as where a person does not make a contract in the course of business or holds himself out as doing so, where the other party makes the contract in the course of business, and where the goods (in sale of goods or hire purchase agreement) are of the type ordinarily supplied for private use or consumption (s. 12). If a part-time electrical contractor used a drill for both private *and* business use the goods would be regarded as in consumer use as he would not be using them exclusively for his business. Difficulties could arise where goods are borrowed from firms (tools, car, machines, typewriters, etc.) for private use by employees. Would their use cease to be for exclusively business purposes in such cases, even though the goods in question had originally been purchased for the firm's use? Importantly the section extends to supply which includes hire and so, for the first time, extends statutory protection for loss or damage to the hirer of consumer goods (*see* 4:11).

(iv) SALE AND HIRE PURCHASE

Liability for breach of implied terms in any sale of goods and hire purchase contracts cannot be excluded or restricted by reference to any contract term as against a person dealing as a consumer (s. 5(1), (2)). Where a person deals other than a consumer such exclusions or restrictions are judged by a reasonableness test (s. 6(3)). In cases where possession or ownership of goods passes in a consumer contract that is not governed by sale of goods or hire purchase law (as in simple hiring) implied terms as to the good's correspondence with description or sample, or quality or fitness for any particular purpose cannot be excluded. Liability in respect of title or quiet possession can be excluded only in so far as the term meets the test of reasonableness. This proviso applies to business contracts as far as exclusion of the implied terms are concerned apart from those dealing with title and quiet possession (s. 7).

(*Note:* this section has no application to goods passing on redemption within the Trading Stamps Act 1965.)

(v) MISREPRESENTATION

The Misrepresentation Act 1967 (*see* p. 36) is amended by substitution for s. 3 of that Act, which deals with exclusion of liability for misrepresentation, of a new section which renders ineffective a term excluding or restricting any liability of a party to a contract for pre-contractual misrepresentation or any remedy available to another party as a result of such a misrepresentation. However, it is open to a person claiming that such a term is reasonable to show that it passes the reasonableness test.

(vi) ARBITRATION OF DIFFERENCES IN CONSUMER DEALINGS

An agreement to refer future differences to arbitration against a person dealing as a consumer cannot be enforced except where that person gives his written consent after differences have arisen or where he has sought arbitration under the agreement (s. 10). This section has no effect on the enforcement of non-domestic (i.e. ordinary commercial) arbitration agreements to which s. 1 of the Arbitration Act 1975 applies or to contracts excluded under Schedule 1 of the Act (these include insurance and land contracts, contracts for creation, transfer or termination of a right or interest in any patent, trade mark, copyright, registered design, technical or commercial information or other intellectual property).

(vii) THE REASONABLENESS TEST

The reasonableness test, to which reference has been made frequently, is contained in s. 11. The guidelines for the test are laid down in Schedule 2 and these are identical to s. 4 of the Supply of Goods (Implied Terms) Act 1973 amending s. 55 of the Sale of Goods Act which has already been discussed (s. 55(5), *see* 4:7). In general the requirement of reasonableness for the purposes of the Act is that the term shall have been a fair and reasonable one to be included having regard to the circumstances which were, or ought reasonably to have been, known to or in the contemplation of the parties when the contract was made. Section 11(3) requires in respect of notices relating to exclusion for negligence that it should be fair and reasonable to allow reliance on the notice, having regard to all the circumstances obtaining when the liability arose, or (but for the notice) would have arisen.

Where restriction of liability to a specified sum of money is sought by reference to a contract term or notice in determining the question of reasonableness (without ruling out the possibility of a court or arbitrator declaring an exclusionary or restrictive term as not being a term of the contract) regard will be given to:

(*a*) the resources of a person seeking the enforcement of the restriction to meet liability if it arose; and
(*b*) how far it was given to him to cover himself by insurance (s. 11 (4)).

Exclusion or restriction of liability is prevented from being subject to restrictive or onerous conditions, excluding or restricting any right or remedy in respect of the liability or subjecting a person pursuing such to any prejudice, or excluding or restricting rules of evidence or procedure (s. 13). This provision does not apply to written agreements to submit present or future differences to arbitration. The reasonableness test has been judicially considered in two cases.

Example

A motor yacht was built by a Norfolk boat yard and sold for cash to J.C.L. Marine. On her maiden voyage the vessel caught fire off the Kent coast and sank. The occupants escaped, but their personal possessions were lost. The fire, it was found, was due to defective electrical wiring in the yacht. It was undisputed that the sale was in the course of business and the yacht constituted 'goods of a type ordinarily bought for private use and consumption'. The status of the buyer was the essence of the case; were the goods sold to a person who did 'not buy or hold himself out as buying in the cause of business'? The purchaser who had previously purchased a similar yacht from the defendants, decided, while the yacht in question was under construction, to purchase it through a company (Rasbora Ltd.) solely owned by himself to be incorporated in Jersey. This was done in order to avoid a large amount of V.A.T. on the vessel. J.C.L. Marine had no objection to this method of payment.

Held: The contract was one of a consumer sale, although the purchase was apparently made by the company. The original contract between J.C.L. Marine and the purchaser had been a consumer sale and the rights and duties passed to the company by novation, remaining those of a consumer sale. Even if the company could be regarded as the purchaser (which the judge Lawson J. held not to be the case) the sale would nonetheless have been a consumer sale. It was also held (obiter) that even if the sale were not a consumer sale, it would not, in all the circumstances, be fair or reasonable to permit the seller to rely on the exclusion clause as the vessel was totally destroyed.

(*Rasbora Ltd. v. J.C.L. Marine*, 1977)

It is difficult to see any real merit in this case as an instance of any realistic issue being raised of consumer protection. Although remarks in the case concerning the application of the reasonableness test were obiter it seems that on the facts both parties were at arms' length, there was no inequality of bargaining power and insurance had covered a risk clearly allocated by an exemption clause in the contract of sale.

A more carefully argued application of the reasonableness test can be found in a case concerning the supply of goods under a standard form contract.

Example

The plaintiffs, seed potato merchants, regularly did business with the defendants on the basis of the standard conditions of the National Association of Seed Potato Merchants (NASPM). These conditions provided that 'notification of rejection, claim of complaint must be made to the seller within three days after the arrival of the seed at its destination' and that any claim to compensation should not amount to more than the contract price of potatoes. In the case of one of three contracts for the sale of twenty tons of seed potatoes, eight months after delivery it appeared that they were infected by a potato virus (virus Y) that could not be detected by inspection at the time of delivery. The plaintiffs sued for the price of the potatoes and the defendants counter-claimed for loss of profits.

Held: The defendant's counter-claim for damages for breach of s. 14 of the Sale of Goods act was allowed. These were, however, limited to the price of the potatoes and set off against the plaintiff's claim for the price. There were no grounds for holding the limitation clause restricting claims to the contract price to be unreasonable. Although it would have been difficult for the buyers to obtain seed potatoes otherwise than on the NASPM conditions, it was possible to obtain seed stock certified as virus free by the Ministry of Agriculture at a much higher price. The standard conditions had been the subject of discussion between the Association and the National Farmers Union; they were not conditions imposed by the strong upon the weak but were rather a set of trading terms on which both sides were apparently content to do business. However, it was a different matter in respect to the requirement that complaints be made within three days of delivery. The plaintiffs had argued that it was quite reasonable, given that potatoes are a very perishable commodity, that all risks be carried by the buyer within a short time of delivery. This would be an acceptable argument in relation to defects such as a virus infection, which was not discoverable on inspection, within the time allowed by the contract. That part of the clause was held to be unreasonable and could not be relied on.

(*R. W. Green Ltd v. Cade Bros. Farm*, 1978)

1:7 CONSIDERATION

All simple contracts must be supported by consideration, that is some element of exchange which is measurable in money or money's worth—e.g. goods in return for cash. It is important to note that a contract for the sale of goods which comes within the Sale of Goods Act 1893 must always be paid for by money. Once there is consideration present in a contract, with the other essentials present, then in the absence of fraud, misrepresentation or mistake, the court will enforce the agreement.

(i) DEFINITION

Consideration has been defined as 'some right, interest, profit, or benefit accruing to the one party or some forebearance, detriment loss or responsibility given, suffered or undertaken by another'.

(Luck, J. in *Currie v. Misa*, 1875)

A simpler definition by Sir Frederick Pollock, is 'the price for which a promise is bought'.

(ii) TYPES OF CONSIDERATION

There are two types of consideration:

(*a*) Executory consideration—where the consideration consists of a promise to do something in the future, e.g. deliver goods.

(*b*) Executed consideration—where the act constituting the consideration is wholly performed—e.g. actual payment for goods delivered.

(iii) CONSIDERATION MUST NOT BE VAGUE OR INDEFINITE

Example

A father promised not to sue his son on a promissory note if the latter in return promised not to bore him with his complaints.
Held: No contract as the consideration was too vague.

(*White v. Bluett*, 1853)

(iv) CONSIDERATION MUST BE LEGAL

That is it must not be a contract to commit an illegal act (*see* illegal contracts).

(v) CONSIDERATION MUST MOVE FROM THE PROMISEE

That means that a person seeking to enforce a simple contract must prove that he has given consideration in return for the promise which he is seeking to enforce.

Example

A father entered an agreement with his son's father-in-law whereby each was to pay a sum of money to the son. The father-in-law never paid and the son-in-law brought an action against the executors of the father-in-law on his death for the money.
Held: Even though made for his benefit the son was 'a stranger to the contract' and could not therefore take advantage of it.

(*Tweddle v. Atkinson*, 1861)

But performance of a contractual duty owed to a third party can be good consideration for a promise.

Example

An uncle promised to pay his nephew, who was about to marry, an annual sum of £150 during his uncle's lifetime. The nephew married and sued on the promise.
Held: The nephew's marriage involving a material and financial change in his life was sufficient consideration for the uncle's promise.

(*Shadwell v. Shadwell*, 1860)

The doctrine of privity of contract—that no stranger to a contract can sue or be sued on the contract—is of considerable commercial importance:

Example

Chemical drums were sent by ship to a firm. A clause in the Bill of Lading limited the shipowners' liability to $500. A firm of stevedores unloaded the ship provided they could take benefit of the limiting clause. Drums valued at $1,700 were damaged by negligence of the stevedoring firm and the firm due to take delivery, unaware of the agreement between the shipowners and the stevedoring firm, sued the latter.
Held: The stevedoring firm were not party to the Bill of Lading and could not take benefit of the limiting clause.

(*Midland Silicones Ltd. v. Scruttons Ltd.*, 1962)

The problem of finding the element of consideration necessary to create a contractual relationship between stevedores and owners of goods was overcome in a decision by the Privy Council where the carrier was regarded as an agent of the stevedores in question.

Example

Stevedores employed by the carrier negligently damaged costly drilling machinery, owned by the plaintiffs, while unloading it in New Zealand. The bill of lading contained a clause expressly limiting the liability of any servant or agent of the carrier or any independent contractor employed by him. The stevedores sought protection of the exemption clause in an action against them by the owners of the equipment for negligence.

Held: An offer shown by the bill of lading was made by the owner through the carrier to the agents or servants of the latter (the stevedores) that, if they, the stevedores as agents of the carriers, performed their duties in relation to the goods they would be exempted from liability by the owners. Consideration was found in the agreement to perform an act which the promisor was under an existing obligation to a third party to do.

(New Zealand Shipping Corporation Co. Ltd. v. A. M. Satterthwaite & Co. Ltd., 1974)

The Privy Council applied the principles of the case above when it recently considered whether a stevedore was entitled to protection of an exemption clause in a bill of lading.

Example

A consignment of razor-blades was shipped on board a vessel for transshipment from Canada to Australia. At the port of discharge, Sydney, a stevedoring company acted for the carrier. The bill of lading extended the benefit of defences and immunities in the bill to independent contractors employed by the carrier. The bill of lading provided amongst other matters that the carrier's responsibility ended as soon as the goods left the ship's tackle. The bill of lading also barred any action not brought within one year after the delivery of the goods (or the date when they should have been delivered). On arrival in Sydney the consignment was discharged from the ship and placed by the stevedore in a shed on the wharf under its control. When the consignee presented the bill of lading the goods were found to be stolen from the wharf, having been delivered by servants of the stevedore to persons who had no right to them. An appeal by the consignee from the court of first instance to the Supreme Court of New South Wales was allowed on the ground that there was no proof of consideration moving from the stevedore to entitle it to the defences in the bill of lading. The High Court of Australia dismissed an appeal by the stevedore which then appealed to the Privy Council.

Held: The stevedores could claim exemption from liability on the basis of the clause in the bill of lading barring an action after one year after delivery of the goods. The appeal would be allowed for reasons including the following:

It was established law that in the normal situation involving the employment of a stevedore by a carrier, commercial practice required the stevedores to enjoy the benefit of contractual provisions in the bill of lading. Shippers, carriers and stevedores knew that such immunity was intended, in principle it was unnecessary to search for the factual ingredients to confer the benefit. In the case at issue, agency had been found as fact and according to established legal principles consideration had been provided by the stevedore.

(*The New York Star*, 1980)

Exceptions

(*a*) s. 27 (2), Bills of Exchange Act 1882, provides that a holder can sue on a bill without proof that he gave consideration personally.

(*b*) s. 25 (1), Restrictive Trade Practices Act 1956 (saving the case of exempted goods under the Resale Prices Act 1964), provides that when goods are sold by a supplier subject to a resale price maintenance agreement the conditions of that agreement can be enforced against any person not a party to the original sale who subsequently acquires the goods with notice of the conditions; e.g. a wholesaler, retailer, manufacturer.

(vi) CONSIDERATION MUST BE REAL, BUT NEED NOT BE ADEQUATE

Example

A widow had been promised by her husband that she should have the house in which he lived or £100. The executors promised to convey the house to her provided she paid £1 a year in rent and kept the house in repair. The executors breached the agreement.

Held: £1 a year rent was 'something of value in the eyes of the law', i.e. consideration.

(*Thomas v. Thomas*, 1842)

Even where a contract requires articles to be sent which are later dispensed within, such articles may validly be part of the total consideration.

Example

The plaintiffs owned the copyright in a tune called 'Rockin Shoes'. This was recorded by another firm who sold the records to the defendants at 4*d* each. These records were advertised to the public at 1*s*. 6*d*. each but three wrappers from Nestlé products were also required. The plaintiffs sued Nestlé for breach of copyright, who pleaded s. 8 of the Copyright Act 1956, which provided that recordings of musical work could be made for retail sale provided the owners of the copyright were paid a royalty of 6¼ per cent of the ordinary retail selling price. The question arose as to whether this royalty was based on the 1*s*. 6*d*. per record or whether the wrappers which were thrown away after receipt by Nestlé were part of the consideration as claimed by the plaintiffs.

Held: The plaintiff's claim would succeed as the wrappers were part of the consideration; '... a peppercorn does not cease to be good consideration if it is established that the promisee does not like pepper and will throw away the corn' (Lord Somervell).

(*Chappell & Co. Ltd. v. Nestlé Co. Ltd.*, 1959)

The courts are not concerned with the commercial adequacy of what is put forward as consideration, but they have laid down guide lines as to what may be insufficient:

(*a*) Where a plaintiff is under an existing contractual duty to the defendant if he does no more than he is already bound to do then no consideration is given.

Example

A ship's captain promised the remaining crew the wages of deserters if they would work the ship home.
Held: The seamen were bound to do this as their duty and so had given no additional consideration.

(*Stilk v. Myrick*, 1809)

The performance of an existing duty constituting consideration was raised in a recent case.

Example

Shipbuilders undertook to build a tanker for shipowners for US$30,395,000. The price was not to be subject to adjustment except in certain events and was payable in five instalments. Further, the shipbuilders were required to open a letter of credit to provide security for repayment of instalments in the event of their defaulting in the performance of the contract. The first instalment was paid on 28 April 1972. On 12 February 1973 the U.S. dollar was devalued by 10 per cent. On 23 April the shipbuilders put forward a claim for a 10 per cent increase in the remaining four instalments. After negotiation the shipowners telexed the shipbuilders on 28 June 1973 agreeing to pay the increased price 'without prejudice to the [owner's] rights'. The shipbuilders wrote on 29 June, acknowledging this letter and assuring the shipowners that the letter of credit would be increased. The shipowners paid the remaining few instalments, together with the additional 10 per cent on each instalment, without protest. They also accepted delivery of the ship on 24 November 1973 without protest. There was no evidence that if the owners had protested and witheld the final instalment the shipbuilders would not have delivered the ship.

In fact the shipowners never intended to affirm the agreement to pay the increased price made on 28/29 June. On 30 July 1975 the shipowners claimed amongst other grounds that the agreement made on the 28/29 June was void for lack of consideration, nominated an arbitrator and claimed that the 10 per cent was recoverable.
Held: The rule that a promise by one party to a contract to fulfil his existing contractual duty towards the other party did not constitute good consideration was still good law. Therefore the builder's original contractual liability to build the ship did not constitute good consideration for the agreement of 28/29 June to pay the further 10 per cent. However, the increase by the builders in their amount of the letter of credit was sufficient consideration on their part for that agreement. By agreeing to increase the letter of credit the builders had undertaken an additional obligation, or had rendered themselves liable to an increased

detriment and were not merely fulfilling their existing contractual duty. Accordingly, there was consideration for the agreement of 28/29 June.

(*North Ocean Shipping Co. Ltd. v. Hyundai Construction Co. Ltd.*, 1978)

(See *Pao On*, section 1:10, for reference to consideration for a promise in the form of an existing contractual duty to a third party and economic duress.)

(*b*) If a plaintiff does no more than his public duty under law he gives no consideration.

Example

A defendant was sued by the plaintiff, an attorney, for six guineas which he alleged had been promised to him for attending as a witness in a case.
Held: The duty was imposed by law, thus no consideration had been given for the promise.

(*Collins v. Godefroy*, 1831)

On the other hand a person can recover a promised payment for doing more than he is obliged to do by law.

Example

Mine owners, fearing strike violence, asked for greater police protection than the authorities thought necessary. The company promised to pay for the protection.
Held: The police authority could recover the payment for providing the additional protection.

(*Glasbrook Bros. Ltd. v. Glamorgan C.C.*, 1925)

(*c*) Payment of smaller sum in place of the full amount due will not discharge the liability of the debtor to pay the balance owed. That is, if a debtor pays £10 in satisfaction of a £20 debt, *unless* this is done at the request of the creditor where the amount owing is unliquidated, i.e. not finally determined, or before the date of repayment, then the debtor remains liable. Payment at a different place or by a third party will provide sufficient consideration to support a creditor's promise to take the lesser sum. This is known as accord and satisfaction—accord is the new agreement; satisfaction is the new consideration. The courts must be satisfied the accord is genuine.

Example

Builders carried out work for the defendants who held up payment knowing the builders were close to bankruptcy, the defendants offered a £300 cheque in satisfaction of the debt of about £482. The builders accepted this, then sued for the balance.
Held: By putting unfair pressure on the builders the defendants could not hold that there had been accord and the payment of the cheque did not provide good satisfaction.

(*D & C Builders v. Rees*, 1965)

The harsh rule that payment of a lesser sum on the day due does not bar the creditor from suing for the balance has been modified by the rule in the High Trees Case which is also known as promissory or equitable estoppel.

This rule laid down by Denning, J., in the case of *Central London Property Trust Ltd. v. High Trees House Ltd.*, 1947, runs as follows:

Where *A* makes a promise to *B* intending legal consequence and that *B* should act on it and *B* does so to his detriment, equity will not allow *A* to go back on his promise and enforce his strict legal rights.

Example

Under a lease a landlord could give a tenant six months' notice to repair the property. In default the tenant could then be evicted. Notice to repair was given and then negotiations for sale opened, it being understood that notice would be suspended during negotiations. These broke down and the landlord sought to evict the tenant at the end of the original notice.

Held: The landlord could not go back on his promise to allow six months' notice from breakdown of negotiations.

(*Hughes v. Metropolitan Railway Co. Ltd.*, 1877)

It should be noted that this rule can only be used as a defence and not to enforce rights.

(*Combe v. Combe*, 1951)

(vii) CONSIDERATION MUST NOT BE PAST

Example

A daughter-in-law completed repairs to property she shared with her husband and his mother. This property was sold on the death of the mother and the sale proceeds shared between the children of the marriage, who signed a document agreeing to pay for the repairs.

Held: At the time when the agreement was signed the consideration was past and the promise to pay could not be enforced.

(Re *McArdle*, 1951)

There are three alleged exceptions:

(*a*) Past consideration carried out at the express request of the defendant.

Example

Joint owners of patents informed *C* that they would give him a one-third share in consideration of services rendered. Sued on their promise, they held that it was not binding as the consideration was past.

Held: At the time services were rendered there was an implication that they would be paid for and the share in the patents would be such a payment.

(Re *Casey's Patents*, 1892)

(*b*) s. 27 (1) of the Bills of Exchange Act 1882. A Bill of Exchange can be supported by an antecedent debt or liability.

(*c*) Under the Limitation Act 1939. Statute-barred debts may be revived by written acknowledgement.

1:8　FORM

All speciality contracts must be in the form of a deed and so no consideration is necessary to enforce the contract except where the contract is in restraint of trade.

The following contracts are *void* unless made by deed:

(i) Promises of gifts.
(ii) Transfers of British ship or shares therein.
(iii) Conditional Bills of Sale (*see* Sale of Goods—Chapter 2).
(iv) The transfer of estates or interests in land and leases for more than three years (Law of Property Act 1925).

The following contracts are *void* unless fully written:

(i) Hire Purchase contracts (Hire Purchase Act 1965).
(ii) Bills of Exchange (Bills of Exchange Act 1882).
(iii) Assignments of copyrights (Copyright Act 1956).
(iv) Contracts of Marine Insurance (Marine Insurance Act 1906).
(v) Transfers of shares in registered companies (Companies Act 1948).
(vi) Articles of association of registered companies.
(vii) Acknowledgement of statute-barred debts (Limitation Act 1939).

The following contracts are unenforceable unless 'evidenced in writing':

(i) Contracts of guarantee—Statute of Frauds 1677, s. 4.
(ii) Contracts for the sale and other disposition of land (Law of Property Act 1925, s. 40).

'Evidenced in writing' means that there is the minimum of necessary written evidence, and provided it contains all the material terms of the contract, any signed note or memorandum of these material terms will suffice, even on scrap paper. It must contain the signature of the party to be charged, names of the parties or sufficient identification, description of the subject-matter (e.g. address of house being sold), and the price or other consideration. Thus an oral agreement to sell land is unenforceable. But if one of the parties has performed his part of the contract then the equitable doctrine of part performance (*see* p. 36) will operate so that the court will order the defaulting party specifically to perform his part of the contract to prevent hardship to the party not in default.

1:9　INTENTION TO CREATE LEGAL RELATIONS

It must be quite clear from the terms of the agreement that the parties intended to create a legally binding contract. Thus any clause that shows an intention to exclude the courts will result in an agreement that cannot be enforced by the courts.

Example

A clause in contract for the purchase of goods stated 'This arrangement is not entered into ... as a formal or legal agreement and shall not be subject to legal

jurisdiction in the Law Courts ... but it is only a definite expression and record of the purpose and intention of the parties concerned'.
Held: Legal relations had been expressly excluded.

(Rose, Frank & Co. v. Crompton Bros., 1923)

On the other hand if the agreement has a business background the courts are more likely to imply an intention to create legal relations.

Example

A pilot was told by an airline of a 15 per cent redundancy of pilot strength and given three months' notice under the terms of his contract of service. During discussions between the employers and the pilot's union (B.A.L.P.A.) it was agreed to make an *ex gratia* payment equal to the employer's pension contribution to each pilot. An action was brought to recover this sum.
Held: The payment was recoverable as the airline would have to disprove an intention to create legal relations in an agreement of this kind.

(Edwards v. Skyways Ltd., 1964)

1:10 GENUINENESS OF CONSENT

An agreement occurs when two minds meet upon a common purpose—*consensus ad idem*. Where there is no such meeting there is no legally binding agreement. In certain circumstances the following factors will act to vitiate an otherwise sound contract:

(i) mistake;
(ii) duress and undue influence;
(iii) misrepresentation.

(i) MISTAKE

(a) General position

Where one party has entered into a contract as the result of a mistake then he will be able to avoid the contract if:

1. the mistake is one of fact and not of law (unless it is a mistake as to foreign law or private rights);
2. the mistake is so fundamental as to negative the agreement.

(b) Inoperative mistake

The following mistakes will *not* affect the validity of the contract:

1. Mistake by one party of the expression of his intention.
2. Mistake as to the meaning of a trade description where goods are sold under that description—e.g. when goods are bought under a trade mark and one party is mistaken as to the quality of the goods. (*See* Chapters 2 and 7.)
3. A mistake or error of judgement. Where one party mistakenly believes an article to be worth more than it is, he has to bear the loss due to his ignorance of the true value of the article.
4. A mistake by one party of his power of performance, e.g. an over-estimate of his ability to complete a contract by a specified time.

(c) Operative mistake

The following mistakes *will* avoid the contract:

1. *Mistake as to the nature of the document itself*

Where a person signs a document in the mistaken belief that it is of an entirely different nature he will be able to plead *non est factum*—it is not his deed.

Example

A car dealer persuaded a customer to sign a partially covered up indemnity form which he represented as 'a release note'.
Held: The customer was not liable.

(Muskham Finance Ltd. v. Howard, 1963)

Unless the document is of a different nature from that intended to be signed the signor will be bound.

Example

A widow of poor sight, without her glasses, executed a deed she believed to be deed of gift to her nephew who was present at the time. In fact it was an assignment to a third party of her house. This person mortgaged the property to a building society who held the deeds. The widow sought to have the agreement set aside.
Held: The assignment was valid as the widow had done what she intended in substance, i.e. divest herself of the interest in the house.

(Gallie v. Lee, 1969)

(Ruling upheld on appeal to the House of Lords under *Saunders v. Anglia Building Society*, 1971)

2. *Mistake as to the identity of the party contracted with*

Example

A Bristol student advertised a car for sale and a rogue convinced the young man and his fiancée that he was Richard Greene of the Robin Hood T.V. series. He asked to pay by cheque and produced a forged Pinewood Studios' pass as identification. The car, log book, and test certificate were handed over and the rogue took the car which he later sold to a student in London. The cheque was dishonoured on presentation.
Held: The plaintiff contracted with the rogue although the contract was voidable for fraud. A sale by the rogue to a purchaser for value with no notice of the fraud was valid and good title was passed. Thus, the only remedy of the plaintiff was an action in fraud against the rogue.

(Lewis v. Averay, 1971)

Note: In this case had the plaintiff notified the A.A. or R.A.C. and the police of the fraud before the car was sold in London, the second sale would have been void.

(Car and Universal Finance Co. Ltd. v. Caldwell, 1965)

Where the identity of the contracting party is important a contract is avoided if it is entered into with any other person than that with which the contractor intends.

Example

A rogue ordered goods from a firm signing his name so that it appeared to read 'Blenkiron & Co.', a company of repute known to the firm. Goods were supplied which the rogue sold to a third party.
Held: The supplying firm could recover the goods or their worth from the third party as there was a mistake as to the identity of the party with whom they had dealt.

(*Cundy v. Lindsay*, 1878)

3. *Common mistake as to the existence of the thing contracted for*

For example, where both parties are unaware that the subject-matter has been destroyed.

Example

Unknown to the parties at the time they contracted, a cargo of corn bound for the U.K. had been sold by the captain at a port en route due to overheating of the commodity.
Held: No contract came into being.

(*Couturier v. Hastie*, 1852)

'Where there is a contract for the sale of specific goods, and the goods, without the knowledge of the seller, have perished at the time when the contract is made the contract is void.'

(s. 6—Sale of Goods Act 1893)

4. *Mutual mistake as to the identity of the thing contracted for*

In this case both parties mistakenly believe that they are contracting for the same article but in fact have different articles in mind—so there is no *consensus ad idem*.

Example

A agreed to purchase a consignment of cotton from *B* arriving 'ex Peerless from Bombay'. By chance two ships of that name were sailing from Bombay. *A* had the one sailing in October in mind, *B* was referring to the one leaving in December.
Held: No contract arose.

(*Raffles v. Wincelhaus*, 1864)

5. *Common mistake as to the fundamental subject-matter of the contract*

If the parties made a contract on the mistaken assumption that a certain state of affairs existed—which was not the case—then the contract will be void.

Example

Two parties entered into a contract for the sale of a life policy believing that the assured was alive. The assured was, in fact, dead.

Held: The assignment could be set aside on the ground of common mistake.

(*Scott v. Coulson*, 1903)

6. *Mistake of one party known to the other*

If one party knows that the other party is mistaken as to the subject-matter of the contract then he will not be allowed to profit by the other party's mistake.

Example

The plaintiff was offered property for £1,250. Previously the plaintiff had been refused on offering £2,000. The offer of £1,250 was accepted. The defendant at once amended the price to the one intended—£2,250.

Held: A decree of specific performance of the contract would be refused.

(*Webster v. Cecil*, 1861)

(*d*) *Equitable remedies for mistake*

Equity can grant three discretionary remedies to modify the strictness of the common law rules relating to mistake, these are:

1. *Rectification*

This will be granted to correct a written contract containing errors of expression, where it can be proved the parties agreed on the terms of the contract but mistakenly wrote them down wrongly.

2. *Refusal of specific performance*

This will be done where the mistake of the defendant makes it unreasonable to enforce the agreement, although it is not an operative mistake at common law.

3. *Setting aside an agreement on terms*

Where both parties mistakenly believe, for example, that a flat is not subject to rent restriction, the court will rescind a contract on grounds of mistake provided a new lease is negotiated at the correct rent level.

(ii) DURESS AND UNDUE INFLUENCE

(*a*) Duress is actual or threatened physical violence or confinement and makes the contract voidable by the person subjected.

(*b*) *Presumption*

Undue influence will be presumed where a close or fiduciary relationship exists between parties, e.g. solicitor and client, parent and child, doctor and patient, but not husband and wife. Its presence, when proved, renders the contract voidable.

Example

An elderly farmer, who had no head for business, guaranteed an overdraft for his son's company which was in financial difficulties. Both were clients of the same bank and the overdraft was secured by a charge on the farmer's house, his sole asset. Later the bank required him to give a charge on the full value of his house as a condition of continuing financial support for the son's firm. At no time did the bank advise the farmer to seek independent advice concerning the company. The farmer signed the documents presented to him by the bank's manager. The bank later enforced both charge and guarantee against the farmer.

Held: The confidential relationship existing between the bank and the farmer imposed a duty of fiduciary care on the bank to advise their client to seek independent advice. As that duty had been breached and undue influence was presumed both the charge and guarantee would be set aside.

(*Lloyds Bank v. Bundy*, 1974)

The Privy Council recently considered the existence of economic duress in *Pao On v. Lau Yiu*, 1979. It held that where the consideration for a promise was an existing contractual duty to a third party which was otherwise valid, consideration for it was not invalidated as against public policy (in absence of proof of duress) merely because the promise had been secured by a threat to repudiate the existing contract or by the unfair use of a dominant bargaining position. Where businessmen were negotiating at arm's length it was unnecessary for the achievement of justice to invoke that principle, for what justice required was that a businessman be held to his bargain unless his consent to it could be shown to have been vitiated by fraud, mistake or duress. To constitute duress of any kind there had to be coercion of will so as to vitiate consent, and in relation to a contract commercial pressure alone did not constitute duress. In addition, there was nothing contrary in principle in recognizing economic duress as a factor which may render a contract voidable. It must be shown that the payment made on the contract entered into was not a voluntary act.

(iii) MISREPRESENTATION

In English Law a person is generally under no duty to disclose all the facts in his possession to the other contracting party. Each person must look after his own interests: *caveat emptor*— 'let the buyer beware'—is still a primary rule. However, if a person makes a statement which is false and which was intended to persuade the other party to enter into the contract he will be guilty of making a misrepresentation.

(*a*) *Definition of misrepresentation*

1. A false statement.
2. Of a material fact.
3. Made by one party to the contract or his agent.
4. Which induces the other party to enter into the contract.

It should be noted that:

1. *The statement must be one of fact and not law or opinion*

This is so, unless the person stating an opinion is a technical expert.

Example

During negotiations for the sale of a New Zealand sheep farm the plaintiff

stated that in his view the land would carry 2,000 sheep, if properly worked—but in fact it could not.
Held: The contract would not be rescinded as the statement as to the carrying capacity of the land was not a misrepresentation but an honest if incorrect opinion.

(Bisset v. Wilkinson, 1927)

2. *It must be material to the transaction*

Example

The plaintiff was asked to make a gun to specifications. The gun when finished was delivered and burst in use due to a defect which had been concealed.
Held: The defendant was liable for the price. The gun had never been inspected by him and so the misrepresentation as to soundness could not have affected his decision to accept the gun.

(Horsfall v. Thomas, 1862)

3. *It must be made by the other party or his agent*

4. *The injured party must have relied upon it*

Example

The defendant during negotiations to sell his solicitor's practice stated it to be worth £300. The papers presented to back his statement, had the plaintiff checked them, would have shown that it was worth only £200.
Held: The plaintiff could have found out the misrepresentation but he had relied on it so he could rescind the contract.

(Redgrave v. Hurd, 1881)

5. *It must be by positive words or conduct*

Silence is not a misrepresentation except where it distorts a positive representation.

Example

A doctor wished to sell his practice to the plaintiff. In January 1934 he stated his income was £2,000 a year. Between January and May when the contract was entered into the practice fell substantially.
Held: The plaintiff could rescind the contract.

(With v. O'Flanagan, 1936)

The effect upon an agreement of a material adverse change in the value of assets of a company was considered in a recent case.

Example

The plaintiffs were shareholders in a fashion company manufacturing and marketing the designs of a Mrs Levison who had a high reputation in the trade. Due to her illness no autumn collection for 1972 and no spring collection for 1973 could be designed. It was decided by the plaintiffs to sell the business and they offered it to the defendants who were competitors in the fashion trade. The defendants were made aware by the plaintiffs that no new collections had been designed, that the company was trading at a loss and was in a traded down state. This was confirmed by the accounts up to 31 December 1972. The plaintiffs were unable to state, as they did not know themselves, how much money was being lost.

On 27 April 1973 the defendants agreed in writing to purchase the company from the plaintiffs for £54,000. The purchase price was made up of a net asset value of the company of £44,000 agreed by the parties on the basis of the December 1972 accounts and £10,000 for goodwill. In the agreement the sellers warranted that between the balance sheet date (31 December 1972) and the completion date 'there will have been no material adverse change in the overall value of the net assets of the company on the basis of a valuation adopted in the balance sheet allowing for normal trade fluctuations.'

After taking over the company the defendants found that between the balance sheet date and the completion date there had been an adverse change in the overall net assets of the company amounting to £8,600. Because of this the defendants refused to pay the first two instalments of the purchase price and indicated they would not pay the balance. In response to an action for the instalments by the plaintiffs it was claimed by the defendants that the plaintiffs had breached the warranty in the agreement.

Held: The defendants were entitled to success as (i) the plaintiffs had breached the warranty as there had been a material adverse change in the overall value of the net assets of the company; (ii) the disclosure of Mrs Levison's illness and the trading down of the company was a general disclosure of the causes of probable losses and was not a disclosure of a quantified reduction in the net asset value or the actual rate of the continuing losses. The disclosure did not protect the plaintiffs from being in breach of warranty therefore as (a) the defendants had no way of knowing what the continuing losses would be, and the actual reduction which occurred was a material adverse change for the purpose of the warranty; (b) the reduction was entirely special to the company and had never occurred before and was not therefore a 'normal trade fluctuation'; and (c) as the disclosure had not been made by specific notice for the purposes of the warranty, the plaintiffs were not, in the circumstances, able to rely on the words 'save and disclosed.'

(*Levison v. Farin*, 1978)

(b) Types of misrepresentation

Misrepresentations are either innocent, fraudulent, or negligent.

1. Innocent misrepresentation

A misrepresentation is innocent if the maker has reasonable grounds for believing the statement to be true. If the maker later discovers that the statement is untrue before the contract is entered into he must inform the other party or the statement will be dealt with as if it was fraudulent misrepresentation. Purely innocent misrepresentation may be remedied by an award of damages, but these lie in the discretion of the court. The person seeking relief has to ask for rescission and the court may award damages in its place (s. 2 (2) Misrepresentation Act 1967).

The right of rescission will be available even though the contract has been performed and even though the misrepresentation has become a term of the contract. The plaintiff will also be entitled to damages unless the maker of the statement can show that he had reasonable grounds to believe and did believe up to the time that the contract was made that the facts represented were true (s. 2 (1) Misrepresentation Act 1967).

2. *Fraudulent misrepresentation*

A misrepresentation is false where the party making it knows that it is false, or makes it without an honest belief in its truth or is careless as to whether it is true or false.

Where fraudulent misrepresentation is proved the plaintiff may sue for damages on the tort of deceit or repudiate the contract or have it rescinded by the court (with or without damages for deceit). The plaintiff may also, if he wishes, affirm the contract and still claim damages.

3. *Negligent misrepresentation*

Negligent misrepresentation is a false statement made by a person who has no reasonable grounds for believing the statement to be true. In this case the person making the false statement is liable in damages unless he can prove that the statement was not made negligently, or there were reasonable grounds for believing the statement was true (s. 2 (1)).

(c) *Remedies under the Misrepresentation Act 1967*

The Misrepresentation Act 1967 allowed rescission for the first time in the case of innocent misrepresentation and also a discretionary award of damages.

An agreement containing a provision excluding or restricting liability for misrepresentation is void except to the extent to which a court will allow it to be relied on as being fair and reasonable in the circumstances (s. 3 Misrepresentation Act 1967).

A contract induced by fraudulent or innocent misrepresentation is voidable at the option of the misled party—but he may lose the right of rescission in the following circumstances:

1. *Affirmation*

If the contract is affirmed either expressly or impliedly by an injured party with full knowledge of the misrepresentation.

Example

A lorry was advertised as being capable of 40 m.p.h. and doing 11 m.p.g., and 'in exceptional condition'. Two days after the purchase defects appeared and the plaintiff accepted the defendant's offer to pay half the cost of a reconditioned dynamo. The next day the lorry broke down on the way to Middlesbrough and was declared to be unroadworthy. The plaintiff sought rescission on the grounds of innocent misrepresentation.

Held: The plaintiff had accepted the lorry and thus lost the right to rescission.

(*Long v. Lloyd*, 1958)

2. *Where the parties cannot be restored to their precontractual position*

Example

A syndicate sold a nitrate mine to a company under a contract with misleading terms. The company sued for rescission of the contract.

Held: Since the mine had been worked by the company the parties could not be restored to their original position; therefore the contract could not be rescinded.

(Laguanas Nitrate Co. v. Laguanas Syndicate, 1899)

3. *Where an innocent third party has obtained an interest in the subject-matter of the contract*

Example

The plaintiff contracted with *A* for the purchase of 50 tons of iron which *A* had obtained by fraud from the defendants, who delivered to the plaintiffs on *A*'s instructions. The plaintiff paid *A* on receipt, but the defendants seized the iron when they discovered they had been defrauded.

Held: Their seizure was wrongful as they could not avoid the contract with *A* after the goods had come into the hands of an innocent third party, the plaintiffs.

(White v. Garden, 1851)

4. *Where there has been unreasonable delay*

Right to rescission will be lost on the grounds of unreasonable delay in bringing the action in the case of innocent misrepresentation.

Example

A painting believed to be a Constable by the plaintiff and innocently misrepresented as such by the art gallery from which it was purchased was found five years later not to be by that painter.

Held: The plaintiff had delayed unreasonably in bringing his action.

(Leaf v. International Galleries, 1950)

(d) *Duty to disclose*

In certain instances a party to a contract is under a duty to disclose all material facts:

1. *Where the contract is uberrimae fidei (of utmost good faith)*

These are certain classes of contract where the material facts are only fully known by one party; he is under a legal duty to disclose these to the other contracting party.

Examples of contracts of utmost good faith are:

(i) contracts of insurance;
(ii) contracts concerning domestic matters;
(iii) contracts for company share allotment.

(i) Contracts of insurance are dealt with in Chapter 11; sufficient to observe here that a person who seeks insurance has to disclose all material facts (those that would influence a careful insurer in either taking on the insurance or calculating the premium) to an insurer.

(ii) Where family property is settled by members of that family, each member has to disclose fully all the material facts he knows.

(iii) Strictly speaking, a contract for the allotment of shares in a company is not a true contract *uberrimae fidei*, although the Companies Act 1948 does make special disclosure provisos. For example, where a company issues a prospectus, inviting the public to subscribe for shares and debentures, such a prospectus must comply with the provisions of the Companies Act 1948 s. 38(1); if it does not, the directors and others responsible for its issue are liable in damages to any person relying on the prospectus who takes up shares or debentures in the company and suffers loss as a result of the Act being contravened. This point is dealt with more fully in Chapter 10.

2. *Where only part of the relevant facts are disclosed*

If only part of the relevant facts are disclosed and the concealed part so alters the part revealed as to make it basically false, then there is a duty to disclose fully the whole truth.

Example

A prospectus described land as 'eminently suitable' for greyhound racing. The land was subject to a local authority planning order which meant prior consent was needed from the local authority before buildings could be put up. The local authority did refuse that permission.

Held: Failure to disclose the facts concerning local authority consent made the description of the land misleading and any who had subscribed on the strength of the prospectus could rescind their contracts with the company.

(*Coles v. White City (Manchester) Greyhound Association Ltd.*, 1929)

3. *Where a representation of fact is made during negotiations which, although true at the time, later becomes false to the person who made it*

This point has already been illustrated by the case of *With v. O'Flanagan*, 1936 (*see* page 34).

1:11 CAPACITY

An adult may enter freely into any contract, subject to the following qualifications:

(i) DRUNKEN PERSONS

Where a person has entered into a contract when he is under the influence of drink to such an extent that he did not realize what he was doing, he may avoid the contract provided he can prove that he did not know what he was doing, and the other party knew of his condition. He will be bound if he ratifies the contract when sober. He will be liable to pay a reasonable price for necessaries.

(*See* Minors below; not s. 2 Sale of Goods Act 1893)

(ii) PERSONS OF UNSOUND MIND

Where a person enters into a contract when his mind is so disordered that he did not realize what he was doing he may avoid the contract providing that he can prove that he did not realize what he was doing and the other party knew of his condition. He will be liable for contracts ratified in a lucid interval or on return to sanity. He will be liable to pay a reasonable price for necessaries.

(s. 2 Sale of Goods Act 1893)

(iii) ALIENS

Aliens have full contractual capacity except that they cannot hold ownership in a British ship. In time of war an enemy alien may not enter into or enforce a contract made before he became an enemy alien. Any contracts made between a British subject and an enemy alien are void but can be ratified at the discretion of the Crown.

(iv) CORPORATIONS

As an artificial legal person a corporation has perpetual succession, a common seal, and a name. It may be incorporated by a royal charter, formed by special Act of Parliament or, more usually, registered as a company under the Companies Act 1948. A corporation can contract only through an agent. A corporation formed by Act of Parliament has its contractual capacity limited by the statute governing it. Any contract outside its power (*ultra vires*) is void and cannot be ratified or made valid. A company formed under the Companies Act of 1948 has its contractual capacity governed by the terms of its memorandum of association. It can contract within those terms or for any objects that the courts will imply from the memorandum. Any acts outside this limit will be *ultra vires* the company and invalid.

(v) MINORS

The contractual capacity of a minor (any person under the age of 18) is governed by common law and the Infants Relief Act 1874. A minor is bound by contracts for necessaries and beneficial service. Necessaries have been defined as goods 'suitable to the condition in life of the infant (minor) at the time of sale and delivery'.

(s. 2 Sale of Goods Act 1893)

A minor must always pay a reasonable price for necessaries sold and actually delivered.

Example

A Cambridge undergraduate, a minor, ordered eleven fancy waistcoats from a local tailor. The student failed to pay the bill and was sued by the tailor.
Held: Although the clothes were suitable to the student's position, it was proved that at the time of delivery of the goods in question he was well supplied with similar clothing. Thus the goods were not necessaries.

(*Nash v. Inman*, 1908)

Contracts for beneficial training and education are binding on a minor providing that they are fundamentally for the benefit of the minor.

Example

A minor commenced work as a porter with the defendant company and joined an insurance scheme as part of the service agreement. This scheme meant he and his personal representatives would not have any claim under the Employers' Liability Act 1880. When injured the minor sued under the Act.
Held: The agreement not to sue was part of the service contract and as a whole the agreement was for the minor's benefit and was therefore binding on him.
(*Clements v. London & North Western Rail Co.*, 1894)

Void contracts under the Infants Relief Act 1874 are:

(*a*) contracts to repay money lent or to be lent;
(*b*) contracts for goods supplied other than necessaries;
(*c*) all accounts stated—e.g. IOUs.

A minor cannot be sued on a cheque. If a minor misrepresents his age to obtain a loan he cannot be sued in order to recover the money.

Example

A minor fraudently represented himself to be of age in order to obtain a loan of £400 from a money-lender. When he refused to repay the sum he was sued for deceit.
Held: Since the loan was void under the 1874 Act, a tort action could not be used as a means of enforcement.
(*Leslie Ltd. v. Sheill*, 1914)

A guarantee of a minor's bank overdraft will be similarly void, but not an indemnity.

Example

A minor entered into a hire purchase agreement and later defaulted. An adult had signed a separate indemnity agreement with the hire purchase company.
Held: The indemnity could be enforced as it was one under which the adult had undertaken principal liability.
(*Yeoman Credit Ltd. v. Latter*, 1961)

Note: Money borrowed to pay for necessaries must be repaid.

The following contracts of a minor are voidable:

(*a*) Contracts requiring express repudiation before or within a reasonable time after reaching 18—e.g. contracts involving a continuing interest in property of a permanent nature such as a lease of land or contracts to take shares in a company.

Example

A minor took a lease of a house, paid £68 towards the lease and furniture it contained. After several months he decided to give up the lease and sought to recover the money.

Held: The lease could be avoided, but since the minor had used the house and the furniture he could not recover the £68 as there had been no total failure of consideration.

(*Valenti v. Canali*, 1889)

(*b*) Contracts not requiring express repudiation, e.g. trading contracts. These remain void even after the eighteenth birthday and cannot be ratified. There must be a fresh promise and additional consideration.

Example

A minor, who had a haulage contracting business, entered into a hire purchase agreement for the purchase of a lorry. When he fell into arrears of instalments due under the agreement he was sued for their recovery by the finance company.

Held: Even if the agreement might be shown to be of benefit to the minor, the action would not succeed as it was brought on a trading contract.

(*Mercantile Union Guarantee Corporation, Ltd. v. Ball*, 1937)

1:12 LEGALITY OF OBJECTS

A contract must not be illegal and, if it is, has no legal effect. Contracts will be illegal because they are contrary to (i) statute or (ii) common law.

(i) CONTRACTS ILLEGAL BY STATUTE

(*a*) *Gaming Act 1845–1892*

Under s. 18 of the Gaming Act of 1845 gaming contracts are void and wagers or sums deposited with stakeholders are not legally recoverable. A wagering contract is a contract under which one party is to win and the other to lose something according to how some unknown fact or event shall turn out, e.g. how many lamp-posts there are on a stretch of road to be passed in a car. A gaming contract is a wager on the result of a skill or chance or a sporting event, such as a greyhound race.

(*b*) *Restrictive Trade Practices Act*—(*see* Chapter 2)

(ii) CONTRACTS ILLEGAL AT COMMON LAW

These are contracts broadly termed as being contrary to public policy, including:

(*a*) Contracts to commit a tort or crime.

(*b*) Contracts tending to corrupt public life—e.g. sale of public offices or bribery.

(*c*) Contracts prejudicial to the administration of justice—e.g. agreements not to appear as witnesses in criminal cases.

(*d*) Contracts of a sexually immoral nature—e.g. those involving prostitution.

(*e*) Contracts that constitute an offence against the laws of a friendly state.

(iii) CONTRACTS VOID AT COMMON LAW

(a) Contracts prejudicial to the sanctity of marriage

These include contracts in absolute (not partial) restraint of marriage, marriage brokerage contracts, and agreements for future separation.

(b) Agreements to oust the jurisdiction of the courts

Where a wife promises not to apply for maintenance in return for an agreed sum.

(c) Agreements in restraint of trade

These are by far the most important in the group and require more detailed study (for agreements to regulate trade *see under* Restrictive Trade Practices, Chapter 2).

All restraints of trade are *prima facie* void unless they can be shown to be reasonable in the interests of the parties and the public. To be reasonable between the parties, the restraint must be no wider than required to protect the interests of the person seeking to enforce the agreement. The person who wishes to avoid being bound by such a contract has the task of proving that the agreement is unreasonable in the interests of the public.

(d) Varieties of restraint of trade

1. *Restraints to prevent employees from competing with their employers*

The courts have laid down guidelines as to what will be reasonable in relation to area, time, and the nature of the employment.

Example

The managing clerk of a solicitor agreed that when his contract of service was terminated he would not practice as a solicitor within seven miles of Tamworth Town Hall.
Held: Since the clerk had access to confidential information he was in a position to injure his ex-employer's business.

(*Fitch v. Dewes*, 1921)

A restraint on the exercise of skill or future competition is void.

Example

A commercial traveller agreed he would not seek orders from any firm in areas in which he had operated.
Held: The restraint included firms that were not existing customers of the employing firm and was void.

(*Gledhow Autoparts v. Delaney*, 1965)

The position of the employee should be taken into account.

Example

A bookmaker's clerk agreed with his employers that he would not be engaged or interested in a similar business within a radius of twelve miles of Cheltenham.

Most of the bets were phoned in. The clerk set up a betting office within the restricted area.

Held: The defendant was in no position to obtain goodwill of customers as he had no direct contact with them. The agreement was designed to prevent ordinary competition and was therefore void.

(*Strange Ltd. v. Mann*, 1965)

The courts will judge whether it is reasonable for the employer to seek protection of confidential information relating to its business.

Example

The plaintiffs, Littlewoods, ran a retail chain store and mail order business in the United Kingdom. Their main competition was Great Universal Stores (GUS) which had two hundred subsidiary companies carrying on various businesses throughout the world. Littlewoods' mail order business was based on a spring/summer and an autumn/winter catalogue. The catalogues were distributed to agents who obtained orders from friends and relatives. The putting together of the catalogues required considerable business skill, long range forecasting being necessary to assess what quantities of goods were required and prices charged. In 1965 the defendant was hired by Littlewoods as a buyer for their retail chain store and mail order business. From 1970, due to his outstanding ability, he was employed exclusively on the mail order side of Littlewoods' business. A written agreement appointing him divisional director of ladies fashions in January 1974 gave him two-year tenure terminable after that by six months notice. The agreement contained a clause which stated that in the event of the agreement ending the defendant would not, within twelve months from that time, enter into a similar agreement, or engage directly or indirectly in trade or business with GUS or any of its subsidiaries. In August 1976 the defendant was appointed executive director of Littlewood's mail order business, which involved planning and compiling that company's catalogues. He immediately began to compile Littlewoods 1977 spring/summer catalogue.

On 4 January 1977 he wrote to Littlewoods tendering his resignation and informing them that he had accepted an offer of employment from the GUS group. Littlewoods accepted his letter as six months notice terminating from 4 July 1977, but asked for a written assurance that he did not intend to breach his service agreement with Littlewoods by taking up employment with the GUS group within twelve months after leaving Littlewoods' employment. When the defendant refused to give such an assurance Littlewoods transferred him to the retail chain store side of their business. They also applied for an injunction restraining him from working with the GUS group for twelve months after he left Littlewoods employment. At first instance the judge found that the defendant had knowledge of the trends of Littlewoods' mail order sales, the percentage and identity of the returns, the sources of manufacture and manufacturers themselves at chairman level, Littlewoods' plans for the foreseeable future, the plans for the 1977 autumn/winter and the 1978 summer/spring catalogues, and the results of their market research. No injunction, however, was granted on the basis that Littlewoods possessed no confidential information requiring protection. Littlewoods appealed.

Held: (i) On the evidence the defendant had acquired much information of a confidential nature about Littlewoods' mail order business in the course of his employment. Littlewoods were therefore entitled to the protection of a reasonable convenant restraining the defendant from working for a rival firm in the mail order business within a limited period after he had left their employment. (ii) Where a covenant in restraint of trade was drafted in general terms which, without alteration of words, could be construed in a sense which was not unreasonably wide in relation to the relevant confidential information or trade secrets for which the convenantee was entitled to protection, the court should construe the covenant in that sense thereby rendering it valid and enforceable. Therefore the clause in the Littlewoods agreement should be construed as applying only to the mail order business GUS carried on in the United Kingdom and not its whole range of business throughout the world. The clause in question was therefore no wider than necessary to protect confidential information about Littlewoods' mail order business and an injunction was therefore granted against the defendant.

(*Littlewoods Organization Ltd v. Harris*, 1978)

The relative bargaining position of the parties will also be considered by the courts.

Example

The plaintiff, a young and unknown song writer, entered into an agreement with the defendants, a music publishing company, whereby they engaged his exclusive services for five years under a standard form agreement. By this the plaintiff assigned to the defendants the full copyright for the whole world in each original work he produced during the agreement and such work prior to it he still owned and controlled. If during the five-year period the plaintiff's royalties and advances equalled or exceeded £5,000 the agreement would be automatically extended for a further five years. The defendants were under no obligation to publish any of the plaintiff's compositions and could end the agreement on one month's notice. The plaintiff sought a declaration that the agreement was in restraint of trade; the defendants argued that the doctrine did not apply to standard form contracts which had become generally accepted commercially.

Held: The House of Lords distinguished between standard form contracts freely made between parties on equal bargaining terms and the case at issue. No presumption in this case could be made that the terms were fair and reasonable. There was no obligation on the part of the defendants to publish the plaintiff's work and he could earn nothing during the contract if the defendants decided not to publish. Lord Diplock: 'The terms of this kind of standard form contract have not been the subject of negotiation between the parties to it.... They have been dictated by the party whose bargaining power ... enables him to say: "If you want these goods and services at all, these are the only terms on which they are obtainable. Take it or leave it."'

(*Schroeder Music Publishing Co. Ltd. v. Macaulay*, 1974)

The reasonableness of the restrictions sought to be imposed and the issue of whether defendants have a sufficient interest to be protected were considered in a recent case involving the attempted revolutionizing of the once gentlemanly game of cricket.

Example

In 1977, a private company, World Series Cricket (W.S.C.), formed by Mr. Kerry Packer in Australia to promote cricket, engaged a number of world-class cricketers from Test-playing countries. Under the terms of their contracts these players were bound to make themselves available to play in a series of 'Test' matches organized by W.S.C. in Australia and possibly elsewhere during the season of September 1977 to March 1978. These contracts varied in length from one to five years.

The International Cricket Conference (I.C.C.) exercised, effectively, sole control over international Test cricket match promotion and has exclusive power to lay down the qualification rules for cricketers in Test matches and to arrange tours for member countries. The Cricket Council governed cricket in the U.K. and the Test and County Cricket Board (T.C.C.B.) was answerable to it; the latter body organized and administered Test matches in the U.K. and M.C.C. overseas tours. The promotion and administration of first-class county cricket and responsibility for registration and qualification of cricketers in such cricket were carried out by the T.C.C.B.

Since a threat was posed to Test match cricket by the W.S.C. development, the I.C.C. altered its rules by resolution by which any cricketer who played for W.S.C. was disqualified from taking part in future Test matches. This followed a similar ban that the T.C.C.B. proposed, subject to Cricket Council and I.C.C. decisions. The I.C.C. strongly recommended that each member country should follow its action. The T.C.C.B. resolved that (subject to the court's decision in the present proceedings) their own rules would be amended to put the I.C.C. decision into effect and thus disqualify any cricketer who was subject to the Test match ban from playing in county cricket.

A declaration was sought by the plaintiffs, who were cricketers contracted with W.S.C., that the change of rules by the I.C.C. and that proposed by the T.C.C.B. would be *ultra vires* as an unlawful restraint of trade.

Held: The new rules were *prima facie* void as being contrary to public policy. The I.C.C. and the T.C.C.B. had a legitimate interest in ensuring that the game of cricket was properly administered and organized. On the evidence the W.S.C. did constitute an immediate threat to the finances of Australian cricket, but not to any of the other Test-playing countries. Long-term such countries might be seriously affected by recruitment of their players by W.S.C. or similar promotions being commenced by local entrepreneurs. Even so, such threats could have been adequately met by simply placing a prospective disqualification from Test cricket on all players who should contract with or play for W.S.C. or other unapproved promoters (although in Slade J's view such a ban would not necessarily have been valid). Taking into account the seriousness of taking away the opportunity to make his livelihood from a professional cricketer and the fact that the I.C.C. ban would add to the deprivation W.S.C. might be causing to the public of Test playing countries, the I.C.C. had not discharged the onus upon it to show that the ban was reasonable and justifiable. The new rules of the I.C.C. (and, as a consequence, those proposed by the T.C.C.B.) were *ultra vires* and void as an unreasonable restraint of trade. The plaintiffs were entitled to a declaration to that effect.

(Greig and Others v. Insole and Others, 1978)

2. *Restraints imposed on the seller by the purchaser of a business*

Such a restriction must only protect the business sold and a proprietary interest.

Example

Manufacturers of road reinforcements purchased the defendant's business which involved loop road reinforcements. The defendant agreed not to open a business in competition within ten miles of any of the purchaser's branches. *Held:* As it was not restricted to the manufacture and sale of loop road reinforcements, the restraint was unreasonable and void.

(British Reinforced Concrete Ltd. v. Schleff, 1921)

3. *Restraints imposed on a mortgagee*

These can be illustrated by 'solus agreements' with petrol companies—i.e. the 'tied' garage situation.

Example

A firm charged one of its garages to a petrol firm by way of mortgage for a loan of £7,000. This was to be repaid over twenty-one years during which time only petrol supplied by the mortgagors was to be sold by the garage. *Held:* The agreement was unreasonable and in restraint of trade. Another mortgage agreement containing similar terms but covering a four and a half year period was held to be valid.

(Esso Petroleum Co. Ltd. v. Harper Garage (Stourport) Ltd., 1968)

Example

In negotiating the sale of a garage, a party entered a solus agreement with a petrol company. As part of this contract only that firm's petrol and lubricating oil was to be sold by the garage. Further, the business would not be sold without giving the petrol company first refusal and then only to a party willing to enter a similar solus agreement. This agreement would run for twelve years. *Held:* As the petrol firm had no proprietary interest, the agreement restricted the garage proprietor's trade on his own land. The restraint on sale of the garage, the lubricating oil restriction, the period of twelve years were all unreasonable.

(Petrofina (Great Britain) Ltd. v. Martin, 1966)

The courts have considered the legal position of a garage breaking a tie in a solus agreement during a petrol price 'war'.

Example

A private company, Lostock, operated a garage which was tied to a solus agreement made between the garage company and Shell in 1955. The agreement required the garage to sell only petrol supplied by Shell and be open for the sale of petrol at all reasonable times. The original agreement was to run to March 1975 but in 1966 the agreement was varied allowing Lostock company to end the agreement on giving twelve months notice at any time after 1971. In December 1975 there was a petrol price 'war'. The garages in Lostock's area, not tied to Shell, cut their petrol prices. Shell began a support scheme (which continued until the end of April 1976) to Shell garages in the area by way of subsidy allowing these garages to compete with the other non-Shell garages in the area. However Lostock was not included in this scheme and was forced to trade at a loss as it could not cut its price and compete with the other Shell garages in the area. In order to meet this competition and mistakenly believing the agreement with Shell ended in 1975, Lostock obtained petrol from another supplying company. This company was threatened with proceedings by Shell for inducing a breach of contract. As a result the other supplying company ceased to supply Lostock. Lostock resumed taking supplies from Shell, claiming they were no longer tied by the solus agreement, However, in case this were so, they gave Shell twelve months notice to end the agreement in March 1977.

Shell then brought an action against Lostock claiming damages for breach of contract by taking supplies from a source other than Shell. Shell also claimed an injunction to prevent Lostock from breaking the tie provision by accepting supplies other than from Shell. Lostock argued that the agreement was unenforceable as an unreasonable constraint of trade. Alternatively, the agreement was subject to an implied term by Shell that it would not normally discriminate against Lostock in favour of competing and neighbouring garages to render Lostock's petrol sales uneconomic. Shell, Lostock claimed, was in breach of that implied term by operating the support scheme and excluding Lostock from it. At first instance it was held that Shell could not enforce the tie so long as Lostock were caused harm by the support scheme. However a declaration that the tie was unenforceable as being in restraint of trade was refused as was an injunction restraining Shell from enforcing the agreement. Lostock appealed.

Held: (i) A term would not be implied that Shell, as the supplier, should not abnormally discriminate against Lostock. The implication of such a term was not necessary to make the agreement effective and could not be precisely formulated. Shell, therefore, was not in breach of the solus agreement by operating the support scheme. (ii) The court dismissed Shell's cross-appeal against the dismissal of its claim for an injunction restraining Lostock from breaking the tie for the following reasons:

(*a*) The court should not enforce an agreement in restraint of trade where, after it had been entered into, it was found to be operating unfairly and unreasonably, in circumstances which had not been envisaged beforehand. The court would therefore not enforce the tie provision, so long as Shell was operating its support scheme to Lostock's disadvantage. Although it appeared reasonable to retain the tie in 1966, when Shell bought in its support scheme in 1975, it had become unfair and unreasonable to enforce the tie.

(*b*) It would not be just and equitable to grant Shell an injunction restraining Lostock from breaking the tie whilst Shell was operating its support scheme and excluded Lostock from it since that scheme operated to Lostock's disadvantage and inflicted hardship upon them.

(*Shell U.K. Ltd v. Lostock Garage Ltd*, 1977)

4. *Severance of terms*

If parts of a restrictive agreement can be enforced, while striking out the invalid terms, the courts will do this.

Example

An estate agent employed the defendant in Kingsbridge and he agreed not to work in a similar post after leaving their employment within a five-mile radius of Kingsbridge and Dartmouth. After dismissal, the defendant opened an estate agency within five miles of Kingsbridge, but outside this radius of Dartmouth.
Held: The restraint in relation to Dartmouth was unreasonable and could be ignored but the restriction in respect of Kingsbridge could be enforced.

(*Scorer v. Seymour Jones*, 1966)

1:13 DISCHARGE OF CONTRACT

(i) DISCHARGE BY PERFORMANCE

(*a*) Complete performance necessary

In general only precise and complete performance of a contractual obligation will discharge a party from his duty.

Example

N agreed to store *E*'s furniture during the Second World War, but arranged storage with another person whose premises were later bombed.
Held: N was liable to *E* as he was under a personal duty under the contract to ensure the goods' safety.

(*Edwards v. Newland & Co.*, 1950)

(*b*) Part performance may be sufficient

However, if part performance is accepted by the defendant then a claim can be made.

Example

A builder agreed to construct two houses for £565. Only part of the work was done and the builder refused to proceed further. The defendant then finished the work and the builder sued on *quantum meruit* (*see under* Remedies) for the work completed—£333.
Held: The defendant had *not* accepted part performance; the builder would not succeed.

(*Sumpter v. Hedges*, 1898)

(c) Payment for part performance

If the contract can be divided and one part is performed then payment can be enforced for that part—e.g. a contract to build a greenhouse and paint a fence. If the contract is substantially performed then the defendant may be able to deduct the cost of finishing the work properly.

Example

A decorator carried out work in a flat and made furniture for the defendant. The job was poorly done and £294 had to be paid by the defendant to bring the work up to standard.
Held: The decorator could claim the contract price (£750 on *quantum meruit*) less the £294 laid out by the defendant.

(*Hoenig v. Isaacs*, 1952)

Where the court regards the work done as falling short of substantial performance the contractor cannot succeed in a claim.

Example

A contractor installed central heating in the defendant's house for a lump sum of £560. After the work was done, the defendant complained that the work was defective in that it failed to heat the house adequately and gave off fumes. He refused to pay the contractor. The lower court found the cost of remedying the serious defects in the system to be £174.50 and ordered payment of the balance, £431.50, to the contractor. The defendant appealed.
Held: The Court of Appeal decided that the plaintiff could only claim on the lump-sum contract, with deductions for defects, where there had been substantial performance of the contract. Taking into account the nature of the defects and the cost of repairs (and the proportion this bore to the contract price) the contract had not been substantially performed. The contractor would therefore recover nothing.

(*Bolton v. Mahadeva*, 1972)

(d) Time the essence of the contract

Example

R agreed to supply a Rolls-Royce chassis to O by 20 March. When it failed to arrive O agreed to wait for later delivery. In June he stated to R that if the chassis did not arrive before 25 July he would refuse to accept it. The chassis arrived in October and O refused delivery. R sued for breach of contract.
Held: O had given reasonable notice he was re-introducing time as an essential element of the contract.

(*Rickards Ltd. v. Oppenheim*, 1950)

(ii) DISCHARGE BY AGREEMENT

(a) Release from obligations

One party to a contract may agree to release the other from his contractual obligations. The second agreement must be under seal or supported by consideration—the latter will be understood by each giving up his earlier promises.

Where one party has completely carried out his part of the agreement then the discharge must be either under seal or by accord and satisfaction. For instance if *A* owes *B* £50 and *B* agrees to accept a cheque for this amount from *C* there will have been accord (agreement) and satisfaction (consideration).

Example

The defendant drew a Bill of Exchange for £18 3*s*. 11*d*. which was returned unaccepted. The plaintiff agreed to accept £9 from the defendant's father in full satisfaction of the debt.
Held: The plaintiff could not recover the balance from the defendant as this would constitute a fraud on the father.

(*Welby v. Drake*, 1825)

(*b*) *Novation*

Where it is agreed that as *A* cannot carry out his obligations to *B*, *C* will take his place, novation occurs. All three parties must agree to this substitution. For instance where a business man sells his business to a company he has formed, the company takes on liability for his trade contracts. Only if the other party agrees to release him from the contract and deal with the company instead has he no liability.

(iii) DISCHARGE BY FRUSTRATION

If performance of the agreement is impossible at the time the agreement is made then the contract is void—there being no consideration for the contract.

(*a*) *Subsequent impossibility*

However, if the contract becomes impossible to perform after it is made then the contract is not as a rule discharged. The courts appear to take the view that the parties should have foreseen certain situations and provided for them in the contract (e.g. by strike and labour dispute clauses, etc.).

But the parties *will* be excused performance in the case of subsequent impossibility in the following circumstances:

1. *Where there has been a change of law*

Example

The grantor of a lease agreed that no building would be erected opposite to the premises leased. A railway company later acquired the land compulsorily under an Act of Parliament and built a station.
Held: The statutory action had discharged the grantor from his obligations.

(*Baily v. De Crespigny*, 1869)

2. *Where the subject matter is destroyed*

Example

A music hall hired to the plaintiff for a series of concerts burnt down before these took place.
Held: The contract was frustrated.

(*Taylor v. Caldwell*, 1863)

3. *Where personal illness prevents performance*

Example

A pianist agreed to play at a concert. He became ill and informed the organizer. The organizer sued the pianist for the loss on the postponed function.
Held: The pianist's illness frustrated the contract.

(*Robinson v. Davison*, 1871)

The situation will depend on the contract.

Example

A works manager was employed under a five-year contract. After two years he became ill and was absent for five months from his job. His employers ended his employment contract.
Held: The manager was entitled to damages for wrongful dismissal as bearing in mind the length of the contract and the period of illness the contract itself was not frustrated.

(*Storey v. Fulham Steel Works Co. Ltd.*, 1907)

4. *Where the contract depends on the occurrence of a certain event*

Example

The defendant hired rooms in Pall Mall to view the coronation procession of Edward VII. When the processions were cancelled the defendant refused to pay the balance of the rent.
Held: The viewing of the processions was the basis of the contract, which had been frustrated.

(*Krell v. Henry*, 1903)

It should be noted the contract must be wholly frustrated.

Example

A boat was chartered to see the royal naval review at Spithead and cruise round the fleet. Due to cancellation of the coronation the review did not take place. The boat owner sued for the hire price.
Held: As the fleet remained in position the whole purpose of the contract was not frustrated and the charge was due.

(*Herne Bay Steam Boat Co. Ltd. v. Hutton*, 1903)

5. *Where the commercial or practical purpose of the contract is frustrated*

Example

A building firm contracted to build reservoirs near Staines within six years. The contract provided that if the work was 'unduly delayed or impeded' extra time for completion would be granted. When the First World War broke out the Ministry of Munitions requisitioned the builder's plant in 1916 and halted work. The water company claimed the contract had been frustrated notwithstanding that their engineers had power under the contract to extend the time limit.

Held: The break in work caused by the Minister's order was of such a kind that the contract when resumed was essentially different from that which was compulsorily ended.

(Metropolitan Water Board v. Dick Kerr and Co. Ltd., 1918)

(b) Performance of the contract must be radically different

Example

A firm of builders contracted to build seventy houses for a council within eight months at a fixed price of £92,425. Due to bad weather and labour troubles the houses took twenty-two months to complete. This resulted in the work costing more than the fixed price. The builders sought discharge of the contract on the grounds of frustration.

Held: The contract's performance had become more onerous to the builders but not radically different from that contemplated by both parties, so it had not been frustrated.

(Davis Contractors Ltd. v. Fareham U.D.C., 1956)

(c) Self-induced frustration of no effect

It should be noted that where a party seeks to set aside a contract he will not be allowed to succeed where he has been responsible for the frustrating act (i.e. self-induced frustration).

Example

Charterers of a ship allowed it to enter the Suez Canal—a known danger zone—in breach of a term of contract. The ship became trapped during hostilities for two months. The charterers claimed that the contract had been frustrated.

Held: Even if there were frustration the charterers could not rely on it as it had been brought about by their own breach in entering a danger zone.

(Ocean Tramp Tankers Corporation v. V/O Sovfracht, 1964)

(d) Effect of the Law Reform (Frustrated Contracts) Act 1943

Under the Law Reform (Frustrated Contracts) Act 1943, the effect of discharge by subsequent impossibility or frustration is covered.

The Act contains the following provisions:

1. All sums paid under a contract before its discharge may be recovered.
2. All sums payable under a contract cease to be payable.
3. If the person who received payment under the contract has incurred expenses in carrying it out he may retain or recover from the payer all or part of the expenses in the discretion of the court where it thinks just.
4. Any valuable benefits obtained from the other party's actions under the contract must be paid for—again at the court's discretion, where it thinks just.
Note: The Act does not apply to charterparties, contracts of insurance, contracts for carriage of goods by sea, agreements for sale of specific goods which perish before the risk has passed to the buyer.

(iv) DISCHARGE OF CONTRACT BY BREACH

(a) Breach of condition

If the contract contains a term that 'goes to the root of the contract'—this term is a condition. If this is broken the other party can treat the contract as at an end. On the other hand he can treat the contract as binding and sue for damages.

Example

A garage proprietor entered into a three-year contract with the plaintiffs under which the garage was to be advertised on litter-bins. The plaintiffs claimed the full contract price on failure by the defendant to pay an instalment; the defendant asked the plaintiffs to cancel the agreement which they refused to do.
Held: The plaintiffs were entitled to recover the sum as they had not accepted the breach so the contract remained.

(*White & Carter (Councils) Ltd. v. McGregor*, 1961)

(b) Breach of warranty

If a term is not essential, but less important, it is a warranty. Breach of warranty does not discharge the contract although the party who is injured may sue for breach and damages. In order to be a breach of condition the action complained of must be such as to destroy the commercial basis of the contract.

Example

H chartered a ship to K for twenty-four weeks. The ship proved to be unseaworthy with ancient engines and an incompetent crew. Fifteen weeks were spent in repair dock at Osaka, Japan—the ship was in fact unseaworthy for twenty weeks out of the twenty-four.
Held: The commercial purpose of the contract was not frustrated. K need not have waited for breach of contract, but should have repudiated the agreement at the outset. H were in breach of warranty only.

(*Hong Kong Fir Shipping Co. Ltd. v. Kawasaki Kisen Kaisha Ltd.*, 1962)

The House of Lords has re-emphasized the rules for construing a contract and, in particular, terms labelled 'conditions'.

Example

In a written contract the appellant company had granted sole selling rights for panel presses to the respondent company. One section of the agreement stated that the respondents send a representative at least once every week to the six largest U.K. motor manufacturers to obtain orders for panel presses. Provision was made for ending the contract if 'material' breaches of the contract occurred which were not remedied within the 4½-year period of the contract. In the first eight months, material breaches occurred followed by a six-month period in which there were lesser breaches. The appellants claimed the right to end the contract on the basis that 'condition' referred to a fundamental term of the contract, breach of which gave the injured party a right to damages and repudiation of the contract itself.

Held: The term 'condition' was not used in its legal sense being fundamental to the contract and therefore the breaches that occurred did not give the appellants the right to repudiate the contract. It was not legitimate for a court to use as an aid in construction of the contract anything the parties did and said after it was made.

(Schuler A.G. v. Wickman Machine Tool Sales Ltd., 1973)

(a) Anticipatory breach

Where one party repudiates before performance is due this is known as anticipatory breach of contract. Here, the injured party may either sue for damages at the time of breach or await performance. If performance is awaited this may frustrate the injured party's right of action, since the defaulting party may take advantage of any circumstance that occurs meanwhile to avoid the contract. Whether such a breach has occurred depends on construction by the court.

Example

Anglia Television decided to make a film of a play *The Man in the Wood* and selected Robert Reed, a well-known American actor, for the leading role, having made prior arrangements such as finding a location, employing a director and production staff. The contract with Reed was entered into on 30 August 1968 which required him to attend rehearsals and act in the play between 9 September and 11 October 1968. Due to a booking in America Reed repudiated the agreement and after a fruitless search for a substitute actor Anglia abandoned the project. Anglia obtained judgement and were awarded damages of £2,750 which included the expenses incurred prior to the agreement. Reed then appealed.

Held: The Court of Appeal in dismissing the appeal ruled that Anglia could claim for wasted expenditure including that incurred before the contract itself, provided it was such as would be reasonably in the contemplation of the parties as likely to be wasted if the contract was broken.

(Anglia Television Ltd. v. Reed, 1971)

1:14 REMEDIES

The following are remedies available to an injured party in contract:

(i) damages at Common Law;
(ii) action on *quantum meruit*;
(iii) specific performance or injunction;
(iv) rescission;
(v) refusal of further performance.

(i) DAMAGES

Damages are a common law remedy for breach of contract and are compensation for actual loss and are awarded as of right to place the injured party in the same financial position that he would have been in if the contract had been performed. There are two types—liquidated and unliquidated damages.

(*a*) Liquidated damages

Liquidated damages represent the amount of damages agreed upon by the parties beforehand as payable in the event of breach. Liquidated damages must not be a penalty but a genuine pre-estimate of loss that may reasonably be expected to occur. If a sum fixed is so high that it amounts to a penalty it is void and only the extent of the proved damage will be recoverable.

Example

Manufacturers supplied tyres to dealers under an agreement whereby the defendants agreed not to sell them below the list price, nor to supply certain named persons and to pay £5 by way of liquidated damages for each breach. *Held:* The payments were enforceable as genuine pre-estimates of loss, as the figure fixed was not extravagant.

(*Dunlop Pneumatic Tyre Co. Ltd. v. New Garage and Motor Co. Ltd.*, 1915)

Example

A dealer agreed not to sell any car or parts below list price, nor resell to other dealers or exhibit cars bought under the agreement. In the event of any breach £250 would be paid by the dealer.
Held: The sum was a penalty—a substantial sum payable on every breach and held as a threat over the dealer's head to compel performance.

(*Ford Motor Co. (England) Ltd. v. Armstrong*, 1915)

It should be noted that if the loss sustained is greater than the liquidated damages, only the agreed damages can be claimed.

Example

A contract for delivery and erection of an acetone recovery plant provided that if the work was not completed by a certain date the contractors were to pay a sum of £20 for every week over the deadline. They were, in fact, thirty weeks late. The defendants claimed for £5,850, the actual loss sustained due to the delay.

Held: The £20 per week was the sum agreed to be paid and so £600 only could be claimed by the defendants.

(*Cellulose Acetate Silk Co. Ltd. v. Widnes Foundry (1925) Ltd.*, 1933)

(b) Unliquidated damages

If the contract fixes no damages the court has to decide the amount to be paid on breach provided the plaintiff can produce evidence of the loss sustained. Unliquidated damages fall into the following main categories:

1. *Ordinary*
Assessed by the court as arising naturally from breach of contract, being genuine financial compensation for the loss actually suffered.
2. *Special*
These cover losses not arising naturally from breach of contract and so must have been in the contemplation of the parties to be recoverable.
3. *Exemplary*
These are in excess of what would normally be awarded. Not normally awarded in contract they may be given where a banker refuses to meet a customer's cheque despite the fact he has adequate funds in his account.
4. *Nominal*
Where a plaintiff has suffered no actual loss but has proved a breach of contract this will be acknowledged by a nominal award—£2.
5. *Contemptuous*
Where the court disapproves of the behaviour of a plaintiff in bringing an action they will award ½p damages.

(c) Remoteness of damage

The main aim of an award of damages is to put the injured party in the same position as if the contract had been performed. However, the result of a breach of contract may be far-reaching and the courts have had to draw a limit beyond which damage incurred is said to be too remote.

Example

H contracted with *B* to take *H*'s crankshaft (part of his mill machinery) to an engineer for repair. Due to *B*'s delay *H*'s mill had to close and *B* was sued by *H* for breach of contract.
Held: The carrier was not liable to compensate *H* for his losses when the mill closed as he did not know that there was only one crankshaft available. *B* could not reasonably have foreseen the damages that resulted from the delay.

(*Hadley v. Baxendale*, 1854)

Example

V Ltd., launderers and dyers, contracted with *N* Ltd. to purchase a second-hand boiler to be delivered on 5 June. The boiler was damaged and arrived in November. *V* Ltd. claimed damages of (1) £16 a week for the loss of new business, (2) £262 per week for the loss of lucrative dyeing contracts.
Held: *N* Ltd. were only liable to pay damages at the rate of £16 a week as these

were normal profits, but damages for losses under (2) were not in the contemplation of the parties at the time the contract was made.

(*Victoria Laundry (Windsor) Ltd. v. Newman Industries Ltd.*, 1949)

It must be pointed out that a plaintiff is under a duty to mitigate his loss as far as he can reasonably do so.

Example

The owner of a Lea Francis 1951 car had an accident and received £80 from his insurance company. Despite advice that repair of the car was uneconomic he had it repaired at a cost of £192, making no attempt to buy a similar car on the open market. He then claimed damages on the basis of the difference between the cost of repair and the insurance payment.

Held: The plaintiff would only get damages based on the market price of the car *not* on cost of repairing it as he had not taken all reasonable steps to mitigate his loss.

(*Darbishire v. Warren*, 1963)

The courts will allow damages for mental distress and inconvenience in an action for breach of contract as an exception to the rule in *Addis v. Gramophone Co.*

Example

The plaintiff booked a fortnight's skiing holiday with defendants, travel agents, in Switzerland. As described in the defendants' brochure the holiday was to be a house party, including an English-speaking hotelier, yodler evenings, a bar in the evening, afternoon tea and cakes, skis for hire and the services of a representative. After the first week the plaintiff was alone, the bar was open one evening only, the hotelier spoke only German, the yodler evenings were brief and performed by a singer in working clothes, no full-length skis were available, there was a representative in the first week only and the tea and cakes proved to be crisps and dried nut cakes. As a result the plaintiff had a miserable holiday and sued the travel firm for damages.

Held: The Court of Appeal awarded damages for mental distress as these might justly be given in cases such as contracts to provide holidays, where the plaintiff suffered loss of enjoyment or inconvenience.

(*Jarvis v. Swans Tours Ltd.*, 1972)

The courts will examine the question of whether the probability of the damage occurring should have been reasonably contemplated by the parties at the time when the contract was made, in the light of their knowledge then.

Example

A ship was chartered for a voyage from Constanza to Basrah in the Persian Gulf to carry sugar. En route the ship deviated to Berbera to load livestock for the shipowners. As a result the ship was ten days late in arriving at Basrah. The charterers claimed damages for the difference between the market price of the sugar at the agreed delivery date and at the actual delivery date.

Held: The House of Lords awarded damages on the basis that the shipowners knew that a market for sugar existed in Basrah and that its price would be subject to daily change. The likelihood existed of the variation being downward and this was the kind of loss the shipowners ought to have realized could arise from a breach of contract causing delay in delivery when the contract was first made.

(Koufos v. C. Czarnikow, Ltd., 1967)

(ii) QUANTUM MERUIT

Under this remedy the plaintiff will be awarded as much as is earned. The court will award what it thinks the work or services are worth. It can be used contractually to recover a reasonable price or payment where there is a contract for the supply of goods or services but no sum has been fixed by the contract. It can also be used quasi-contractually to recover money for work done under a contract repudiated by the defendant, where there has been partial or substantial performance, where a benefit has been received which should be paid for, or where the contract is void or frustrated.

Example

The plaintiff was appointed managing director of a company, but the contract was void, although he was not aware of this for some months.
Held: He could recover on a *quantum meruit* for his services.

(Craven-Ellis v. Cannons Ltd., 1936)

(iii) SPECIFIC PERFORMANCE

This is an express order by the court, available at its discretion, to a contractual party instructing him to carry out his part of the agreement. It must be sought within a reasonable time. It will not be granted where it would cause undue hardship to the defendant or if the court cannot supervise the agreement. The remedy must be available to both parties and the person seeking it must be willing and able to carry out his obligations. There must be consideration for the promise the plaintiff seeks to enforce. Normally specific performance will not be granted for performance of a contract for personal services.

Injunction

This is a discretionary order of the court requiring a person to stop doing an action complained of, or ordering a person to do something. It can be used to prevent an act that would cause a breach of contract. Although specific performance is not normally granted to compel performance of a contract for personal services, an injunction may be awarded to enforce a negative term of an agreement.

Example

Miss Bette Davis, the film actress, agreed with a film company not to work for any other employer during the term of her contract without written consent of the producer.

Held: An injunction would be granted to enforce the negative terms for the period of contract or three years, whichever was the shorter.

(*Warner Bros. v. Nelson*, 1936)

Note: The conditions that apply to the award of specific performance also applies to the injunction.

(iv) RESCISSION

In granting rescission the courts must be satisfied that it is possible to restore the parties to their pre-contractual positions. Part payments must be returned unless there are circumstances that indicate these are guarantees for performance on the part of the payer. If this is the case they will be forfeited if the contract is not proceeded with.

(v) REFUSAL OF FURTHER PERFORMANCE

A person suffering from a breach of contract who wishes to end his obligations under it can refuse to carry them out and set up the other parties' breach as a defence to his own. To strengthen his case he may decide to bring an action for rescission.

1:15 ASSIGNMENT

METHODS

Assignment, that is the passing of rights or liabilities under a contract to another person, can be accomplished in a variety of ways. Liabilities and rights can be assigned only with the consent of the other party to the contract.

The chief ways in which rights under a contract are assigned are:.

(*a*) legal assignment;
(*b*) equitable assignment;
(*c*) assignment by operation of law;
(*d*) novation.

(a) Legal assignment

All debts and other legal things in action (including rights under a contract) may be assigned (s. 136 Law of Property Act 1925); however, the assignment must be in writing and signed by the person making the assignment, be absolute and not solely by way of charge and express notice must be given to the debtor, trustee or other party from whom the assignor could claim the thing in action or debt. If only part of the interest is assigned the assignment is not absolute, as, for example, where part of a salary is assigned to a creditor under a repayment scheme.

(*Hughes v. Pump House Hotel Co. Ltd.*, 1906)

The effect of the assignment is to transfer to the assignee the legal right to the debt or thing in action, with all the corresponding legal and equitable remedies as well as empowering the assignee with the authority to give a good discharge for the debt.

The assignee takes the assignment subject to all the defences and claims open to the debtor arising from the contract and existing when the debtor had notice of the assignment.

(b) Equitable assignment

If there is a clear intention to assign but the assignment does not conform to the formalities of legal assignment then the assignment may still stand as an equitable one. In this instance the assignment may be informal and need not be in writing. In practice notice should be given to the debtor so that priority is gained over any subsequent assignee without notice of his assignment. Similarly, the debtor can set up defences against the assignee he had against the assignor up to the date he received notice of assignment. Any payment made by the debtor to assignor before notice is received is good against the assignee.

Contracts of a personal nature cannot be either equitably or legally assigned; for example, a contract of service or even a contract for the sale of goods if this contains a distinct element of personal service.

(*Kemp v. Baerselman*, 1906)

(c) Assignment by operation of law

Contracts may be assigned by operation of law in two ways:

1. death;
2. bankruptcy.

1. Death of a party to a contract results in all his rights and liabilities passing to his personal representatives, except those contracts of personal service.
2. Bankruptcy results in the bankrupt's rights and liabilities being passed to his trustee in bankruptcy.

(d) Novation

When the membership of a firm changes and creditors agree, expressly or by implication, to accept the new management in place of the old, then what is termed novation occurs. This is a fresh contract between the creditors and the old firm agreeing that the new firm step into their shoes and take over their liability thus releasing the former debtors. A similar situation arises when membership of a partnership changes.

QUESTIONS

1. Smith advertises his car in the local paper for £200 or near offer. On Friday at 10.00 a.m. Jones telephones Smith and offers £150. Smith replies that he will not take less than £175 and Jones agrees to £175 'subject to inspection', which is arranged for noon. At 11.00 a.m. Brown telephones and offers £200. Smith accepts and at 11.30 a.m. Brown arrives, pays over the £200 and drives away the car. When later in the day Jones arrives to inspect the car he is told that it has already been sold. Advise Jones as to whether he has legal redress and if so against whom.

(Institute of Purchasing and Supply, December, 1970)

2. (*a*) With the aid of illustrations, explain the main rules which apply to the making, acceptance and termination of an offer.

(*b*) Auctioneers, Adam Bede and Partners, advertised the sale of antique furniture for which offers were to be submitted 'in sealed envelopes not later than 10.00 on Monday, 11 June, 1979'. The usual practice was to accept the highest bid. The auctioneers reserved the right to withdraw the goods from sale 'if bids tendered fail to reach a reserve price, or if the goods have been sold by private treaty before the aforementioned time or for any other reason which the auctioneers deem fit'. Charles made a bid of £3,000 for the furniture; his offer was not exceeded by any other bidder. Through a misunderstanding at the auctioneers' office, a bid for £2,275 from Dorian was accepted by letter which never reached its destination. The letter of confirmation of acceptance of his bid was posted on Friday, 8 June 1979. Over the telephone on Tuesday, 12 June, 1979, Dorian is informed that the letter of acceptance had been sent to him in error. Charles and Dorian both claim title to the furniture. The auctioneers assert a legal right to refuse delivery of the goods to either (i) Charles or (ii) Dorian. Advise the auctioneers.

(Certificate in Marketing, Part II, June 1979)

3. (*a*) What is meant by the phrase, 'intention to create legal relations', when applied to the law of contract?

(*b*) Albert is Brian's friend. They form a syndicate with Brian's two brothers, Charles and David, in order to submit a football pool coupon which bears the clause: 'This coupon is accepted on the clear understanding that the agreement subsisting between the persons submitting the coupon and the Company is binding in honour only.' The coupon is sent to the company, the Neverlose Football Pool Company, in Charles' name. When the football results are declared at the weekend, it becomes apparent that the syndicate has made an accurate forecast of the results which entitles the winner to a dividend of £250,000. Albert, who had made his equal contribution to the stake invested on the coupon now seeks payment of £62,500. The other members of the syndicate refuse to pay him anything. Would you advise Albert to sue?

(Diploma in Marketing, Part II, November 1975)

4. (*a*) What is consideration and by what rules is it governed?

(*b*) In his will, *A* left his home to *B*, one of his daughters, but gave his wife a life interest in the property. During her occupation of the property, *A*'s wife carried out certain improvements to the property at a cost of £500. Some time later, *B* signed a document promising to pay *A*'s widow when she *B*) received a capital sum due under an endowment policy. *B* subsequently refused to make the payment whereupon *A*'s widow brought an action for recovery. State, with reasons, whether the action would or would not succeed.

(Diploma in Marketing, Part II, May 1970)

5. (*a*) What is the legal position of a minor who enters a contractual agreement?

(b) Two teenagers, Ian and Joan, who had studied music together, lived in the same block of flats. Both are music critics for national newspapers. Before they married, Joan bought an expensive record-player from Kenneth on credit. She requested Kenneth to send the bill to Ian. The transaction has been guaranteed by Leonard. The shop-keeper, Kenneth, was under the impression, because of close similarity of facial features, than Ian and Joan were brother and sister. The bill for the record-player arrived a month after the marriage between Ian and Joan. What is the legal position if Ian fails to pay for the record-player?

(Certificate in Marketing, Part II, November 1979)

6. (a) What is an exemption (or exception or exclusion) clause? To what extent may a party rely upon such a clause?

(b) Figure-conscious Caroline asks David to supply her with some slim-ming tablets for herself and her friend, Elaine. David, a herbalist, states that he has only one small box of tablets, bearing the trade mark of a well-known manufacturer of pharmaceutical products. As Caroline wants an additional quantity, she agrees to supply David with a formula under which he would prepare the balance of the order. Before committing himself to the production of the tablets, David asks Caroline to sign a document, which she does without reading it, on which the following clause is printed:
'The signatory to this document agrees to exempt the supplier from all liability for any injury, damage or loss howsoever arising.'
Over the years David has supplied tablets, based on formulae supplied by customers, for the treatment of common ailments. Caroline and Elaine use first the tablets bearing the manufaturer's brand name. When the supply, sufficient for three days, is exhausted, they use the tablets specially made by David. Within a few hours of taking them Caroline and Elaine become ill. Caroline, who had taken an excess dose, soon recovers; but Elaine, who has an allergy to one of the ingredients in the tablets, suffers from lesions of the intestine after using the tablets and she is off work for five weeks. Assess Elaine's entitlement to damages, if any, from David.

(Certificate in Marketing, Part II, June 1979)

7. (a) Certain contracts are required by statute to be evidenced in writing, otherwise they cannot be enforced. Mention these contracts and say how they are affected by the doctrine of part performance.

(b) *A* verbally agreed to lease a flat from *R*, provided *R* made certain specified alterations to meet *A*'s wishes. *A* himself supervised and approved the work, but upon its completion refused to take the lease, pleading absence of writing. Advise *R*.

(Diploma in Marketing II, November 1970)

8. (a) What is the effect of the incorporation of an exemption clause in a contract?

(b) Eve telephoned her local dry-cleaners to discover whether they removed stains from suède jackets. Following an affirmative reply, Eve asked the Manageress, Faith, the fee charged for this service. Eve then inquired about business hours before the conversation continued:

Eve: 'I will bring the jacket in this afternoon.'

Faith: 'We will be delighted to offer you our services, Madam.'

Eve: 'That's fine! The price seems very reasonable.'

Faith: 'In these days of inflation, we regret we are unable to offer any lower fee. Simply deposit the jacket with us and we will do the rest.'

At Faith's shop, a notice is displayed on the wall close to a door through which customers enter. The notice excludes liability 'for any damage to goods deposited with the Company by customers for processing'. The exemption clause is repeated on the reverse of the document handed to Eve by Faith against receipt of the goods. Carbon paper used for preparation of an office duplicate copy smudges the exemption clause on the copy handed to Eve.

Eve's jacket is returned to her in a more stained condition than when she left it at the shop. A diamond ring, which had been inadvertently left in a pocket of the jacket, was returned buckled. Eve insists that the company must pay her damages for her loss. Solicitors acting for the company claim that the company is protected by the exemption clause. Which of the parties to this dispute has the stronger claim?

(Diploma in Marketing, Part II, November 1975)

9. (a) What is misrepresentation? What forms does it take? Indicate the legal remedies available for misrepresentation.

(b) In a letter, Harry, an executive employed by Jamboree & Co. Ltd., informs Ian that a particular model of tractor 'is eminently suitable for hill farming' and supports his statement by citing technical data from a brochure produced by Jamboree & Co. Ltd. on the advice of technical experts who have acted as consultants to Jamboree & Co. Ltd. In several material particulars the brochure is inaccurate. On a previous occasion, Harry had received data from the same consultants which carried several major technical errors. Throughout the remainder of an extensive business connection between Jamboree & Co. Ltd., and the consultants, the quality of advice tendered by the same consultants was of a high standard. Ian buys one of the tractors which is not suitable for hill farming. Advise Ian.

(Certificate in Marketing, Part II, June 1979)

10. (a) By what principles must an employer be guided when imposing restrictions on the present and future activities of his employees?

(b) *T* was employed by *E* as a traveller for children's wear and gave a signed undertaking that he would never engage in similar work for any competitor should he terminate his employment with *E*. Upon leaving *E*'s employment, however, he accepted a similar post with *C*, a competing manufacturer. Give reasons why *E* could, or could not, enforce *T*'s undertaking.

(Diploma in Marketing II, May 1969)

11. The General Engineering Co. Ltd. place an order with the Swift Telephone Co. Ltd. for a complete internal communications system. The contract contains the following clause: 'The system supplied will be of the most

modern design, and in accordance with latest applicable internationally recognized engineering standards.' Six months after having placed the contract, General Engineering discover that the equipment being supplied was first designed ten years ago, and that both Japanese and Swedish companies can offer a more up to date system with improved facilities and lower operating costs. Advise General Engineering as to their contractual rights against the Swift Company.

(I.P.S., December 1971)

12. Under what circumstances is a supplier entitled to claim that a contract is frustrated? Give two examples illustrating where a contract would be considered frustrated and contrast these with a case when the supplier would not be successful in a claim for frustration.

(I.P.S., December 1971)

13. Jones & Co. send a letter to one of their equipment suppliers which states 'we accept your tender—subject to the preparation of a formal contract to be drawn up by our respective lawyers'. No formal contract is ever prepared, but the supplier proceeds with manufacture. When manufacture is nearly complete, Jones & Co. decide that they no longer want the goods. They seek your advice as to their legal position. What advice would you give?

(I.P.S., May 1969)

14. (*a*) To what extent will a party to a contract be able to plead successfully that a mistake has released him from his legal obligations?

(*b*) During negotiations for the sale of a painting, Fred offered to buy it at an inflated price in the mistaken belief that the painting was the work of a Dutch master. The painting was the work of a forger. The vendor, Hogg, thought that he was selling the painting to Fred's twin brother, George. Twice during the negotiations Hogg addressed Fred as George. To avoid embarrassment, Fred did not draw Hogg's attention to the misuse of names. Fred pays for the painting by cheque which is later dishonoured. By the time that the cheque has been returned to Hogg, accompanied by a note from the bank that it has been dishonoured, Fred has sold the painting to Ilka. Advise Hogg.

(Certificate in Marketing, Part II, November 1978)

15. A heating contractor is three months late in completing the heating installation for a new factory. The contract contains a fixed date for completion but no liquidated damages clause. During the delay there was exceptionally cold weather and the factory production had to be suspended for four weeks. Advise the purchaser on what basis he would recover damages for the delay.

(I.P.S., May 1970)

16. (*a*) Outline the main remedies for a breach of contract.

(*b*) Under a verbal agreement Jack agreed to grant the lease of a shop and an adjoining forecourt to Kenneth for £98,000. The written agreement refers exclusively to the lease of the shop for £99,000; no mention is made of the forecourt. The written agreement provided that 'the said premises shall be used solely as a shop'. Kenneth begins trading as Lampoon Ltd., a business engaged in light industry. At the time of the negotiations Kenneth did not disclose that he proposed to change the use of the premises from being a shop to their present use. Jack occupies a luxury maisonette over the premises. Advise the parties as to any legal remedies available to them. (Knowledge of planning law is not required.)

(Certificate in Marketing, Part II, November 1978)

17. (*a*) In what circumstances will a contract be discharged?
    (*b*) Tour operators, Medihols Ltd., had agreed to fix up a holiday in Paris for Nicholas and his wife. Included in the holiday arrangements were several trips around Paris by coach. When Nicholas and his wife arrived in Paris, coach drivers, who normally drove sightseers around Paris, were on strike, and the hotel where they had been reserved accommodation was infested with vermin. After staying in Paris for three days, at another hotel of inferior quality found for Nicholas and his wife by the tour operators, Nicholas' wife returned home. Nicholas, on completion of his holiday, seeks your advice as to which remedies he is entitled, if any?

(Certificate in Marketing, Part II, November 1979)

18. Smith obtains a provisional price from his garage for carrying out certain repairs costing £30 to his car and instructs the garage to proceed. When the work is complete the garage submit a bill for £50 and when Smith refuses to pay they refuse to return his car to him. Advise Smith as to his legal position.

(I.P.S., December 1967)

19. (*a*) Mention the exceptions to the general rule that a party to a contract is under no obligation to disclose material facts of which the other party is unaware, and comment briefly on each.
    (*b*) Smith was employed by Andrews as a sales representative, whose duties included the collection from customers of amounts due to Andrews. Andrews took out a fidelity guarantee with the *X* company, under which the customer agreed to be answerable for any loss, not exceeding £500, which Andrews might sustain through Smith's dishonesty. In January 1968 Smith embezzled £55 and, without informing the *X* company, Andrews continued to employ Smith provided he repaid the amount at £5 a week. This Smith did, but in February 1969 he embezzled a further £174, whereupon Andrews dismissed him and called upon the *X* company to make good the £174. State, with reasons, whether the company is liable.

(Diploma in Marketing II, May 1969)

2. *Restrictive Trade Practices*

2:1 RESTRICTIVE TRADE PRACTICES ACT 1976; RESTRICTIVE PRACTICES COURT ACT 1976; RESALE PRICES ACT 1976

Before 1956 trade associations commonly made contracts with their members under which it was agreed that if a member of the association sold goods below a stated price the others would jointly cut off his supplies. This was made illegal by the 1956 Restrictive Trade Practices Act.

The Restrictive Trade Practices Act 1976 and the Restrictive Practices Court Act 1976 and the Resale Prices Act 1976 have now consolidated the Restrictive Trade Practices Acts 1956 to 1973 together with sections of the Fair Trading Act 1973 (*see* 2:2).

(i) REGISTRATION

The 1976 Restrictive Trade Practices Act requires restrictive trade agreements to be registered in a public register which the Director-General of Fair Trading is under a duty to compile and maintain.

The Act requires registration of agreements of a restrictive character made between two or more persons carrying on business in the U.K., in the production, supply, or processing of goods. Such agreements by s. 6 include those with regard to:

(*a*) the prices to be charged, quoted or paid for goods supplied, offered or acquired, or for the application of any process or manufacture to goods;

(*b*) the prices to be recommended or suggested as the prices to be charged in respect of the resale cf goods supplied;

(*c*) the terms or conditions on or subject to which goods are to be supplied or acquired or any such process is to be applied to goods;

(*d*) the quantities or descriptions of goods to be produced, supplied or acquired;

(*e*) the processes of manufacture to be applied to any goods, or the quantities or descriptions of goods to which any such process is to be applied; or

(*f*) the persons or class of persons to, for or from whom, or the areas or places in or from which, the goods are to be supplied or acquired, or any such process applied.

It is immaterial whether any restrictions accepted by the parties to the agreement relate to the same or different matters specified above, or have a similar or different effect to them and whether the parties accepting restrictions carry on the same or different classes of business. An agreement which confers privileges or benefits only on parties complying with conditions listed above or which imposes obligations on parties who do not comply will be treated as an agreement under which restrictions are accepted by each of the parties in respect of those conditions.

Recommendations by trade associations to their members with regard to prices members are to charge are subject to registration (s. 8 (2)).

An agreement where one party is obliged to make payments will be treated as a restrictive agreement where payment is calculated by reference:

(*a*) to the quantity of goods produced or supplied by him, or to which any process of manufacture is applied by him; or
(*b*) to the quantity of materials acquired or used by him for the purpose of or in the production of any goods or the application of any such process to the goods.

Note: Agreement covers any agreement even if it is not intended to be legally enforceable. 'An agreement for the supply of goods' refers to any agreement under which one person agrees to supply goods to another even though it may include agreement on other matters.

(ii) FURNISHING PARTICULARS

Particulars of agreements registrable under the Act made before 1 November 1973 must be furnished within three months from that date (i.e. before 1 February 1974) unless ended before that date.

New registrable agreements made on or after 1 November 1973, or, in the case of agreements (whenever made) which extend or add to the restrictions accepted under an agreement or which add to or reduce the scope of the application of a continuing restriction as regards the classes of persons, goods, process of manufacture, areas or places to which it relates, must also be furnished before they take effect (or within three months if that is earlier).

With regard to registrable information agreements (*see* (iv) below), provision for the furnishing of information in respect of prices or terms or conditions of supply is treated as a restriction.

Procedure to be followed is laid down in s. 27 of the Act and detailed in Registration of Restrictive Trading Agreements Registrations Order 1976 (S.I. 183). All documents required for registration must be sent to:

The Office of Fair Trading (Registration),
Chancery House, Chancery Lane, London WC2A 1SP.

The office provides copies of the necessary forms for furnishing particulars and all details of requirements on request. The person sending the documents to the office must certify on an official form that the particulars given are complete as to the parties and all the terms of the agreement.

(iii) FAILURE TO REGISTER

In respect of every agreement subject to registration the following must be furnished to the Director-General:
(*a*) the names and addresses of the persons who are parties to the agreement; and
(*b*) the whole of the terms of the agreement, whether or not relating to any such restriction or information described in the Act.

Failure to furnish particulars of any registrable agreement or registrable variation within the time laid down by the Act (s. 24, Schedule 2 Table at para. 5 (1)) means that such an agreement will be void in respect of all restrictions (or provisions for the exchange of information) to which the default applies and it will be unlawful for any party carrying on business in the United Kingdom to give effect to the agreement, enforce or try to enforce it in respect of these restrictions (ss. 35(1), 24 (2)). This rule applies to agreements and variations made before 1 November 1973 and not furnished for registration within three months of that date as well as to new agreements or variations which must be furnished before restriction is effective.

The Director-General may take proceedings in the Restrictive Practices Court for injunctions restraining the parties from enforcing an existing agreement or from giving effect to all other unregistered agreements, or enforcing or trying to enforce them. If any person suffers loss through the operation of the void restriction they may sue for damages (s. 35 (1)).

If there is doubt as to whether an agreement or variation is subject to registration a safe procedure is to give particulars within the stipulated time to the Director-General. The particulars will not be registered if not registrable, but the parties concerned will have carried out their legal obligations. Any such application must identify the agreement or variation to which it relates, state the further time requested and the reason why it is impracticable to furnish the particulars within the time specified.

(iv) INFORMATION AGREEMENTS

The Secretary of State is empowered (ss. 7 and 12) to call up for registration by means of an order under statutory instrument any class of information agreements. These are agreements between two or more persons carrying on business in the U.K. under which provision is made for furnishing information covering supply and acquisition of goods or supply of services as well as prices charged under past agreements.

Not included as services described as designated services in an order of the Secretary of State are, for example (the list given is not exhaustive), legal, medical and dental services, architect's, accounting, auditing, surveyor's, professional engineering or technologist's services; see also Restrictive Trade Practices (Services) Order 1976 S.I. 98. It was recently decided that a lease was not prevented from being an agreement under the above Services Order. To be caught by this Order there need to be two persons carrying on business in the U.K. in the supply of services. It was recently accepted in a case where the ambit of the order was at issue that where a landlord was only involved in letting property he was not carrying on a business in the provision of services.

(*Re Ravenseft Properties Ltd. and Others*, 1976)

(v) EXEMPT AGREEMENTS

The Restrictive Trade Practices Act does not apply to agreements specifically exempted including those in Schedule 3 of that Act, and so do not require registration.

These include agreements expressly authorized by statute, agreements important to the national economy, exclusive dealings between two persons for the supply of goods (neither being a trade association), agreements between two parties for the use of patents, registered designs, know-how or trade marks, agreements for supplying services with overseas operations and export agreements. Certain of these will now be considered in more detail.

(a) *Export agreements*

Export agreements are exempt from registration if all the restrictions relate to:

(*a*) supply of goods by export from the U.K.;
(*b*) the production of goods or the application of any process of manufacture of goods outside the U.K.;
(*c*) the acquisition of goods delivered outside the U.K. and not imported into the U.K. for home use; or
(*d*) the supply of goods to be delivered outside the U.K. otherwise than by export from the U.K.

Particulars of agreements in which all the relevant restrictions relate exclusively to the supply of goods by export have to be sent by the parties to the Director-General although these restrictions do not have to be registered (s. 28). Particulars that need to be given to the Director-General regarding every export agreement are:

1. the names and addresses of the persons who are parties to the agreement;
2. the whole of the terms of the agreement, whether or not relating to the restrictions.

Particulars of an export agreement that is varied or determined must be given to the Director-General even where the effect of a variation is to remove all the restrictions relating to the supply of exports to the U.K. Particulars of specific recommendations made by trade associations relating exclusively to exports of the type mentioned must also be furnished to the Director-General.

Note: The Secretary of State is empowered by s. 29 to make an order to exempt from registration for a specified period any agreements considered reasonably necessary to enable the carrying out of a project or scheme of substantial importance to the economy with the aim of promoting trade or industrial efficiency. Certain government departments are empowered to exempt price restriction agreements (s. 30).

(b) *Patents and registered designs*

Exemption from registration was given under the 1956 Restrictive Trade Practices Act for licences and assignments and agreements to grant licences and assignments relating to a patented invention, or for which application for a patent had been made, where no relevant restrictions were accepted save in respect of the invention.

The exemption was removed by s. 101 of the Fair Trading Act now re-enacted in Schedule 3 of the Restrictive Trade Practices Act 1976 for the purposes of patent and design pooling agreements granted or made (directly or indirectly) in pursuance of a patent or design pooling agreement. Agreements must be registered whereby patent holder cross-licence one another or grant the patents to a central organization for the purpose of licensing.

A patent or design pooling agreement is defined (Schedule 3 para. 5 (5)) as an agreement between three or more persons (principal parties) each of whom has an interest in one or more patents or registered designs whereby one of the principal parties agrees to grant existing or future interests in one or more such patents or registered designs to one or more of the principal parties, or to one or more of such parties and to other persons, whether directly or indirectly through a third person (e.g. a patent holding company or a trade association). A person has an 'interest' in a patent or registered design if he is a proprietor or licensee of, or has applied for, or has acquired the right to apply for a patent or the registration of a design.

(c) Agreements relating to coal or steel

In determining whether or not an agreement is registrable no account is to be taken of any restriction relating to coal and/or steel accepted under two or more coal or steel undertakings (as defined by the European Coal and Steel Community Treaty) (s. 9 (1), (2)). An agreement is exempt from registration so long as there is in force in relation to that agreement an authorization given for the purpose of any provision in the European Coal and Steel Community Treaty relating to restrictive trade practices (s. 34). Agreements containing restrictions relating to other than coal and steel undertakings (including parties outside these industries) are still registrable.

(d) Subscriptions to trade associations

An obligation on a party to an agreement to make payments based on the quantities of material acquired, or goods produced and supplied by him is treated as a restriction in respect of the quantities of goods to be produced or supplied by him if the payments are calculated, or calculated at an increased rate, regarding quantities of goods or materials exceeding any quantity specified or calculated in accordance with the agreement. Such agreements are still registrable but this does not apply to bona fide membership subscription payments a person is obliged to make to a trade association of which he is a member (s. 6). Agreements for graduated payments on sales or output other than as a trade association membership must still be registered.

Note: Agreements to comply with standards of dimension, design, quality or performance approved by the British Standards Institution or prescribed or adapted by any trade association or other body and approved by the Secretary of State are not caught by the Act (s. 9 (5)). Industrial and provident societies (as defined under s. 15 of the Friendly and Industrial Provident Societies Act 1968) are within the definition of interconnected bodies corporate for the purposes of the Act (s. 43 (1)).

(e) Loan finance and credit facilities

The Restrictive Trade Practices Act 1977 ensures that agreements between banks and financial institutions for the provision of loan finance and credit facilities through consortium lending do not have to be registered with the

Director-General of Fair Trading and referred to the Restrictive Practices Court. This exemption applies so long as the restrictions accepted under the agreements are directed towards the protection of the security for the loan (e.g. preventing the borrower or guarantor pledging the security elsewhere) or limiting the level of further borrowing, and not at distorting competition. The Restrictive Trade Practices (Services) Order 1976 S.I. 98 is accordingly amended by s. 1 and Schedule, Part I of the Restrictive Trade Practices Act 1977.

(vi) RESTRICTIVE PRACTICES COURT

A restrictive trade agreement is invalid as being contrary to the public interest unless the Restrictive Practices Court can be satisfied that under s. 10 of Restrictive Trade Practices Act that:

(*a*) the restriction is reasonably necessary, with regard to the character of the goods, to protect the public against injury;
(*b*) the removal of the restriction would deny specific and substantial benefits to the public as purchasers, consumers or users;
(*c*) the restriction is reasonably necessary to counteract measures by a person not a party to the agreement;
(*d*) the restriction is reasonably necessary to enable the persons party to the agreement to negotiate fair terms with a person not a party to it who controls a major part of the trade, business or market in the goods concerned;
(*e*) the removal of the restriction would have serious repercussions on the general level of unemployment;
(*f*) the removal of the restriction would be likely to cause a reduction in the volume or earnings of an export business which is substantial either in relation to the whole export business of the U.K. or in relation to the whole business (including export business) of the trade or industry;
(*g*) the restriction is reasonably required for purposes connected with the maintenance of any other restrictions accepted by the parties;
(*h*) the restriction does not directly or indirectly restrict or discourage competition to any material degree in any relevant trade or industry and is not likely to do so.

'Purchasers', 'consumers' and 'users' under s. 10 include persons purchasing, consuming or using for trade or business or for public purposes and references to any one person include references to two persons being interconnected corporations or individuals in business partnership with each other.

The Restrictive Practices Court set up by the Restrictive Practices Court Act 1956 and now administered under the Restrictive Trade Practices Act 1976 is a superior court of record presided over by a High Court judge; four other judges and up to ten laymen may be members, the latter chosen for their knowledge of or experience in commerce. The Court declares on application by the Director-General whether a restriction in an agreement is contrary to the public interest. The Director-General by s. 1 (2) of the Trade Practices Act 1976 is charged with the duty of taking proceedings with regard to agreements filed or entered on the register he maintains but this duty is subject to such directions the Secretary of State may give as to order of proceedings. The Director-General may also refrain from taking proceedings before the Court when an agreement is void under any relevant provision of the E.E.C. (s. 21). The Court itself is authorized either to decline or postpone its jurisdiction, or exercise this, should it appear to the Court right to do so in view of the E.E.C. provision or the purpose and effect of any authorization or exemption it might grant (s. 5 and *see* ss. 1 and 2; *see* 2:4).

The Director-General may take civil proceedings in the Court to obtain an injunction to restrain continuation or repetition of such unlawful action. Civil proceedings for damages can be brought by any person who has suffered a loss through the void restrictions being operated. the Director-General has a discretion regarding reference to the Court of an agreement which has been determined for adjudication. The Secretary of State may discharge the Director-General from the duty of referring agreements to the Court where it is considered that the restrictions are not of such significance as to call for investigation by the Court.

(vii) RESALE PRICES ACT 1976

The Resale Prices Act 1976 prohibits manufacturers and other suppliers of goods from imposing conditions for maintenance of minimum prices at which goods are to be sold and prohibits the enforcement of such prices by withholding supplies from dealers who do not follow them (ss. 1 and 2).

Any agreement relating to the sale of goods providing for minimum prices to be charged on resale in the U.K. is void (s. 9). Such a provision or its inclusion or publication of minimum resale prices is unlawful, but suppliers can recommend resale prices for goods although an agreement fixing the price recommended must be registerd (s. 6 Restrictive Trade Practices Act 1976). It is also unlawful for a supplier to withhold supplies from a dealer on the grounds that he has sold or is likely to sell the supplier's goods at less than the stipulated minimum resale price (s. 11); however, supplies can be withheld where a dealer has been selling the same or similar goods as loss leaders in the past twelve months (s. 13).

Particular classes of goods can be exempted by order of the Restrictive Practices Court where:

(*a*) the quality or varieties of such goods would be substantially reduced to the detriment of the public or consumers or users of these goods; or
(*b*) the number of establishments for the sale of such goods would be substantially reduced to the detriment of the public etc., or
(*c*) the prices at which the goods are sold by retail would in general and in the long run be increased to the detriment of the public etc., or
(*d*) the goods would be sold by retail under conditions likely to cause danger to the health in consequence of their misuse by the public, etc., or
(*e*) any necessary services actually provided in connection with or after the sale of goods by retail would cease to be so provided or would be substantially reduced to the detriment of the public, etc.

Note: Exemption from resale price maintenance will be granted only where it can be shown to be in the public interest (s. 14).

2:2 FAIR TRADING ACT 1973

The Fair Trading Act 1973 created a substantial reform of restrictive trade practices law and further extended consumer protection. The Act created the post of Director-General of Fair Trading. The Act provides the Director-General of Fair Trading with far-ranging powers in relation to 'unfair consumer trade practices'; these powers he has used.

(ii) THE DIRECTOR-GENERAL OF FAIR TRADING

The general functions of the Director-General of Fair Trading (appointed in September 1973) are as follows (s. 2):

(*a*) keeping under review commercial activities in the United Kingdom relating to the supply or intended supply of goods and services to consumers;
(*b*) collecting and receiving information about activities and practices that may adversely affect the economic and other interests of the consumer;
(*c*) reviewing commercial activities and obtaining information about monopoly situations or uncompetitive practices;
(*d*) at the request of the Secretary of State or on his own initiative the Director will make recommendations to the Secretary of State with regard to the matters listed above.

As a matter of public policy the Director-General of Fair Trading has used persuasion to curb practices unfair to the consumer, a point borne out in the Act itself:

> 'Where it appears to the Director that the person carrying on business has in the course of that business persisted in a course of conduct which
> (*a*) is detrimental to the interests of consumers in the United Kingdom, whether those interests are economic interests or interests in respect of health, safety or other matters, and
> (*b*) in accordance with the following provisions of this section is to be regarded as unfair to consumers,
> the Director shall use his best endeavours, by communication with that person or otherwise, to obtain from him a satisfactory written assurance that he will refrain from continuing that course of conduct and from carrying on any similar course of conduct in the course of that business' (s. 34(1)).

> 'A course of conduct unfair to a consumer consists of contraventions of one or more enactments which impose duties, prohibitions or restrictions enforceable by criminal proceedings, whether any such duty, prohibition or restriction is imposed in relation to consumers as such or not and whether the person carrying on the business has or has not ben convicted of any offence in respect of any such contravention ... (or) consists of things done, or omitted to be done, in the course of that business in breach of contract or in breach of duty (other than contractual duty) owed to any person by virtue of any enactment or rule of law and enforceable by civil proceedings, whether (in any such case) civil proceedings in respect of the breach of contract or breach of duty have been brought or not' (ss. 34(1) and (2)).

The Director-General notes information on such practices from complaints of consumers' organizations gathered by virtue of s. 2 of the Act (*see* above). If a firm fails to give an assurance to the Director-General that an unfair consumer practice will cease or does not abide by an undertaking to discontinue a practice, proceedings can be taken by the Director-General against such a body in the Restrictive Practices Court (s. 35).

In the case of individual offenders or corporate organizations of under £10,000 share capital, the Director-General has a discretion (which it seems appropriate that he will exercise from the viewpoint of practicality) to bring proceedings in an alternative court (s. 41).

Legal sanctions that the Director-General can impose are up to £400 in fines and two years imprisonment.

In his work the Director-General is assisted by the Consumer Protection Advisory Committee.

(iii) CONSUMER PROTECTION ADVISORY COMMITTEE

The Consumer Protection Advisory Committee consists of a maximum of fifteen members appointed by the Secretary of State who can increase this number. These include persons qualified to advise on practices relating to goods or services supplied to or produced for supply to consumers, others experienced in the operation of the Trade Descriptions Act 1968, besides those who have a practical knowledge of consumer protection organizations.

A consumer trade practice for the purposes of the Act which may be referred to the Consumer Protection Advisory Committee by the Director-General, Secretary of State, or any other Minister is defined as:

'any practice which is for the time being carried on in connection with the supply of goods (whether by sale or otherwise) to consumers or in connection with the supply of services for consumers which relates:

(*a*) to the terms or conditions (whether as to price or otherwise) on or subject to which goods or services are or are sought to be supplied, or

(*b*) to the manner in which those terms or conditions are communicated to persons to whom goods are or are sought to be supplied or for whom services are or are sought to be supplied, or

(*c*) to promotion (by advertising, labelling or marking of goods, canvassing or otherwise) of the supply of goods or the supply of services, or

(*d*) to methods of salesmanship employed in dealing with consumers, or

(*e*) to the way in which goods are packed or otherwise got up for the purpose of being supplied, or

(*f*) to methods of demanding or securing payment for goods or services supplied' (s. 13).

On any reference being made to them the Committee, assisted by information, powers, and facilities generally available to the Director-General, will make a report to the Director-General with a copy to the Secretary of State (s. 14). No reference will be made under s. 14 if the consumer trade practice concerns supply of services of a description covered by Schedule 4 of the Act. These include legal, medical, dental, and veterinary services, nursing and midwifery services, those of architects, accountants and auditors, surveyors, patent agents and professional engineers or technologists and public educational services. Further, unless the appropriate Minister consents, no reference will be made in respect of a consumer trade practice except where

(*a*) carried on in connection with the supply of goods or services by a corporate body including the supply of gas, electricity, carriage of passengers and goods by retail and the transmission, collection and delivery of letters (Schedule 5, Part I), or
(*b*) carried on in connection only with the supply of goods and services by a corporate body including apparatus used for electrical purposes under the Post Office Act 1969, s. 24(1), and related subscriber services (e.g. telephones and similar provision) (Schedule 5, Part II).

The Director-General may propose to the Secretary of State that he make an order against a consumer trade practice where it either does or is likely to have the effect:

'(*a*) of misleading consumers as to, or withholding from them adequate information as to, or an adequate record of their rights and obligations under relevant consumer transactions or
(*b*) of otherwise misleading or confusing consumers with respect to any matter in connection with relevant consumer transactions, or
(*c*) of subjecting consumers to undue pressure to enter into relevant consumer transactions, or
(*d*) of causing the terms and conditions, on or subject to which consumers enter into relevant consumer transactions, to be so adverse to them to be inequitable' (s. 17(1)).

In the case of such a reference by the Director-General it will be published in full by him in the *London*, *Edinburgh*, and *Belfast Gazettes*. The Director-General in making his proposals under s. 17 will have regard:

'(*a*) to the particular respects in which it appears to him that the consumer trade practice specified in the reference may adversely affect the economic interests of consumers in the United Kingdom, and
(*b*) to the class of relevant consumer transactions, or the classes (whether being some or all classes) of such transactions, in relation to which it appears to him that the practice may so affect those consumers' (s. 19(1)).

The Director-General's proposed recommendation will be for an order preventing or modifying the consumer trade practice. The Advisory Committee will have three months in which to report following a reference unless the Secretary of State permits further extensions. The Committee can either agree or disagree with the proposals in the reference or suggest modifications.

The Secretary of State may, after a report of the Advisory Committee has been laid before Parliament, make an order by statutory instrument which may contain supplementary provisions at the discretion of the Secretary of State (s. 22).

(iv) PENALTIES AND DEFENCES

Failure to comply with a requirement under an order made by the Secretary of State or contravention of a prohibition imposed under s. 22 will constitute an offence and such a person will be liable to a fine of up to £400 on summary conviction or a term of imprisonment of up to two years or a fine or both on conviction on indictment (s. 22). Where an offence is due to the act of default of another person they may be charged and convicted.

It will be a defence to a charge under s. 22 for a person to prove

'(*a*) that the commission of the offence was due to a mistake, or to reliance on information supplied to him, or to the act of default of another person, an accident or some other cause beyond his control and
(*b*) that he took all reasonable precautions and exercised all due diligence to avoid the commission of such an offence by himself or any person under his control' (s. 25).

(v) ENFORCEMENT

The local weights and measures authorities will have the duty of enforcing orders under s. 22 and they will be able to authorize their officers to make test purchases of goods or obtain services to check whether an order is being complied with (s. 28).

(vi) MONOPOLIES AND MERGERS COMMISSION

The Monopolies and Mergers Commission may consist of a maximum of twenty-five members. The main duty of the Commission, assisted by the Director-General, is to investigate any report on any question referred to it:

(*a*) with respect to the existence, or possible existence, of a monopoly situation, or
(*b*) with respect to a transfer of a newspaper or of newspaper assets, or
(*c*) with respect to the creation or possible creation of a merger situation qualifying for investigation (s. 5).

A monopoly situation will exist (for the purposes of the Act) in relation to supply of goods or services if

(*a*) at least one quarter of all the goods (or services) of that description which are supplied in the United Kingdom are suppled *by* one and the same person, or are supplied *to* one and the same person, or
(*b*) at least one-quarter of all the goods of that description which are produced in the United Kingdom are produced by members of one and the same group of inter-connected bodies corporate;
(*c*) one or more agreements are in operation which in any way prevent or restrict, or prevent, restrict or distort competition in relation to the export of goods of that description from the United Kingdom, and
(*d*) that agreement or agreements are operative with respect to at least one-quarter of all the goods of that description which are produced in the United Kingdom.

Exports of goods of any description to any *particular market* will come within the monopoly situation reference if they fall within categories (*c*) and (*d*).

Apart from a reference to export goods, one can be made, if it is appropriate in the circumstances, to a monopoly situation limited to a part of the United Kingdom.

For the purposes of monopoly reference in respect of goods and services, these may be treated as being the subject of different forms of supply where the transactions differ as to nature, parties, terms, and surrounding circumstances and the difference is a material one in the view of those making the reference or the Commission. In determining whether the one-quarter proportion is met for the purposes of a monopoly reference the most suitable yardstick will be applied (e.g. value, cost, price, capacity, number of workers employed).

(vii) MERGERS

In relation to merger policy the intention is to deal with a minority of cases that raise important public issues. If a merger or proposed merger creates or intensifies a monopoly, formerly created by a $33\frac{1}{3}$ per cent control of the market but now taken as 25 per cent, or involves the acquisition of assets of £5 million gross value, then the Secretary of State has complete discretion in referring the merger in question to the Monopolies Commission for investigation. In practice a stop order is imposed on the merger during investigation and also while it is being investigated by the Commission. The 25 per cent provision covers those mergers that have an important direct effect on horizontal competition: the £5 million criteria is especially relevant to vertical and conglomerate mergers.

With regard to merger references, these may be made by the Secretary of State to the Commission where any two enterprises have ceased to be distinct. For the purposes of the Act this will come about, if:

(*a*) they are brought under common ownership or common control (whether or not the business to which either of them formerly belonged continues to be carried on under the same or different ownership or control), or
(*b*) either of the enterprises ceases to be carried on at all and does so in consequence of any arrangements or transactions entered into to prevent competition between the enterprises (s. 65 (1)).

A person or group of persons are treated as bringing an enterprise under his or their control if

(*a*) they acquire a controlling interest in the enterprise or body corporate being already able to control or influence the policy of that firm, or
(*b*) they become able to control the policy.

This type of merger reference is given a six-month time limit for report by the Commission unless the Secretary of State gives a maximum of three months' extension. In making their report the Commission may suggest what action should be taken to remedy the situation where they find it is adverse to the public interest. Following such a report the Secretary of State may make an order under statutory instrument which may provide for the division of any business or interconnected body corporate by sale or any other methods needed to make this effective, including:

(*a*) the transfer or vesting of property, rights, liabilities or obligations;
(*b*) the adjustment of contracts including discharge or reduction of liability or obligation;
(*c*) creation, allotment, surrender or cancellation of any stocks, shares or securities;
(*d*) the formation, or winding up of a company or other association, corporate or unincorporate, or the amendment of the memorandum and articles or other regulatory instruments of company or association;
(*e*) the registration of any alterations of the share capital, constitution, or other matters alterable by a company or association;
(*f*) the continuation of any legal proceedings with any change of parties necessary (Schedule 8, Part II).

Before making such an order the Minister must publish a notice stating his intention to make the order, indicating the nature of the provisions in that order and making it clear that anyone whose interests are likely to be affected by the order and who wish to make representation must do so before a date specified in the notice (s. 91)

There is no legal requirement under the Act for firms that are proposing or considering mergers to notify or obtain prior permission from the Department of Trade. In practice the firms concerned will make approaches to seek information as to whether their actions will conflict with the statutory provisions or the D.O.T. itself will initiate enquiries.

(viii) NEWSPAPER MERGERS

The Act prohibits the transfer of a newspaper or its assets to a newspaper proprietor whose own newspapers have an average daily circulation of 500,000 (including that of the newspaper concerned in the transfer) unless written consent is given by the Secretary of State. This may be given if he is satisfied that the newspaper to be transferred is not economic as a going concern and as a separate publication or if the daily circulation is not more than 250,000 copies. If the newspaper is not intended to continue as a separate publication (and the Secretary of State is satisfied on this point) consent will be given unconditionally and without a report from the Commission (s. 58).

Where an application is made to the Secretary of State for his consent to a merger he must refer the matter to the Commission one month after the application which will report three months after reference unless a maximum three months' extension is permitted by the Secretary of State.

Any person who is knowingly concerned in an attempted transfer which is unlawful under s. 58 is liable to imprisonment of up to two years, or a fine, or both.

(ix) RESTRICTIVE TRADING AGREEMENTS

The functions of the Registrar of Restrictive Trading Agreements under the former Restrictive Trade Practices Acts 1956–68 are transferred to the Director-General under the 1973 Fair Trading Act (s. 94(1)). The 1976 Restrictive Trade

Practices Act repealed and re-enacted sections of the Fair Trading Act which dealt amongst other matters with registration of restrictive trade practices and reference has already been made to them earlier (*see* 2:1).

(x) PYRAMID SELLING

The Fair Trading Act provides for regulations to make it an offence to solicit payments from participants in pyramid selling or similar schemes if these are induced to make payments by the prospect of benefiting from the recruitment of further participants. The Acts' Pyramid Selling Provisions have been in force since 14 September 1973 and new regulations effective from 15 November 1973 further prohibit the objectionable usages of pyramid selling, the additional limitations being:

(*a*) *Joining fees*

An essential feature of any pyramid scheme is that intending participants pay a substantial sum to join, which is often represented as being for stock or training. The payments are now limited to a maximum of £25 for stock and there is a complete ban on payments for training and other services.

(*b*) *Buying back goods*

Since pyramid schemes make it impossible in most cases for participants who wish to leave to get a refund for unsold goods, the new regulations give a right to any participant who is supplied with goods to require the promoter of the scheme to buy them back at 90 per cent of the price paid if the participant wishes to leave the scheme, provided that the goods to be returned are in a satisfactory condition.

(*c*) *Information*

Recruiting advertising and other documents *must* give basic information about the schemes and claims that any particular income can be earned by joining are completely banned.

(*d*) *Cooling-off period*

Anyone who joins a scheme must be given a seven-day cooling-off period, during which he can withdraw from the scheme without loss.

(*e*) *Written contracts*

All participants must be given written contracts which set out the rights given under the regulations. Contravention of the regulations is a criminal offence punishable by a fine not exceeding £400 or three months' imprisonment or both on summary conviction, or a fine or imprisonment up to two years or both on conviction on indictment.

The 1973 Act empowers the Secretary of State to make further regulations to control pyramid selling or direct trading (s. 119). It should be stressed, however, that the existing and future regulations are not intended to impede genuine direct selling that works on conventional techniques and is not operated on the unscrupulous lines of some pyramid selling that has rightly attracted the attention of the legislature.

(xi) CODES OF PRACTICE

The Director-General is under a duty to encourage the preparation and disemination by relevant associations of codes of practice giving guidance with regard to safeguarding and promotion of consumers' interests in the U.K. Relevant associations here mean any association whose membership consists wholly or mainly of members producing or supplying goods or services or representing those so engaged.

Where a code of practice contains restrictions covered by the Restrictive Trade Practices Act 1976, s. 6 (1) and the code was either agreed to by the members of the association or recommended to them by the association, the code would be registrable. Although such a code would be capable of reference to the Restrictive Practices Court by the Director-General he may make representation to the Secretary of State under s. 21 (2) of the Restrictive Trade Practices Act, already noted, to discharge him from taking proceedings before the Court on the grounds of the insignificance of the restrictions in the code.

A number of codes have been prepared since the Fair Trading Act in consultation with the Office of Fair Trading and the Institute of Marketing has played a significant role in this development. Codes now cover a wide range of industries and services, including the motor vehicle body repair and second-hand car industries, footwear, electrical retail and servicing industries and laundry cleaning services and travel agents's associations.

The codes of practice contain machinery and procedures to deal with unresolved disputes between customer and trader. It is not possible to discuss the details of a number of specific individual codes but the Scottish Motor Trade Association Used Car Code contains a concise illustrative provision. This states that in the case of an unresolved dispute about the standard warranty the Association's Customer Complaint Service will investigate the dispute and recommend a settlement. In the event of either party disagreeing with the recommended settlement independent arbitration will be conducted by an arbiter chosen by the Institute of Arbitrators from a panel approved by the Director-General. The party seeking arbitration is required to lodge a deposit; £10 in the case of the customer and £20 for the garage, which is returnable if the arbiter finds in favour of that party.

2:3 COMPETITION ACT 1980

The Competition Act 1980 provides for the abolition of the Prices Commission and the control of anti-competitive practices in relation to goods and services. The Act also deals with references of certain public bodies and other corporate bodies to the Monopolies and Mergers Commission. Investigation of prices and charges by the Director-General of Fair Trading is also dealt with in the Act as are suspension of declarations under s. 1 (3) of the Restrictive Trade Practices Act 1976 and the repeal of the remaining provisions of the Counter-Inflation Act 1973.

(i) CONTROL OF ANTI-COMPETITIVE PRACTICES

The aim of this part of the Act is to control anti-competitive practices. A person engages in such practices if, in the course of a business, they pursue a course of conduct which is intended to have or is likely to have the effect of restricting, distorting or preventing competition in connection with the production, supply or acquisition of goods or supply or securing of services, in the U.K. or any part of it.

Conduct amounting to anti-competitive practices

Conduct by a person will constitute engaging in anti-competitive practices either of itself or when taken together with a course of conduct pursued by persons associated with him (s. 2(1)).

A course of conduct will not be regarded as constituting an anti-competitive practice for the purposes of the Restrictive Trade Practices Act if the course of conduct is required or envisaged by a material provision of, or a material recommendation in, an agreement which is registered or subject to registration under that Act.

A material provision of an agreement is one that, because of its existence (alone or with other provisions), makes that agreement one to which the Restrictive Trade Practices Act applies. A material recommendation is one in an agreement to which a term is implied by any provision of s. 8 or s. 16 of that Act. These are terms implied into trade association and services supply agreements (s. 2 (2)) (*see* p. 67).

A course of conduct will not constitute an anti-competitive practice if excluded for the purposes of the Act by an order made by the Secretary of State; such an order may limit the exclusion given by reference to particular persons or circumstances (s. 2(3)). An order may exclude the conduct of any person by reference to the size of his business by reference to turnover (as defined in the order), his market share or in any other manner (s. 2(4)). To enable the Director to establish whether any person's course of conduct is excluded under an order, this may provide for application of ss. 44 and 46 of the Fair Trading Act 1973 (power of the Director to require information) with appropriate modifications (s. 2(5)).

Any two persons are treated as associated under s. 2 if:

(*a*) one is a body corporate of which the other has direct or indirect control, either alone or with other members of interconnected bodies corporate of which he is a member, or
(*b*) both are bodies corporate of which one and the same person or group of persons has direct or indirect control.

A person or group of persons able to control or materially influence the policy of a body corporate, directly or indirectly, without having controlling interest in that body corporate may be treated as having control of it (s. 2(7)).

Investigations by the Director-General

The Director-General may (if it so appears to him) carry out an investigation with a view to establishing whether a person has been or is pursuing a course of conduct which does amount to an anti-competitive practice. Before he does so the Director-General shall:

(*a*) give the Secretary of State and the person or persons whose conduct is to

be investigated notice of the proposed investigation. This is given with an indication of the matters to be investigated, the person or persons concerned and the goods or services to which the investigation is to relate; and
(*b*) arrange for notice of the proposed investigation, together with an indication of the matters to be investigated, the persons concerned and the goods or services to which the investigation is to relate. This notice is to be published in a such manner the Director-General considers most suitable for bringing the proposed investigation to the attention of any other persons who, in the Director-General's opinion, would be affected by or be likely to have an interest in the investigation (s. 3 (2)).

Once (*a*) and (*b*) have been carried out the Director-General is to proceed with the investigation as expediently as possible. The Secretary of State may direct the Director-General not to proceed with the investigation if he does so before the end of two weeks from the day on which he (the Secretary of State) received notice under s. 2 (a). In such a case the Secretary of State shall:

(*a*) give notice of the direction to the person or persons whose conduct was to be investigated; and
(*b*) arrange for the direction to be published in such a manner that he considers most suitable for bringing to the attention of any other person who, in his opinion, would have been affected by, or likely to have had an interest in, the direction (s. 3 (6)).

The Director-General may (by notice in writing signed by him) require for the purposes of investigation under s. 3:

(*a*) any person to produce to him or any person appointed for the purpose, at a time and place specified in the notice, any documents described by the notice and which are documents in the person's custody or control relating to any matter relevant to the investigation; or
(*b*) any person carrying on business to furnish him with estimates, returns or other information specified or described in the notice and the time, manner and form of furnishing these. However, no person shall be compelled to produce any document or give any information for such an investigation which he would not be compelled to produce or give in civil proceedings in the High Court (or in Scotland, the Court of Session) (s. 3 (7)).

The enforcement provisions of s. 85 (5)–(8) of the Fair Trading Act relating to notices requiring production of documents and furnishing of information apply to notices under s. 3 (1) and (7) of the Competition Act (s. 3 (8)).

If the Director-General, with the Secretary of State's consent, decides not to proceed with the investigation the Director-General shall give notice of this to the person or persons whose conduct was being investigated. He shall also arrange for his decision to be publicized on the same basis as s. 3 (2) (a) (s. 3 (9)) (*see* above).

When an investigation has been completed, as soon as is practicable, the Director-General is required to publish a report. This must, giving reasons, state whether he regards a course of conduct described in the report as constituting an anti-competitive practice and, if so:

(*a*) specifying the person or persons concerned and the goods or services in question; and
(*b*) stating, with reasons, whether he considers it is appropriate for him to make a competition reference under s. 5 (*see* below) (s. 3 (10)).

In this latter case the Director-General shall consider any written representations made to him by a person the report specifies as one who was or is engaged in an anti-competitive practice, such representations containing proposals as to what should be done as a result of the report's conclusions as they relate to that person (s. 4 (1)). Such person may include an undertaking in his representation to be bound for a period if this undertaking is accepted by the Director-General.

The Director-General has a duty to keep under review any undertaking he accepts and to consider, if circumstances change, whether the undertaking is no longer appropriate or can be varied, replaced or whether the person concerned can be released from it (s. 4 (4) (a)). He must also give notice to the person giving the undertaking of his failure to carry it out.

If the Director-General concludes that under s-s. (4) (a) that any person can be released from an undertaking, or it needs to be varied or superseded by a new one, he shall give a notice to that effect to the person specifying s. 4 (5). The Director-General may at any time, by notice to the person concerned, agree to the continuation of an undertaking under s-s. (5) or accept a new and varied undertaking offered by that person as a result of the notice. Where the Director-General makes a competition reference (s. 5) in relation to a notice under s. 4 (5) he shall not, after the making of reference, agree to a continuation of, or accept a new or varied, undertaking as a result of that notice (s. 4 (8)). The Secretary of State is empowered to make regulations by statutory instrument governing notices (s. 4 (9)).

(ii) COMPETITION REFERENCES
The Director-General may make a reference under s. 5 to the Monopolies and Mergers Commission in particular cases. This will be so where:

(*a*) a report has been published under s. 3 that it is appropriate for the Director-General to make a competition reference and he has not accepted undertaking(s) from each of the persons specified in the relevant report, as in his opinion, cover(s) every course of conduct described in the report as constituting an anti-competitive practice; or
(*b*) the Director-General has given notice to any person who has failed to carry out an undertaking; or
(*c*) the Director-General has given notice to any person under s. 4 (5) specifying a variation of an undertaking or a new undertaking which is required and has not accepted a new or varied undertaking from that person or agreed on the original undertaking being continued [s. 5 (1)].

A competition reference is a 'report reference' if made under (*a*) and a 'notice reference' if made under (*b*) or (*c*). No competition reference may be made within four weeks of, or eight weeks after, the date on which the report of the Director-General was published in the case of a report reference or in the case of a notice reference within or after the same period on which the notice was given in (*b*) or (*c*). This eight-week period can be extended for both types of reference up to a maximum of twelve weeks by the direction of the Secretary of State only if, on representations by the Director-General, it appears to the former that it would be appropriate in the case in question to allow more time for the Director-General to negotiate an undertaking (*see* s. 4) (s. 5 (5)).

Scope of competition references

In a competition reference the Director-General shall specify:

(*a*) the person or persons whose activities are to be investigated by the Commission, that is subject to the reference;
(*b*) the goods or services to which the investigation is to extend; and
(*c*) the course or courses of conduct to be investigated (s. 6 (1)).

The Director-General may not specify in a competition reference any person, goods or services or conduct not specified or described in the relevant report (either arising from a report or notice reference). However, if the Director-General regards an undertaking he has accepted under s. 4 as covering any of the items above he shall exclude that person, goods or services or course of conduct from the reference (s. 6 (2), (3)). This provision does not apply to an undertaking which a person the Director-General regards as having failed to have carried out or one that needs to be varied or superseded by a new undertaking (s. 4 (4) (b), (5) (b)).

The Commission shall, on a competition reference report on the following questions:

(*a*) whether a person, subject to the reference, twelve months before the date of the reference was pursuing a course of conduct or one similar in form and effect in relation to goods and services specified in the reference; and
(*b*) whether the person, by pursuing such a course of conduct, was in that period engaging in an anti-competitive practice; and
(*c*) whether that practice operated or might be expected to operate against the public interest (s. 6 (5)).

A competition reference may be restricted in scope by the Director-General by excluding from the reference some or all of the activities of any person subject to the reference or any goods, services or conduct specified in it. The commission, on receiving a notice to this effect from the Director-General, shall discontinue their investigation as far as it relates to any excluded matter which they will not refer to in their report. (This is subject to s. 7 (below).)

Supplementary provisions dealing with varying of competition references are dealt with in s. 7. Sections 70 (time limit for report on merger reference), 84 (public interest), and 85 (attendance of witnesses and production of documents) of the Fair Trading Act 1973 and Part II of Schedule 3 of that Act (performance of functions of Commission) apply to competition references (s. 7 (6)).

Conclusions and reports of the Commission

A report on a Commission reference is required to be made to the Secretary of State. This report must state:

(*a*) whether any person whose activities were investigated over twelve months was pursuing a course of conduct that amounted to anti-competitive practice; (*b*) and if so whether that practice operated, or might be expected to operate, against the public interest, in which case what are, or were likely to be, the effects adverse to that interest (s. 8 (1)).

If the course of conduct is a material provision or recommendation of an agreement registered or subject to registration under the Restrictive Trade Practices Act 1976 then the Commission shall make no recommendations. However, if the Commission conclude a person has engaged in an anti-competitive practice in terms of s. 8 (1) they shall consider what action (if any) should be taken to remedy or prevent the adverse effects of that practice and make recommendations in their report for action, including action by a Minister or Ministers or other public authorities.

The Secretary of State, where a report of the Commission finds a person has engaged in an anti-competitive practice and he regards the effects as adverse to the public interest, may request the Director-General to seek an undertaking from that person to remedy or prevent such effects. The Director-General is under a duty to keep the carrying out of the undertaking under review. He is to advise the Secretary of State on whether the undertaking has not been, or is not being, fulfilled, or needs to be varied or superseded. A person can be released from an undertaking by the Director-General where the Secretary of State considers this appropriate (s. 9).

The Secretary of State is empowered to make orders to prohibit a person named in the order from engaging in any anti-competitive practice specified in the report or pursuing any course of conduct which has substantially the same effect as that practice. An order operates, in extent and manner the Secretary of State thinks fit, to remedy or prevent any adverse effects specified in the report.

The power to make orders is stated to be as if s. 56 of the Fair Trading Act applied; ss. 90, 91, 93, Part II of Schedule 8 (s. 10).

Further references and investigations

The Secretary of State may refer to the Commission any question relating to the efficiency and costs of the service provided or possible abuse of a monopoly situation, by a body as defined by the Act. These are:

(*a*) any corporate body supplying goods or services by way of business, its affairs being managed by members who are appointed under an enactment (e.g. National Coal Board); or
(*b*) a similar body providing a bus service, including one in London; or
(*c*) any statutory water undertaker; or
(*d*) any body administering a scheme under the Agricultural Marketing Act 1958; or
(*e*) any corporate body with a statutory duty to promote and assist any of the

bodies (*a*)–(*d*) in the maintenance and development of the efficient supply of any goods or services;
(*f*) any subsidiary, within the meaning of the Companies Act 1948 connected with (*a*)–(*d*).

A monopoly situation for the purposes above includes such a situation limited to a part of the U.K. Reference to the U.K. in ss. 6 and 7 of the Fair Trading Act includes references to part of the U.K.

On a reference being made to it by the Secretary of State the Commission shall investigate and report with its reasons and conclusions on any question referred to them. The following will be excluded from their investigation and report:

(*a*) any financial obligations or guidance as to financial objectives imposed on or given to the body in question by or under any enactment, or by a Minister; and
(*b*) any course of conduct pursued under a material provision or recommendation of an agreement registered or subject to registration under the Restrictive Trade Practices Act 1976.

A reference under this section is subject to s. 70 (time limit for report on merger reference), s. 85 (attendance of witnesses and production of documents) and Part II of Schedule 3 (performance of functions of the Commission) of the Fair Trading Act (s. 11). The Secretary of State has powers to make orders in respect of s. 11 (Part I of schedule 3 of the Fair Trading Act, excluding s. 10) (s. 12).

(iii) INVESTIGATION OF PRICES DIRECTED BY THE SECRETARY OF STATE

The Director-General is required to carry out an investigation into any price specified in a direction by the Secretary of State. This investigation is to provide the latter with the information required. This does not prevent the Director-General from initiating an investigation under s. 3 into a course of conduct pursued by a person by or to whom the price is charged. Such a direction is not to be given unless the Secretary of State is satisfied that the price in question is of major public concern. In this connection he shall have regard to whether:

(*a*) the provision or acquisition of the goods is of general economic importance;
(*b*) consumers are significantly affected, directly or indirectly by the price (s. 13).

2:4 RESTRICTIVE TRADE PRACTICES AND E.E.C. LAW

(i) AIMS

One of the aims of the E.E.C. is to set up an effective system of competition within the Common Market. Thus, there is a general prohibition of all restrictive practices, agreements and dominant trading positions and concentration under the Rome Treaty of 1957 and the European Coal and Steel Community Treaty of 1951. With the U.K.'s accession to the E.E.C. on 1

January 1973 it is increasingly necessary to know the basic laws that underlie the business arrangements of our trading partners in the Community.

(ii) AGREEMENTS AUTOMATICALLY NULL AND VOID

Restrictive agreements and decisions are made null and void by Article 85(2) of the E.E.C. Treaty and by Article 65(4) of the European Coal and Steel Community Treaty. With regard to the E.C.S.C. provisions, the European Commission has sole jurisdiction to declare the agreement or decision invalid, whereas under the E.E.C. Treaty either the Commission or the national courts can make similar declarations.

(iii) EXEMPT RESTRICTIVE PRACTICES

Certain restrictive agreements, decisions, and practices can be exclusively exempted by the Commission under the judicial control of the European Court of Justice. These are of a nature that generally improve distribution or production or aid economic or technical advance. This power of the Commission is exercised by means of a system of notification of the agreements, decisions, and practices. The Commission can then provide retrospective exemption or seek modification to make these either exempt or valid.

(iv) ARRANGEMENTS NOT REQUIRING NOTIFICATION

The following need not be notified:

(*a*) *Price maintenance or industrial property agreements between only two enterprises*

These will be exempt where:

1. The only effect is to restrict the freedom of one party to the arrangement to fix the re-sale prices or conditions of trading in goods purchased from the other party.
2. A limitation is imposed on the assignee or licensee of a patent, design, trade mark, utility model or on the concessionary of a know-how agreement (*see* Chapter 8).

(*b*) *Confined within a member state*

If the parties are both within one member state and there are no imports or exports involved between member states of the E.E.C.

(*c*) *Standardization or joint research arrangements*

1. Where the aim is to develop or to apply standards or types.
2. Where the only object is the pooling of joint research with a view to technical improvement as long as the rsults are virtually accessible to, and exploitable by, both sides.

(v) RESTRICTIVE AGREEMENTS

'The following shall be prohibited as incompatible with the common market: all agreements between undertakings, decisions by associations of undertakings and concerted practices which may affect trade between

Member States and which have as their object or effect the prevention, restriction or distortion of competition within the common market, and in particular those which:

(*a*) directly or indirectly fix purchase or selling prices or any other trading conditions;
(*b*) limit or control production, markets, technical development, or investment;
(*c*) share markets or sources of supply;
(*d*) apply dissimilar conditions to equivalent transactions with other trading parties, thereby placing them at a competitive disadvantage;
(*e*) make the conclusion of contracts subject to acceptance by the other parties of supplementary obligations or which, by their nature or according to commercial usage, have no connection with the subject of such contracts.'

Such agreements or decisions are automatically void under Article 85(1). To illustrate the operation of Article 85(1) in the *Dyestuffs* case (*ICI and others v. Commission EC*, 1972) the European Court of Justice ruled that it was not necessary for the parties to draw up a common plan for their activity to fall within the meaning of concerted practices. '... the concerted practice does not combine all the elements of an agreement, but may ... result from a coordination which becomes apparent from the behaviour of the participants.' It would be sufficient to inform each other in advance of the line they would take so that each could decide its action relying in its competitors acting in the same way. In *Dyestuffs* it was found that on three occasions, nine or ten of the leading producers of dyestuffs in the Common Market, who together produced 80 per cent of the dyes sold there, each announced price rises. There was evidence of actual collusion and in deciding that the increases were concerted and fining all firms concerned the Commission did not seek to discover an agreement as such (*see also* 8:5).

The Belgian Tobacco Case

In a recent decision, *The Tobacco Case* (FEDTAB) (*Van Landewyck and others v. Commission*, 1980) the European Court considered infringements of Article 85(1) by agreements, decisions and recommendations of members of the Belgian and Luxembourg tobacco manufacturers association. The agreements and decisions were under the following headings:

(i) a system under which FEDTAB granted approval to wholesalers and retailers with different margins allowed for different categories, with lower margins for non-approved retailers;
(ii) a system of resale price maintainence;
(iii) a refusal from 1971 onwards to grant approval to new wholesalers in certain categories;
(iv) a prohibition on wholesalers reselling to other wholesalers who were not directly supplied by the manfacturer;
(v) an imposition of a uniform time limit of fifteen days for payments by the wholesalers to manufacturers; and
(vi) an obligation for certain retailers to carry a minimum selection. The recom-

mendations were in respect of (a) a system of different margins for different wholesalers and retailers; (b) an annual rebate calculated on the basis of total sales; (c) the imposition of a system of immediate payment, with a possible delay of fifteen days in exceptional cases.

The Court's basic view of the agreements, decisions and recommendations was that they prevented competition with regard to profit margins. The Court held that there was nothing in Belgian national legislation to prevent different and individual profit margins being allowed within the scope of the fixed resale price, and that effective competition would be possible with regard to profit margins. The Court also held that FEDTAB's distribution system was not justifiable as intended to preserve a specialist tobacco trade as tobacco sales did not require qualified outlets.

It was found that members of FEDTAB carried out more than half the imports of cigarettes and 12–15 per cent of the imports of cigars into Belgium. Therefore the imposition of FEDTAB's uniform conditions removed any financial incentive for wholesalers or retailers to sell one imported brand rather than another by removing any competition with regard to profit margins, rebates or conditions for payment, and so was capable of affecting trade between Member States.

The Court did not accept that the recommendations were capable of exemption under Article 85 (3). While recognizing that FEDTAB's distribution system might be beneficial in keeping a large number of small retailers in business, the Court doubted whether the advantages stemming from the recommendations were sufficient to outweigh the severe restrictions on competition which they imposed. The view of the Court was that, given the market share held by FEDTAB's members, the recommendations would give them the possibility of eliminating competition in respect of a substantial part of the product in question.

Distillers Case

The issue of export restriction and Article 85 can be exemplified in decisions involving a large U.K. whisky company, Distillers.

Distillers' U.K. price structure offered much more favourable terms to U.K. dealers who did not buy for export (about £8 a case in bond against about £13). This system, introduced in June 1975, replaced earlier conditions on home sale of complete prohibition on exports. The earlier conditions were notified in June 1973 and the import restriction was abandoned in the same letter that introduced the new price structure. The 1975 price structure was not formally notified but a copy was sent to the Commission at the date of introduction. In May 1976 five firms controlled by the Bulloch family complained that Distillers would not sell to them at U.K. prices because some whisky sold to Bullock at U.K. prices had been found in Belgium. The Commission issued a decision in December 1977 that Distillers' price structure came within Article 85 (1) and could not be exempted under Article 85 (3) because it had not been notified and because it was not part of Distillers' exclusive dealing agreements with its continental distributors.

On appeal to the European Court (*The Distillers Co. Ltd v. E.C. Commission,*

Bulloch and others intervening, 1980) it was considered that Distillers had established that there was no commercially practical alternative to some sort of export restriction on U.K. sales and that its price structure could therefore be approved under Article 85(3). However as the price structure had not been notified it could not be approved.

A later Commission decision in 1980 involved Distillers' standard agreement with victuallers (traders who supply duty-free customers such as ships and airport shops). The agreements included a term that the victuallers would supply whisky only to persons who would use it duty-free or sell it for such use. It was held by the Commission that the agreements were not caught by Article 85(1).

(vi) MONOPOLY SITUATIONS

Under Article 86 of the E.E.C. treaty it is prohibited for one or more enterprises to exploit improperly a dominant position within the Common Market or a substantial part of it. Abuse of this position is illustrated in four ways:

(*a*) direct or indirect imposition of any inequitable purchase or selling prices or of any other inequitable trading conditions;
(*b*) limitation of production, markets, technical developments, to the prejudice of consumers;
(*c*) the application of unequal conditions to parties undertaking equivalent transactions, thereby placing them at competitive disadvantage;
(*d*) making the conclusion of a contract subject to the acceptance by the other party to the contract of additional obligations which by their nature or according to commercial usage have no connection with the subject matter of such contract.

Acquisition and abuse of a dominant position (monopoly) is achieved either by natural growth or through mergers. To determine whether or not an organization or organizations are subject to substantial competition within the Common Market or a substantial part of it, the enterprise or enterprises under review are to be considered relative to:

(*a*) the given market,
(*b*) the existence and importance of competitors within or outside the E.E.C.,
(*c*) the availability of other services and products to customers.

The operation of Article 86 can be illustrated by the following cases.

In the *Continental Can* case (1973), Continental Can (an American firm), through a wholly owned subsidiary, Europeanballage, held a controlling participation in Schmalbach-Lubeca-Werke (S.L.W.) which, the Commission alleged, accounted for 70 to 80 per cent of the market in West Germany for meat tins, 80 to 90 per cent of that market for fish tins, and 50 to 55 per cent for metal caps (other than crown corks). In 1971 Europeanballage acquired control of Thomassen and Drifver-Verblifa (T.D.V.), the largest manufacturer in Holland of the products in which S.L.W. specialized. The Commission held this merger to violate Article 86 on the basis that through S.L.W. Continental Can occupied a dominant position in the relevant markets in Germany, a substantial part of the E.E.C. T.D.V. was a potential competitor of S.L.W.

since although it did not export to Germany it was capable of doing so. As the merger resulted in the elimination of competition with S.L.W. Continental Can was guilty of abuse of dominant position capable of affecting trade between member states.

On appeal to the European Court of Justice the Court upheld the Commission's interpretation of Article 86, but decided that the Commission had failed to provide a sufficiently rigorous analysis of the economic factors relevant to the alleged abuse and the decision was annulled. The Court did state that '... while the existence of a dominant position is not objectionable in itself, the extension of such a position beyond a certain point may amount to an abuse within the meaning of Article 86'.

The Commission subsequently submitted a draft regulation to the Council of Ministers for the control of concentrations, which was adopted in a resolution of December 1973 by the Council. This went beyond the *Continental Can* position by making the regulation applicable to concentrations which distort competition without necessarily resulting in suppression of all market participants other than those which the composite undertaking controls. The Commission was also enabled by the subsequent directive to take preventive measures where the proposed merger was thought incompatible with the Common Market.

In the *Chiquita* case (1975) the Commission found that the United Brands Corporation, created by a merger of the United Fruit Co. and A.M.K. Corporation (a major U.S. meat producer), as the world's largest seller of bananas held a dominant position in the banana market in a substantial part of the Community. As well as handling 40 per cent of the trade in bananas within the E.E.C., U.B.C. wielded overwhelming economic power, due chiefly to the vertical integration of its banana business and the holding of other advantages as a result of its multi-national and conglomerate nature. These included ownership of numerous plantations in tropical banana-growing countries and a fleet of refrigerated banana boats. It also controlled banana ripening in consumer countries and had direct charge of advertising and sales campaigns related to its own brand of bananas. U.B.C. was the only firm in the banana market to possess all these advantages and was in a position to use them to block effective competition by existing competing firms, while potential competitors were confronted with major barriers to market entry. Investigation showed that market shares held by U.B.C. in the northern area of the E.E.C., backed by the marketing policy it pursued, gave it a dominant position in that region.

The Commission held that U.B.C. had been abusing its dominant position in the following ways:

(*a*) it prohibited its distributors and ripeners from reselling green bananas, which meant there was market fragmentation;
(*b*) it charged its customers prices which differed according to the Member States in which they were located, although there were no objective reasons for such discrimination;
(*c*) it charged unfair prices for sales to its customers in Germany, Denmark, and the Benelux;

(*d*) for no objectively valid reason, it refused to supply one of its main Danish customers.

Due to the seriousness of the violations of Article 86 the Commission fined U.B.C. one million units of account and ordered U.B.C. to end its infringements of the Treaty (except the refusal of supply, which had already ceased). In order that it could check on compliance U.B.C. was instructed to notify the Commission once it had withdrawn its ban on the resale of green bananas by its distributors and ripeners in the northern half of the E.E.C. and inform the Commission of actual prices charged in the countries in that area over the next two years.

(vii) NEGATIVE CLEARANCE AND EXEMPTION

Any party to an arrangement which is either restrictive under Article 85 or dominant under Article 86 can apply for a negative clearance from the Commission. This may give guidance to the party concerned but does not prevent national courts from enforcing Article 85 and Articles 86 (1) and (2).

Negative clearance and exemption are applied for on the same form. The exempting decision must give reasons and can be reversed by the European Court of Justice. The exemption is conditional and temporary and the Commission can revoke or modify its decision or prohibit certain activities if some essential fact alters, or a condition of the decision is broken by an interested party, or they abuse the exemption, or if the decision was obtained either by fraud or by the giving of inaccurate information

QUESTIONS

1. (*a*) What are the main provisions of the Resale Prices Act 1964?
   (*b*) *R*, a retailer of gramophone records, placed an order for certain records with *M*, a record manufacturer. *M* declined to supply the records on the ground that it was *R*'s practice to resell records at less than list prices, unless he was prepared to give a written undertaking that he would not in future sell below list prices. Advise *R* as to his legal position.
2. To what extent have restrictive trade practices, monopolies, and mergers been affected by the Fair Trading Act 1973?
3. What are the main provisions made under existing E.E.C. law to regulate restrictive practices?

3. *Contracts of Employment*

3:1 SCOPE

The law relating to the formation of the contract of employment is fundamentally similar to the law of contract. In this chapter we are concerned only with the contractual rules and statutory regulations that govern employment contracts and will not consider the law relating to trade unions, collective bargaining and disputes. This area of the law has been subjected to what can only be described as prolonged legislative upheaval. Only the main statutes relevant to contracts of employment for the purposes of this text are dealt with here. The Trade Union and Labour Relations Act 1974 constitutes the main statute together with the Employment Protection (Consolidation) Act 1978 which repealed and re-enacted the Contracts of Employment Act 1972, and the Employment Protection Act 1975. The Employment Protection (Consolidation) Act brings together in one statute the many individual employment rights previously scattered over many statutes. The Health and Safety at Work Acts 1975 and 1980 deal with the area of industrial safety.

3:2 FORMATION OF THE CONTRACT

A contract of employment may take any form, either oral or written. However, a contract of apprenticeship must be in writing but under the Apprentices Act of 1814 need no longer be under seal. Employment contracts for merchant seamen under the Merchant Shipping Act 1894 have also to be written.

(i) EMPLOYMENT PROTECTION (CONSOLIDATION) ACT 1978

The Employment Protection (Consolidation) Act 1978 makes it a duty for an employer to give a written statement to the employee containing the terms of employment within thirteen weeks of the commencement of the contract of employment. These terms are:

(*a*) the name of the parties;
(*b*) date of commencement of the contract;
(*c*) rate of remuneration or method of calculation;
(*d*) intervals of payment;
(*e*) hours of work;
(*f*) holiday and holiday pay arrangements;
(*g*) sickness and sick pay;
(*h*) pensions and pension schemes;
(*i*) length of notice on both sides;

(*j*) in the case of fixed-term contracts, the date of expiry;

(*k*) an indication of the employee's right in relation to trade union membership and the effect, where it is in force, of an agency shop agreement or an approved closed shop agreement;

(*l*) entitlement to holidays and holiday pay in a form that makes the employee's entitlements exactly calculable, including entitlement to accrued holiday pay on termination of enmployment (where this applies);

(*m*) the method by which an employee can take up a grievance, whom he should approach, and the steps in the grievance procedure or reference to an accessible document that explains them.

This written statement is not itself a contract but is evidence of the terms of the contract. Any changes in these terms should be communicated to the employee within one month of such alterations. It is not necessary to give these written terms to an employee engaged under a written contract already containing them or if he can obtain a document or copy containing these terms.

Any employee who does not receive such a statement or receives one that is incomplete or inaccurate may ask an Industrial Tribunal to make a decision which will have the effect of incorporating the new terms in the statement.

There is no need for the written statement to be signed, but if the employer signs the statement and the employee signs and gives back a copy to the employer this has the effect of:

(*a*) introducing a personal element into the relationship;

(*b*) establishing greater trust between the parties;

(*c*) giving evidence to the employer of receipt of the statement.

The 1978 Act does not apply in the following cases:

(*a*) employees normally working less than twenty-one hours a week;

(*b*) registered dock workers;

(*c*) where the employee is father, mother, husband, wife, daughter, or son of the employer;

(*d*) certain marine workers and fishermen;

(*e*) crown employees;

(*f*) employees working mainly or wholly outside the U.K.;

(*g*) employees who leave during the first thirteen weeks of their employment.

(ii) COLLECTIVE AGREEMENTS

The collective agreement has legal effect by its terms being implied in the individual contract of employment. Therefore, if an employee enters into a contract of employment with a firm on terms that apply to the other employees he is deemed to accept these terms. The collective agreement also may be expressly incorporated into the individual contract of employment. For a detailed discussion of this complex topic reference should be made to specialist texts on Labour Law.

In a recent case alteration of a collective agreement was considered by the Employment Appeal Tribunal. In *Land and Wilson v. West Yorkshire Metropolitan County Council* the employers and the Fire Brigades Union had agreed to phase out the system of employing firemen, known as retained duties, and to make provision only for wholetime duties. The number of firemen on retained duties experienced a substantial loss in pay as a result.

The employer (West Yorkshire Metropolitan County Council) wrote to Land and Wilson in October 1976 asking them to agree to a variation of their contracts abolishing retained duties. This the firemen refused to do and as a result their employers gave them three months' notice of termination of the retained element. Both men terminated their employment. The industrial tribunal held that there had been only one contract containing both wholetime and retained duties and since the complainants continued to be employed by the authority, there had been a variation, but no repudiation of the contract; as a result there had been no dismissal. On appeal the Employment Appeal Tribunal held that although a single contract existed, a dismissal had taken place since the retained element was an important part of the contract as a whole. However the dismissal was held not to be unfair.

The Court of Appeal found that although a single contract existed it was severable into two parts. The part containing the retained duties could be terminated separately, while the rest of the contract remained intact. Since employees could give up retained duties without terminating the contract (as 1,500 firemen had done), the employer had the related right of terminating the retained element on reasonable notice. As the complainants continued with their wholetime duties there was no dismissal and their claim failed.

(iii) CLOSED SHOP

Closed shop agreements have been the subject of considerable political contention. Their relationship with unfair dismissal is considered later (see 3 : 7).

In *Young, James and Webster v. U.K.*, the European Court adjudicated on whether dismissal as a consequence of a closed shop agreement constituted a breach of Article 11 of the Convention for the Protection of Human Rights and Fundamental Freedoms 1950. The basis of the claimants' arguments was that enforcement of the British closed shop legislation, which permitted their dismissal from employment when they objected on reasonable grounds to joining a trade union, interfered with their freedom of thought, conscience, expression and association with others. Article 11 states:

1. Everyone has the right to freedom of peaceful assembly and to freedom of association with others, including the right to form and join trade unions for the protection of his interests.
2. No restrictions shall be placed upon the exercise of these rights other than such as are prescribed by law and are necessary in a democratic society in the interests of national security or public safety, for the prevention of disorder or crime, for the protection of health or morals or for the protection of the rights and freedoms of others.

The main issue was whether Article 11 in giving a positive right of freedom of association also implied a negative right not to be compelled to join a union. The European Commission expressed its view that Article 11 had been violated, it referred the matter to the European Court which upheld the Commission's opinion by eighteen votes to three. The Court's reasons were: (a) the compulsion to join a union, where there had been no such requirement at the time of engagement, allied to the threat of dismissal as an alternative to joining one of the British Rail unions, was an interference with the freedom guaranteed under Article 11; (b) for all practical purposes, the applicants were prevented from belonging to any other trade union of their choice; and (c) they were being compelled to join an association contrary to their convictions (*see* 3:7 and the Employment Protection (Consolidation) Act 1978 s. 58 (3A–C)).

(iv) PARTIES TO THE AGREEMENT

Initially it is vital to distinguish between an employee and others who might appear to be employees but who in fact are not. It is important to distinguish between a contract of service, in which the relationship of employer–employee arises, and a contract for services, which establishes a relationship with an independent contractor and his employees. Various tests have been applied by the courts to determine, in specific instances, which of these relationships has obtained between the parties.

(a) The control test

One person is the employee of the other where the employer can determine the job to be done and the manner of doing it. This is not a satisfactory test as it does not match modern conditions where highly qualified people such as research chemists, architects, lawyers, and accountants know more about the nature and operation of their work than their employers.

(b) The organization test

Lord Denning has laid down another test based on the concept of work in relation to its organization:

> 'Under a contract of service, a man is employed as part of the business and his work is done as an integral part of the business; whereas, under a contract for services, his work, although done for the business, is not integrated into it but is only an accessory to it.'
>
> (*Stevenson, Jordan and Harrison Ltd. v. McDonald and Evans*, 1952)

This test certainly covers relations not touched by the control test, but it was applied in the case above to a professional worker and may not be easily extended to other employees. One of the difficulties is to determine the meaning of 'integration' and 'organization'. Without knowing the meaning of these terms interpretation is bound to be discretionary on the part of a court of law.

(c) The mixed test

In view of the fact that both the control and organizational tests have defects it appears that the courts are more likely to take into consideration other factors, such as the nature of the work, who pays the employee, dismissal and hire arrangements.

Example

Women were employed part-time by a company to do market research.
Held: Using the control test, there was evidence of service, but a basic test

suggested was 'Is the person who has engaged himself to perform these services performing them in business on his own account?' It was decided on the facts of the case that the women were employees of the company.

(Market Investigations Ltd. v. Ministry of Social Security, 1969)

Additional tests were also suggested in *Ready Mixed Concrete (South East) Ltd. v. Ministry of Pensions* (1968) to determine the existence of a contract of employment. In that case such a contract was held to exist where:

(*a*) the employee agreed for a wage or salary to provide his own work and skill in the performance of some service for his employer;
(*b*) that in carrying out that service the employee agreed to be subject to the control of the employer;
(*c*) the remaining provisions in the contract were consistent with its being a contract of employment.

(iv) EFFECT OF DISTINCTION BETWEEN EMPLOYEE AND INDEPENDENT CONTRACTOR

The differences between independent contractors and employees have important practical results:

(*a*) An employer does not have to stamp the insurance cards of an independent contractor.
(*b*) An employee is entitled to written notice of his terms of employment and to certain minimum periods of notice of dismissal.
(*c*) An employee may be entitled to a redundancy payment under the Redundancy Payments Act 1965.
(*d*) An employer is liable for wrongful acts of his employees committed in the course of their employment, but is not generally liable for the wrongful acts committed by an independent contractor.
(*e*) The employer owes a higher duty at common law to secure the safety of his employees than he owes to independent contractors.
(*f*) An employer may benefit from any invention made by an employee in the course of his employment, but not from that of an independent contractor.

(British Syphon Co. Ltd. v. Homewood, 1956)

Note: In law there is a strong presumption against the transfer of an employee from his general employer to a temporary one. If, while working for a temporary employer, a loaned employee commits a wrongful act, his general employer will be liable.

Example

A Harbour Board hired out a crane and driver to a stevedoring firm. The contract included provision that the driver was the hirer's servant. The Board paid the driver during the hire period and had sole power of dismissal. The driver injured another while on hire.
Held: The Board was liable as being the general employer.

(Mersey Docks and Harbour Board v. Coggin & Griffiths Ltd., 1946)

However, by making an express provision in the contract the general employer may exempt himself from liability.

Example

A driver and a crane-excavator were both hired out to another firm. The contract stated that the driver was to be regarded as the servant of the hirers who would be solely responsible for any claims against the driver during his work. The driver injured another during the hire period.

Held: The hiring firm were liable.

(Arthur White Ltd. v. Tarmac Civil Engineering Ltd., 1967)

3:3 DUTIES OF THE EMPLOYEE

Apart from certain terms expressed in the contract of employment itself certain duties on the part of the employee are implied.

(a) *To do the work personally*

The employee is normally under a duty to carry out his work personally. Where an employee has the right under the contract of employment to bring in a substitute the relation may be one of employer and independent contractor.

(b) *To obey all reasonable and lawful orders*

Disobedience to reasonable and lawful orders is a ground for summary dismissal, but only if the employee's conduct shows a clear intention to flout the essential conditions of the contract.

Example

A head gardener worked satisfactorily for an employer for three months, after which he became surly and awkward. On asking the gardener about arrangements concerning the greenhouse the employer was met with the colourful phrase 'I couldn't care less about your bloody greenhouse or your sodding garden'. The employee was dismissed on the spot.

Held: The abuse, together with the earlier unco-operative attitude, justified summary dismissal.

(Pepper v. Webb, 1969)

However, a conflict of loyalties may have arisen in certain cases.

Example

An advertising representative was present at a conference when an argument broke out between her immediate superior, the advertising manager, and the managing director of the company. The advertising manager left the room followed, despite an instruction by the managing director to stay, by the advertising representative. On the following day the advertising representative was dismissed.

Held: The dismissal was wrongful as the act of following her immediate superior out of the room was one of loyalty to him and not one that evinced a complete disregard for the essential conditions of her contract of employment.

(*Laws v. London Chronicle*, 1959)

(*c*) *Not to compete against the employer*

During his contract of employment the employee must not act against his employer's interests or compete against him.

Example

Employees of a hearing-aid manufacturer worked in their own time for a rival firm.

Held: Such conduct amounted to a breach of contract and an injunction would be granted against the defendant company to prevent the continued employment of the plaintiff's employees.

(*Hivac Ltd. v. Park Royal Scientific Instruments Ltd.*, 1946)

(*d*) *Not to accept bribes or secret commissions*

Even if the employee remains uninfluenced by bribes or secret commissions he receives while employed, such action constitutes a breach of his contract.

Example

After a managing director was dismissed the company who had employed him discovered that he had been taking commission from firms who had placed contracts with the company.

Held: The company were within their legal rights to dismiss him because he had breached his duty to give faithful service.

(*Boston Deep Sea Fishing and Ice Co. Ltd. v. Ansell*, 1888)

(*e*) *To conduct himself properly*

Apart from the instances noted already, continued laziness, poor time-keeping, and drunkenness may be breaches of duty, but whether they justify immediate dismissal depends on the circumstances. Dishonesty always justifies dismissal (*Cunningham v. Fonblanque*, 1833). In a decided case it was held that persistent drunkenness even outside working hours would justify dismisal if such conduct was habitual and directly interfered with the employer's business. However, it would be unlikely that acts of private sexual immorality on the part of an employee would justify dismissal where, for example, the employee was employed as a market researcher.

(*f*) *To account to employers for any patent or invention made in the course of employment*

If an employee invents a new process while working for a firm, an agreement may be made for mutual development of the patent (*see* Chapter 8).

Example

A chief technician invented a new type of soda syphon, and after leaving to work for a rival firm patented the invention in his own name.
Held: The patent was the property of the ex-employers.

(*British Syphon Co. v. Homewood*, 1956)

(g) To attend the place of work

This duty may appear self-explanatory, but a problem may arise where the employer moves his place of business. A removal to a place close to the former site will not discharge the contract but a shift to a more distant site may alter the situation.

Example

Electricians employed at the Liverpool branch of a company refused to work at Barrow-in-Furness, 120 miles away. They were dismissed by their employers.
Held: There was no implied term in their contracts of employment that the employees had to work anywhere within the company's area of operations. They were therefore entitled to redundancy pay.

(*O'Brien v. Associated Fire Alarms Ltd.*, 1969)

(h) Duty to indemnify the employer

An employee is implied to possess the necessary skill for his job and must exercise it with reasonable care. Thus, dismissal for incompetence is perfectly valid.

Example

A father and son, both employed by the same firm, took out a company lorry on business. While reversing the vehicle the son injured the father. The father obtained damages against the employers for the son's negligence and the firm sued the son for breach of an implied term in his contract that he would use reasonable care in driving.
Held: The son was liable and the company were entitled to the indemnity.

(*Lister v. Romford Ice and Cold Storage Co. Ltd.*, 1957)

(i) Duty of disclosure

Since the contract of employment is not one of *uberrimae fidei* an employee is under no duty to inform his employer of facts that may be to the latter's disadvantage, provided no actual misrepresentation is made.

Example

A director was given £30,000 compensation for loss of office by his firm. Later it was found that he had been making secret profits during his term of employment which would have entitled the company to dismiss him, without notice. The firm sued for return of the payment.
Held: The contract was valid and the ex-director was entitled to retain the payment.

(*Bell v. Lever Bros.*, 1932)

But if the employee is injured because he did not reveal certain information to his employer, the employee may have to accept reduced damages in a civil action against the employer.

Example

An employee suffered from epileptic fits making work at high levels dangerous. He did not disclose this fact to his employers and was injured in a fall.
Held: Damages awarded to the employee would be reduced because of his failure to inform the employer of his illness.

(*Cork v. Kirby Maclean*, 1952)

DUTIES OF FORMER EMPLOYEES

An employee on leaving his employer's service is entitled to use the knowledge and skill that he has acquired during the course of that employment, but he owes a duty to the ex-employer not to reveal his trade secrets or confidential information—e.g. secret formulae or lists of customers.

Example

The former managing director of a company utilized trade secrets concerning the correct method of employing a plastic strip to hold together the walls of an above-ground swimming pool.
Held: An injunction would be granted in favour of the ex-employers to restrain the defendant and any other company from using the information.

(*Cranleigh Precision Engineering Ltd. v. Bryant*, 1965)

As already noted in Chapter 1 the employer may insert a clause or clauses in the employee's contract restraining him from working in the same trade after leaving the present employment. Such restrictions are subject to tests of reasonableness by the courts (*see* p. 42).

3:4 DUTIES OF THE EMPLOYER

The chief duties of the employer are as follows:

(i) TO PAY THE AGREED WAGES, SALARY, OR OTHER REMUNERATION

(a) *Wages in general*

Wages are fixed by personal negotiation or under a collective agreement negotiated locally or nationally between the employee's trade union and the employer or his federation or by wages councils. The Terms and Conditions of Employment Act 1959, s. 8, provides that if an employee brings a complaint to the Industrial Court that an employer is paying below the usual wage rate the Court may make an order that the normal wage level be read into the individual contract of employment as an implied term. Wage rates provided under collective agreements additionally can be either implied or expressly incorporated into the individual contract of employment.

Under the 'Fair Wages Clauses' all government departments arrange for fair wages and conditions to be provided under contracts given by them to contractors. These include:

1. That contractors should pay wages and follow hours and conditions of work commensurate with those commonly accepted in the area where the work is being done. If there are none these should be on a par with those governing other employers in the industry. These terms should apply to all the contractor's employees, not merely those involved in the government contract.
2. The contractor is responsible for observance of the clauses by his subcontractors. In default of friendly resolution of a dispute the Industrial Court may be asked to arbitrate.

(b) *Payment of wages*

The Truck Acts 1831–1940 make it an offence to pay workmen (generally meant to apply only to manual workers) their wages in any form other than the coin of the realm. If an employer wishes to pay this category of employee by any other method then he must do so under the provisions of the Payment of Wages Act 1960.

1. An employee may request his employer in writing to pay his wages by cheque, money, or postal order, or directly into his back account. The employer may comply either by agreeing in writing, or simply by carrying out the request, but if the employer delays fourteen days in taking action then the request will lapse and will need to be renewed.
2. The employee must provide the manual worker, paid in the ways authorized by the 1960 Act, with a statement in writing that sets out the gross wages, the amount of each deduction and the reason for each, with the next amount payable.
3. A manual worker who is absent from work and who has made no request as to payment under the 1960 Act can be paid by postal or money order (but not by cheque).

Note: It has always been legal to pay staff by any method, including cheque.

(c) *Bonuses*

Payment of bonuses and commission depend on the contractual agreement and on interpretation by the courts. Commission that is based on each year's profits has been held to mean that no commission is payable where a loss is made in one year, but a loss cannot be carried over to a year when a profit is made. In general an advance commission must be repaid if not earned, although an agreement may provide otherwise. Bonuses may be payable under the contract of employment or merely be gratuitous. In *Powell v. Braun* it was held that an employee was entitled to a reasonable sum in wages due when he contested the right of his employer to give him a bonus instead of a pay rise. In *Grieve v. British Tobacco Corporation Ltd.*, however, the court decided that an annual bonus paid by a company to its employees for fifty years but withheld from employees who went on strike was a gratuitous payment and could not be converted into a contractual obligation even by repetition.

(ii) TO PROVIDE FOR THE SAFETY OF THE EMPLOYEE

This duty can be suitably sub-divided into three parts:

(a) *Provision of safe plant and appliances*

An employer is under a duty to provide safe plant, tools, and equipment that are best suited to the work and nature of the employment.

Example

A van driver was instructed by his firm to drive 500 miles in very cold weather and due to the van being unheated the driver suffered frostbite.
Held: The employee would receive damages for negligence on the part of his employers as the risk was foreseeable.

(Bradford v. Robinson Rentals, 1967)

Under the Employer's Liability (Defective Equipment) Act 1969, an employer is primarily liable for defective equipment and must pay damages to an employee injured by such an appliance. An indemnity may be sought from the manufacturer of the equipment. Since 1 January 1973 all employers must display a certificate indicating that they are compulsorily insured against employees' claims.

(*b*) *Provision of safe system of work*

A safe system of work will include not only the work itself, but factors such as safety provisions, special protective clothing, safety instructions, alarm systems, training of personnel, and layout of plant or offices.

Example

An employee working on a grinding machine was injured by a piece of metal flying into his face. Goggles were available but the employee had not been told where to find them.
Held: The firm were liable to the employee.

(Finch v. Telegraph Construction & Maintenance Co. Ltd., 1949)

If the employer provides the safety equipment and instructs his employees as to their use and location it will be up to the employees to use them unless the employee is at special risk (e.g. has only one eye or is similarly handicapped).

Example

Protective clothing was made available to employees working on a molten metal process and large notices stating that such clothing should be used and where it could be found were widely displayed. Due to non-compliance with the safety instructions an employee was injured by hot metal.
Held: The employer was not liable as he had done all that was necessary in the circumstances to bring both the desirability of wearing the clothing and notification of its whereabouts to employees.

(James v. Hepworth & Grandage Ltd., 1967)

(*c*) *Competent staff*

If an employee is injured during work due to the carelessness or lack of competence by another employee, the employer will be liable in negligence.

Example

An employee was injured by a stupid and dangerous practical joke played on him by a fellow-worker. The activities of this employee were known to the firm who had frequently warned him about such actions. The injured employee sued his firm.

Held: As the workman who had caused the accident was known to be a source of danger to his fellow-workers, the firm had failed in their duty to the plaintiff.

(Hudson v. Ridge Manufacturing Co. Ltd., 1957)

The general duties of employers to their employees in connection with health and safety are laid down in statutory form in the Health and Safety at Work Act 1975 based on the proposals of the Robens Report. The general duties are set out in s. 2 (2) of the Act. These include, as far as is reasonably practicable:

(*a*) the provision and maintenance of plant and systems of work that are safe and without risks to health;

(*b*) arrangements for ensuring safety and absence of risks to health in connection with the use, handling, storage, and transport of articles and substances;

(*c*) the provision of such information, instruction, training as is necessary to ensure the health and safety of employees;

(*d*) as regards any place of work under the employer's control the maintenance of it that is safe and without risks to health and provision of safe means of access and exit;

(*e*) the provision and maintenance of a working environment for employees that is without risk to health, and adequate as regards facilities and arrangements for their welfare at work.

(iii) PROVISION OF REFERENCES

No employer is under a duty to provide a reference to an employee who seeks other employment. If an employer does give a reference which contains statements that are defamatory of the employee, the employer may successfully claim that the statement was true and that, provided the reference was not communicated to outside parties, he had a duty to make it and the prospective employer had an interest in receiving it. However, if the defamatory reference has been motivated by malice the employer will be liable in damages to the employee.

If a reference is given falsely or carelessly the employer may have to pay damages to the new employer who suffers loss as a result of taking on the employee.

(iv) DISCLOSURE OF INFORMATION

A statutory general duty on employers to disclose information at all stages of collective bargaining is laid down by the Employment Protection Act 1975, s. 17. Such information shall be disclosed to representatives of an independent trade union, provided this information is in the employer's possession and relates to his undertaking or that of an associated employer and is information without which the trade union representatives would be impeded in their collective bargaining with the employer or such that he should disclose to them for collective bargaining purposes in accordance with good industrial practice. Section 18 of the Act provides that no employer will be required to disclose:

(*a*) any information the disclosure of which would be against the interests of national security; or

(*b*) any information which he could not disclose without contravening a statutory prohibition; or

(*c*) any information given to, or obtained by, the employer in confidence; or

(*d*) any information relating specifically to an individual unless they consent to disclosure; or

(*e*) any information which would cause substantial injury to the employer's undertaking apart from its effect on collective bargaining; or

(*f*) any information obtained by the employer for the purposes of bringing, prosecuting or defending any legal proceedings.

Subject to these exceptions where an employer fails to disclose information on the terms of s. 17 an independent trade union may present a written complaint to the Central Arbitration Committee who may then deal with it themselves or refer it to the Conciliation Service for conciliation.

3:5 LIABILITY OF THE EMPLOYER TO THIRD PARTIES

An employer will be liable for the acts of his employee committed in the course of his employment which result in injury to third parties, if these acts were condoned or authorized or they arose from the actual work performed by the employee.

Example

A driver of a petrol lorry lit a cigarette and threw away the match while he was delivering petrol to a garage. A fire followed by an explosion did considerable damage to the premises.

Held: As the negligent act of the driver was done in the course of his employment his employers would be held liable for his action.

(*Century Insurance Co. Ltd. v. Northern Ireland Road Transport Board*, 1942)

On the other hand if the action complained of has no connection with the employment, the employer will not be liable.

Example

A customer was punched by a petrol pump attendant who mistakenly believed that the customer had not paid.

Held: As the employee was taking up a personal quarrel, his actions were outside the course of his employment.

(*Warren v. Henleys Ltd.*, 1948)

Where an employer has expressly forbidden an action this will exempt him from liability if a third party is injured as a result of a forbidden act.

Example

A lorry driver was prohibited by his employers from giving lifts to unauthorized passengers and a notice to this effect was displayed on the dashboard. Such a person was given a lift and injured due to the employee's negligent driving. *Held:* The prohibition effectively took the driver's action out of his course of employment and his employers were not liable.

(*Twine v. Bean's Express Ltd.*, 1946)

3:6 TERMINATION OF THE CONTRACT

Either party can end the contract of employment lawfully by giving the appropriate notice (unless it is a fixed term agreement) which will depend on the terms of the contract. The position is chiefly governed by statute. Under the Employment Protection (Consolidation) Act 1978 (Part IV), an employer must give in the case of:

(i) an employee with between thirteen weeks' and up to two years' continuous employment—one week's notice;

(ii) an employee with two years' or more but less than five years' continuous employment—two weeks;

(iii) an employee with five years' or more continuous employment but less than ten years'—four weeks;

(iv) an employee with continuous employment of ten years or more but less than fifteen years—six weeks;

(v) an employee with continuous employment of fifteen years or more—eight weeks' notice.

Although continuous employment is defined as employment by one employer, this continuity is not broken by transfer of business, by change of firm, or death of the employer, nor by the employee going on strike.

Similarly, the continuity is not affected by a lock-out by the employer. Subject to the strike rules, weeks that count for the calculation of continuous employment under Schedule 1 of the Contract of Employment Act are;

(*a*) A week in which an employee was employed for sixteen hours or more.

(*b*) A week in which an employee had a contract normally involving employment for sixteen or more hours. In certain cases this is reduced to eight hours under the Employment Protection Act 1975 (Schedule 16, Part II).

(*c*) A week in which the employee is:

(i) incapable of work through sickness or injury;

(ii) absent due to a temporary break in work other than a strike; or

(iii) absent in a situation where still in employment by reason of an arrangement or custom; or

(iv) absent due to pregnancy or confinement.

A strike will not count for the purposes of continuous employment.

If the individual contract of employment contains terms similar to or better than those provided by the Act, those contractual provisions apply, but if the contractual terms are inferior to those stipulated by statute, the Act applies. The employee is not prevented from taking wages or salary in lieu of notice or from foregoing his right to notice if he chooses.

Payment of employees during the statutory notice period is dealt with in

detail under the Employment Protection Act 1975 (Schedules 4 and 5), whereby employees are divided into three groups:
(1) employees with normal working hours where payment does not vary with the number of hours worked;
(2) those whose payment does vary in which case the week's pay is calculated by reference to the average hourly rate over the previous twelve weeks; and
(3) those with no normal working hours where the basis is the average weekly pay for the previous twelve weeks.

The Employment Protection Act 1975 for the first time, by s. 71, entitles an employee at his request to written notice from an employer on termination of his contract of employment, whether this is done without notice by the employer, or being a fixed term contract expires without being renewed under the same contract. The employer must provide the written statement giving particular reasons for the dismisal within fourteen days of the request. An employee is not entitled to a written statement unless on the effective date of termination he has been, or would have been, continuously employed for a period of twenty-six weeks ending with the last complete week before that date.

3:7 UNFAIR DISMISSAL

The provisions relating to unfair dismissal are now contained in the Employment Protection (Consolidation) Act 1978 (Part V).

In every employment to which the provisions apply an employee has the right not to be unfairly dismissed by his employer. Where this is alleged to have occurred, the employee may present a complaint against an employer to an industrial tribunal (s. 67).

The unfair dismissal provisions do not apply in the case of an employee not continuously employed for a period of not less than twenty-six weeks ending with the effective date of termination of employment. They do not apply either to employees close to retirement (s. 64).

An employee will be treated as dismissed for the purposes of the Act only if:

(*a*) the contract under which he is employed by the employer is terminated by the employer, whether with or without notice; or
(*b*) where being employed under a fixed term contract, that term expires without being renewed under the same contract; or
(*c*) the employee terminates the contract, with or without notice, in circumstances such that he is entitled to do so without notice by reason of the employer's conduct (s. 55).

Therefore apart from (*c*) if the contract ends by mutual agreement, or the employee gives notice himself, he will not have a claim.

Effective date of termination of the contract is the date on which notice of termination expires, or, in the case of fixed term contracts, the date on which that term expires (s. 55). From court and tribunal decisions it appears additionally that the date of termination will be when the employer makes it clear that the contract is at an end immediately, as with dismissal with salary in lieu of notice. In the case of dismissal by notice this terminates when the notice expires. The Employment Protection (Consolidation) Act 1978 provides that if an employer has failed to give notice to which the employee was entitled under the Act and that notice would have resulted in a later date of termination, that later date is to be treated as the effective date of termination (s. 55).

In order to establish that there was a substantial reason for the dismissal the employer must show that this:

(*a*) related to the capability or qualifications of the employee for performing work of the kind which he was employed to do; or
(*b*) related to his conduct; or
(*c*) that he was redundant; or
(*d*) that the employee could not continue to work in the position which he had held without breaking a statutory requirement.

Capability is assessed by reference to skill, aptitude, health, or any other physical or mental quality. Qualifications mean any degree, diploma, or other academic, technical, or professional qualification relevant to the position held by the employee (s. 57).

Even where a substantial reason is proved the employer still has further to prove that it was fair in the circumstances to dismiss the employee. For example, if dismissal was for bad time-keeping, it would be open to the industrial tribunal to examine the overall record of time-keeping by all the firm's employees, as well as the employee's own record, to assess the relative meaning of the term 'bad'.

Dismissal of an employee by an employer because he was, or proposed to be, a member of a trade union or had taken, or proposed to take, part in their activities constitutes unfair dismissal. Similarly, this will be so where an employee is dismissed who has refused, or proposed to refuse, to become a member of a trade union that is not independent. Dismissal of an employee will be regarded as fair if it is the practice, in accordance with a union membership agreement, for employees for the time being in the same category as the dismissed employee to belong to either one of a number or a specified independent trade union. Dismissal will be regarded as fair also if the employee was not a member of such a trade union or had refused to belong to one. If the employee has genuine objections on grounds of religious belief to being a member of a union, then the dismissal is unfair (s. 58).

It will be unfair dismissal for an employee to be dismissed for redundancy where the circumstances could have been equally applied to one or more employees in similar positions to the dismissed employee, who have not been dismissed. This dismissal will be unfair if either the employee was principally dismissed for an inadmissable reason or he was selected for dismissal in breach of a customary arrangement or agreed procedure relating to redundancy, with no special reasons for departing from these (s. 59).

An employee dismissed for reason of pregnancy, or any other reason connected with this situation, is to be treated as unfairly dismissed. This will not be the case if she is, or will become, incapable of adequately carrying out the work she is employed to do at the effective date of the termination of her employment. Dismissal will also be valid if the employee cannot or will not be able to continue to carry on her work due to her pregnancy without either herself or her employer breaching a duty or restriction laid down by an enactment. Such an emloyee will be unfairly dismissed if she is dismissed on the valid grounds given above, but neither the employer nor any successor makes an offer to engage her on a new contract of employment before, or on, the effective date of termination (s. 60).

The unfair dismissal provisions apply where an employee claims he was unfairly dismissed by his employer if the employer was conducting or instituting a lock-out or the employee was on strike or involved in other industrial action. It must be shown, in claim to an industrial tribunal, that one or more of the employees so involved, of the same employer, have not been dismissed or they have been offered re-engagement, but the employee has not (s. 62).

Once an employee has proved unfair dismissal he must also show his loss. The complaint must be presented within three months of the effective date of termination of employment, unless the industrial tribunal gives a further period if they consider it was not reasonably practicable for the complaint to be presented within the time specified (s. 67). The tribunal may recommend re-engagement by the employer on terms they consider reasonable if the complainant seeks this and it is practicable and just to do so (s. 69). If an employer refuses to re-employ a dismissed employee this may increase the compensation awarded; similarly, an unreasonable refusal of an offer by the employee may reduce the damages given.

If an employer does not comply with an order by the tribunal to reinstate or re-engage an employee, unless the employer can prove that compliance was not practicable, the tribunal must make an award in addition to the usual compensation for unfair dismissal. This consists of:

1. not less than thirteen and not more than twenty-six weeks' pay; or
2. where the dismissal involved racial or sex discrimination, or was for an inadmissible reason, not less than twenty-six and not more than fifty-two weeks' pay.

The employee is under the normal duty to mitigate his loss. If he does not do this the tribunal will take this into account in making an award for unfair dismissal (s. 71). The amount of compensation awarded to a person for unfair dismissal shall not exceed £5,200 (s. 73(1)).

The reports of industrial tribunal decisions concerning unfair dismissal claims indicate frequent use of the statutory provisions.

Dismissal of a site engineer for reluctance to leave head office and work on site was held to be fair as the employee had failed to reach the capability expected of a person of his experience (*Abernathie v. Mott Hay*, 1973). Dismissal was held to be unfair in the case of an employee promoted and then dismissed for alleged incompetence in his new position when it was shown that his employers had failed to provide him with adequate training for his new post (*Burrows v. Ace Caravan Co.*, 1972).

The decision in *Marley Tile Co. Ltd. v. Shaw*, 1980 may have significantly reduced the organizing power of lay trade union representatives. Section 58 (above) states that dismissal of an employee taking part in the activities of a trade union at an appropriate time is dismissal for an inadmissable reason. An 'appropriate time' means either outside working hours or during working hours (excluding meal times) with the employer's consent. In *Marley Tile* the employer had refused to recognize the shop steward credentials of Shaw at a meeting he had called with his employer to discuss a wage grievance of one of his constituents. Shaw then left the meeting stating that he would telephone the union district secretary, and to call a meeting of his constituents, the maintainence craftsmen. No permission was sought from his employer, although no objection was raised at the time. The meeting which was called, which resolved on a one-hour protest stoppage, was also attended by shop-floor workers. The company decided to dismiss Shaw on the grounds that he had failed to follow the company's grievance procedure. Shaw complained to the industrial tribunal that his dismissal was for the inadmissable reason of participating in union activities at the appropriate time, thereby allowing him to circumvent the six month qualifying period (now one year in most cases) required for unfair dismissal claims.

The Court of Appeal, in reversing the decision of the industrial tribunal and the Employment Appeal Tribunal, decided that although it could be implied that the employer had given consent to participation in trade union activities during working hours, this could not be inferred from the present case. In allowing the employer's appeal, the Court of Appeal concluded that implied consent could not have been given for the particular activity of calling the maintainence men to the canteen in working hours.

A recent case involving closed shop dismissals should be noted. In *Leyland Vehicles Ltd v. Jones* the employee was required, under a union membership agreement, to belong to either the AUEW or to the National Union of Sheet Metal Workers (NUSMW). He had been a member of the AUEW but had attempted to resign in order to join the NUSMW. The AUEW refused to accept his resignation and so his membership of the NUSMW was cancelled. He was then expelled from the AUEW and his subscription to that union was in arrears he was unable, under the Bridlington Agreement, to join the NUSMW. As a consequence of the union membership agreement his employers dismissed him believing him to be a member of neither union, even though he insisted the NUSMW had not cancelled his membership. The TUC's Independent Review Committee subsequently found that his expulsion from the NUSMW was invalid so that at the time of his dismissal he was a member of the NUSMW.

On appeal by the employer against the finding of the industrial tribunal that the employee had been unfairly dismissed, the Employment Appeal Tribunal held that a geniune belief by the employer that an employee was not a member of a union was not sufficient to enable him to justify dismissing an employee in accordance with s. 58 (3) of the Employment Protection (Consolidation) Act 1978. The Appeal Tribunal also decided that a genuine belief on the part of an employer could constitute another substantial reason justifying dismissal under s. 57 of the above Act. However, this argument would not stand because, as a matter of fact found by the industrial tribunal, the employers had failed to carry out a sufficient examination into whether the employee was a member of a specified union.

3:8 EMPLOYMENT PROTECTION (CONSOLIDATION) ACT—GENERAL PROVISIONS

Certain important provisions that the above Act consolidates can be conveniently summarized here.

1. An employee is entitled to a 'guarantee payment' for a day on which no work is available (ss. 12–18).
2. A pregnant woman is entitled to be paid maternity leave and be re-engaged (ss. 33–48).
3. An employee while suspended on specified medical grounds is entitled to payment (ss. 19–22).
4. An employee is entitled to a reasonable amount of time off work to look for work and arrange for training in cases of redundancy; to take part in the activities of an independent trade union of which he is an officer and a member; to take part in public duties (ss. 23–32).
5. On insolvency of an employer most sums payable under the Act are preferential debts and the employee is entitled to eight weeks' arrears of pay and certain other payments including a guarantee payment (s. 121).
6. An itemized pay statement must be provided by a wage-paying employer showing gross and net pay and deductions (ss. 8, 9).

Any questions as to the right of an employee to a redundancy payment is referred to an industrial tribunal (s. 91). From it an appeal lies to the Employment Appeal Tribunal with a further appeal to the House of Lords.

In the event of non-compliance with these and certain other provisions of the Act a complaint may be made to an industrial tribunal.

3:9 EMPLOYMENT ACT 1980

The Employment Act 1980, which effectively came into operation on 1 October 1980, covers the following main areas: trade union ballots and codes of practice (ss. 1–3), exclusion from trade union membership (ss. 4–5), unfair dismissal amendments (ss. 6–10), maternity rights (ss. 11–13), other rights of employees such as guarantee payments (ss. 14–15), picketing, secondary industrial action, and acts to compel union membership (ss. 16–18).

(a) Trade union ballots and codes of practice

Independent trade unions are offered financial support under sections 1 and 2 to enable them to conduct secret ballots covering the calling or ending of a strike or other industrial action, certain trade union elections, amending the rules of a union, and trade union amalgamations or transfers of engagement. The certification officer is empowered with administering the scheme which will be laid down by ministerial regulation. An employer with more than twenty workers must abide by the request of a recognized trade union to provide premises where such a secret ballot as laid down in the scheme can be carried out. Non-compliance by an employer may lay him open to an award for compensation by an industrial tribunal on the application by the union. The Secretary of State may issue codes of industrial relations practice admissible in evidence before a tribunal (s. 3).

(b) Trade union membership

An individual is given the right, where there is a closed shop, not to be unreasonably excluded or expelled from a trade union (s. 4). Persons have their common law rights preserved and the test of reasonableness is determined 'in accordance with equity and the substantial merits of the case'. Reasonableness on the part of the union is specifically stated not to be established by the mere fact that a union acts in accordance with its rules. It is a matter for the tribunals to inquire into the matter of unreasonable exclusion or expulsion from trade unions. Where a tribunal makes a declaration in favour of a complainant, compensation is payable (s. 5).

(c) Picketing

A person's right to picket is limited to picket his own place of work or to a location near his place of work (s. 16). Sympathetic picketing will lay participants open to civil action by the employer whose premises are being picketed (Trade Union and Labour Relations Act, 1974, ss. 13 and 15). It is, however, lawful for picketing to be conducted by a trade union official who accompanies a member of his union, whom he represents, where the member is himself picketing at or near his place of work. If an employee normally works at more than one place or at a place where attendance for the purposes of picketing is impracticable, then his place of work for purposes shall be any premises of his employer from which he works or from which his work is administered. In the case of a worker who is not in employment and whose last employment was terminated in connection with a trade dispute, then he may lawfully picket his former place of work.

(d) Secondary industrial action

Section 17 imposes restrictions on secondary industrial action. This limits the scope for interference by trade unions with the supply of goods and services between their employer and an employer engaged in a dispute with his employees in support of whom the above trade unionists are undertaking their secondary action. Immunity will only be granted where:

1. the purpose or principal purpose is directly to prevent or disrupt, during the dispute, the supply of goods or services between an employer who is party to the dispute and the employer of those taking the secondary industrial action;
2. the action was likely to achieve that purpose (in other words, not too remote from 1.);
3. it arises from interference with or inducement of breach of contract of employment (not breach of a commercial contract) or threats thereof;
4. the secondary action is restricted to a first supplier or customer whose employees are engaging in sympathetic industrial action reasonably likely achieve that principal purpose of interference.

Secondary industrial action often occurs where a shop steward or union official of company *X* calls on (or induces) employees of company *Y* not to handle goods or services running between company *X* and company *Y*, where company *Y* is not a party to the dispute between company *X* and its employees. Such secondary action (subject to 1–4 above) will be immune from tort liability.

Where the supply of goods or services between company X and company Y are disrupted by the actions of X's employees and company Y is an associated employer of an employer in dispute (company Z for example) and the goods and services supplied between X and Y are substitutes for goods 'blacked' due to the dispute at Z, then, the organizers of the actions (X's employees) are protected. This will also be the case where a person induces employees of Y to 'black' substitute goods or services. Y supplies to Z where Y is an associated employer of Z, the original party in the dispute. It should be noted that peaceful picketing in support of secondary industrial action is permitted (s. 17 (5)) subject to the limitations of s. 16 (noted above).

(e) Closed shop and unfair dismissal

Dismissal for non-membership of an independent trade union where there exists a union membership agreement will be unfair in the following circumstances:

1. where the employee genuinely objects on grounds of conscience or other deeply held personal conviction to union membership or any particular union;
2. where the employee had continued to remain outside the specified union both before and after the agreement had been reached;
3. where, in the case of new agreements entered into from 15 August 1980, there was less than eighty per cent support for the agreement by secret ballot by those covered by it (s. 7).

Employees coming under 1–3 also have the right not to have action short of dismissal taken against them (s. 15 (2)). The right to participate in union activities on the employer's premises only on behalf of a union specified in a closed shop agreement (under the Employment Protection (Consolidation) Act 1978 s. 58 (3)) now only applies, in the case of an agreement reached on or after 15 August 1980, where at least eighty per cent of those covered by it approve of the agreement in secret ballot.

An employer is permitted to join a trade union or other person in unfair dismissal proceedings where the employer alleges that the party joined induced him by threats of, or by actual, industrial action to dismiss the applicant to the tribunal for refusing to join a union (s. 10). The party joined, if the allegations are well founded, may be compelled to contribute some or all of the compensation payable by the employer to the applicant. Where the employer dismisses a non-unionist employee after pressure by a contractor insisting on contract work being performed by union members, then the contractor may also be joined as a party by the employer, under similar compensation provisions.

(f) Coercion to join a union

Immunity is removed from the calling of industrial action the purpose of which is to compel workers to join a particular union. Inducement of, or threats to induce, a breach of contract of employment will be actionable except where the employee concerned works for the same employer or at the same place as the workers subject to 'coercive' union recruitment (s. 18). A general right is also given to an employee not to have action short of dismissal taken against him by his employer to compel him to join a union (s. 15 (1)).

(Note: The Employment Act 1980 by s. 19 (b) repeals the statutory trade union recognition procedure contained in the Employment Protection Act 1975 ss. 11–16, and Schedule 11 of that Act which makes provision for the extension of recognized terms of collective bargaining (s. 19 (c)).

3:10   REDUNDANCY

(i) REDUNDANCY PAYMENTS

The rights of an employee who has been made redundant to a redundancy payment are now dealt with in the Employment Protection (Consolidation) Act 1978. The 1978 Act substantially (but not entirely) repeals the Redundancy Payments Act 1965. Contributions are paid by employers to a Redundancy Fund set up by the Secretary of State for Employment (Part VI, s. 103).

An employee is not entitled to a redundancy payment unless within six months of dismissal:

(a) the payment has been agreed and paid; or
(b) the employee has made a claim in writing against the employer; or
(c) a question as to the right of the employee to the payment, or the amount, has been referred to an industrial tribunal; or
(d) a complaint relating to the employee's alleged unfair dismissal has been presented by him (s. 101).

If it seems just and equitable to the tribunal that the employee should receive a payment the tribunal may have regard to the reason shown by employee for not taking the steps above under (a), (b), or (c).

(ii) EXCEPTIONS

The Act applies to all employees with the following exceptions;

(a) self-employed persons;
(b) public employees under the Superannuation Act 1965 or as defined in Schedule 5 of the Employment Protection (Consolidation) Act (s. 99);
(c) domestic employees (but not domestic employees as such) who are close relatives of the employer (s. 100 (2));
(d) employees who attain retiring age before the date of expiry of their notice or when their employment was otherwise terminated (60 in the case of women, 65 in the case of men) (s. 82).

(iii) RIGHT TO REDUNDANCY PAYMENT

The right to a redundancy payment will arise when an employee has lost his job for one of the following reasons:

(a) the employer has ceased to carry on the business in which the employee was employed;
(b) the employer has ceased to carry on the business in the place where the employee worked;
(c) the employer has continued his business but his need for the employee's service has ended;
(d) the employee is laid off or is kept on short time for either a continuous

period of four weeks or six weeks of which no more than three were consecutive within an overall period of thirteen weeks (s. 88).

The Act does not apply where an employee is dismissed because of misconduct or disobedience unless a refusal to do another type of job was motivated by his own work ceasing or falling off, in this case an employee would be redundant.

Where an employer offers to re-engage the employee in a suitable alternative employment or to renew his present contract this will not be a dismissal, but the courts have found a number of cases difficult to interpret on their facts.

Example

An employee working as a tanker driver was given a circular letter which notified employees that the firm was selling out to another firm and wanted existing employees to remain in the business. After working with the new firm for two weeks the driver in question received a notice under the Contracts of Employment Act 1963, setting out the terms of his employment which differed from those under his old contract. He claimed a redundancy payment.
Held: The circular letter was not a sufficient offer in writing for the purpose of the Redundancy Payments Act 1965, s. 3 (2), as it did not show the main differences between the new terms of re-employment and those then in existence. The driver was therefore entitled to a redundancy payment.

(Havenhand v. Thomas Black Ltd., 1968)

One of the key points arising in redundancy cases may involve the question of a change in work organization and its effect on an employee.

Example

A skilled craftsman employed in repair and construction of wooden boats was told, after the firm had gone over to fibre glass building and a work study, that his performance was 'too good and too slow'. He claimed a redundancy payment.
Held: His work had not ceased to exist but his dismissal was due to unsatisfactory performance. No payment would be granted.

(Hindle v. Percival Boats Ltd., 1969)

By giving a wide interpretation to the notion of work of a particular kind, where there is no change in the name of the work, the courts appear reluctant to take the view that demand for work of a particular kind has ceased or diminished.

Example

A quiet middle-aged barmaid was dismissed on the take-over of a pub in order to replace her with a young blonde 'bunny-girl' type to attract a new clientele.
Held: Not a dismissal for redundancy as both were barmaids doing barmaid's work.

(Vaux and Associated Breweries Ltd. v. Ward, 1968)

(iv) PAYMENTS

The basis of calculation is the period of continuous employment from:

(*a*) the date on which notice expires in the case of dismissal by notice, or the date when termination takes effect in the case of termination on either side without notice; the date when the contract ends in the case of a fixed term agreement;
(*b*) the date at the end of the employee's notice in the case of notice by the employee.

The period of continuous employment is calculated according to the Employment Protection (Consolidation) Act 1978 (Schedule 4). The employee must have at least 104 weeks' continuous employment since attaining the age of 18 to qualify.

If an employee takes part in a strike after notice of termination of employment the employer can serve a notice of extension which asks the employee to extend his contract beyond the expiry date equal to the days lost by the strike. Non-compliance with this notice results in a loss of right to payment on the part of the employee.

Payment is made as follows:

(*a*) for every year of service between 18 and 21—$\frac{1}{2}$ week's pay;
(*b*) for every year of service between 22 and 40—1 week's pay;
(*c*) for every year of service between 41 and 65 (men), 41 and 60 (women)—$1\frac{1}{2}$ weeks' pay.

There is a maximum of twenty years' continuous employment and a maximum of £80 per week, so that the highest payment possible under these criteria would be £2,400.

It should be noted that as methods of wage and salary payment vary, this places tribunals in some difficulty in making their calculations.

(v) NOTIFICATION OF REDUNDANCIES

The Employment Protection Act 1975 requires an employer, who proposes dismissing an employee or employees for redundancy, to consult the appropriate trade union representatives at the earliest opportunity (s. 99). In certain circumstances notice must be given of impending redundancies to the Secretary of State (s. 100). There are sanctions for non-compliance with these provisions including fines of up to £400 (ss. 102, 104).

3:11 DISCRIMINATION

There are main areas where statute has dealt with discrimination in employment. Only a brief note of them is made here.

(*a*) *Sex and marital discrimination*

Men and women are required to be given equal treatment with regard to pay in the case of like work or work rated as equivalent by the Equal Pay Act 1970. The Sex Discrimination Act 1975 adds to this by incidentally prohibiting sex or marital discrimination in recruitment, training, promotion, or dismissal.

(b) *Racial discrimination*

It is unlawful, subject to certain exceptions under the Race Relations Act 1968, to discriminate against a person on grounds of colour, race, national or ethnic origins, including anyone in employment, seeking or dismissed from it. Actions can be commenced in the courts only by the Race Relations Board or Secretary of State.

(c) *Offenders*

A person who has been convicted of a criminal offence and undergone punishment is under no obligation to disclose a 'spent conviction' (as defined) by virtue of the Rehabilitation of Offenders Act 1974. Such a conviction is not a proper ground for dismissing or excluding a person from any office, profession, occupation or employment. There is no sanction under the Act for refusing employment. It would appear that dismissal on discovering an employee had spent conviction would constitute unfair dismissal.

QUESTIONS

1. 'Was the contract a contract of service with the meaning which an ordinary person would give to the words.'
   (*Somervell, L. in Cassidy v. Ministry of Health*, 1951)
   Do you feel that this test of the existence of a contract of service is adequate?
   What other tests have been suggested?
   Why is it important to determine whether such a contract exists?
   (Institute of Cost and Management Accountants, December 1971)
2. Discuss whether or not summary dismissal is justified in the following circumstances:
   (a) Jane, a secretary, has been absent from work through illness on a number of occasions during the past two years. Her present illness has continued for six weeks.
   (b) Richard, an accounts clerk, is criticized by the office manager for careless work. An argument develops and Richard walks out of the office, slamming the door behind him.
   (Institute of Cost and Management Accountants, May 1972)
3. B. Laboratories Ltd. discover a new and profitable method of pregnancy testing. Since the process is so simple, they are afraid that some employees may be tempted to engage in this work either as a part-time activity or by leaving and setting up in competition.
   Draft a report to the directors of the company explaining the extent to which they may protect themselves against competition from employees:
   (a) whilst they are employed by the company,
   (b) after termination of employment.
   (Institute of Cost and Management Accountants, December 1970)
4. Albert is employed by a drug firm as the manager of a department in which new drugs are tested on animals. He refuses to administer a particular drug on the grounds that it would cause unnecessary suffering to the animals,

whereupon the firm closes down the department and dismisses Albert without notice.

Discuss Albert's right to claim:

(a) damages for unfair dismissal,

(b) redundancy payment.

(Institute of Cost and Management Accountants, June 1971)

5. (a) In what circumstances will a contract in restraint of trade be deemed by the courts to be (i) valid and (ii) invalid?

(b) For several years, Simon worked as a research chemist. Disillusioned with his role, he decided to see whether a career in lecturing would offer him more job satisfaction. Simon is appointed to an academic post at the local technical college, which has its main buildings and administration offices about one mile and a half from the laboratories of his former employers. Most of Simon's teaching and his research programme are carried out at an annexe of the college eight miles away from the main building. When Simon had joined his former employer, he agreed not to compete with them for a period of twelve years and within a radius of seven miles from their laboratories. Is Simon in violation of his contract with his former employers if he now lectures in the field covered by his research experience?

(Diploma in Marketing, Part II, November 1975)

4. *Sale of Goods*

4:1 INTRODUCTION

The law governing contracts for the sale of goods is chiefly found in the Sale of Goods Act 1979 which came into operation on 1 January 1980. This Act repeals and re-enacts the original 1893 Act and does the same, partially, for the Supply of Goods (Implied Terms) Act 1973. It also repeals minor provisions of the Misrepresentation Act 1967, the Consumer Credit Act 1974, and the Unfair Contract Terms Act 1977, and makes marginal amendments to other statutes such as the Hire Purchase Act 1965. Under the Sale of Goods Act (referred to subsequently as S.G.A.) parties are no longer free to exclude implied conditions in respect of consumer sales. The Supply of Goods and Services Act 1982 passed on July 13 1982 deals with contracts for the transfer of property in goods, for the hire of goods and for the supply of services. It has been included in this chapter for convenience.

4:2 DEFINITION

A contract of sale is defined as:

> 'a contract whereby the seller transfers or agrees to transfer the property in goods to the buyer for a money consideration called the price' (s. 2 (1), S.G.A.).

A sale exists where transfer of property (i.e. ownership) is conveyed at once; an agreement to sell exists where the property passes in the future or on fulfilment of certain conditions.

Under s. 61 (1), S.G.A., goods include 'all chattels personal other than things in action and money'. The definition covers ships, goods in process of manufacture (termed future goods) and things attached to or forming part of land, such as crops which are to be separated before the contract of sale. Although no longer of vital distinction, the difference between a contract of sale and one for work and materials needs explanation. If a contract is for work and materials the implied condition under s. 14 (3), S.G.A., that the goods sold are reasonably fit for the purposes required by the buyer if he has made the seller aware of the purpose, either expressly or impliedly, cannot be applied. But a similar condition may be implied at common law where the contract is for work and materials.

Example

A car owner took his vehicle to a garage for repair and agreed to their suggestion that specialists should do the work of relining the brakes. Due to unsuitable materials being used and poor workmanship by the specialists the car was damaged in an accident.

Held: The garage were liable under an absolute warranty of fitness for the intended purpose of the work as this was held out as being of the type they or sub-contractors could perform and the car owner had relied on the garage's skill and judgment.

(*Stewart v. Reavell's Garage*, 1952)

4:3   CAPACITY

Capacity to buy and sell is governed by the general law of contract. Liability of minors, drunkards, and persons of unsound mind for goods deemed necessaries has already been noted in Chapter 1.

4:4   TRANSFER OF PROPERTY

It is often important to knew when property in goods has passed to a purchaser. Unless there is an agreement to the contrary the risk of loss as a general rule lies on the owner. The Sale of Goods Act 1979 distinguishes between 'specific' and 'unascertained' goods and lays down rules as to when ownership passes from the seller to the buyer.

(*a*) Specific goods are goods that have been identified and agreed on at the making of the contract; e.g. 'Triumph Herald 1200—JJN 3D'.

(*b*) Unascertained goods are those that have been agreed on only in general terms; e.g. 'A Triumph Herald'.

The following rules under s. 18, S.G.A., provide guidelines:

RULE 1

'Where there is an unconditional contract for the sale of specific goods, in a deliverable state, the property in the goods passes to the buyer when the contract is made, and it is immaterial whether the time of payment or the time of delivery, or both, be postponed.'

Deliverable state means in a condition that the buyer is bound to accept. Rule 1 applies even if the parties agree that the property is not to pass until a certain time, although the contract has already been made.

Example

An auctioneer knocked down a van to the highest bidder and took a cheque from him on the written undertaking that the property in the van would not pass until the cheque was paid. The purchaser took the van and sold it to a third party who was sued for its return by the auctioneer.

Held: The property passed on the fall of the hammer under s. 58, S.G.A., the subsequent written undertaking was therefore ineffective and the third party had good title to the van.

(*Dennant v. Skinner*, 1948)

RULE 2

'Where there is a contract for the sale of specific goods and the seller is bound to do something to the goods, for the purpose of putting them into a deliverable state, the property does not pass until such thing be done, and the buyer has notice thereof.'

Example

The sellers sold a condensing engine to the buyers for £650 ((free on rail) which was bolted to concrete bases. On loading at the railway the engine was accidentally damaged. The buyers refused to accept the machine.
Held: They were entitled to do so as the property had not passed to the buyers as the machine was not in a 'deliverable state'.
   (*Underwood Ltd. v. Burgh Castle Brick and Cement Syndicate*, 1921)

RULE 3

'Where there is a contract for the sale of specific goods in a deliverable state, but the seller is bound to weigh, measure, test, or do some other act or thing with reference to the goods for the purpose of ascertaining the price, the property does not pass until such act or thing be done and the buyer has notice thereof.'

The rule does not apply where the weighing, measuring, etc., is to be done by the buyer or by the seller at the buyer's request.

Example

Cocoa was sold to a buyer who was to resell to a third party, who were to weigh it to determine the price the original buyer should pay.
Held: The property in the goods passed to the original buyer and the third party thus had good title. The fact the weighing was to be done by a person other than the seller excluded the operation of s. 18, r. 3, S.G.A.
   (*Nanka-Bruce v. Commonwealth Trust Ltd.*, 1926)

RULE 4

'When goods are delivered to the buyer on approval or "on sale or return" or other similar terms the property therein passes to the buyer:

(*a*) When he signifies his approval or acceptance to the seller or does any other act adopting the transaction;
(*b*) If he does not signify his approval or acceptance to the seller but retains the goods without giving notice of the rejection then if a time has been fixed for the return of the goods, on the expiration of a reasonable time. What is a reasonable time is a question of fact.'

Example

A jeweller delivered jewellery to a dealer on sale or return. The dealer pawned it with a third party.
Held: The act of pawning the jewellery was an adoption of the transaction and so property had passed to the dealer who could give good title to the pawnbroker.
   (*Kirkham v. Attenborough*, 1897)

Note: If there is a contrary intention in the contract the rule will not apply; e.g. if the property in goods delivered on sale or return is clearly stated to pass *only* on payment. Where goods are retained ownership will pass after the approval period lapses, or after a reasonable time.

Example

A car was left with car dealers on 'sale or return terms', but without stipulation of time limit. The car was unsold for three months, despite several requests during this period by the owner for the car's return. Due to unauthorized use by the dealer's staff the car was returned in a damaged state.
Held: The property in the car passed to the dealers as it had not been returned in a reasonable time and they were liable for the price.

(*Poole v. Smith's Car Sales* (*Balham*) *Ltd.*, 1962)

RULE 5 (1)

'Where there is a contract for the sale of unascertained or future goods by description, and goods of that description and in a deliverable state are unconditionally appropriated to the contract, either by the seller with the assent of the buyer, or by the buyer with the assent of the seller, the property in the goods thereupon passes to the buyer. Such an assent may be express or implied, and may be given either before or after the appropriation is made.'

RULE 5 (2)

'Where in pursuance of the contract, the seller delivers the goods to the buyer or to a carrier or other bailee or custodier (whether named by the buyer or not) for the purpose of transmission to the buyer, and does not reserve the right of disposal, he is deemed to have unconditionally appropriated the goods to the contract.'

In deciding whether goods of the agreed description in a deliverable state have been 'appropriated' all the circumstances and facts must be considered.

Example

A seller sold 140 bags of rice to a buyer, the bags in question being unascertained. The buyer paid by cheque and asked for a delivery order which was duly sent for 125 bags, the seller stating that the remaining 15 bags were awaiting delivery at his place of business. The buyer waited for nearly one month after paying by cheque to collect the remaining bags, which were found to have been stolen, without negligence on the seller's part.
Held: The seller had appropriated the 15 bags to the contract and the buyer had agreed by his conduct, so the property in the bags and the risk had passed to the purchaser.

(*Pignataro v. Gilroy*, 1919)

Example

The sellers sold to the buyers 600 boxes of frozen kidneys out of a consignment of 1,500 in a cold store. The buyer's carrier took delivery the next day at 8.0

a.m. of 600 boxes, when the delivery note was handed over, and loading was completed by 12 midday. The carrier did not start the refrigeration in the van until 10.0 a.m. and it did not become effective until 1.0 p.m. On reaching the buyer's premises the meat was found to be unfit for human consumption. The sellers held the loss fell on the buyers.

Held: The property had passed under s. 18, r. 5 (1), as there had been an 'unconditional appropriation of goods to the contract'. When the carrier handed over the delivery order to the cold store official and this was accepted the goods were held on the buyer's behalf and he accepted the risk of deterioration.

(*Wardar's (Import & Export) Co. Ltd. v. W. Norwood & Sons Ltd.*, 1968)

4:5 TRANSFER OF TITLE

As a general rule only the owner is capable of passing a good title to a buyer—'*nemo dat quod non habet*'—no one can give what he has not got. No one can give a better title than he himself possesses; however, the need to protect commercial transactions has modified the rule.

(i) GENERAL EXCEPTIONS

(*a*) *Agency*

If the seller of goods does so with the consent or authority of the owner, the buyer obtains a good title (s. 21 (2), S.G.A.).

Example

X agreed with *Y* that *X* would sell a car to a finance company which would let it on H.P. to *Y*. Before completion of the arrangements *X* handed the vehicle and registration book to *Y*. The finance company refused to complete; in the meantime *Y* sold to a third party.

Held: *Y* had no title to give to the third party as the mere handing over of the car by *X* did not prevent him from disputing *Y*'s authority.

(*Central Newbury Car Auctions Ltd. v. Unity Finance Ltd.*, 1956)

(*b*) *Sale under Common Law or Statutory Power*

At common law a pawnbroker may sell goods pawned if the pawner defaults. Landlords, innkeepers, and bailees have statutory power to pass good title, e.g. an innkeeper may sell a guest's goods when his bill is unpaid (Innkeepers' Act 1878). Under the rules of the Supreme Court a court has wide powers to order a sale of goods.

(ii) SPECIAL EXCEPTIONS

(*a*) *Market overt*

Under s. 22, S.G.A., 'where goods are sold in market overt according to the usage of the market, the buyer acquires a good title to the goods, provided he buys them in good faith and without notice of any defect or want of title on the part of the seller'. A market overt is every open, public, and legally constituted market, including every sale made in the course of business by any shop in the City of London (Sundays excepted).

Example

A hirer of a car under an H.P. agreement tried to sell it in breach of this agreement by auction at Maidstone Auction Market, but failed to do so, later selling it privately in accordance with the custom of the market. The hire purchase company sought the return of the car from the purchaser.
Held: As the custom of the market had been followed, the sale was perfectly valid and the purchaser had a good title.
(*Bishopsgate Motor Finance Corporation v. Transport Brakes Ltd.*, 1949)

(b) Sale by a person with a voidable title

A person who has a voidable title (e.g. one as in *Lewis v. Averay*, 1971, *see* Chapter 1) can pass good title to a bona fide purchaser for value without notice of the fraud unless the true owner has already avoided the sale—e.g. by informing the A.A. or R.A.C. and the police before the sale takes place (*Car and Universal Finance Co. Ltd. v. Caldwell*, 1965—*see* Chapter 1).
Note: Where goods are stolen or obtained by fraud or other wrongful means, the title to that or any other property will not be affected by the conviction of the offender, despite any contrary enactment (s. 31 (2), Theft Act, repealing s. 24, S.G.A. 1893). On conviction of an offender a court can order the restitution of goods to the owner (s. 28, Theft Act 1968).

(c) Purchase of a car on hire purchase terms

Where a person sells to a private buyer a car he has obtained under hire purchase terms or conditional sale, the title in the car will pass to that purchaser as long as he buys in good faith and without notice of the seller's defect of title.
(Hire Purchase Act 1964, s. 27 (2))

The same rule applies where a garage purchases from the hirer a vehicle under a hire purchase agreement and then sells to a private purchaser buying in good faith and without notice of the seller's defect of title (Hire Purchase Act 1964—s. 27 (3)). This rule does not apply where the garage sells to another garage; the second garage would not get a good title (*see* Chapter 6).

(d) Sale by a mercantile agent

A factor is defined by the Factors Act 1889 as 'a mercantile agent having in the customary course of his business as such agent authority to sell goods, or to consign goods for the purpose of sale, or to buy goods, or to raise money on the security of goods'.
The mercantile agent will bind the owner where the agent has possession of goods or documents of title to goods (such as bills of lading) with consent of the owner and pledges, sells, or otherwise disposes of such goods in the ordinary course of business, with or without the owner's authorization.

Example

A car owner delivered to a mercantile agent for sale at not less than £575. The agent sold to a buyer at £340 who purchased in good faith and without notice of any fraud. The agent defaulted with the purchase price and the original owner sued to recover the car from the purchaser.

Held: As the agent was in possession with the original owner's consent the purchaser had a good title.

(*Folkes v. King*, 1923)

A mercantile agent does not sell a car in the ordinary course of business unless it is sold with the registration book, but a good title will be passed to the purchaser even if the book is obtained by larceny or trick, though the sale is voidable for fraud.

Example

A car owner left his car with a mercantile agent to see what offers were made, but he was not authorized to sell it. The agent intended to steal the car and on obtaining possession he sold to a third party.

Held: Even though the possession of the car had been obtained by a trick, the agent was in possession 'with consent of the owner' under s. 2(1) of the Factors Act 1889. As the sale, although voidable for fraud, had not been avoided before purchase by a bona fide purchaser for value without notice of the fraud, this purchaser obtained good title.

(*Pearson v. Rose & Young Ltd.*, 1951)

(e) Sale by possessors of goods or documents of title to them

Where a person who buys or agrees to buy goods obtains, with the consent of the seller, possession of goods or documents of title to them and disposes of the documents or goods to a bona fide third party, that third party gets a good title (s. 25(1)).

Example

A sold copper to *B* and sent him a bill of lading with a draft for the price. *B* was insolvent and did not accept the draft, but handed a third party, *C*, the bill of lading in fulfilling a sale contract of the copper to him. *C* paid for the copper and took the bill of lading without notice of *A*'s right as an unpaid seller. *A* stopped the copper in transit.

Held: *B* was in possession of the bill of lading with *A*'s consent so *C* could obtain good title.

(*Cahn v. Pockett's Bristol Channel Co.*, 1899)

In a recent case the fiduciary position of the buyer was examined by the Court of Appeal in relation to a resale.

Example

The plaintiffs sold aluminium foil to the defendant for manufacture and resale, under a contract which contained the following condition: that ownership of the material delivered would be transferred to the purchaser only when he had paid all that was owing to the plaintiffs. The contract also provided that if the foil was processed into other articles ownership of these would be given to the plaintiffs and the defendants would keep them in their capacity as 'fiduciary owner', although they were expressly empowered to sell such articles in the normal course of business. Nothing was provided in the contract concerning sale of foil not made up into other articles. The defendants went into liquidation and the receiver eventually received £35,000 which represented the proceeds of aluminium foil resold by the defendants to third parties, the latter having obtained good title under s. 25 (2). The plaintiffs included in the claims one for the £35,000 under a tracing action.

Held: The condition was clearly intended to protect the plaintiffs against the risk of non-payment if the buyer became insolvent. So the defendants held the foil, processed or not, as agents or bailees and there was implied, in addition to a power to sell unprocessed foil, a duty to account as fiduciary owners. On the facts, following resale to the third parties the plaintiffs were not mere creditors and claimed the £35,000 under a tracing action and thereby gained priority over the defendant's general creditors.

(*Aluminium Industries Vaassen B.V. v. Romalpa Aluminium Ltd.*, 1976)

The common use of what are now known as Rompala clauses which seek to reserve proprietary rights to a seller of goods was noted in a recent case.

Example

The sellers supplied synthetic fibre to the buyers who use it in the manufacture of carpets. The fibre was supplied by separate deliveries each of which was a separate contract. Each contract laid down that the risk in the property (fibre) passed to the buyers on delivery, but 'the equitable and beneficial ownership' of the fibre was to remain with the sellers until full payment had been made for the fibre delivered or until prior resale where the sellers' entitlement would attach to the proceeds of sale. If the fibre became part of, or was converted into, other products the sellers were to have equitable and beneficial ownership in those products or in the proceeds of their sale. In the course of the buyers' production the fibre was spun into yarn with other fibre and the yarn processed and woven into carpets. As a result the fibre supplied by the sellers became an inseparable part of the yarn and the carpets. The buyers became insolvent and receivers were appointed. On that date the buyers owed £587,397 for twenty-nine unpaid deliveries of fibre. The buyers held little raw fibre but did have large stocks of yarn and finished carpets. The yarn included fibre supplied by the sellers, reprocessed fibre owned by the buyers and yarn purchased from a subsidiary of the buyers. It was impossible to separate the unpaid fibre from the yarn and carpets or determine accurately how much unpaid fibre these contained! The buyers claimed that, under the retention of the title clause in the contracts, they were entitled to trace their fibre into the stocks of yarn and carpets held by the buyers or the proceeds of sale of carpets in which it had been used. The receivers argued that the only rights given to the sellers by the retention of title clause were those under a floating charge which was void against the other creditors for want of registration under s. 95 (1) of the Companies Act 1948. The sellers, on their part, argued that they were in a position to be a beneficiary under a trust or alternatively, if only a charge had been created to secure the purchase price they, not the buyers, had created it and it was not void under s. 95 (1).

Held: The contracts between the buyers and sellers were primarily contracts for the sale of goods under which the property and risk in the goods passed on delivery to the buyers who were free to resell them or use them in manufacture. This was subject to the intention of the parties that the sellers should retain rights of equitable and beneficial ownership until payment was made. The buyers were entitled to redeem the sellers' interest in the property remaining in the fibre by paying the money owing. If the sellers exercised their power of resale any surplus belonged to the buyers and not the sellers. On true construction of the retention of title clause the rights given to the sellers were merely by way of equitable charge over the fibre (or subsequent products or proceeds of sale). The entire beneficial interest of sale remained with the buyers as the buyers' equity of redemption (in paying off the purchase price) was inconsistent with the existence of a trust for the sellers' benefit.

The equitable charge, or true construction of the contract, was created by the buyers by way of an implied grant back to the sellers after the whole of the property in the fibre had first passed to the buyer. Since the buyers were free to use the fibre in the course of their business the charge was a floating charge not a specific charge. The charge had not been registered and was therefore void under s. 95 (1) against the buyers' creditors.

(Re Bond Worth Ltd., 1979)

(for information on floating and specific charges see Chapter 10, p. 274)

4:6 IMPLIED CONDITIONS

The main purpose of the Sale of Goods Act 1979 is to lay down a series of rules so that the parties to a sale know what their rights and duties are. As far as buyers are concerned, among the most important rules are the 'implied conditions' laid down in the Act. These implied conditions are automatically incorporated into every contract for the sale of goods, irrespective of any action or knowledge of the parties. Sections 12–15 of the S.G.A. contain these conditions and place a number of duties on sellers for the protection of buyers.

The implied conditions are:

(i) *That the seller has the right to sell the goods and, where there is an agreement to sell, that he will have the right to sell the goods at the time when the property is to pass* (s. 12 (1) (a))

If it turns out that the goods do not belong to the seller, and the buyer has to give them up to the true owner, under s. 12 (1), S.G.A., the seller is liable in damages for the price of goods to the buyer.

Example

A buyer of a car used it for three months, and then found that it was stolen property, and had to return it to the true owner.
Held: Even though the car had been used for three months, the buyer could recover the price, as there had been a total failure of consideration.

(Rowland v. Divall, 1923)

(ii) *There is an implied warranty that the goods are free, and will remain so until the property is to pass, from any charge or encumbrance not disclosed or known to the buyer before the contract is made and that the buyer will enjoy quiet possession of the goods except so far as it may be disturbed by the owner or other person entitled to the benefit of any charge or encumbrance so disclosed or known* (s. 12 (1) (b))

Example

The plaintiffs, who had manufactured a road-marking machine, sold it to the defendant between the date when a patent application had been made by a third party to protect an invention embodied in it, and publication of the application. In defence and in counter-claim to an action for part of the purchase price the defendants pleaded breach of the implied condition by the plaintiffs of the right to sell the goods and of the implied warranty of quiet possession.

Held: The Court of Appeal held that there was no breach of the right to sell as at the time of sale the plaintiffs did have that right. However, there had been a breach of the implied warranty that the buyer shall have and enjoy quiet possession of the goods; the natural meaning of the future tense was that the warranty applied to events occurring after the sale.

(*Microbeads A.C. v. Vinhurst Road Markings Ltd.*, 1975)

Note: Although this case was decided before the Sale of Goods Act 1893 was amended by the Supply of Goods (Implied Terms) Act 1973 s. 1 (*see* s. 12 above) the form of s. 12 does not suggest that the case would be decided differently under the present law. Section 12 (2) provides that where there appears from the contract or to be inferred from its circumstances an intention that the seller should transfer only such title as he or a third party may have, there is:

(*a*) an implied warranty that all charges and encumbrances known to the seller and not known to the buyer have been disclosed to the buyer before the contract made; and

(*b*) an implied warranty that neither

(i) the seller, nor

(ii) in a case where the parties to the contract intend that the seller should transfer only such title as a third party may have, that person; nor

(iii) anyone claiming through or under the seller or that third person otherwise then under a charge or encumbrance disclosed or known to the buyer before the contract is made;

will disturb the buyer's quiet possession of the goods.

(iii) *In a case of contract for sale of goods by description, there is an implied condition that the goods shall correspond with the description; and if the sale be by sample, as well as by description, it is not sufficient that the bulk of the goods corresponds with the sample if the goods do not also correspond with the description* (s. 13 (1), (2))

Goods are purchased by description where they are described by the buyer in detail or he uses a descriptive word; e.g. the buyer asks for a bicycle, a hot water bottle, underpants, or a bottle of wine.

A sale of goods is not prevented from being a sale by description by reason only that, being exposed for sale or hire, they are selected by the buyer (s. 13 (3)). Therefore a sale of goods is still a sale by description even though the buyer selects the goods, as for instance in a self-service store.

Example

A shopper in a store asked for underwear and was shown some woollen underpants, which he purchased. They contained an irritating substance (sulphide traces) which caused him dermatitis.
Held: This was a sale by description and the goods were not of merchantable quality or fit for the purpose for which they were required.
(Grant v. Australian Knitting Mills, 1936)

Example

A purchaser asked for a bottle of Stone's ginger wine at a shop, which was licensed for the sale of wines. On opening the bottle the purchaser was injured when it broke.
Held: This was a sale by description and the bottle was not of merchantable quality—the purchaser could therefore recover damages.
(Morelli v. Fitch and Gibbons, 1928)

Note: If the wine had been purchased at 35p and there was a $2\frac{1}{2}$p deposit on the bottle and the buyer injured under similar circumstances the Act would not have applied to the bottle as it would have been *hired* and not purchased.
(Beecham Foods Ltd. v. North Supplies (Edmonton) Ltd., 1959)

Example

Seller agreed to sell tinned pears, which were to be packed in cases containing thirty tins each. When the goods were delivered, half the cases contained twenty-four tins in each case. The buyers refused to accept them.
Held: The goods had been sold by description and the method of packing was part of the description; the buyers were justified in refusing delivery.
(Re Moore & Co. Ltd. v. Landauer & Co., 1921)

(iv) *Where goods are sold by description by a seller who deals in goods of that description there is an implied condition that the goods shall be of merchantable quality* (s. 14 (2))

Goods are of merchantable quality within the meaning of the S.G.A. if they are as fit for the purposes for which goods of that kind are commonly bought as is reasonable to expect having regard to any description applied to them, the price (if relevant) and all the other relevant circumstances (s. 14 (6)).

Example

A purchaser ordered Coalite from a coal merchant. When burnt on a domestic fire it exploded due to the presence of gelignite in the coal.
Held: There was a breach of the implied condition that the goods were of merchantable quality.
(Wilson v. Rickett, Cockerell & Co. Ltd., 1954)

There will be no such condition of merchantable quality implied where a seller sells goods in the course of a business (*a*) as regards defects specifically drawn to the buyer's attention before the contract is made; or (*b*) if the buyer examines the goods before the contract is made, as regards defects which the examination ought to reveal (s. 14(2)(a)(b)). This change in the S.G.A. made by s. 3 of the 1973 Act would appear to negate the ruling in *Thornett & Fehr v. Beer & Sons* where nominal examination of goods (representative of purchasers checking only exteriors of glue barrels containing vegetable glue) was held to prevent a buyer from claiming damages for breach of merchantable quality. Where the defect is not discoverable on examination the seller is still liable (*Wren v. Holt,* 1903; arsenic in beer).

The condition of merchantable quality applies only where the seller sells in the course of business. In a recent Scottish case application of the condition was considered when goods sold formed part of the equipment used for the purposes of the seller's business.

Example

A farm and livestock were sold by farmers to the defendants. Before the latter took over the farm it was found that one of the cows was tubercular. After it had been slaughtered the Department of Agriculture and Fisheries for Scotland issued a notice prohibiting cattle movement from and to the farm. When the purchasers took over the farm they wished to move some stock and it was only then that they discovered the fact of the slaughtered cow and the restriction. Later a second cow had to be killed. The purchasers held back part of the purchase price as a result of the losses. Amongst other matters the buyers relied on s. 14 (2) and argued that, as the cattle were sold in the course of the seller's business, there was an implied condition as to merchantability. This had been breached, it was claimed, since at the time of sale the cattle were positive tuberculosis reactors. The sellers argued that the private sale which ended the business was not a sale in the course of business.
Held: Rejecting the sellers' argument the court held that anyone who sells any part of business equipment must sell that part in the course of his business. It made no difference whether the sale was of one item or the whole of the goods used by the seller for the purpose of a business.

(*Buchanan-Jardine v. Hamlink*, 1981)

(v) *Where the seller sells goods in the course of a business and the buyer, expressly or by implication, makes known to the seller any particular purpose for which such goods are being bought, there is an implied condition that the goods supplied under the contract are reasonably fit for that purpose except where the circumstances show that the buyer does not rely, or that it is unreasonable for him to rely on the seller's skill and judgement* (s. 14(3))

The Sale of Goods Act 1979 has amended this section by placing a credit-broker under a similar obligation to a buyer (who has made known to the credit-broker any particular purpose for which the goods are being bought) where the purchase price, or part of it, is payable by instalments and the goods were previously sold by the credit-broker to the seller.

Example

A prospective purchaser told a firm of car dealers that he required a comfortable car for touring. The garage recommended a Bugatti and this was purchased by the plaintiff, but he found the car uncomfortable and unsuitable for touring purposes.
Held: The purchaser was entitled to reject the car for breach of the implied condition of fitness implied under s. 14(1) (now s. 14(3)). The car had not been sold under a trade name, but the buyer had relied on the judgement and skill of the seller. (*Baldry v. Marshall*, 1924)

Where the buyer orders goods under their patent or trade name, the seller does not undertake that they are fit for any particular use.

The implied condition as to fitness for purpose applies to goods 'supplied under a contract of sale', although no property in the goods may pass to the buyer.

Example

Bottles of mineral water sold by a manufacturer to a retailer. The bottles were not part of the sale, but had to be returned to the manufacturer. Due to a defect one of the bottles burst and injured the buyer.
Held: The sellers were liable to the buyer of the bottle for breach of the condition that the goods should be reasonably fit for the purpose; although the bottle had not been sold it had been supplied under a contract of sale.
(*Geddling v. Marsh*, 1920)

For s. 14(3) to operate, the goods must be of a description which it is in the course of the seller's business to supply.

Example

A buyer purchased quantities of material from gum and adhesive manufacturers. He explained the material was required for manufacturing fly papers. The first consignment was made of natural materials but a later consignment was made of synthetic materials and proved unsatisfactory. The manufacturing firm, in an action against them under s. 14(1), pleaded that the second consignment was not 'of a description which it is in the course of the seller's business to supply' as it had not been previously supplied and was made specially for the buyer.
Held: The manufacturers being dealers in adhesives and gums were liable although the supplies in question took a special form.
(*Spencer Trading Co. Ltd. v. Devon Fixol & Stickphast Ltd., Third parties*, 1947)

A House of Lords case indicates the complexity that may occur in relation to the application of the conditions of fitness and purpose and merchantable quality to a particular set of facts.

Example

Animal food compounders who had never supplied food for mink agreed to supply to a mink farm a trade food made up to the purchaser's formula, being told the food was required for mink. The purchaser's formula included herring meal; that used by the sellers obtained from a Norwegian supplier, Norsildmel, contained a chemical substance that reacted with the preservative in the compound creating a substance that caused the death of the mink that ate it. *Held:* The suppliers were not liable under s. 13—(sale by description)—as the meal was certainly herring meal. The supplier and Norsildmel were, however, liable under s. 14(1). Although the mink farm supplied the formula they relied on the sellers to ensure that the ingredients were of a quality that would be fit for feeding to animals, including mink. The herring meal had been shown to contain a degree of toxic matter. The suppliers were suppliers of animal foods and thus the goods came under s. 14(1). There was also liability under s. 14(2) as they were sellers dealing in goods 'of that description', since they had accepted the order to supply them in the way of business, whether or not orders for goods of that description had been previously accepted.

(*Ashington Piggeries Ltd. v. Christopher Hill Ltd.*, 1971)

The Court of Appeal has dealt with the application of the implied condition of fitness of purpose to a second-hand car sale.

Example

A second-hand Jaguar car was purchased for £390 from a garage with over 82,000 miles on the mileometer and described by the salesman as, for the make, 'hardly run in'. It passed its M.O.T. the following day but after minor problems and being driven 2,354 miles in the next three weeks the car's engine seized up on a motorway and eventually a new engine was fitted. The plaintiff brought an action incidentally claiming damages on the grounds that he had relied on the seller's skill and judgement and that the car was not fit for the purpose for which it was required. The dealers denied liability, relying on the high mileage covered by the car since purchase and claiming that the plaintiff had inspected the car. The dealers appealed from the lower court's decision that there had been a breach of the implied condition on the basis of the previous owner's evidence that the car was 'clapped out' when sold to the dealer's for resale.

Held: Dismissing the appeal; that despite the fact that the car had been driven for over 2,300 miles after sale the judge was entitled to find evidence of its condition as not then fit for use on the road when sold to the dealers and thus the condition as to fitness of purpose had been breached.

(*Crowther v. Shannon Motors Co.*, 1975)

Note: Lord Denning in the above case drew a distinction between that case and *Bartlett v. Sidney Marcus Ltd.*, 1965, where it was emphasized that a buyer should expect defects in a second-hand car. In *Bartlett's* case it was held to be no breach of the implied condition as to fitness of purpose where a second-hand car required a clutch repair costing £45 after 300 miles.

No provision is made under s. 14 regarding sales under trade names, but the implied term as to fitness will not apply where circumstances show that it is unreasonable for the buyer to rely on the seller's skill and judgement or that the buyer did not rely upon this. The court will probably be able to find that the buyer relied entirely on the manufacturer rather than on the retailer in the case of goods sold by a trade name. Section 14(5) provides that the provisions of s. 14 apply to a sale by a person acting in the course of business as an agent as they apply to a sale by a principal, except where the buyer knows the agent is not so acting or reasonable steps are made to bring this fact to his notice before the contract is made.

(vi) *Where goods are sold by reference to a sample the following conditions are implied:*
(*a*) that the bulk shall correspond with the sample in quality;
(*b*) that the buyer shall have a reasonable opportunity of comparing the bulk with the sample;
(*c*) that the goods are free from defects rendering them unmerchantable which would not have been apparent on reasonable examination of the sample s. 15 (2).

A contract for sale by sample is created where there is an express or implied term to the effect that the sale is based on the sample.

Example

A retailer purchased two dozen catapults by sample at 12½p a dozen from Burton & Son (Bermondsey) Ltd. A six-year-old boy purchased a catapult for 2½p in the retailer's shop. While using the catapult it broke due to a hidden defect and his eye was so damaged it had to be removed. His father sued the retailer, alleging the retailer was in breach of s. 14(1), fitness for purpose, and s. 14(2), merchantable quality. In turn the retailer sued the wholesalers for breach of s. 15—freedom from defects not apparent in sample, rendering goods unmerchantable. The wholesalers, on their part, sued the importers under s. 15. *Held:* The boy had relied on the retailer's skill and judgement (s. 14(1)) and it was also a sale by description (s. 14(2)). The shopkeeper recovered damages of £2,500 from the wholesalers, who then obtained an indemnity from the importers.

> (*Godley v. Perry; Burton & Sons (Bermondsey) Ltd., Third Party; Graham, Fourth Party*, 1960)

Where a defect is not apparent from a sample a buyer can bring an action either under s. 14(2) or s. 15(2)(c). Where a defect was discoverable the buyer might bring an action under s. 14(2) but not under s. 15(2)(c).

Note: The Law Commission and the Scottish Law Commission in a Working Paper published in October 1983 on Sale and Supply of Goods (Law Commission Working Paper No. 85) have suggested a new definition to replace the existing statutory definition of merchantable quality. It is recommended that the new definition, which would not include the word merchantable, would cover both consumer and commercial transactions. The working paper suggests the formulation of a flexible standard coupled with a clear statement of certain important elements included within the idea of quality, such as freedom from minor defects, durability and safety and a list of important factors such as price and description, to which regard should be paid in determining the standard in a particular case.

4:7   MODIFICATION OF THE 1979 ACT

The Act is modified in its application to contracts of sale of goods made on certain dates by Schedule 1.

(i) CONTRACTS MADE BEFORE 18 MAY 1973

A contract made before 18 May 1973 is governed by Schedule 1. This provides that, unless the circumstances of the contract show otherwise, there is an implied condition on the part of the seller that he has the right to sell the goods and in the case of an agreement to sell he will have such a right at the time when the property is to pass. Such a contract is also subject to an implied warranty that the buyer will have and enjoy quiet possession of the goods and that the goods will be free from any charge or encumbrance in favour of a third party, not declared or known to the buyer before or at the time when the contract is made (Schedule 1, para. 3). In relation to a sale by description s. 13 (3) does not apply (Schedule 1, para. 4).

Where the buyer, expressly or impliedly, makes known to the seller the particular purpose for which the goods are required so as to show that the buyer relies on the seller's skill or judgement, and the goods are of a description which it is in the course of the seller's business to supply (whether he is the manufacturer or not), there is an implied condition that the goods will be reasonably fit for such purpose. However, in the case of a contract for the sale of a specified article under its patent or other trade name there is no such implied condition.

Where goods are bought by description from a seller dealing in goods of that description (whether he is the manufacturer or not) there is an implied condition that the goods will be of merchantable quality. If the buyer has examined the goods, no such condition will apply as regards defects which the examination ought to have revealed. An express condition or warranty does not negate a condition or warranty implied by the Act unless inconsistent with it (Schedule 1, para. 6).

In relation to sale by sample in contracts made before 18 May 1973 'unmerchantable' does not apply as defined in the body of the Act by s. 14 (6) (Schedule 1, para. 7).

(ii) CONTRACTS MADE ON OR AFTER 18 MAY 1973

Contracts made on or after 18 May and before 1 January 1980 have certain modified conditions applying to them. There is an implied condition that goods are of merchantable quality in terms identical to s. 14 (2) (*see* 4:6). Where the seller sells goods in the course of a business and the seller, expressly or impliedly, makes known to the seller any particular purpose for which the goods are bought there is an implied condition that the goods supplied under the contract are reasonably fit for that purpose, whether or not such goods are commonly supplied for such a purpose. This condition will not apply where the circumstances show that the buyer does not rely, or that it is unreasonable for him to rely, on the seller's skill and judgement.

The condition above, in applying to an agreement for the sale of goods under which the purchase price or part of it is payable by instalments, includes as a seller any reference to a person by whom any negotiations prior to the contract are conducted (applying s. 58 (3), (5) of the Hire Purchase Act 1965, s. 54 (3), (5) Hire Purchase (Scotland) Act 1965, s. 65 (3), (5) Hire Purchase Act (Northern Ireland) 1966 (Schedule 1, para. 5)).

Note: Exclusion of the implied terms is dealt with below (4:8).

The Sale of Goods Act 1979 consolidates changes made to s. 55 of the Sale of Goods Act 1893 by s. 4 of the Supply of Goods (Implied Terms) Act 1973. Under Schedule 1, para. 11, contracts made on or after 18 May 1973 and before 1 February 1978 that are for a consumer sale cannot have the protection of the implied terms and conditions taken from them. In a consumer contract of sale any term of that or any other contract exempting from all or any provisions of s. 12 shall be void (para. 11 (3)). Any term exempting any provisions of ss. 13–15 in any other case (i.e. a non-consumer sale) shall not be enforceable to the extent that it would not be fair or reasonable to allow reliance on the term (para. 11 (4)).

(iii) COURT DISCRETION REGARDING EXEMPTION CLAUSES IN NON-CONSUMER SALES

In order to determine whether reliance on such a term would be reasonable the circumstances shall be taken into account including the following matters:

(*a*) the strength of the bargaining position of the seller and buyer relative to each other, taking into account, among other things, the availability of suitable alternative products and sources of supply;
(*b*) whether the buyer received an inducement to agree to the term or, in accepting it, had an opportunity of buying the goods or suitable alternatives without it from any source of supply;
(*c*) whether the buyer knew or ought reasonably to have known of the existence and extent of the term (having regard, among other things, to any custom of the trade and any previous course of dealings between the parties);
(*d*) where the term exempts from all or any of the provisions of ss. 13, 14 or 15 if some condition is not complied with, whether it was reasonable at the time of the contract to expect that compliance with that condition would be practicable;
(*e*) whether the goods were manufactured, processed or adapted to the special order of the buyer (para. 11 (5)).

A consumer sale is defined as a sale of goods (other than a sale by auction or competitive tender) by a seller in the course of a business where the goods:

(*a*) are of a type ordinarily bought for private use or consumption and
(*b*) are sold to a person who does not buy or hold himself out as buying them in the course of business (para. 11 (7)).

It is up to a party who is arguing that a sale is not a consumer sale to prove this (para. 11 (8)).

The discretion given to the court in deciding the fairness or reasonableness of an exclusionary term in a non-consumer contract of sale is guided by para. 11 (5). Where a seller is the sole supplier he is in a more favourable position to place restrictive terms on a buyer than if there were competition amongst suppliers. However, if a buyer, who can obtain identical or similar goods elsewhere, is offered goods on special terms the restriction imposed by a seller may be more justifiable (*see* (*c*)). In respect of (*d*) the question of reasonableness is referred to the time of the contract and not whether reliance on a limit was fair in the situation that occurred. For example, where goods are manufactured or processed to the special order of a buyer, it may be reasonable for the seller to limit his liability in a non-consumer sale. The implied terms can be excluded or varied by express agreement in a contract made before 18 May 1973 or by the course of dealings between the parties, or by usage binding both of them (para. 12).

(iv) DEFINITION OF A CONSUMER SALE

With respect to the definition of a consumer sale (para. 11 (7)) difficulties may arise in interpreting 'sale in the course of a business'. Where a private seller sells through a commercial agent who then resells in the course of business then this is clearly a sale by the agent in the course of a business. But in other instances of agency (*see* Chapter 6) the principal is the seller and if he does not act in the course of a business then the sale is not a consumer sale; this is subject to s. 14(5) where the implied terms of s. 14 apply when a private seller sells through an agent acting in the course of business, unless the buyer knows, or means have been used to inform him, that the seller is a private seller.

Goods do not necessarily fall into the category of 'a type ordinarily bought for private use and consumption'; some goods may be purchased for both private and business use (e.g. cars, furniture, carpets). The main test is whether the goods are of a type ordinarily bought for household use and consumption. Therefore, it can be argued (although there is conflict of legal opinion on this point) that if a firm of solicitors purchases a carpet for their office and the carpet is of similar quality to that used in a domestic house this is a consumer sale. Difficulties may arise with the not uncommon practice of bulk buying frozen food for deep freezes by consumers; would the purchase of fifty frozen pork chops rank as a consumer sale? Clearly bulk sales of chemical bleach to a purchaser would not come under the heading of a consumer sale as even the keenest bargain-hunting housewives would not normally buy in such quantities, but problems exist for mail order and cash and carry firms who may have to check the type of goods sold and their clientele in order to determine whether their liability is that under a consumer or a non-consumer sale.

Similar problems may emerge from interpreting what is meant by 'course of a business'. Where large-scale purchases are made by non-profit making institutions the question may arise as to whether these are consumer sales. As with other points raised this matter awaits interpretation by the courts.

(v) CONSUMER TRANSACTIONS (RESTRICTIONS ON STATEMENTS) ORDER 1976

Although the Supply of Goods (Implied Terms) Act 1973 made exclusion of the implied terms of the S.G.A. void in respect of a consumer sale it did not prevent a seller, or an owner of goods under a hire purchase agreement from putting such exclusionary provisions in a contract. This has now been changed by the Consumer Transactions (Restrictions on Statements) Order 1976 made under s. 22 of the Fair Trading Act 1973.

This prohibits the following acts by persons acting in the course of a business:

1. the display of certain notices where consumer transactions are carried out. These are notices which would be void under s. 55 of the S.G.A. (in the case of hire purchase transactions s. 12 (3) of the 1973 amending Act);
2. the publication of any advertisement intended to induce consumers to enter consumer transactions containing statements similarly void;
3. supplying to a consumer goods bearing on the container a void term, or which would be if it were a term;
4. furnishing to any consumer party, or prospective party, to a consumer transaction of a document containing a void term, or which would be if it were a term;
5. supplying goods, containers, and furnishing documents to a consumer which contain a statement detailing certain rights or obligations of a consumer. Goods, containers or documents must not contain a statement relating to the right or obligations of the consumer where the goods are defective, not fit for a particular purpose or do not correspond with their description unless there is a clear conspicuous statement in close proximity to the other which informs the consumer that his statutory rights are not affected;
6. the supplying by the retailer, anticipating a subsequent consumer transaction, of any goods, container bearing, or furnishing a document containing, a statement limiting the liability of the supplier to the retailer. This can only be done if there is a clear conspicuous statement as in (5).

Anyone contravening the provisions of the order is liable on summary conviction, to a fine not exceeding £400 and, on conviction or indictment, an unlimited fine, or a term of two years' imprisonment or both (s. 23, Fair Trading Act 1973).

4:8 SUPPLY OF GOODS AND SERVICES ACT 1982

The Supply of Goods and Services Act 1982, which was passed on 13 July 1982, makes changes in the law concerning implied terms in contracts for the transfer of property in goods, for the hire of goods and for the supply of services. The Act stems from recommendations of the Law Commission report 'Implied Terms in Contracts for the Supply of Goods' (Law Com. No. 95, 1979). The Supply of Goods and Services Act 1982 deals with Supply of Goods in Part I (which comes into operation with s. 17 and related parts of ss. 18 and 19 on January 1 1983) and with Supply of Services in Part II (which, with related parts of ss. 18 and 19 comes into operation on a day to be appointed by the Secretary of State). Part II deals with supplementary matters.

(a) Supply of Goods
A contract for the transfer of goods for the purposes of the Act means a contract under which one person agrees to transfer property in goods to another, other than an excepted contract. An excepted contract (i.e. one the Act does not cover) means a contract

(*a*) for a sale of goods;
(*b*) for a hire purchase agreement;

(c) under which the property in goods is (or is to be) transferred in exchange for trading stamps or their redemption;

(d) for a transfer or agreement to transfer which is made by deed and for which there is no other consideration other than the presumed consideration imported by the deed;

(e) intended to operate by way of mortgage, pledge, charge or other security (s. 1 (2)).

Under the Act a contract is regarded as a contract for the transfer of goods whether or not services are provided (or to be provided) under the contract and whatever the nature of the consideration for the transfer or the agreement to do so (subject to s. 1 (2)). The latter provision will therefore cover such items as goods supplied in return for product labels or packet tear off coupons (see *Chappell & Co Ltd. v. Nestle's Co Ltd*, p. 24).

Part I deals with implied terms in the supply of goods.

The implied terms are, with one important difference, similar to those in the Sale of Goods Act 1979 ss. 12-15 concerning title (s. 2), correspondence with description (s. 3), merchantable quality and fitness of purpose (s. 4) and sale by sample (s. 5). (See 4:6 above.)

Where the transferor transfers the property in goods in the course of a business and the transferee either expressly or impliedly makes known any particular purpose for which the goods are being acquired to the transferor and to a credit broker (where the consideration (or part) for transfer is a sum payable by instalments and the goods were previously sold by a credit broker to the transferor) there is an implied condition that the goods supplied under the contract are reasonably fit for that purpose, whether or not that is a purpose for which such goods are commonly supplied (s. 4 (4), (5)). The background to this provision is to be found in cases such as *Spencer Trading Co* (see p. 131) and *Ashington Piggeries* (see p. 132). These provisions will not apply when the circumstances show that the transferee does not rely or that it is unreasonable for him to rely, on the skill or judgement of the transferor or credit broker (s. 4 (6). A credit broker is defined by the Act as a person acting in the course of a business of credit brokerage carried on by him (s. 18). The above provisions also apply to a transfer by a person who in the course of business is acting as agent for another. They also apply to a transfer by a principal in the course of a business, except where the other person is not transferring in the course of a business and either the transferee knew this or reasonable steps are taken to bring it to the transferee's notice before the contract concerned is made (s. 4 (8)).

An implied condition or warranty about quality or fitness for a particular purposes may be annexed by usage to a contract for the transfer of goods (s. 4 (7)).

(b) Hire of Goods

A contract for the hire of goods is defined as a contract under which one persons bails or agrees to bail goods to another by way of hire. This does not include a hire purchase agreement or a contract under which goods are (or are to be) bailed in exchange for trading stamps on their redemption (s. 6 (1), (2)). A contract is a contract for hire whether or not services are also provided or to be provided under the contract whatever is the nature of the consideration for the bailment or agreement to bail by way of hire (s. 6 (3)).

A bailor is defined, in relation to a contract for the hire of goods, as a person who bails the goods under the contract or a person who agrees to do so, or a person to whom the duties under the contract of either of those persons have passed. A bailee is described in similar terms as a person to whom goods are bailed under the contract. In each case the definition will be dependent on the context (s. 18 (1)). Essentially a bailment occurs where one person (the bailor) gives over possession of goods to another (the bailee).

Implied terms concerning hire by description (s. 8), quality and fitness (s. 9) and hire by ample (s. 10) are similar to those governing supply of goods (ss. 3–5). Additionally in a contract for the hire of goods there is an implied condition on the part of the bailor that in the case of a bailment he has the right to transfer possession of the goods by way of hire for the period of the bailment and in the case of an agreement to bail he will have such a right at the time of bailment. There is also an implied warranty that the bailee will enjoy quiet possession of the goods for the period of bailment except so far as the possession may be disturbed by the owner or other person entitled to the benefit of any charge or encumbrance disclosed or known to the bailee before the contract is made (s. 7 (1), (2)). These provisions do not affect the right of the bailor to repossess the goods under an express or implied term of the contract (s. 7 (3)).

In the case of a contract for the transfer of goods for the hire of goods a right, duty or liability which would otherwise arise under such a contract may be negatived or varied by express agreement, by a course of dealing between the parties, or by such usage as binds both parties to the contract. This is subject to the provisions of concerning consumer supply under the Unfair Contract Terms Act 1977 (see 1: 6) and the provision that an express condition or warranty does not negative a condition or warranty implied by preceding provisions of the Supply of Goods and Services Act unless inconsistent with it. Nothing in those preceding provisions prejudices the operation of any other enactment or rule of law thereby any condition and warranty (apart from one relating to quality and fitness) is to be implied in a contract for the transfer of goods or for the hire of goods (s. 11).

(c) *Supply of services*

A contract for the supply of services is defined as a contract under which the supplier agrees to carry out a service. A contract of service or apprenticeship is expressly excluded from the definition of a contract for the supply of services. A contract is one for the supply of services under the Act whether or not goods are also transferred or to be transferred, or bailed or to be bailed by way of hire under the contract, and whatever is the nature of the consideration for which the service is to be carried out (s. 12 (1)–(3)). In a contract for the supply of service, where the supplier is acting in the course of a business, there is an implied term that the supplier will carry out the service with reasonable care and skill (s. 13). Where the contract does not fix the time for the service to be carried out, or left to be fixed in a manner agreed by the contract or to be determined by the course of dealing between the parties, there is an implied term that the supplier will carry out the service within a reasonable time. What is a reasonable time is a question of fact (s. 14). There is an implied term in similar circumstances as s. 14 that the party contracting with the supplier will pay a reasonable charge (again, a question of fact) as consideration for the supply of a service (s. 15).

The Secretary of State may provide by order (the power exercisable by statutory instrument) that one or more of ss. 13–15 shall not apply to services of a description specified in the order which may make different provision for different circumstances (s. 12 (4), (5)). Exclusion of the implied terms is governed by s. 16 which is identical to s. 11. Nothing in this part of the Act is to prejudice any rule of law which imposes on the supplier of services a duty stricter than under s. 13 or s. 14 or one whereby any term is implied not inconsistent with this part of the Act. This part of the Act has effect subject to any other enactment which defines or restricts the rights, duties or liabilities arising in connection with a service of any description (s. 16).

Note: The Supply of Goods and Services Act by s. 18 amends the Unfair Contract Terms Act 1977 in that liability for breach of s. 7 of the 1982 Act (implied condition as to title, etc.) cannot be excluded or restricted; see s. 7 (3A) Unfair Contract Terms Act 1977 at 1:6.

4:9   CONSUMER SAFETY ACT 1978

Under the Consumer Safety Act 1978 the Secretary of State is given power to make regulations to ensure that goods are safe and appropriate information is provided with goods supplied. Such safety regulation may contain such provisions dealing with the following matters:

(*a*) composition, design, construction, finish or packing of goods;
(*b*) conformity to a particular standard or one to be approved or of a kind approved by a particular person;
(*c*) testing or inspection, in determining the manner in which, and persons by whom, any test or inspection is carried out and the standards to be applied;
(*d*) requiring warnings or instructions or other information to be applied to goods and ensuring that inappropriate information is not given by misleading marks or otherwise;
(*e*) prohibiting persons from supplying goods which the Secretary of State considers are not safe and do not satisfy the requirements of the regulations;
(*f*) prohibiting persons from supplying goods designed as component parts of other goods and which would, if used as such, cause the other goods to breach the requirements of the regulations (s. 1 (2)).

Note: Supply in (*e*) and (*f*) includes offering to supply, agreeing to supply, exposing for supply or possessing for supply.

The safety regulations may:

(*a*) make different provision for different circumstances or provision relating only to specified circumstances;
(*b*) provide for exemptions from any provision of the regulations;
(*c*) contain such incidental and supplementary provisions as the Secretary of State considers appropriate (s. 1 (3)).

The Secretary of State has to consult such organizations he considers as representative of interests substantially affected by a proposal to make safety regulations and also other appropriate persons. He is under a duty to consult the Health and Safety Commission in the case of proposed regulations relating to goods suitable for use at work. It is an offence if a person breaches safety regulations prohibiting them from supplying goods. Similarly, where safety regulations require a person who makes or processes goods in the course of a business:

(*a*) to carry out or use a particular test or procedure; or
(*b*) to deal or not to deal in a particular way with a quantity of the goods which either partly or wholly do not satisfy tests or standards connected with the procedure, an offence is committed if that person does not comply with the requirement (s. 2 (2)). Such offences are punishable by imprisonment on summary conviction of a maximum of three months and a fine not exceeding £1,000.

A civil action may be taken for the statutory breach of any obligation imposed on a person by safety regulations or by a prohibition order (an order made under s. 3 by the Secretary of State to prohibit supply of goods or to give warning of danger from goods).

The Secretary of State may also serve a 'prohibition notice' which prohibits the person on whom it is served from supplying the goods referred to in the notice without the consent of the Secretary of State. A 'notice to warn' may also be served which requires the person on whom it is served to publish a warning in relation to the goods he is selling. Breach of the above notices, as with prohibition orders, constitutes a criminal offence.

The Act is enforced by the Weights and Measures authorities.

4:10 THE CONSUMER'S REMEDY IN TORT

In particular cases a consumer may be able to bring an action in tort against the manufacturer of goods that have caused them injury or damage.

Example

A shop assistant drank some ginger beer which the manufacturers had sold to a Paisley café proprietor who in turn sold it to the shop assistant's friend. As a second glass was poured for her from the opaque bottle a decomposed snail floated out. As a result the woman became ill from the glass of ginger beer she had already drunk and suffered nervous shock from the gruesome sight of the desiccated mollusc. She claimed damages from the manufacturer for negligence. *Held:* The manufacturers owed the plaintiff a duty to take care that the bottle did not contain harmful material. A manufacturer of food, medicine, or similar article, who sold these in circumstances where the distributor or consumer could not discover any defect on a reasonable inspection (in this case because the bottle was opaque and sealed by a metal press cap) was under a legal duty to the ultimate consumer or purchaser to take reasonable care that the article was free from any defect likely to cause injury.

(*Donoghue v. Stevenson*, 1932)

This important case also contained a useful guide from one of the judges, Lord Atkin, on how wide the duty of care might be. In his view 'You must take reasonable care to avoid acts or omissions which you can reasonably foresee would be likely to injure your neighbour. Who then in law is my neighbour? The answer seems to be—persons who are so closely and directly affected by my act that I ought reasonably to have them in contemplation as being so affected when I am directing my mind to the acts or omissions which are called in question.'

The duty of care laid down in this case (and re-affirmed in the many that have followed it) is owed by the manufacturer to the 'ultimate consumer' (i.e. the person who finally uses the product) completely independent of contract. The lady who suffered in *Donoghue v. Stevenson* had not purchased the bottle of ginger beer from the café proprietor; her friend had. So the liability of the manufacturer was not in contract, but tort—a breach of the duty of care.

If the manufacturers have given clear instructions on the products regarding their use and these are ignored they will not be liable:

Example

Manufacturers of hair dye gave warning on the bottles and in brochures issued with the product that the dye might be dangerous to certain skins and recommended testing before use. A hairdresser ignored these warnings and as a result one of his clients contracted dermatitis.

Held: The client could recover damages from the hairdresser, but *not* from the manufacturers.

(*Holmes v. Ashford*, 1950)

In considering the question of financial injury the courts have had to draw a line not only to limit foreseeability but also to determine whether the plaintiff was owed a duty of care in the first place.

Example

An agricultural research station used a virus in experimental work which escaped and infected cattle in the area. An order was made closing cattle markets with the result that the plaintiffs, auctioneers, temporarily had to stop dealing at those markets and suffered financial loss.

Held: The institute was not liable to the plaintiffs in negligence as their duty to take care to prevent the escape of virus that could infect cattle in the area was owed to cattle owners. As the plaintiffs were not cattle owners no duty was owed to them.

(*Weller & Co. v. Foot & Mouth Disease Research Institute*, 1965)

In an earlier case it had been decided that although a duty of care might be owed to a plaintiff who suffered financial loss due to a negligent statement, such a duty could be avoided by liability being specifically exempted.

Example

Hedley Byrne Ltd. sought through their bankers to discover the financial viability and investment-worthiness of a company known as Easipower Ltd.

Heller & Partners, in reply to the bank's enquiry as to whether Easipower Ltd. were trustworthy to the extent of a £100,000 investment, stated: 'Respectably constituted company, considered good for ordinary business engagements.' In reliance on this statement Hedley Byrne Ltd. invested in Easipower and lost over £17,000 when the company went into liquidation. Hedley Byrne Ltd. sued Heller & Partners Ltd. for the financial loss due to the negligently prepared statement.

Held: Heller & Partners Ltd. were not liable as they did not undertake to exercise a duty of care in giving their replies, the statement being expressly given without responsibility on the part of Heller & Partners Ltd., or their officials.

(*Hedley Byrne & Co. Ltd. v. Heller & Partners Ltd.*, 1964)

However, all the judges in the case just quoted dealt with the position which might have arisen if the firm giving advice had *not* put in express disclaimer of liability. In those circumstances the firm would have been liable to Hedley Byrne as they owed them a duty of care. In a situation where it could be inferred that a maker of a statement was guaranteeing its accuracy knowing that the person to whom it was made, or someone to whom it was passed on, would rely upon it then there was a duty on the maker of the statement to take reasonable care that the statement was accurate. Therefore anyone who gives advice in his ordinary professional capacity (as distinct from a casual conversation at a social function) needs to be aware of the possible legal consequences if he does not exercise reasonable care in framing his advice and a client or customer suffers financial or economic loss as a result.

The duty of care in giving advice has recently been considered where a special relationship arose between a large petrol company and a station tenant.

Example

A petrol company began negotiations with a prospective tenant interested in acquiring a petrol station tenancy. The company's dealer sales representative had encouraged the company to acquire and develop a site which had deficiencies with regard to passing trade which were apparent to the prospective tenant when he inspected it. The representative and other company agents informed the tenant that the sales on the site would be about 200,000 gallons a year in the third year of development although the tenant felt up to 150,000 gallons was a more realistic figure. However, in view of the representative's experience and expertise, the tenant took a three-year tenancy. The business never prospered despite the tenant's efforts and petrol sales reached less than 90,000 gallons in the third year. After three years the tenant gave up the tenancy and in proceedings by the company for arrears of rent counter-claimed for damages for negligence by the company for statements made on its behalf.

Held: In making statements during the course of negotiations for the tenancy agreement concerning the station's prospects the company owed the tenant a duty of care as there was a special relationship between the company and the tenant which gave rise to the duty of care as the company had a financial interest in the advice they gave and knew that the tenant relying on their knowledge and expertise sought information on which to base his decision concerning the tenancy. The defects of the layout of the site were apparent to the company. The fact that the statements were made prior to contract did not relieve the company of a duty of care in making them.

(Esso v. Mardon, 1975)

Cases have laid down a general rule that, apart from *Hedley Byrne* situations, there will be no liability for economic loss due to negligence. It is doubtful, however, that this rule can now be applied in all situations in the light of a recent decision by the High Court of Australia. Here economic loss was held to be recoverable where an oil pipeline was negligently damaged by a harbour dredge operating in Botany Bay, Sydney.

Example

A pipeline owned by a refining company, which passed oil across Botany Bay to an oil terminal operated by Caltex, was broken by a dredge, *Willemstad*, which was deepening the shipping channel. The operators of the dredge knew of the pipeline and the vessel was equipped with navigation aids, which included a unit that incorrectly showed the area safe for dredging. Caltex retained ownership of the crude oil both when in the pipeline and in the refinery supplied. By agreement with the refinery that company carried the risk of loss or damage to the oil until it reached Caltex's terminal. An action was brought by the refinery against the dredge and the installers of the navigation equipment, Decca. The Supreme Court of New South Wales found both liable and awarded $125,000 damages for damage to the pipeline and oil it contained. Caltex also brought actions against the dredge and Decca for damages of $95,000, being the costs of arranging alternative means of carrying the petroleum products until the pipeline was repaired. The judge refused to award these damages as he held they were economic losses unrelated to any injury to Caltex's property. Caltex appealed.

Held: In all the circumstances, both the dredge and Decca owed a duty to Caltex to take reasonable care to avoid causing damage to the pipeline and thereby causing economic loss to Caltex. '... it is still right to say that as a general rule damages are not recoverable for economic loss which is not consequential upon injury to the plaintiff's person or property. The fact that the loss was foreseeable is not enough to make it recoverable. However, there are exceptional cases in which the defendant has knowledge or means of knowledge that the plaintiff individually, and not merely as a member of an unascertained class, will be likely to suffer economic loss as a consequence of his negligence, and owes the plaintiff a duty to take care not to cause him such damage by his negligent act.' (Gibbs, J.)

(Caltex Oil v. 'Willemstad', 1977)

A manufacturer of a defective product will potentially attract liability for compensating an injured party under the tort of negligence or on the basis of contractual obligations as to quality. A recent case illustrates a situation where no remedy may be available to a supplier along the chain of distribution.

Example

A manufacturer produced a tow-hitch which failed while being used to link a trailer to a car. The trailer becoming unsecured as a result of the failure hit a vehicle travelling behind it and killed and injured the occupants. It was found that the cause of the tow-hitch failing was a combination of faulty design and inadequate maintainence.

Held: Liability for the accident was split: 75 per cent to the manufacturers and 25 per cent to the owner of the car with the defective tow-hitch. The owner was held to be entitled to recover from the supplier of the tow-hitch in a claim for breach of contract, both for damages and costs, as well as interest on both, covering the car owner's liability to the accident victims. The Court of Appeal held that the test was not whether the car owner had been negligent towards the injured parties but whether he had been as careful as his contract with the supplier required. It was a question of the contemplation of the parties when the contract was made. The liability of the seller who breaks a contract may not be increased by unreasonable conduct by the buyer. Where, however, a seller sells equipment as 'foolproof' or 'fit and forget' or with similar undertakings he cannot complain if the purchaser does exactly that. The test was 'whether in all the circumstances, the owner's carefulness was so unreasonable as to be beyond the contemplation of the sellers, or such as to break the chain of causation between their breach of warranty and the accident which resulted in the owner's liability'. It was held that the lack of maintenance by the owner did not amount to such unreasonable carelessness and the supplier was therefore liable to the car owner.

The Court of Appeal, however, classified the loss suffered by the supplier (and impliedly by the car owner) as 'pure economic loss' and was excluded by the rules concerning remoteness of damage (see above). As the supplier had failed to keep a record of the sale to him by the manufacturer the supplier could not sue the manufacturer in contract. The Court refused to accept the argument that there was a collateral contract on the basis of the manufacturer's promotional literature, both to the trade and to the public. The hitch had been promoted by the manufacturer as requiring 'no maintenance', 'foolproof', 'once the pin is pushed home it is locked – absolutely', 'no metallic springs to break or rust'. The suppliers argued that these claims were intended to be serious and to be acted upon by users, which the evidence of the manufacturer supported. However, in the Court's view: '. . . the difficulty is to show that what the manufacturer stated in the literature advertising and accompanying their products as to their safety and suitability was intended to be a contractural warranty of binding promise. It is one thing to express or imply it in a contract of sale, another to treat it as expressed or implied as a contract or as a term of a contract, collateral to a contract of sale. There may be cases where the purchase from the intermediate seller may be regarded as fortuitous and the original supplier or seller can properly be held liable for breaches of warranty given by the intermediate seller as well as for those given by him: see *Wells (Mersham) Ltd v. Buckland Sand and Silica Ltd*. But that is not in our judgement this case.'

(*Lambert v. Lewis*, 1980)

The supplier in the *Lambert* case subsequently appealed to the House of Lords both on the grounds of the claim of the indemnity to the car owner against the supplier, and the refusal of the Court of Appeal to allow the supplier to pass this liability to the manufacturer. In *Lexmead (Basingstoke) Ltd v. Lewis and Others*, 1981 the House of Lords held that the car owner, in using the towing hitch knowing it to be defective, was not allowed to plead that his use of a dangerous piece of equipment was the result of the supplier's breach of warranty of fitness. On the issue of the supplier's claim against the manufacturer there was therefore no liability the supplier could pass on to the manufacturer.

Lord Diplock, however, did make the following observations (obiter) on the application by the Court of Appeal of the 'pure economic loss' rule:

'The Court of Appeal rejected this ground of liability because, in their view, they were bound by authority to hold that what may be conveniently referred to as the *Donoghue v. Stevenson* principle was restricted to damage by physical injury but did not extend to purely economic loss; and that the loss sustained by the dealers was purely economic loss. While in the absence of argument it could not be right to express any final view, I should *not* (emphasis added) wish the dismissal of the dealers' appeal to be regarded as an approval by this House that where the economic loss suffered by a distributor in the chain between the manufacturer and the ultimate consumer consists of a liability to pay damages to the ultimate consumer for physical injuries sustained by him, or consists of a liability to indemnify a distributor lower in the chain of distribution for his liability to the ultimate consumer for damages for physical injuries, such economic loss is not recoverable under the *Donoghue v. Stevenson* principle from the manufacturer.'

4:11 PRODUCT LIABILITY: E.E.C. DEVELOPMENTS

The consumer, although normally having no direct contractual relationship with a manufacturer of goods he purchases, is encouraged by modern methods of production, distribution and advertising to regard the manufacturer as primarily responsible for the safety and quality of such goods.

It is against this background that two developments will be considered although space does not permit any more than an essential outline.

(i) THE DRAFT EUROPEAN CONVENTION ON PRODUCTS LIABILITY

In 1970 a committee of experts was set up by the Committee of Ministers of the Council of Europe to propose measures to harmonize the law of Member States in the area of product liability with regard to personal injury and death. The Draft European Convention was published in 1975 with a draft Explanatory Report and submitted for observation by governments of Member States of the Council of Europe. The Convention in its final form opened for signature on 21 January 1977.

The Convention imposes strict liability on the producer only for death or injury caused by a defect in his product irrespective of the existence of a contract between the producer and the person suffering damage (Art. 3(1)). The Convention provides that compensation payable may be reduced or disallowed if the plaintiff or person entitled to compensation contributed to the damage by his own fault (Art. 4(1)). The importer who imports a product for putting it into circulation in the course of business incurs liability as a producer (Art. 3(2)). The producer is the party, according to the Explanatory Report, who puts the product into the state in which it is offered to the public.

This essentially means that for practical purposes a producer will include both the manufacturer of finished products and the producer of natural products. Product is defined as including all moveables, natural or industrial, whether raw or manufactured, even if incorporated into another moveable or an immoveable (Art. 2(a)). Clearly this covers parts made up into machinery and domestic appliances and includes agricultural produce and animal products. A producer of a component is liable only where damage is caused by a defect in his own product as is the producer incorporating the product (Art. 3(4)). A supplier is liable as a producer where the product does not indicate the identity of any of the persons liable as producers, unless the supplier discloses within a reasonable time, and at the request of the claimant, the identity of the producer or the person who supplied him with the product (Art. 3(3)).

Where a plaintiff has shown that he suffered damage caused by a defect in the product, the producer will not be liable if he proves that he did not put the product into circulation or that it was not defective when he put it into circulation. A producer's liability will not be reduced when the damage is caused both by a defect in the product and an act and omission of a third party (Art. 5).

Not only are manufacturers of products both finished and natural liable but also included are those in the commercial links of product preparation and distribution, including warehousemen and repairers and their agents and employees. The Convention is concerned only with the choice of legal rules that will determine the national substantive law to be applied. The distributor's liability will therefore be governed by the appropriate national law. The provisions of the Convention do not apply to the liability of producers between themselves and any rights of contribution and indemnity against third parties. In a situation akin to *Godley v. Perry* (*see* 4:6) the liability of the importer to a distributor of a product still falls to be considered by national law.

Although the Convention rules out the exclusion or limitation of liability by a producer (Art. 8) and has no limit on the financial liability of a producer, in a claim against him, States are allowed to reserve the right to limit the liability of a producer to a minimum ceiling (expressed in special Drawing Rights (S.D.R.) as defined by the International Monetary Fund) of 70,000 S.D.R. per injured or deceased person with a limit of 10 million S.D.R. for all damage caused by identical products with the same defect e.g. as in situations like the thalidomide tragedy (Art. 15). This provision is intended to prevent incalculable risks being placed on producers and an inflation of product prices due to high insurance cover. A limitation period of three years applies to proceedings for recovery of damages running from the day when the plaintiff has knowledge, actual or assumed of the damage, the defect and the producer's identity (Arts. 6, 7).

(ii) THE E.E.C. DIRECTIVE ON LIABILITY FOR DEFECTIVE PRODUCTS

In September 1976 a proposal was made to the Council of the European Communities by the European Commission for a directive relating to the harmonization of laws, regulations and administrative provisions of Member States concerning liability for defective products (Bulletin Supplement 11/76). Like the Convention the proposal was accompanied by an explanatory Memorandum and the Draft Directive itself is substantially similar to the Convention already considered, although certain differences between the two will be examined.

In the view of the Commission current differences in the national laws of Member States adversely affected the establishment of the Common Market in three ways. These were in distortion of competition within the market, the free movement of goods being affected and differing degrees of consumer protection within the E.E.C. being incompatible with a common market of all consumers.

The directive is wider in scope than the Convention in that it imposes strict liability on producers of defective articles, but in certain instances for damage of property.

Under the directive a producer is liable for damage caused by a defect in the article produced, whether or not he knew or could have known of the defect. Liability rests with the producer even if the article could not have been regarded as defective in the light of scientific and technological development (Art. 1). It will not be a defence for the producer to prove that, when he put the article into circulation he could not have known it was defective (Art. 6). Nor will it be a defence for him to prove that the defect was caused by the fault of a person employed by him (Art. 7). A producer will not be liable if he proves that he did not put the article into circulation or that it was not defective when he put it into circulation (Art. 5).

A producer is defined as the producer of the finished article, the producer of any material or component, and any person who, by putting his name, trade mark or other distinguishing feature on the article, represents himself as its producer (Art. 2). This provision is similar to that of the Convention. As in the Convention an importer is liable as a producer (Art. 2). A product is defective when it does not provide for persons or property the safety which a person is entitled to expect (Art. 4). Damage means death or personal injuries and damage to or destruction of any item of property other than the defective article itself where the item is of a type ordinarily acquired for private use or consumption and was not used or acquired by the claimant for his trade, business or professional purposes (Art. 6).

The total liability of the producer for all personal injuries caused by identical articles having the same defect is limited to 25m E.U.A. (£10.4m) (that is European units of account defined by a Commission decision of 18 December 1975; the equivalent in national currency is determined by applying the conversion rate on the day preceeding that date when compensation is finally fixed). Liability of the producer in respect of property is limited to 15,000 E.U.A. (£6,300) per head in the case of moveable property and 50,000 E.U.A. (£21,000) in the case of immoveable property (Art. 7).

Liability under the directive cannot be excluded or limited (Art. 10). The liability of a producer shall be extinguished after ten years at the end of the calendar year in which the defective article was put into circulation by the producer, unless the injured person has in the meantime commenced proceedings against the producer (Art. 9).

The main distinction between the Convention and directive is that, apart from the former dealing with death and injury only and the latter governing in certain instances damage to property, the Convention states that contributory negligence by the injured person or claimant (in the case of fatal injury) may give rise to a reduction or disallowance of the claim. The Convention also provides that similar reduction or disallowance will apply where the fault contributing to the injury is that of an employee or agent of a claimant.

(iii) THE PATTERN OF FUTURE PRODUCT LIABILITY LEGISLATION

The House of Lords Select Committee on the European Communities, in a report prepared by Lord Diplock which appeared at the end of 1976, pointed out the differences between the Convention and directive already mentioned in relation to contributory negligence. The report noted that the only defences open to the producer under the directive were for him to prove that he did not put the article into circulation or that it was not defective when he did so. The Committee felt that this ruled out reduction or disallowance of a claim on the basis of contributory negligence and it was essential that the directive should deal expressly with the legal consequences of fault by the injured person or claimant which contributed to the damage he sustained.

The Committee were also critical of the limit of £10.4 m on the producer's liability for all personal injuries caused by identical articles with the same defect. Although this is intended to provide liability limits that can be covered by an insurance premium which will not require an unreasonable price increase in a product the Committee felt it was necessary to provide expressly for application of the limitation between various claimants. It did not appear clear to the Committee if each claimant was to be paid in full until the limitation amount was exhausted or, as under the Convention, to be divided rateably among all the claimants. The situation also appeared to be further complicated in the Committee's view by the fact that an injury caused by a defective article might not become apparent until long after articles having the same defect had been put on the market, or even long after they had been consumed by the claimant or their parent. This period of uncertainty concerning the proportion an individual claimant might recover could be prolonged until the end of the maximum period of claim, ten years. The Committee's main recommendation was that because of the directive's serious deficiencies Parliament should not proceed with further consideration until the law commissions had reported; the Royal Commission on Civil Liability and Personal Injury under Lord Pearson did so in March 1978.

(iv) THE PEARSON REPORT

The Pearson Report (Cmnd. 1754) covers three separate volumes dealing with many aspects that cannot be mentioned here; therefore only those principal recommendations that touch on the question of product liability are noted.

The Report found no justification at present for introducing a no-fault liability scheme for injuries caused by defective products. It was felt that strict liability would meet most problems and the Report favoured a scheme broadly based on the Convention and the draft directive (para. 132). Producers should be strictly liable in tort for death or injury caused by their products (para. 132) and a producer should not be able to contract out of this liability which should have no financial limit (paras. 146, 147). Defects should be defined in terms of Art. 2 of the Convention whereby 'a product has a defect when it does not provide the safety which a person is entitled to expect having regard to all the circumstances including the presentation of the product' (see Art. 14 of the directive) (para. 134).

Both producers of finished products and components should be strictly liable in tort for defective products. However, a distributor who sold such a product in the course of a business should be obliged to disclose to the person injured by the product either the name of the producer of the goods or the name of his (the distributor's) own supplier. Failure to do so within a reasonable time should render the seller himself strictly liable in tort (paras. 135, 136). Importers should be treated as producers for the purpose of products liability (para. 139). In respect of own brand products strict liability in tort should apply to those who brand them as well as to their producers (para. 137). Producers should not be exempt from strict liability in respect of defective finished products made to a specification (para. 138).

The Report favoured the defence of contributory negligence being available to a producer (para. 143), also that it should be a defence for a producer to prove that either he did not put the product into circulation or the product was not defective when he did so, or that he did not put it into circulation in the course of a business (para. 140). However, it should not be a defence for a producer merely to prove he had withdrawn or attempted to withdraw his product (para. 141), nor should he be allowed the defences of development risk or official certification (paras. 144, 145). Of particular interest in view of the complex litigation following the DC 10 Paris aircrash, the Report recommended that a manufacturer of aircraft should be given a right to be indemnified by a user operator who has wilfully ignored his (the producer's) instructions to rectify defects or modify service schedules (para. 142).

The Report did not favour the introducton of compulsory liability insurance for products (para. 148), but recommended that damages for non-pecuniary loss should not be excluded from product liability actions (para. 151).

The producer's strict liability in tort should be subject to a cut-off period of ten years from the date of the circulation of the product and the Report recommended the adoption of the Convention's provisions on the limitation period within which the person injured by a defective product can start proceedings (paras. 149, 150).

The Report recommended that human blood and organs should be regarded as products and that the authorities responsible for distributing them should be regarded as products producers (para. 152). It was also recommended that moveable products incorporated into immoveable products should be regarded as products for the purposes of products liability (para. 153).

It is therefore difficult to predict what form legislation might take to carry out the provisions of the directive in this country. In view of the limitations of claim that the directive provides it is unlikely that product liability claims will reach the high levels currently experienced in the United States. There in the last decade product liability claims have grown by 1,000 per cent and it is reported that since the Consumer Product Safety Commission was set up in 1972 with powers to impose civil penalties of $2,000 for each violation of the Consumer Product Safety Act and criminal penalties up to $50,000 and a year's imprisonment for each offence insurers have lost $2,500 m. However, one should take into account the contingency fee system in America which permits lawyers to share in damages obtained for clients, a practice illegal in Western Europe. However, strict liability for products on the part of a producer may well become English law provided the inconsistencies between the Convention and directive, already noted, are dealt with. Companies manufacturing consumer products may need to review their insurance cover and check their product quality control. The Office of Fair Trading in their 1974 report showed that 400,000 consumers made complaints about goods and services. Tougher product liability laws would increase that level; if they also had the effect of making the unit costs of production unreasonably high, which would be necessary if insurance premiums rose steeply to meet increased liability, improved consumer protection might be purchased at too high a price.

4:12   PERFORMANCE OF THE CONTRACT

The seller is under a duty to deliver the goods and the buyer to accept and pay for them under the terms of the contract (s. 27, S.G.A.). Payment and delivery, unless otherwise agreed, take place simultaneously, as with cash sales in shops.

(i) DELIVERY

Delivery may be performed in five ways:
(a) by physical transfer (the commonest method);
(b) by delivery of documents of title (e.g. bills of lading);
(c) by delivery of means of control (e.g. key to a store);
(d) where a third party in possession of goods acknowledges that he holds them on the buyer's behalf;
(e) where the seller sends the goods to the buyer under the contract and delivers to a carrier, this is taken as *prima facie* delivery to the buyer.
   (*Wardar's (Import & Export) Co. Ltd. v. W. Norwood & Sons Ltd.*, 1968)

The place of delivery is the seller's business premises; if he has none, his residence. Delivery must be within a reasonable time. Where the seller agrees to deliver goods to a buyer other than at the place of sale, the buyer takes the risk of deterioration of the goods necessarily incident to transit, unless there is a contrary agreement (s. 33, S.G.A.). If the goods are delivered to a buyer's business premises or residence and given to an apparently authorized person, who later misappropriates them, the risk is with the buyer.

Example

A consignment of champagne was delivered at the buyer's residence to a person who appeared to be authorized to receive the goods. This person made off with the cases.

Held: The sellers, having made a valid delivery, were entitled to be paid the price of the goods by the buyer.

(Galbraith & Grant Ltd. v. Block, 1922)

The buyer will be liable to the seller for a reasonable charge for care and custody of the goods and any loss borne by the seller due to the buyer's refusal to take delivery of the goods, after request by the seller, within a reasonable time (s. 37, S.G.A.).

(ii) DELIVERY OF THE WRONG AMOUNT

If the buyer is sent more or less than ordered under the contract he may

(*a*) reject the whole consignment;
(*b*) accept the whole; or
(*c*) accept what was ordered and reject the remainder.

Where goods are delivered in accordance with the contract together with goods of a different kind he can accept the goods agreed on and reject the rest, or reject the whole consignment (s. 30, S.G.A.).

Example

A firm agreed to sell to the buyers 50 tons of galvanized steel sheets 'assorted over 6, 7, 8, 9, and 10 feet long'. The whole of the purchase price was paid by the buyers in advance. On arrival the sheets were found to consist of 50 tons of 6-foot lengths. The buyers claimed to accept one-fifth of the consignment and recover the balance of the money advanced to the sellers.

Held: They were entitled to do so.

(Ebrahim Dawood Ltd. v. Heath Ltd.)

Example

In a contract for the sale of 4,000 tons of meal a variation of 20 per cent either way was allowed. An amount considerably in excess of 4,000 tons was delivered.

Held: The buyers could reject the whole.

(Payne & Routh v. Lillico & Sons, 1920)

If the difference is small, this will not entitle the buyer to reject.

Example

Sellers agreed to sell to the buyers a cargo of wheat of 4,000 tons '2 per cent more or less', with an option to tender another 8 per cent if the sellers wished it. This would have given an amount of 4,950 tons. In fact 4,950 tons 55 lbs were tendered.

Held: The difference of 55 lbs was insignificant and the buyers could not reject under s. 30 (2), S.G.A.

(*Shipton, Anderson & Co. v. Weil Bros. & Co. Ltd.*, 1912)

Where a contract states that each consignment is to be treated as a separate contract the seller can treat the contract as a unity or make separate deliveries, when the contract will become severable.

Example

Goods were shipped by the seller from Hong Kong to Liverpool stating each shipment was a separate contract; the goods were shipped under two bills of lading, each relating to one-half of the shipment. The buyers accepted only one-half.

Held: There was only one contract, the buyers had accepted half the goods, they could not reject the rest.

(*J. Rosenthal & Sons Ltd. v. Esmail*, 1965)

(iii) INSTALMENT DELIVERIES

Where goods are to be delivered by instalments which are to be paid for separately and there is a breach on either side it will depend on the circumstances as to whether this amounts to a repudiation of the whole contract or is a severable breach giving a right only to claim damages. If it is likely that breaches will take place relating to future deliveries the contract can be repudiated.

Example

A sold *B* 1,500 tons of meat and bone meal of a specific quality, to be shipped in equal weekly instalments of 125 tons a month. After half the meal was delivered and paid for *B* found it was not of the quality agreed on and refused further deliveries.

Held: *B* could do so, as he did not have to risk taking future deliveries which did not come up to the contract quality.

(*Robert A. Munro & Co. v. Meyer*, 1930)

Contrast:

Example

In an agreement for 100 tons of rag flock, weekly deliveries were to be paid for separately, which were to be at the rate of three loads a week. The flock was to adhere to a government standard relating to chlorine content. The first fifteen instalments were satisfactory, but the sixteenth one had more chlorine content than allowed by the contract. Four later deliveries were satisfactory. The buyers sought to repudiate the contract.

Held: The defective delivery did not amount to a repudiation by the sellers of the whole agreement so the buyer could not repudidiate.

(*Maple Flock Co. Ltd. v. Universal Furniture Products (Wembley) Ltd.*, 1933)

Example

A purchased 5,000 tons of steel from *B*—delivery at 1,000 tons monthly. A petition to wind up *B*'s company was presented after 2,000 tons had been delivered, but before payment was due. *A* mistakenly refused to pay unless the court sanctioned further transactions, whereupon the liquidator refused to make further deliveries on the grounds that *A*'s failure to pay amounted to a repudiation of the contract.

Held: *A*'s refusal to pay did not excuse the company's liquidator from making further deliveries, as *A*'s conduct did not show an intention to repudiate the contract.

(*Mersey Steel & Iron Co. v. Naylor*, 1884)

(iv) ACCEPTANCE

Acceptance takes place when the buyer indicates acceptance to the seller, or does any act which is inconsistent with the seller's ownership, or retains the goods after a reasonable time, not having indicated rejection.

If the buyer has had no opportunity of previously examining goods sent by the seller he is not reckoned to have accepted them until he has had a reasonable opportunity of doing so.

Example

A sold *B* barley by sample, delivery to be at a named railway station. *B* resold the goods to *C*. *B* inspected a sample of the barley at the station and sent the consignment to *C*. *C* rejected it as not being according to sample and *B* also claimed to reject as against *A*.

Held: *B*'s act of inspection and ordering the transmission of the barley to *C* was an acceptance and he could not later reject the goods.

(*Perkins v. Bell*, 1893)

(v) RIGHTS OF THE SELLER

A seller is entitled to be paid and have the goods accepted. The buyer has a right to examine the goods if he has not done so already. A seller, generally, cannot force the buyer to return the goods he has rejected; he is entitled only to notice of the rejection. If the buyer breaks the contract the seller has other rights—against the buyer and in some cases against the goods.

(vi) ACTIONS AGAINST THE BUYER

Where property in the goods has passed the seller may bring an action for the price if the buyer defaults, or an action for damages for non-acceptance if the buyer refuses or neglects to accept. The measure of damages will be the estimated loss that directly and naturally arises in the ordinary course of events from the buyer's breach of contract (s. 50 (2), S.G.A.).

(*a*) *Measure of damages*

The amount of damages recoverable will depend on whether the goods have been specially made for the buyer, or the goods are sold generally on the open market. Under s. 50 (3) where there is an available market for the goods in question the measure of damages is *prima facie* to be worked out by the difference between the contract price and the market or current price at the time or times when the goods ought to have been accepted. If no time is fixed for acceptance the time of refusal is referred to.

Example

The sellers sold an amount of tinned ham to the buyers. It was wrongfully rejected by the buyers and the sellers claimed damages for non-acceptance under s. 50 (3)—i.e. the difference between the contract price and the market price at the date of the breach.
Held: The sellers were justified in their claim. The fact that the market price for the goods rose after the date of breach could not be taken into consideration.
                    (*Campbell Mostyn* (*Provisions*) *Ltd. v. Barnett Trading Co.*, 1954)

The loss suffered by the seller must arise directly and naturally in the ordinary course of events from the buyer's breach.

Example

A Vanguard car was sold by a garage to a buyer who later repudiated the sale. The car could only be sold at a fixed price and Vanguard cars were in plentiful supply in the area. The car was returned to the garage's suppliers and they (the garage) claimed from the defaulting buyer damages amounting to the profit they would have made on the sale of the car if the purchase has been completed:
Held: Due to the lack of demand the sellers had lost their sale and were entitled to damages for loss of profits.
                    (*W. L. Thompson Ltd. v. R. Robinson* (*Gunmakers*) *Ltd.*, 1955)

Note: An available market was defined in this case by Upjohn, J.: 'the situation in the particular trade in the particular area was such that the particular goods could be freely sold, and that there was a demand sufficient to absorb readily all the goods that were thrust upon it, so that if a purchaser defaulted the goods in question could readily be disposed of'.

Contrast:
Example

A car dealer agreed to sell a Hillman Minx to buyer (at a time when such cars were in short supply) for £773.75, a fixed retail price. The purchaser failed to complete and the car was sold to another buyer. The car dealer claimed as damages loss of the profit (£97.75) he would have made if the car had been sold to the defendant, or another buyer.
Held: Only nominal damages (£2) would be given to the dealer as he had not proved a loss of profit as he had sold the same number of cars as he would have done if the sale had been completed.

                                        (*Charter v. Sullivan*, 1957)

Where goods are specially made and the buyer refuses to accept them, the seller can recover as damages the cost of making them plus the loss of profit.

If the goods are saleable in the open market by alteration the seller must do what he can to mitigate his loss.

(b) Action for price

A seller has a personal remedy for the price against the buyer where:
1. The property in the goods has passed to the buyer. This action will not apply where credit has been given and the credit period is not at an end.
2. The price must be paid on a fixed date and the buyer neglects or refuses to pay, although the property in the goods has not passed.

(vii) ACTIONS AGAINST THE GOODS

The rights of an unpaid seller (defined under s. 38, S.G.A., as one who has not been paid the whole price, or who has received a dishonoured cheque or other negotiable instrument) are as follows:

(a) lien;
(b) stoppage in transitu;
(c) resale.

(a) Lien

This is the seller's right to hold goods in possession which he does not own, when the price is not paid. If property in the goods has not passed to the buyer the unpaid seller may withhold delivery. An unpaid seller can exercise a lien where:

1. goods have been sold without credit terms;
2. goods have been sold on credit, but the term has ended;
3. the buyer has become insolvent.

A lien will be lost in the following circumstances:

1. the seller delivers goods to a carrier for transmission to the buyer, without reserving right of disposal; or
2. the buyer or his agent obtain lawful possession of the goods; or
3. the seller waives the lien.

(b) Stoppage in transitu

This can only be exercised where the buyer is insolvent. A person is judged as insolvent if he has ceased to pay his debts in the ordinary course of business, or is unable to pay debts as they come due, whether an act of bankruptcy has been committed or not. It may be that the seller stops the goods before actual insolvency but, if the buyer proves to be solvent at the end of the transit then the seller must deliver and will be liable for any loss due to delay in delivery caused by the stoppage. The effect of stoppage in transitu is to restore the right of possession to the seller. It does not rescind the sale. Transit will be at an end when:

1. the buyer or his agent takes delivery of the goods from the carrier, even before arrival at their destination;
2. the carrier or his agent informs the seller that he holds the goods as warehouseman for the buyer, the goods having arrived at their destination;

3. the carrier or his agent wrongfully refuses to deliver to the buyer or his agent;

4. the goods, in certain circumstances, are delivered to the master of the buyer's ship.

The unpaid seller may exercise a right of stoppage in transitu either by taking possession of the goods or by giving notice to the carrier. On being given such notice the carrier must re-deliver according to the seller's directions, at the seller's expense.

Stoppage in transitu is not affected by a sale or any other disposition by the buyer unless the seller agrees to this. But if the documents of title have been lawfully transferred, and that holder transfers such documents to another who takes them bona fide and for value by way of sale, this defeats the unpaid seller's right of stoppage in transitu (and of lien).

(c) Resale

If the unpaid seller resells, although this is normally a breach of contract, the new buyer will have a good title to the goods as against the original buyer. There are three cases where the unpaid seller may resell:

1. where the right of resale was expressly reserved in the contract of sale;
2. where the goods are perishable;
3. where the unpaid seller gives notice to the buyer of his intention to resell and the buyer does not tender the price within a reasonable time.

In these instances the seller can resell and claim for any loss caused by the buyer's breach of contract. The exercise of the right to resell under the conditions above rescinds the original agreement and the unpaid seller may keep any profit made on resale (s. 48 (3), S.G.A.).

Example

On 6 May the seller sold to the buyer a Vanguard car and a Ford Zodiac for £850. The buyer put down a deposit of £25 but then refused to pay the balance. The buyer was told via the seller's solicitors that if the balance was not paid by 11 May, the seller would resell the cars. On the buyer's failing to respond the Vanguard was resold on 24 May for £350, but no purchaser could be found for the Zodiac. The seller claimed the balance of the purchase price of £475 plus costs of advertising the cars amounting to £22.50.

Held: Resale of the Vanguard rescinded the contract. The price of the Zodiac could not be recovered as this was the seller's property, only the loss caused by the buyer's default. The remedy in damages for non-acceptance which was £850, less the £25 deposit, less the £350 for the Vanguard, less an agreed value for the Zodiac, £450, plus advertising costs of £22.50, giving a final total figure for damages of £47.50.

(*R. V. Ward Ltd. v. Bignall*, 1967)

(viii) RIGHTS OF THE BUYER

Non-delivery

If the seller fails to deliver the goods under the contract to buyer, the buyer is entitled to damages based on the estimated loss arising directly and naturally, in the ordinary course of events from the breach (s. 51, S.G.A.). If the goods can be easily obtained on the open market the measure of damages is *prima facie* the difference between the contract price and the market price at the time when the goods should have been delivered.

Example

On 3 November the seller sold a quantity of unascertained wheat at a fixed price. The contract contained provisions relating to resale by the buyers. Both parties knew the buyers might resell or keep the goods. The market price rose on 21 November and the buyers resold. On 10 February the sellers appropriated the wheat from the cargo. On 22 March, following a fall in the price, the sellers failed to deliver. The sellers held they were only liable for damages based on the difference between 3 November and 22 March.
Held: The buyers were entitled to their own loss of profit on resale and damages they had to pay to their own purchasers as these had been contemplated by the parties, for express mention of sub-sales had been made in contract.

(*R. & H. Hall Ltd. v. W. H. Pim (Junior) & Co.'s Arbitration*, 1928)

Where there is no available market the buyer's damages will be based on the loss naturally arising from the breach.

Example

Russian wheat not normally available in Britain was purchased at £2.84 per 480 lbs. The purchaser had contracted to resell at £3.025. The original seller failed to deliver.
Held: The buyer was entitled to damages for loss of profits on the resale.

(*Patrick v. Russo-British Grain Export Co. Ltd.*, 1927)

(ix) SPECIFIC PERFORMANCE

Specific performance will be granted to the buyer only if the goods are of special value to the buyer or are unique. The goods must be specific or ascertained.

Example

Purchasers bought 500 tons of wheat to be shipped c.i.f. Avonmouth, part of a consignment of 1,000 tons belonging to the seller. The wheat was purchased before the seller became bankrupt. The 500 tons of wheat had not been appropriated to the contract when the vessel arrived at Avonmouth. When the seller's trustee in bankruptcy refused to deliver the buyers claimed specific performance.
Held: As the goods were not specific or ascertained as required under s. 52, S.G.A., specific performance would not be granted.

(Re *Wait*, 1927)

If the price has already been paid and the seller fails to deliver the buyer can recover the price.

(X) BREACH OF WARRANTY

A warranty is defined as 'an agreement with reference to goods which are the subject of a contract of sale, but collateral to the main purpose of such contract, the breach of which gives rise to a claim for damages, but not to a right to reject the goods and treat the contract as repudiated'. Where there is a breach of warranty or the buyer decides, or is forced to treat a breach of condition as a breach of warranty, the buyer may set up the breach of warranty in reduction or cancellation of the price, or maintain an action against the seller for damages for breach of warranty. Under s. 53 (3) damages are *prima facie* equal to the difference between the value of the goods at the time of delivery to the buyer and their value if they had been up to the warranty. If personal injury is caused—e.g. by a defect—larger damages can be obtained, if the goods have been accepted in whole or in part by the buyer and unless the contract is severable or there is a provision to the contrary, the buyer is bound to treat the breach of condition as a breach of warranty (S.G.A., s. 11 (1), as amended by the Misrepresentation Act 1967, s. 4 (1)).

4:13 TORTS (INTERFERENCE WITH GOODS) ACT 1977

This Act, based on the eighteenth Report of the Law Reform Committee (1971 Cmnd. 4774), amends the law of conversion and detinue and other unlawful interferences with goods. The Disposal of Uncollected Goods Act 1952 is repealed and replaced by ss. 12 and 13 of the new Act. Only a basic outline of the 1977 Act is given.

(i) ABOLITION OF DETINUE AND MODIFICATION OF CONVERSION

Detinue, wrongful holding of another's goods, is abolished (s. 2). An action can still be brought in conversion for any loss or destruction of goods which a bailee has permitted to happen in breach of his duty to the bailor. Conversion, the tort of unauthorized used of another's goods, is modified. Denial of title accompanied by refusal of access to the goods, or some dealing or interference with them, may still amount to conversion (s. 11 (3)). In cases where goods are jointly owned it is no defence to an action by one co-owner against another that the goods are co-owned where the defendant, without the other's authority, either:

(*a*) destroys the goods, or disposes of them to give good title to them, or does anything tantamount to destroying the interest of the other co-owner in them; or (*b*) purports to dispose of them in such a way to give good title to the goods as if he was acting with the other co-owner's (or co-owners') authority (s. 10).

(ii) THIRD PARTY RIGHTS

A defendant in an action for wrongful interference with goods (defined below) may use as a defence the fact that a third party has a better right than the plaintiff as to all or part the latter claims, or in right of which he sues. The Act abolishes any rule of the law to the contrary. Therefore, if the defendant establishes the existence of a third party's right then the plaintiff must fail in his action. This will be so even if the plaintiff's claim is based on interference with, or damage to, goods in his possession (s. 8). Wrongful interference not only includes conversion, but is defined to include trespass to goods, negligence or any other tort as far as it results in damage to goods or to an interest in goods (s. 1).

(iii) REMEDIES AND DAMAGES

Relief that the court can award in proceedings for wrongful interference with goods against a person in possession or control of the goods is as follows:

(*a*) an order for delivery of the goods, and for payment of any consequential damages, or
(*b*) an order for delivery of the goods, but giving the defendant the alternative of paying damages by reference to the value of the goods, together, in either alternative, with payment of any consequential damage, or
(*c*) damages (s. 3).

Under (*a*) relief is given at the discretion of the court; under (*b*) and (*c*) the successful claimant can choose between them.

The plaintiff's title to goods is extinguished where the defendant pays damages assessed for the plaintiff's whole interest in the goods. This is subject, where appropriate, to any reduction in damages for contributory negligence. This also applies where the plaintiff's claim is settled out of court. Payment of damages will not affect any third party's interest in the goods, except where the third party is compensated for the whole of his interest in the goods by another plaintiff (s. 5). Defendants are not liable to pay damages to two or more plaintiffs (e.g. to a finder and then an owner) (s. 7). Double liability of this kind is avoided. If the defendant is sued by two or more plaintiffs and any one of them has received a remedy he would not have received if the other claimants had been parties then the plaintiff with the 'unjust enrichment' has to account for such sums as avoid double liability to the other claimant or claimants or defendant, as appropriate (s. 7 (3)).

Contributory negligence is no longer a defence in proceedings based on conversion or intentional trespass to goods (s. 11 (1)).

(iv) IMPROVEMENTS TO GOODS

In any action for wrongful interference with goods against a person who has improved goods in the mistaken but honest belief that he had good title to them, or against a person who has purchased goods so improved, the defendant has a right to be granted an allowance by the plaintiff to the extent to which the goods have been increased in value by the improvement (s. 6). If a person in good faith buys a stolen car from the improver and is sued in conversion by the true owner the damages may be reduced to reflect the improvement. However, if the person who bought the car sues the improver for failure of consideration and the improver acted in good faith then there will be a comparable reduction in damages the purchaser will receive from the improver (s. 6 (2)).

(v) UNCOLLECTED GOODS

The Act allows a bailee to sell goods belonging to a bailor who has failed to take delivery of them. This will be so if the bailee first serves a statutory notice on the bailor notifying him of the intention to sell, or takes reasonable steps to serve the notice. The bailee is liable to account to the bailor for the net proceeds of sale. The bailee can give good title against the bailor, but not against the true owner if the bailor was not the owner of the goods (s. 12). The bailee can obtain the court's sanction to such a sale and pay the net proceeds into court, less any sum payable to the bailee on the goods (s. 13).

4:14 F.O.B. CONTRACTS

In contracts involving international shipment of goods contractual obligations are generally indicated by initials.

An f.o.b. contract (free on board) on the terms 'sold to Phillips n/v (Eindhoven) 20 tons platinum wire f.o.b. Avonmouth', means that the seller must put the goods on board at Avonmouth at his own cost for the buyer's account. The goods (whether specific or not) are at the risk of the buyer, who is also regarded as the shipper. Under such a contract the buyer must name a ship or authorize the seller to do so. The seller must give the buyer sufficient notice so that he can arrange insurance to protect against risks at sea during the voyage.

Unless there is an agreement to the contrary the property and risk in the goods do not pass to the buyer until they are placed aboard the ship concerned.

Example

A consignment of unascertained leather goods was sold to buyers f.o.b. Liverpool. No ship was named by the buyers and the goods were left at the port. The sellers sued for the price.
Held: The action failed; since the goods had not been shipped the property in them had not passed so the sellers were not entitled to sue for the price.

(*Colley v. Overseas Exporters (1919) Ltd.*, 1921)

The seller is entitled to insist on making delivery on board the ship concerned though the buyer may wish to take delivery beforehand.

Example

The sellers sold to the buyers a quantity of wool 'delivery Liverpool' for export to America. Although the buyers wished to obtain delivery of the goods before they were loaded on the ship the sellers insisted on delivering on board.
Held: 'F.o.b. Liverpool' meant the sellers could insist on delivery on board. The place of delivery was intended for both parties' benefit and could not therefore be waived without the other's consent.

(*Maine Spinning Co. v. Sutcliffe & Co.*, 1916)

4:15 C.I.F. CONTRACTS

In a contract under which a dealer agrees to sell goods at '£2 per ton c.i.f. Swansea Docks', the sum will include the price of goods, the insurance premium, plus the freight charge for carriage to Swansea. The seller is under the following obligations;

(i) to make out an invoice of goods sold;
(ii) to ship at the shipment port goods described in the contract;
(iii) to procure an affreightment contract under which goods will be delivered to the agreed destination;
(iv) to arrange an insurance cover for the buyer on current trade terms;
(v) with all reasonable speed to send forward to the buyers the following shipping documents: (*a*) invoice, (*b*) bill of lading, (*c*) insurance policy.

Delivery of the above documents to the buyer symbolizes delivery of the goods bought and entitles the seller to their price.

A c.i.f. contract normally provides for payment of 'cash against the document' and the fact the goods have not arrived when the documents are tendered does not excuse the buyers from paying immediately. A seller who has shipped appropriate goods under an ordinary c.i.f. contract can tender the proper documents to the buyer and demand payment even though he knows the goods have been lost at sea.

Example

A quantity of corn syrup was sold c.i.f. London. On 14 March 1917 the sellers tendered the shipping documents to the buyers, although they knew the ship carrying the goods had already been sunk by a German submarine.
Held: The tender was good as the buyers obtained the documents bargained for and if the loss was covered by insurance they could recover on the policy.
(*Manbre Saccharine Co. Ltd. v. Corn Products Co. Ltd.*, 1918)

The buyer has a right to reject the goods and recover money paid if the goods on arrival do not conform to the contract. Similarly, if the documents are not in order they can be rejected.

Example

The sellers agreed to sell to the buyers a consigment of bleaching chemical under a c.i.f. contract. The goods were to be shipped not later than 31 October 1951. The goods arrived for loading on 31 October but were not loaded until 3 November. The bill of lading was endorsed 'Received for shipment and since shipped 31 October'. All but the date was later erased from the bill and on tender of the shipping documents to the bank, the seller's draft was accepted on behalf of the buyers. When the goods arrived, the buyers found that the true date of shipment was 3 November and held they were entitled to reject them.
Held: This the buyers could do as they had this right and the right to reject the documents under a c.i.f. contract.
(*Chao v. British Traders & Shippers Ltd.*, 1954)

A recent case arose from one of the many arbitrations following the United States Department of Commerce embargo on soya bean meal in June 1973. General trade practice was referred to by the court in order to determine the nature of a series of 'contracts' between the buyer and sellers of a c.i.f. contract.

Example

The sellers had *inter alia* two branches, one in Hamburg (H) and another in Munich (M). Office H were the original shippers of soya bean meal from the U.S.A. and they sold a quantity to the buyers under two contracts of five hundred tonnes each, shipment June 1974 c.i.f. Rotterdam. A dispute arose concerning these two contracts. Office H also sold soya bean meal to Office M on May 12 1974 and on June 6 Office M resold to Office H so that the latter could use them to carry out the Rotterdam shipment. The market for soya bean meal was erratic with the result that there were considerable price differences in the four contracts. All contracts were made on GAFTA (Grain and Feed Trade Association) Form No. 100. Under cl. 10 of this form notice of appropriate of goods was required with ten consecutive days from the date of the bill of lading. Office H gave notice down the string of 'contracts'—thus from H-M-M-H-buyer. The buyers rejected the notice as being out of time. If the notice had to be given down the string then the appropriation was given within cl. 10 of GAFTA 100. If Offices M and H were treated as one person, then the notice was given out of time. The GAFTA arbitrators, the Board of Appeal and the Commercial Court held that Offices M and H were to be treated as separate sellers and buyers, although branches of one company.

Held: On appeal, the Court of Appeal held *inter alia* that the Board of Appeal were entitled to rely on what they knew of the general practice of the trade. Once it was found that there was a general trade practice to regard these inter-office transactions as part of a string the important point was not whether some particular transaction down the string was enforceable as a matter of law, but whether it was a genuine trading transaction.

(*Bremer Handelgesellschaft m.b.H. v. Toepfer*, 1980)

4:16   EX SHIP CONTRACTS

In the case of an 'ex ship' contract the seller must deliver to a buyer from a ship that has arrived at the delivery port and has docked at a normal unloading point for the goods in the contract. The property and risk in the goods do not pass to the buyer until the goods are delivered at the port of destination.

The seller must pay the freight and give the buyer an effective direction to the ship to deliver. Until this is done the buyer does not have to pay for the goods.

4:17   LETTERS OF CREDIT

Where it is the buyer's duty to pay cash against documents it is a usual condition that the buyer instructs his own bank to open a credit in favour of the seller in the seller's country. The buyer's bank instructs the overseas bank either to pay the seller or to accept a bill of exchange drawn by the seller when he hands the shipping documents over. In each case the buyer must provide the credit at a reasonable time before the first day of shipment and if the shipment is due between two dates the creditor must stay open for the whole of the period. If the documents tendered do not on the face of them correspond to what a banker has been instructed to accept he may then refuse to pay the seller.

Example

The sellers sold the buyers a quantity of steel bars. The Midland Bank Ltd. issued an irrevocable credit to the sellers under which it promised to pay them up to £23,000 on presentation of the shipping documents including the bills of lading. On the back of the bills was a clause stating that the shipowners were not responsible for correct delivery unless every bar was marked with oil paint. The bills of lading presented to the bank described the goods but the shipowners did not acknowledge that the marking stipulation had been followed. The bank refused to pay on the ground that the bills were not 'clean' and therefore not a good tender under the credit.

Held: The bank was wrong in its claim as the bills were 'clean' even though they contained no acknowledgement that the clause had been complied with. It was no concern of the bank's to see that conditions on the back of a bill of lading have been complied with.

(*British Imex Industries v. Midland Bank*, 1958)

4:18 AUCTION SALES

The following rules apply to auction sales:

(i) Each lot is presumed *prima facie* to be a separate contract of sale.
(ii) When the auctioneer's hammer falls the sale is complete.
(iii) Neither the seller nor his agent can bid, and for an auctioneer knowingly to take such a bid is unlawful unless there is notice given before that the sale is subject to such a right. A sale in breach of this rule can be treated by the buyer as fraudulent.
(iv) Where a sale is subject to a reserve price, each bid is accepted on condition that this reserve is reached.

An auctioneer undertakes the following implied obligations:

(i) that he knows of no defect in his principal's title;
(ii) that possession will be given following payment of the price;
(iii) that the possession will not be disturbed by the auctioneer or his principal;
(iv) that he has authority to sell.

Under the Auction (Bidding Agreements) Act 1927, it is a criminal offence for a dealer to agree to give any person any consideration for abstaining from bidding at an auction sale. Additionally, the Mock Auctions Act 1961 makes it a criminal offence to assist, promote, or conduct a mock auction at which one or more lots are offered for sale. The Act applies where a lot is sold to a bidder at a price lower than his highest bid or where part of the price at which it is sold is repaid or credited to him. The Act applies too where articles are given away or offered as gifts, or where the right to bid is restricted to persons who have agreed to buy one or more articles.

4:19 UNSOLICITED GOODS AND SERVICES ACT 1971

This Act provides the following rules governing unsolicited goods and services. If unsolicited goods are sent or delivered for sale or hire these will become the property of the recipient as a gift provided he gives notice to the sender within thirty days of receiving the goods and they are not retrieved by the sender. The same result will occur if the sender does not collect the goods within six months.

The Act does not apply to goods that the recipient reasonably believes were sent to be acquired for a trade or business he deals with. Nor are goods sent by a firm in response to a reply-paid card filled in without the knowledge of the recipient.

It is a criminal offence under the Act to send out unsolicited books that describe or illustrate sexual techniques. A criminal offence is also committed where payment is demanded for the entry of a person's name or other details in a trade or business directory without having obtained the person's signature on a note giving details of the directory and supplying him with a copy of the note.

The Unsolicited Goods and Services (Amendment) Act 1975 amends the 1971 Act in the following ways. It enables the Secretary of State to make regulations with respect to the contents and form of notes of agreement, invoices, and similar documents. These regulations may require specified information to be included, the manner in which this is to be done, and requirements as to type, size, colour and disposition of lettering (s. 1 adding new s. 3A to principal Act).

4:20 UNIFORM LAWS ON INTERNATIONAL SALES ACT 1967

In 1964 the United Kingdom together with a number of other states signed two conventions at the Hague. Both of these, the Uniform Law on the International Sale of Goods and the Uniform on the Formation of Contracts for the International Sale of Goods, are now included in the Uniform Law on International Sales Act 1967, which is now in force.

(i) EFFECT

Parties to an international sale may now contract by reference to the 1967 Act in preference to the Sale of Goods Act 1979 (s. 56 of the S.G.A. allows for exclusion or modification of rights or duties under Act; *see* Schedule 1, para. 13). Thus where such a choice is made the 1967 Act will wholly or partly govern the contract. However, an international sale is restricted by definition to a sale between two parties dealing in states that were parties to the 1964 Hague Convention.

The main provisions are:

(a) Fundamental breach

A breach will be regarded as fundamental where the party in breach either knew or should have known when contracting that a reasonable man in similar circumstances would not have entered into the contract if he could have predicted the breach and its results.

(b) Delivery

Where there is a fundamental breach regarding the time or place of delivery the buyer can either insist on performance or avoid the contract; the buyer must communicate his intention within a reasonable time and if he does not the contract is regarded as avoided.

If the goods do not correspond to the quantity or quality under the contract, or to sample, or are unfit for ordinary commercial use or particular purpose under the contract, then the seller will not have performed his duty of delivery. However, if defective goods are rectified before the delivery date (as long as this does not result in expense or inconvenience for the buyer) the seller will have performed his duty.

(c) Examination

Normally the buyer must examine the goods at the place of destination promptly unless the goods are re-despatched and the seller either knew or should have known this, in which instance examination can be delayed until the goods arrive at their new delivery point.

Prompt notice must be given by the buyer of any non-conformity in the goods; failure to give notice after the defect was discovered or should have been noted means the buyer cannot rely on the defect. Where the defect occurs at any time within two years after delivery, the buyer can exercise his rights if he gives prompt notice. Unless the seller is in breach of a longer running guarantee the buyer cannot rely on the defect after two years.

(d) Damages

Damages under the 1967 Act for non-delivery and non-acceptance are basically similar to the provisions of the Sale of Goods Act 1893.

(ii) AMENDMENTS TO THE 1967 ACT

In relation to a contract made on or after 18 May 1973 and before 1 February 1978, Schedule 1, para. 13, of the Sale of Goods Act 1979 amends s. 1 (4) of the Uniform Laws on International Sales Act 1967 which provides that no provision of the laws of any part of the United Kingdom shall be regarded as a mandatory provision for the purposes of the Uniform Law on the International Sales of Goods so as to override the choice of the parties. Section 56 (1) of the 1979 Act provides that where the proper law of the contract of the sale of goods would be the law of part of the United Kingdom were it not a term that it should be the law of some other country or a term or similar effect, or where any such contract substitutes or tries to substitute by a term the provision of the law of another country for all or any of ss. 12–15 and 55 of the Sale of Goods Act, those sections apply despite such a term. Nothing in the Sale of Goods Act shall prevent the parties to a contract for the international sale of goods from negativing or varying any right, duty or liability otherwise arising impliedly under ss. 12–15 of the Act (s. 56 (2)).

QUESTIONS

1. Smith, a local shopkeeper, orders some goods from a travelling salesman. They fail to arrive. Later he receives an invoice for the goods which he refuses to pay. Advise Smith whether legally he is obliged to pay for the goods.

   (I.P.S., December 1967)

2. (a) What conditions and warranties are implied by the Sale of Goods Act 1893 as amended?

   (b) Maurice runs a small nursery to supplement his salary. A large horticultural establishment sells him some weedkiller, in error for liquid fertilizer, as the container was wrongly labelled. It is applied to his lawn with ruinous consequences. Maurice also asked for some named product to rid his prize roses of a troublesome disease. The sellers are out of stock and, at Maurice's invitation, they suggest an alternative product. On the label of the container there appears the statement: 'Effects are permanent'. Soon after the contents are applied the roses die. A notice suspended in a prominent position by the sellers states: 'Goods sold on these premises are sold subject to exclusion of all implied conditions and warranties.' Advise Maurice.

   (Diploma in Marketing, Part II, May 1975)

3. (a) What conditions and warranties are implied under the Sale of Goods Act 1893 as amended?

   (b) Peter asked a sales representative to supply him with a quantity of outer garments suitable for wear by shop assistants. The catalogue described the material used as 'fine denim material in light blue'. The suppliers, Quality Retailers, sent Peter the garments which were in a darker colour than that shown in the catalogue, with slight variation in colour, but falling short of dark blue. The material used in the manufacture of the garments was a coarse denim fabric. Are the suppliers liable under the Sale of Goods Act, 1893 as amended?

   (Certificate in Marketing, Part II, June 1979)

4. When buying certain standard components Smith & Sons specify that they must be packed suitably for export to the Middle East. When put into use the components were found to be totally incapable of withstanding the extremes of dust and temperature encountered and have to be replaced by Smith & Sons at substantial additional cost. Advise Smith & Sons as to whether they can recover any of these additional costs from the supplier of the components.

   (I.P.S., December 1970)

5. (a) What are the rights of an unpaid seller of goods?

   (b) The Petrol Pump Garage services Quenlon's car. Before he can settle the bill with the garage, Quenlon receives a telephone message that his sister has been taken seriously ill. As the garage has shut down for the night, Quenlon asks his brother, Ronald, who works as a mechanic at Petrol Pump Garage, to allow him (Quenlon) to take the car away so that he (Quenlon) may visit his sister as soon as possible. If Quenlon refuses to pay the bill, alleging that the work has been inefficiently carried out, what rights, if any, does the garage have against him?

(Certificate in Marketing, Part II, November 1978)

6. Jones buys 300,000 items value 10p each. He samples 300 of these and finds 20 are not in accordance with the contract specification. Jones then claims to reject the whole 300,000 which in fact he no longer has any use for. Advise Jones whether legally he is entitled to take this action.

(I.P.S., May 1970)

7. Brown pays Smith & Son a deposit of £25 towards the purchase of a lounge suite and agrees to pay the balance within a month. Before he can do so, however, Smith's store is badly damaged by fire and the contents destroyed. Is Brown entitled to claim the return of the deposit or is he obliged to pay the balance of the purchase price?

(I.P.S., May 1969)

8. Henry & Co. purchase a quantity of paint with which to paint the steel frame of a structure at their works. Within six months of the paint having been applied it all peels off. Henry & Co. complain to the paint supplier, who rejects their claim on the grounds that (*a*) the preparation was inadequate and (*b*) the chemical fumes at the works were of a corrosive nature. Advise Henry & Co. whether they have any legal claim against the paint supplier, and if so on what grounds?

(I.P.S., May 1969)

9. Jones buys a second-hand car from a garage for £200. After two days the car breaks down and after inspecting it a motor engineer advises that repairs which would cost £250 would be needed to put it in good running order. When Jones bought the car he signed a form of order which stated 'this vehicle is sold as it lies and all warranties and conditions statutory or otherwise are hereby excluded'. Advise Jones as to his rights against the garage either to reject the car or to claim damages.

(I.P.S., May 1971)

10. Goods are being sold under a purchase order which states 'these goods are warranted first quality and free from defect'. The goods supplied could be used in their present condition but not for the particular process which the buyer had in mind without first being purified. Advise the buyer whether he would be entitled either to reject the goods or to claim from the supplier the purification costs.

(I.P.S., December 1971)

11. Brown orders goods to be delivered from Hong Kong c.i.f. London. The ship sinks and the goods are lost. Advise Brown as to his liability to pay the supplier.

(I.P.S., May 1971)

12. Distinguish between buying goods on f.o.b. and c.i.f. terms. Which method do you consider is more advantageous to the purchaser and why?

(I.P.S., May 1969)

13. In a contract of sale, the property in specific goods passes to the buyer when the parties intend it to pass. What rules are applied in the Sale of Goods Act for ascertaining this intention?

(Diploma in Marketing II, May 1970)

5. *Consumer Credit*

5:1 THE CONSUMER CREDIT ACT: BACKGROUND

The Consumer Credit Act 1974 which has completely remodelled the law relating to consumer credit arose from the recommendations of the Crowther Committee on Consumer Credit which reported in 1971 (Cmnd. 4596). Provision of consumer credit is essentially a loan of money for the acquisition of goods and services, although this provision may take the form of hire purchase, conditional sale, credit sale, personal loan, and credit card. Before the 1974 Act different statutes governed different forms of consumer credit even though the transactions performed similar functions. In order to resolve the tangle of illogical legislation the Crowther Committee recommended one statute to regulate loans and securities generally (including registration of security interests) and another to protect the consumer in consumer transactions. The Consumer Credit Act 1974 gives effect to some of the Committees' recommendations with respect to the second recommendation.

The Consumer Credit Act repeals the Hire Purchase Act 1965, the Advertisements (Hire Purchase) Acts 1964, the Moneylenders Act 1900–1927 and the Pawnbrokers Acts 1872–1960. All the forms of consumer credit previously governed by these statutes are now governed by the Consumer Credit Act and by regulations, orders, and determinations made under it.

The Act does not cover all matters likely to affect a consumer credit agreement. Common law rules relating to formation of the contract will be relevant as will implied conditions in hire purchase agreements under the Sale of Goods Act 1979 (as amended) (ss. 8–12 of the Supply of Goods (Implied Terms) Act 1973) which also covers conditional and credit sales. The Hire Purchase Act 1965 will govern agreements made before the 1974 Act came into operation which do not exceed £2,000 and where the hirer or buyer is not a body corporate. Part III of the Hire Purchase Act 1964 which deals with purchase of a car on hire purchase and conditional sale terms is retained with minor modifications (*see* Schedule 4 of the Act; 5:11).

5:2 REGULATED AGREEMENTS

The Act only applies to a regulated agreement that is defined as a consumer credit agreement or consumer hire agreement other than an exempt agreement (*see* s. 189 where definitions are given and Schedule 2 where there are detailed examples of how these terms operate in particular cases).

(i) CONSUMER CREDIT AGREEMENT

A consumer credit agreement is an agreement between an individual (the debtor) and any other person (the creditor) under which the creditor provides the debtor with credit not exceeding £5,000 (s. 8). The term consumer will include partnerships and sole traders and would cover solicitors renting photocopying equipment, and non-corporate firms purchasing office equipment on credit sale as long as the transaction is within the limit laid down by the Act. 'Credit' includes a cash loan and any other form of financial accommodation (s. 9), which brings in every type of credit agreement, hire purchase, credit card and unsecured loans and overdrafts. Credit in hire purchase cases is 'the total price of the goods less the aggregate of the deposit (if any) and the total charge for credit'.

Example

Hire purchase price £7,500 including £1,000 down payment and £1,500 charge for credit. Total credit is: (£7,500 − 1,000 − 1,500) = £5,000.

The agreement is a consumer credit agreement (Schedule 2, example 10). Where a debtor can obtain money, goods or services up to a specified limit (as with a Barclaycard or a bank overdraft or budget account) the Act provides a means of measuring whether this credit is within the £5,000 limit; it will not be a consumer credit agreement if—

(*a*) the credit limit does not exceed £5,000; or
(*b*) whether or not there is a credit limit, and if there is, notwithstanding that it exceeds £5,000:

(i) the debtor is not enabled to draw at any one time an amount which, so far as it represents credit, exceeds £5,000, or
(ii) the agreement provides that, if the debit balance rises above a given amount (not exceeding £5,000), the rate of the total charge for credit increases or any other condition favouring the creditor or his associate comes into operation, or
(iii) at the time the agreement is made it is probable, having regard to the agreement and any other relevant considerations, that the debit balance will not at any time rise above £5,000 (s. 10 (3)).

Example

J owns a shop which normally carries a stock worth about £1,000. *K* undertakes to provide, on short-term credit, the stock needed by *J* without any specified limit. Under (iii) above the agreement is a consumer credit agreement (Schedule 2, example 7).

This provision (iii) will incidentally benefit a finance house making stocking loans on an overdraft to an unincorporated motor dealer where at the time of the agreement it is considered unlikely that the debit balance will be held to £5,000.

(ii) CONSUMER HIRE AGREEMENT

This is an agreement made by a person (the owner) with an individual (the hirer) for bailment of goods to the hirer where it

(*a*) is not a hire-purchase agreement and

(*b*) operates for more than three months and
(*c*) the hirer is not required to make payments exceeding £5,000 (s. 15).

(*See* Schedule 2, Example 24.)

(iii) HIRE PURCHASE, CONDITIONAL SALE AND CREDIT SALE
AGREEMENTS

1. A hire purchase agreement is defined as an agreement other than a conditional sale agreement, whereby goods are bailed in return for periodical payments and the property in the goods is to pass on the exercise of the option to purchase, or the doing of a specified act or the happening of some other specified event.
2. A conditional sale agreement is one for the sale of goods or land under which the purchase price or part of it is payable by instalments and the property in the goods or land is to remain in the seller, notwithstanding that the buyer is to have possession of the goods or land until such conditions as may be specified in the agreements are fulfilled.
3. A credit sale agreement is one under which the price is payable by instalments not being a conditional sale agreement; that is, property passes to the buyer at once.

(iv) RESTRICTED USE AND UNRESTRICTED USE CREDIT

The distinction between restricted use and unrestricted use credit is as follows. The first limits the use of granted credit facilities, as for example in a hire purchase agreement for vehicle purchase. The second enables the debtor to use a loan as he wishes, for example as in the case of a cash loan. A loan may be an unrestricted use loan even if granted for specific application. This will be so if the credit is provided in such a way as to leave the debtor free to use it as he chooses, even though certain uses would contravene that or any other agreement (s. 11).

(v) DEBTOR–CREDITOR–SUPPLIER AND DEBTOR–CREDITOR
AGREEMENTS

A debtor–creditor–supplier agreement involves credit financing a transaction between debtor and supplier when credit is provided by the supplier himself or by a distinct creditor with a business arrangement with the supplier to finance the transaction, as, for example, in the case of a hire purchase, conditional sale and credit sale agreement. A debtor–creditor agreement is one where the creditor finances a transactions between debtor and supplier where the creditor has no business arrangement with the supplier to provide credit, for example in the case of moneylender's loans and personal bank loans (ss. 12, 13).

(vi) CREDIT-TOKEN AGREEMENT

A credit-token agreement is a regulated agreement for the provision of credit and is defined as 'a card, check, voucher, coupon, stamp, form, booklet or other document or thing given to an individual by a person carrying on a consumer credit business' (s. 14). Such a person undertakes:

(*a*) that on production of the token he will supply cash, goods and services (or any of these) on credit (e.g. credit tokens issued by a department store to regular customers to purchase goods on short-term credit);

(*b*) that where the credit token is produced to a third party who supplies cash, goods, or services (or any of these) to the holder of the token, he will reimburse the supplier in return for payment to him by the holder (as in the case of a Barclaycard).

(vii) LINKED AGREEMENTS

In entering into a regulated agreement a debtor may either be obliged or persuaded to enter into another agreement linked to the first one. These would include agreements to insure goods or purchase of an article such as a deep freeze with an ancillary agreement to purchase food with which to stock it (Schedule 2, Example 11). To classify as a linked transaction the agreement in question.

(*a*) must have been entered into in accord with a term of the regulated agreement, or

(*b*) must have been financed by a debtor–creditor–supplier agreement, or

(*c*) must have been initiated by the creditor or owner or his associates or a person representing both creditor or owner and the seller; as in the case of a door-to-door canvasser representing a trade selling on credit.

A linked transaction entered into before the main agreement is made has no effect until that main agreement is made (s. 19).

(viii) EXEMPT AGREEMENTS

The Secretary of State is empowered to exclude certain types of agreement from the Act's provisions except in the case of extortionate bargains (s. 16; *see* 5:7). Save for this exception the Act does not apply where a building society, local authority or a body of a kind specified in an order made by the Secretary of State enters into a debtor–creditor–supplier agreement to finance land purchase or provision of dwellings on land, and takes a mortgage of that land as security, or makes a loan secured by a land mortgage.

5:3 REGULATION OF THE AGREEMENT

(i) DISCLOSURE AND NEGOTIATION BEFORE CONTRACT

Before any agreement is made the debtor must be given such information as is required by any regulations made by the Secretary of State (s. 55). If such information is not given a subsequent agreement is regarded as improperly executed and will be enforceable only by a court order. In this connection the Act provides for regulations to be made laying down how the true cost of credit is to be determined and these may require disclosure of information in advertisements and other documents. Negotiations are regarded as being conducted by the negotiator as agent for the creditor as well as in his actual capacity. On the basis of *Andrews v. Hopkinson* where a statement by the salesman as to the quality of a vehicle, 'It's a good little bus—I'd stake my life on it', was held to be a collateral warranty, this would now also bind the finance company. A creditor cannot exclude liability for default of the negotiator in forming the agreement nor make valid provision by which such a negotiator is treated as the agent of the debtor (s. 56).

A party can withdraw from a prospective agreement provided an offer made is effectively revoked. Under the Act withdrawal operates as cancellation of a concluded agreement (s. 57) (*see* below) and can be carried out by the debtor informing the credit broker or supplier who negotiated with him or anyone acting on the debtor's behalf, such as a solicitor.

(ii) FORM AND CONTENT OF THE AGREEMENT

A regulated agreement to be properly executed must be:

(*a*) in writing;
(*b*) comply in form and content with any regulations made by the Secretary of State under s. 60;
(*c*) contain all the express terms in readily legible form;
(*d*) be signed by the debtor in person, and by or on behalf of all other parties (s. 61).

Where a document is personally presented to the debtor or hirer for signature it is not executed on his signature unless previously signed by or on behalf of the other party to the agreement. If this has not been done a copy of the agreement must be given to the debtor or hirer when the agreement is given to him to sign with any document that the agreement refers to. Within seven days a further copy of the agreement must be sent to him (s. 62). If the agreement has been signed by or on behalf of the other party a copy must be given when the hirer or debtor signs, but a second copy is not required under the Act.

Where an agreement is sent by post for signature by a hirer or debtor this must be accompanied by a copy of the agreement (s. 62). Again, if the agreement is executed on the signature of hirer or debtor no second copy is needed; if the agreement does not become executed on his signature a further copy of the agreement must be sent within seven days of the agreement being made (s. 63).

In the case of a cancellable agreement (*see* below) a notice in the prescribed form must be included in every copy given to the hirer indicating the right of the debtor or hirer to cancel the agreement, when and how the right is exercisable and the name and address of a person to whom notice of cancellation may be given.

A second copy of a credit-token agreement, where this is prescribed, need not be sent within seven days of the agreement being made if a copy was given to the debtor at or before the time of delivery of the token (s. 64).

(iii) CANCELLATION

A regulated agreement may be cancelled by the debtor if notice is given before the end of the fifth day following the day on which he received either the copy of the executed agreement or notice of his rights. A right of cancellation will exist only:

(*a*) where in antecedent negotiations, oral representations were made in the presence of the debtor by an individual acting as or on behalf of the negotiator; (*b*) where the agreement was signed by the debtor at a place other than the place of business of the creditor, or of any party to a linked transaction, or of the negotiator (s. 37).

The effect of notice of cancellation cancels both an agreement and a linked transaction except where regulations prescribe otherwise (s. 69). Notice of cancellation may be served on the creditor, by the person specified in the notice informing the creditor of his right to cancel, by credit-broker or supplier who was the negotiator or by anyone who, in the course of his business, acted on the debtor's behalf in the negotiations (s. 69). Notice of cancellation by post is effective when posted, even if not received.

On cancellation the debtor must be repaid any money paid under the agreement and he may retain such goods under the agreement in his possession until he is repaid. The debtor ceases to be liable to pay further money under the agreement except so far as he is obliged to pay for work done or goods supplied to meet an emergency or for goods supplied which have been incorporated in land or thing not part of the agreement or a linked transaction. The debtor must repay any credit with interest, except in the case of debtor–creditor–supplier agreements, but no interest is payable on an amount repaid within one month of cancellation by instalments under an agreement, before the last instalment is due (s. 71).

Goods supplied under a debtor–creditor–supplier restricted use agreement must be returned by the debtor on cancellation. A restricted use credit agreement (as defined by s. 11) is a regulated agreement to finance a transaction between the debtor and the creditor, or re-finance an existing debt of the debtors; this would include a hire purchase agreement. Goods under such an agreement do not have to be returned where they:

(*a*) were perishable;
(*b*) have been consumed;
(*c*) were supplied to meet an emergency;
(*d*) have become incorporated in any land or thing not forming part of the agreement.

The debtor is under a duty to take reasonable care of goods in his possession and allow their collection on receiving a written request. The duty ceases after twenty-one days unless the debtor fails or refuses unreasonably to comply with a request for redelivery in which case he is still liable for the goods until he complies with the request (s. 72). If the debtor attempts to redeliver the goods after cancellation he must take reasonable care of them and will be liable for damage occurring in transit.

In the case of goods taken in part-exchange under a cancelled agreement these must be returned within ten days of cancellation in essentially the condition in which they were taken. If this is not done the debtor can recover the sum allowed in part-exchange, or a reasonable sum if no exact amount was agreed. The debtor can retain goods in his possession supplied under the agreement until his goods are returned or the part-exchange allowance is paid (s. 73).

A right to cancel does not apply to non-commercial agreements, to debtor–creditor agreements (where the Director-General so directs) which enable the debtor to overdraw on a current account or which finance payments in connection with the death of a person. Nor does the right apply to agreements secured on land, or which are for restricted use credit, or for a bridging loan in connection with the purchase of land (s. 74).

(iv) GENERAL EXCLUSIONS

Non-commercial agreements, that is those not made by the creditor owner in the course of a business, are excluded for the purposes of entry into hire or credit agreements except so far as the agency provisions apply (s. 56). In the case of a small debtor–creditor–supplier agreement for restricted use credit the only provisions that apply are those relating to disclosure and agency, (ss. 55, 56). A small agreement is defined as a regulated consumer credit agreement either not exceeding £30 other than a hire purchase or a conditional sale agreement or where the hirer does not have to make payments over £30 (s. 17). In either case the agreement must be unsecured or secured only by a guarantee or indemnity only. To prevent avoidance of this section provisions are made to prevent a transaction from being divided into a number of smaller agreements (s. 18). The Director-General is empowered to exclude (save for s. 56 purposes) any overdraft arrangement or a debtor–creditor agreement to finance such payments on or in connection with the death of a person.

Bankers within the meaning of the Bankers' Books Evidence Act 1879 are exempted from the protective formalities of the Consumer Credit Act in relation to overdrafts in general, so long as the position of depositors is not considered to be prejudiced (s. 38(1) Banking Act 1979 inserting s. 74(3A) in the Consumer Credit Act.)

5:4 MATTERS ARISING DURING THE AGREEMENT

(i) MISREPRESENTATION AND BREACH OF CONTRACT

If the debtor under a debtor–creditor–supplier agreement has a claim against the supplier for misrepresentation or breach of contract in respect of a transaction financed by the agreement the debtor also has a claim against the creditor. Unless otherwise agreed, however, the creditor is entitled to an indemnity from the supplier. In the case where a debtor purchases with a Barclaycard defective goods from a supplier which breach the implied conditions of the Sale of Goods Act (*see* 4:6) the debtor can claim damages from the creditor or use the breach of contract as a defence to an action by the creditor on the loan agreement (s. 75). This section does not apply to a claim under a non-commercial agreement nor to one relating to a single item cash-priced by the supplier at not over £30 or more than £3,000. This section will apply even if the debtor exceeds the credit limit or breaches some other term of the regulated agreement.

(ii) ADDITIONAL INFORMATION

The hirer or debtor is entitled on a written request and on tendering 15p to an additional copy of the executed agreement, any document referred to in it and a statement signed by or on behalf of the creditor or owner giving details of the total sum due, future instalments and sums accrued. These provisions do not apply to non-commercial agreements nor where no sums are payable, nor if a request is made within one month of the date when a previous request was complied with. The creditor or owner cannot enforce the agreement which he defaults in complying with a request within the prescribed period. If default continues for one month an offence is committed punishable on summary conviction with a fine of not over £200.

The debtor or hirer who, under a regulated agreement, is required to keep goods in his possession or control must tell the creditor or owner where the goods are within seven days of receiving a request in writing to that effect. In the case of default for fourteen days he commits an offence punishable on summary conviction with a fine not less than £500 (s. 167 and Schedule 1).

(iii) APPROPRIATION OF PAYMENTS

In the case of a debtor owing two or more debts to the same creditor under two or more regulated agreements who makes a payment insufficient to cover the sums due, the debtor can indicate the debt or debts to which the money is to be applied. If he fails to do so where one or more of the agreements are a hire purchase, conditional sale, consumer hire or any agreement in relation to which security is provided, the payment has to be applied in satisfaction of the sums due in the proportion which those sums bear to each other (s. 81). In the case of payment of £12 for two items under separate agreements where £10 and £5 are due respectively the payment would be split in those proportions so that £8 would go to pay the £10 owing and £4 to pay the £5 owing.

(iv) VARIATION OF REGULATED AGREEMENTS

Variation of a regulated agreement by a later one revokes both the earlier one and the incorporation of the unamended terms into the later one. Where the earlier, but not the later, agreement is regulated that later is treated as regulated (s. 82). An earlier agreement remains cancellable even if the later is not.

(v) CREDIT-TOKEN AGREEMENTS

The debtor under a regulated consumer credit agreement is not liable to the creditor for loss arising from the use of the credit facility by another who is not, or cannot be taken as, the debtor's agent; for instance in the case of a credit card. If persons using the token acquired with the debtor's consent the debtor may be liable without limit to the creditor for loss the latter incurs by such use. The debtor is liable up to £30 (or less if the credit limit is lower) for the tokens' use while in unauthorized possession. The debtor is not liable in either circumstance if he gives oral (confirmed within seven days in writing) or written notice to the creditor that the token has been stolen or is otherwise open to misuse (s. 84).

5:5 TERMINATION

(i) STATUTORY RIGHT TO TERMINATE: DEBTOR

The debtor or hirer can terminate the agreement by either completing his payments or exercising his statutory right to terminate (ss. 99–101).

The statutory right to terminate before the end of the agreement cannot be excluded and regulations can be made to provide for a rebate in this case other than where a sum becomes payable earlier than otherwise (ss. 94, 95, not yet in force). Early settlement ends any future liability of the debtor or his relative under a linked transaction (s. 96). The creditor is under an obligation on demand from the hirer or debtor to give a statement to the hirer or debtor giving details of the sum required to clear the debt and to give a similar statement confirming clearance and stating that the agreement is no longer in force (s. 103).

The right to terminate a regulated hire purchase or conditional sale agreement before the final instalment falls due may be exercised by giving notice to the person entitled or authorized to receive payments under the agreement. This is so except in the case of a conditional sale of land if the title has passed to the debtor or under a conditional sale agreement if the property, vested in the debtor, is transferred to a third person.

On lawful termination of the agreement referred to the debtor is liable to

(*a*) pay all sums accrued due;
(*b*) bring his total payments up to one-half of the total price at once before termination unless the agreement is more favourable to him. The court may order a lesser sum to be paid if it is satisfied that this is enough to compensate the owner;
(*c*) compensate the creditor if he, the debtor, is in breach of his duty to take reasonable care;
(*d*) allow the owner to retake the goods.

(ii) STATUTORY RIGHT TO TERMINATE: HIRER

A hirer may terminate his agreement in the manner outlined above except that this right does not arise until the agreement has been in existence for eighteen months unless the agreement provides for an earlier termination.

Unless the agreement is more favourable the minimum period of notice is as follows:

(*a*) where sums are payable at equal intervals, one interval or three months, whichever is less;
(*b*) where sums are payable at unequal intervals, the shortest interval or three months, whichever is less;
(*c*) in any other case, three months (s. 101).

There is no right to terminate where:

(*a*) the agreement requires the hirer to make payments in total exceeding £300 a year;
(*b*) the goods are hired for a business or are to be hired out in turn in the course of a business and freely selected by the hirer from a supplier and the hiring arrangement was not made until the goods were selected;
(*c*) the Director-General exempts from the termination rules the agreements made by a person carrying on a consumer hire business on that person's application.

(iii) RESTRICTIONS ON THE RIGHTS OF CREDITOR OR OWNER IN DEFAULT

Where the debtor is in breach of the agreement the creditor must serve a default notice before:

(*a*) terminating the agreement; or
(*b*) demanding earlier payment; or
(*c*) recovering possession of land; or
(*d*) treating any debtor's right (except that of drawing credit) as terminated restricted or deferred; or
(*e*) enforcing any security (s. 87).

The default notice must be in the prescribed form and specify the nature of the alleged breach, the remedial action required and the time within which it must be taken; that is not less than seven days after service of the notice. In the case of a breach not capable of remedy the notice must state the compensation required which must be paid not less than seven days after service of the notice. Any notice served must give details of failure to comply with it (s. 88). Where the debtor complies with the notice the breach is regarded as not having occurred (s. 89).

Goods are treated as 'protected goods' when they are subject to a regulated hire purchase or conditional sale agreement and:

(*a*) the debtor has paid or tendered one-third or more of the total price of the goods;
(*b*) the creditor retains the property in the goods;
(*c*) the debtor has not ended the agreement (s. 90).

Such goods can only be recovered under a court order if the debtor has agreed to surrender the goods.

Where a creditor is required to carry out installation under a credit sale or hire purchase agreement and the agreement specifies the amount to be paid for installation as a part of the total price, the one-third of the total price in (*a*) is calculated as a reference to the aggregate installation charge and one-third of the remainder of the total price.

If protected goods are recovered without a court order having been obtained the agreement is at an end and the debtor is no longer liable under it and can recover all money paid under the agreement (s. 91).

The creditor or owner is not entitled to enter premises to recover any goods subject to a hire purchase or conditional sale agreement without the debtor's consent unless he has a court order (s. 92).

5:6 LICENSING

The Act sets up a wide licensing system administered by the Director-General of Fair Trading, the details of which are filled out by regulations. A licence is required by all (except a local authority) who carry on a consumer credit or consumer hire business or an ancillary credit business. An ancillary credit business is any business which includes or is related to (*a*) credit brokerage (*b*) debt adjusting, (*c*) debt counselling, (*d*) debt collecting or (*e*) the operation of a credit reference agency (s. 145 (1)); these definitions include motor-dealers and those introducing business to finance houses by hire purchase and similar agreement and the activities of the clearing banks. A licence is restricted to the activities specified in the licence these being those listed in (*a*) to (*e*) above. An offence will be committed if a licensable activity is carried on under a name not specified in the licence (ss. 39 (1), (2)). A regulated agreement will only be enforceable if entered into by an unlicensed creditor or owner where the Director-General makes an order which treats the regulated agreement made in the unlicensed periods as if made under licence (s. 40). Regulated agreements made on the introduction of unlicensed credit brokers are unenforceable unless the Director-General makes an order similarly validating such agreements (s. 149).

The usual licence issued is the *standard licence* which is issued to a person named making the application covering the activities described in the licence. A standard licence cannot be issued to more than one person except in the case of a partnership or unincorporated body. A *group licence* is one that is issued on application to the Director-General or by him for such a period as he decides (under regulations made by the Secretary of State (s. 189 (1)) to cover such persons and activities described in the licence. The group licence is intended to cover those who are only dealing incidentally with consumer, hire or ancillary credit, as is the case with solicitors engaged in debt collection, for, or making of bridging loans to, clients, or advisory centres such as citizens' advice bureaux giving advice on consumer credit matters. The standard licence runs normally for three years unless suspended or revoked (s. 32).

A person has a right to apply for a licence if he satisfies the Director-General that he is a fit person to engage in the activities covered by the licence and that the name or names under which he applies to be licensed are not misleading or otherwise undesirable (s. 25 (1)). However, the Director-General has a wide discretion in granting a licence. The Director-General in making this decision is required to take into account any evidence tending to show that the applicant, or any of his past or present employees, agents or associates or, in the case of a corporation, anyone who appears to be a controller or his associate, has

(*a*) committed any offence involving fraud or other dishonesty or violence;
(*b*) contravened any provision made by or under the Act or any other enactment regulating the provision of credit to individuals or other transactions with individuals;
(*c*) practised discrimination on grounds of sex, colour, race or ethnic or natural origins in, or connection with, the carrying on of any business; or
(*d*) engaged in business practices appearing to the Director to be deceitful or oppressive, or otherwise unfair or improper (whether unlawful or not).

The Director-General cannot refuse a licence application in the terms made unless he first gives notice, with reasons, of his intended refusal, allowing the applicant to make written or oral representations (ss. 27, 34). The Director-General may refuse, suspend or revoke a licence, but the licensee can appeal to the Secretary of State and a further appeal, on a point of law, can be made to the High Court (ss. 41, 42).

Licensing, which is in three stages, first, credit reference agencies, debt collectors, debt adjusters and debt counsellors, secondly, consumer credit and hire business, ended on 1 December 1977 with the completion of the third stage, credit brokers.

5:7   ADVERTISING AND CANVASSING

The Act in Part IV makes provision for protection of consumers with regard to advertising and canvassing for business which are subject to detailed regulations.

The Act regulates any advertisement published for the purposes of a business carried on by the advertiser indicating his willingness to provide credit or enter into an agreement for the hiring of goods by him (s. 45 (1)). Those businesses included are a consumer credit or hire business, those in the course of which credit is provided to individuals secured on land and those which comprise or relate to unregulated agreements where the proper law is of a country outside the U.K., or would be a regulated agreement if the proper law were the law of a part of the U.K. (s. 45 (2)). Advertisements are not within the Act if they indicate credit must exceed £5,000, and that no security is required, or the security is to consist of property other than land, or the credit is available only to a corporation or that the advertiser is unwilling to enter into a consumer hire agreement (s. 43 (4)).

An offence is committed in the case of an advertisement for credit in the acquisition of goods and services under restricted credit use agreements where the person providing goods or services does not hold himself out as prepared to supply them for cash (s. 45). An advertiser commits an offence if an advertisement contains information which is false or misleading in a material respect (ss. 46, 47), but defences available are:

(*a*) that the act or omission was due to a mistake or to reliance on information supplied to the advertiser or to an act or omission by another or other cause beyond his control and
(*b*) he took all reasonable precautions and exercised all due diligence to avoid such an act or omission by himself or anyone under his control (s. 168 (1)).

In respect of canvassing the Act creates four specific offences. An offence is committed where an individual visits premises other than the business premises of the creditor, owner supplier, canvasser, debtor or hirer and makes oral representations there to induce another to enter a debtor–creditor agreement unless the visit is in response to a previous written request signed by the person making it (ss. 48, 49). Similar provisions apply to canvassing off trade premises by a person carrying on the business of credit brokerage, debt adjusting or debt counselling (ss. 153, 154). An offence is also committed where a person, with a view to financial gain, sends to a minor any document inviting him to borrow money, obtain goods on credit or hire, obtain services on credit, or apply for information or advice in connection with the above. If the person had no knowledge or reasonable cause to suspect that he was a minor this will be a defence (s. 50). In relation to other canvassing offences defences under s. 168 are available (*see* above).

5:8 ROLE OF THE DIRECTOR-GENERAL

The role of the Director-General of Fair Trading in connection with the Consumer Credit Act is that of enforcing the Act and keeping a watching brief over the entire field of consumer credit. Apart from his function in relation to licences he has the following general duties and powers:

(*a*) to enforce and supervise the Act and regulations made thereunder;
(*b*) to make orders in appropriate cases dispensing or permitting enforcement of agreements with unlicensed traders;
(*c*) to make an annual report to the Secretary of State and disseminate information and advice.

The enforcement of the many duties under the Act is the responsibility of the Director-General and the Consumer Standards Offices of local authorities (s. 161).

5:9 JUDICIAL CONTROL

(i) EXTORTIONATE BARGAINS

The wide discretionary powers given the courts in relation to the enforcement of regulated agreements extend to the reopening of extortionate credit bargains, regulated or not (Schedule 3, para. 42). In deciding whether a bargain is extortionate the following factors and any other relevant considerations are among those to be considered by the courts; generally a bargain is regarded as extortionate if the debtor or his relative is required by it to pay grossly exorbitant sums:

(*a*) the current interest rates when the agreement was made;
(*b*) the debtor's personal situation such as age, health, experience, business knowledge and financial restraints;
(*c*) the creditor's personal situation such as the risk involved, relationship to the debtor and whether the rate of interest was reduced artificially by a specious cash price (s. 138).

The courts can rewrite the credit bargain, avoid liabilities and order repayment of sums and the taking of accounts but not affect a judgement by an order (s. 139). It is for the creditor to prove that the bargain is not extortionate if the debtor provides some evidence to show that it is.

(ii) ENFORCEMENT ORDERS

The courts can make a variety of orders. An enforcement order can be made only where an agreement is not properly signed unless an additional document exists with all the prescribed terms signed by the debtor (s. 127(3)). Power to make such an order may be made where the court considers it just to do so with regard to any prejudice caused by the contravention to any person (usually minor) and the powers it has to make conditional and suspended orders and to vary agreements. The amount payable by the debtor to compensate for the prejudice caused by the contravention can be reduced or discharged by an enforcement order by the court (s. 127(2)).

(iii) TIME ORDERS

Additionally the court can make a time order if the creditor or owner applies for an enforcement order or brings an action to enforce a regulated agreement or any security to recover possession of any goods or land covered by the agreement. This order can also be made on application by a hirer or debtor when served with a notice under ss. 76, 87 (not yet in force) or 98 relating to the duty by the creditor to give notice before taking certain action, or in cases of default or termination. A time order is defined as one which provides for payment by the debtor or hirer or any security of any sum owed under a regulated agreement by such instalments and at times that the court thinks just with regard to the means of the debtor or hirer and to any security. It also includes an order requiring that the debtor or hirer remedy any breach (except the non-payment of money) within a period specified by the court (s. 129 (2)). In hire purchase and conditional sale cases, the time order can relate to both future as well as to due instalments (s. 130). No enforcement can be commenced by a creditor or owner in the case of non-money breaches until the specified period has expired and rectification of the breach within that period cures the breach itself.

(iv) PROTECTION ORDERS

The court may make such orders as it thinks just for protecting any property of the creditor or owner on their application, or property subject to any security, from damage or depreciation pending the determination of any proceedings under the Act, including orders restricting or prohibiting use of the property or giving directions as to its custody (s. 131).

(v) HIRER'S RELIEF

In the case of regulated consumer hire agreements where an owner recovers possession of goods under the agreement other than by an action the hirer can apply to the court for an order that the whole or any part of any sum paid by the hirer to the owner for the goods be repaid and the obligation to pay the whole or any part of such sum shall end. The court may grant the application fully or partly if it considers it just with regard to the extent of the enjoyment of the goods by the hirer (s. 132).

(vi) HIRE PURCHASE AND CONDITIONAL SALE AGREEMENTS

The court can additionally make orders in hire purchase and conditional sale cases in an action for a time or enforcement order or an action to recover possession. In such proceedings the court may either make a return order ordering the debtor to return goods under the agreement to the creditor or make a transfer order ordering the debtor to return some of the goods to the creditor and vesting the remaining goods in the debtor. The debtor cannot receive more than the paid-up sum less one-third of the unpaid balance. Where the debtor pays the price before recovery of possession by the creditor the debtor obtains title which nullifies any return or transfer order. Failure by the debtor to conform with either order gives the creditor the right to ask the court to cancel the order and substitute an order for the payment of the price of the unrecovered goods (s. 133).

(vii) CONDITIONAL SUSPENDED ORDERS AND VARIATIONS

The court may make any provision of an order conditional on performance of a specified act by any party to the proceedings or suspend the operation of such a term until the court directs or the specified act or omission occurs. This is subject to the qualifications that an order for delivery of goods by any person will not be suspended unless the court is satisfied that the goods are in that person's control or possession and the hiring period in a consumer hire agreement cannot be extended by the court. The return order can be postponed in the case of a hire purchase or conditional sale agreement on condition the debtor pays the balance or on terms fixed by the court. Finally, the court has wide powers to amend any agreement or security as a consequence of a provision of an order it has made (s. 136).

5:10 CONTROL OF CREDIT REFERENCE AGENCIES

The operation of credit reference agencies, whose function is to collect and keep a register of information on an individual's credit-worthiness, is dealt with by the Act. Such information is supplied to finance companies so that the latter may assess the risk involved in giving credit in specific cases. The Act seeks to redress the atmosphere of secrecy that has previously surrounded such registers. A debtor or hirer is entitled to discover the name and address of any credit reference agency which has been consulted concerning the debtor or hirer's credit-worthiness from the creditor, owner or negotiator in any preliminary negotiations. Failure to supply such information by the creditor, owner or negotiator after a written request has been received constitutes an offence (s. 157). On receiving this information the debtor or hirer can make a written request, with a payment of 25p, to a credit reference agency for a copy of his file; failure by the agency to do this is also an offence (s. 158). The request can be made if an attempt has or has not been made to obtain credit.

Any consumer who regards an entry relating to him on a file to be incorrect and prejudicial to him unless corrected can request the agency to remove or amend the entry (s. 159). The agency has twenty-eight days either to comply or not and to notify the consumer. Failure to alter or amend the file by the agency in these circumstances entitles the consumer to require the agency to add a notice of correction to the consumer's file of not more than 200 words drafted by the consumer. Refusal by the agency to do so gives the consumer or the agency the right to apply to the Director-General who has a discretion to make an order; it is an offence to fail to obey such an order.

5:11 PURCHASE OF A CAR ON H.P. AND CONDITIONAL SALE TERMS

If a person agrees to hire a motor vehicle on hire purchase or to buy it under a conditional sale and before the property has passed to him he sells the vehicle to a private person, then as long as that person buys in good faith and without notice of the seller's want of title he gets a good title to the vehicle (s. 27 (2), H.P.A. 1964).

Example

H took a car on hire purchase from a finance company then misled a private purchaser, *N*, into buying the car by telling him that, although the car had been subject to a hire purchase agreement, all the instalments had been paid off. *H* also produced false documentation to give substance to his story. *N*, after repairing the car, sold it to a dealer, Bell, who then resold it to another dealer, Barker. The finance company claimed possession of the car from Barker, who returned it. Barker sought to recoup his loss by suing Bell for breach of the implied condition as to the title of the car; *N* being brought in as a third party. Section 27 (2) would protect *N* provided he took in good faith and without notice of the hire purchase agreement. This depended on the interpretation by the court of s. 29 (3) which states:

> 'a person shall be taken to be a purchaser of a motor vehicle without notice of a hire-purchase agreement if at the time of the disposition made to him, he has no actual notice that the vehicle is or was the subject of any hire-purchase agreement'.

In the lower court it was held that *N* was *not* protected by s. 27 (2) as he had notice that the car had at some time been subject to a hire purchase agreement. Thus *N* had received no title.

Held; On appeal: *N* was not liable as, within s. 27 (2), he took in good faith and without notice of the hire purchase agreement and thus obtained a good title. Thus, a purchaser will only be affected where he has *actual notice* that the vehicle is at present subject to a hire purchase agreement.

(Barker v. Bell, 1971)

An accelerated payment clause was recently adjudicated in a conditional sale agreement for a car.

Example

The buyer entered into a conditional sale agreement with the sellers in order to finance the purchase of a car. The agreement was subject to the Hire Purchase Act 1965, but expressly gave the buyer the right to terminate the agreement on the terms of the statutory notice. under the Act regarding a buyer's right to terminate, the notice being deemed to form part of the agreement. Under the agreement the buyer was to pay the purchase price of £2,145 by a deposit and thirty-six monthly instalments. The agreement included an 'accelerated payment clause' which provided that if the buyer defaulted in the punctual payment of two or more of the instalments the sellers could elect to call on the buyer, on giving the buyer written notice to pay within ten days, for the accelerated payment. This was made up of the unpaid balance of the purchase price together with certain fees and charges. If the accelerated payment was not paid within ten days the clause provided for $1\frac{1}{2}\%$ per month interest to be charged on the amount of the accelerated payment. After the end of the ten-day period, title to the car would pass to the seller. The buyer paid the deposit but failed to pay any of the instalments. The sellers elected to call for accelerated payment and when the buyer failed to pay the outstanding amount within the ten-day period, brought an action against her claiming the amount of the accelerated payment, £1,386. The buyer argued that the accelerated payment restricted her right under s. 27(1) of the 1965 Hire Purchase Act to terminate the agreement at any time before the final payment under the agreement fell due and so was void under s. 29(2)(b) of the Act. The buyer also argued that the final instalment did not fall due until the last of the thirty-six instalments became payable and the accelerated payment clause was therefore an attempt to interfere with her right under s. 27(1) to terminate the agreement at any time until then. Alternatively the buyer contented that the provision in the clause for payment of interest on non-payment of the accelerated payment within the prescribed period prevented the accelerated payment, when due, from being final payment under the agreement. If s. 27(1) did not make the clause void it was void either under s. 29(2)(b) or s. 29(2)(c) of the Act. In the case of s. 29(2)(b) if the buyer were to exercise her statutory right to terminate the agreement after she became liable to pay the accelerated payment she would be under a liability on terminating the agreement in excess of that under s. 28(1)(b). In the case of s. 29(2)(c) although exercise by the sellers of their rights under the clause terminated the agreement, the amount payable by the buyer under the clause exceeded the amount required by s. 29(2)(c) to be paid on termination of the agreement. Lastly, the buyer argued that the accelerated payment clause was a penalty clause and not a genuine pre-estimate of the sellers' loss on early termination of the agreement.

Held: The buyer was liable to the sellers for the accelerated payments claimed for the following reasons:

(*a*) The accelerated payment clause was not void under s. 29(2)(b) as when it fell due after the expiry of ten days from the notice it became as 'final payment' under the agreement for the purposes of s. 27(1). Therefore the buyer's right by s. 27(1) to terminate the agreement was lost. As the buyer expressly kept the right to terminate the agreement up to the date when the accelerated payment fell due the accelerated payment clause did not restrict or exclude the buyer's right to terminate under s. 27(1) and so was not void under s. 29(2)(b). Nor was the provision in the clause for payment of interest void under s. 29(2)(b) because the additional liability was the exercise by the sellers of their rights under the clause and not imposed by reason of termination of the agreement.

(*b*) The fact that an accelerated payment had fallen due under the clause did not terminate the agreement which remained in force until both parties had performed their obligations under the clause. Even though the buyer's liability exceeded the amount specified in s. 29(2)(c) it was not a liability which arose after termination of the agreement within that section.

(*c*) The accelerated payment was in the circumstances a genuine pre-estimate of what the sellers would lose as a result of the early termination of the agreement and was not void as a penalty.

(*Wadham Stringer Finance Ltd v. Meaney*, 1980)

QUESTIONS

1. In relation to the Consumer Credit Act 1974 what are the hirer's rights with respect to:
   (*a*) cancellation of the agreement;
   (*b*) termination of the agreement?
2. Outline the terms implied in hire-purchase contracts by statute.
3. Jim, a private person, enters into a contract to acquire a car from Alf. Unknown to Jim the car is subject to a hire purchase agreement. Jim takes possession of the car, but later the true owner of the car, a finance company, Credit Facilities, claim that the vehicle is still under a hire purchase agreement. What is the legal position?
4. A salesman impresses a prospective hirer that the car he wishes to sell him is a 'first-class vehicle'. On the strength of this statement the hirer enters a hire purchase agreement with Easicredit Ltd., a finance company. After paying the first instalment the hirer has an accident due to brake failure. What are the hirer's remedies and against whom can he proceed?

6. *Agency*

Agency is based on the principle that one who acts through another is deemed to act in person (*qui facit per alium facit per se*).

6:1 DEFINITION

Agency is the legal relationship that exists between two persons when one, called the agent, is employed by the other, called the principal, to bring the principal into legal relations with third parties. The relationship of principal and agent may arise in the following ways:

(i) express appointment;
(ii) estoppel;
(iii) ratification;
(iv) necessity.

(i) EXPRESS APPOINTMENT

Such appointments may be made orally or in writing. However, if the agent is to sign deeds on behalf of his principal then his appointment must be made by deed; such an appointment is called *Power of Attorney*.

(ii) ESTOPPEL

Estoppel means that a person who has allowed another to believe that a certain state of affairs exists, with the result that there is reliance on such beliefs, cannot afterwards be heard to say that the true state of affairs was far different, if to do so would involve the other person in suffering some kind of detriment. Applied to agency this means that a person who by words or conduct has allowed another to appear to the outside world to be his agent, with the result that third parties deal with him as his agent, cannot afterwards repudiate this apparent agency if to do so would cause injury to third parties; he is treated as being in the same position as if he had in fact authorized the agent to act in the way in which he had done.

If, for example, a member of a partnership retires without notifying the public, he will be bound by contracts made by the remaining partners with persons who had previously had dealings with the firm or who were aware of his membership, providing that they had no notice of his retirement.

(iii) RATIFICATION

If a person without previous authority from another purports to make a contract with a third party on that other's behalf, then the person for whom the contract is made may ratify and adopt it. The effect of ratification is to establish the relationship of principal and agent between the unauthorized person who made the contract and the person who ratified it, and the contract becomes binding on the principal. The requirements for ratification are as follows:

(*a*) The agent whose act it is sought to ratify must have purported to act for the principal.

Example

A firm instructed Roberts, a corn merchant, to buy wheat from another party on a joint account at £2 5*s*. 3*d*. [£2.26] a quarter. The merchant agreed with the other party to purchase at £2 5*s*. 6*d*. [£2.28] a quarter, but did not disclose he was purchasing on a joint account. The firm purported to ratify the contract. The price was not paid to the other party, who claimed the firm were liable on the agreement. *Held:* The purported ratification was ineffective because Roberts had not disclosed he was acting for a principal. Only a principal whose existence had been disclosed could ratify.

(*Keighley, Maxsted Co. v. Durant*, 1901)

(*b*) at the time when the act was done the principal must have had capacity to act and have been in existence at the time of contracting.

Example

L. Newborne arranged a contract for the purchase of tinned meat for a company he was forming. The contract was signed 'Leopold Newborne Ltd., Leopold Newborne, Director'. The company, when formed, tried to enforce the agreement.
Held: The company could not do this as when the agreement was made it was not in existence. Newborne himself incurred no rights or liabilities as he signed his name not as an agent but simply to show his responsibility in fixing the signature of the company.

(*Newborne v. Sensolid (Great Britain) Ltd.*, 1954)

Note: S. 9 (2) of the European Communities Act 1972 provides that pre-incorporation contracts shall have effect as contracts entered into by the persons purporting to act for the company or as agents for it. (*See* Chapter 10.)

(*c*) At the time of ratification the principal must be in possession of all the facts of the contract or be willing to adopt it without such information. The ratification must be complete and not partial.
(*d*) Ratification must take place before the contract is performed.

Example

On 15 September the defendants offered to supply eggs to the plaintiffs for six months commencing 30 September. On 22 September the clerk of the plaintiffs, without authorization, informed the defendants that their offer had been

accepted. On 24 September the defendants withdrew their offer as they realized they had made an error with regard to the price of the eggs. On 6 October the plaintiffs decided to hold the defendants to their agreement and put their seal to the contract. The defendant held that the contract was not binding on them.
Held: The contract was not binding on the defendants. They were not entitled to withdraw their offer, but the purported ratification by the plaintiffs was too late as it had not been made by the date when the contract was to be performed.

(*Managers of the Metropolitan Asylums Board v. Kingham & Sons*, 1889)

(iv) NECESSITY

There are some circumstances in which, although no relationship exists, or covers the exact situation which has arisen, the law regards what has been done by someone as having been done with the authority of some other person, and therefore as his agent, for whose acts he will be responsible. The basis for this type of agency is 'necessity'. The bulk of the decided cases seem to have arisen where an agency was already in existence and circumstances have occurred requiring action to preserve goods or property belonging to the principal.

The pre-requisites of an agency of necessity are;

(*a*) It must have been impossible to obtain the principal's instructions regarding the disposal of goods.

Example

A consignment of tomatoes was sent from Jersey to London. Due to a rail strike unloading at Weymouth was delayed for two days. On unloading, the tomatoes were found to be bad, so the rail company sold them locally, without obtaining instructions from the party to whom they were consigned.
Held: The company were liable in damages to the principal as they should have got in touch with him before selling the consignment.

(*Springer v. G.W. Railway*, 1921)

(*b*) There must have been a definite commercial necessity.

Example

Skins were purchased by agents for *X* in 1915 and 1916 valued at £1,900, for which *X* paid. When enemy forces occupied Rumania it became impossible to communicate with *X* in Bucharest. The skins were sold by the agents in 1917 and 1918 at a greatly increased profit.
Held: As the skins were unlikely to deteriorate they should have been stored; there was no need for the earlier sale and the agents were liable in damages (for conversion) to *X*.

(*Prager v. Blatspiel, Stamp & Heacock Ltd.*, 1924)

(*c*) The agent must have acted bona fide:

Note: A wife's agency of necessity (pledging her husband's credit for necessaries) was abolished by s. 41 of the Matrimonial Proceedings and Property Act 1970. A court may nevertheless order maintenance to be awarded on granting a decree of divorce, nullity or separation.

6:2 CAPACITY

A principal contracting through an agent must have contractual capacity. Such capacity is governed by the rules considered in Chapter 1 in reference to the general law of contract. Corporations, minors, and mentally incapacitated persons have either no capacity, or only a limited capacity.

A corporation can only appoint an agent within the terms of the memorandum; any other appointment will be beyond the powers (*ultra vires*) of the corporation.

A minor can only appoint an agent where the minor has power to make a valid contract. Unless a married woman, a minor cannot give a power of attorney.

However, there is nothing to prevent a person of limited contractual capacity being appointed an agent of a principal who has full contractual capacity.

6:3 AUTHORITY OF THE AGENT

An agent may bind his principal in contract by virtue of actual or apparent authority.

Actual authority is that authority given by the principal under the agreement between them. It has been defined as follows in a recent case as a 'legal relationship between principal and an agent created by concessional agreement to which they alone are parties. Its scope is to be ascertained by applying ordinary principles of construction of contracts, including any proper implications from the express words used, the usages of the trade, or the course of business between the parties.'

(Diplock, L.J., in *Freeman & Lockyer v. Buckhurst Park Properties (Mangal) Ltd.*, 1964)

The authority may be implied from the business that the agent is employed to transact.

Example

The defendant authorized a firm of estate agents to sell his house to the plaintiff for £840. The agents entered into a contract with the plaintiff to sell the property to him on terms laid down by the agents which were that the defendant sold as beneficial owner, and title would commence with a document giving a good root of title dated 20 years back. When the plaintiff claimed specific performance of the contract the defendant contended he had not authorized the agents to enter into the contract.

Held: An agent who was instructed to sell property at a stated price, had no authority to enter into contract with the intending purchaser. On the facts, however, it had been shown that the defendant had authorized the making of the contract, so a decree of specific performance would be ordered.

(*Wragg v. Lovett*, 1948)

An estate agent's authority to create a tenancy has been judicially considered.

Example

The plaintiffs (husband and wife) wished to lease on a short term basis premises which they eventually wished to sell with vacant possession. Having seen an estate agent's advertisement in which he stated he could arrange occupation of property without the possibility of it becoming a protected tenancy, the agreement concluded by the wife with the estate agent gave him authority to seek occupants for the flats but gave him no authority to enter into any agreement for occupation of the flats without reference to the wife. The defendants wished to enter an agreement for not less than six months. The agent stated that he was not prepared to grant a term of more than three months but that the term would be renewable. The defendants entered the agreement on the assurance that they would occupy the flat to the exclusion of anyone else. Amongst other matters not directly relevant to agency, the question arose as to whether the agent had authority to enter into an agreement so as to bind the plaintiffs.

Held: The agent had clearly been held out by the wife as having full authority to enter into a contractual agreement with the defendants. Therefore the plaintiffs (husband and wife) were bound by whatever agreement the agent made with the defendants, even though the agent had been expressly denied any authority to create a tenancy.

(*Walsh v. Griffiths-Jones*, 1978)

An agent's actual authority may include his usual or customary authority. This is the authority which persons dealing with the agent of the trade or business would expect him to have. Unless the third party knows that the usual powers have been withdrawn, the agent will bind the principal as long as the contract is one which an agent of the class has usual authority to make, even though the agent has exceeded his express authority.

Example

H owned the Victoria Hotel which he sold to F, who employed H as manager and allowed his name to remain over the door. F forbade H to buy cigars on credit. H bought cigars on credit from W, who discovered the existence of F, and claimed the price from him.

Held: The claim would be successful. It was within the usual authority of a hotel manager to buy cigars on credit. A principal, disclosed or not, was liable for the acts of his agent. A secret limit on this authority was no defence when the principal was sued by a third party.

(*Watteau v. Fenwick*, 1891)

Apparent or ostensible authority is an authority which has not been given by the principal, but which the law regards the agent as possessing notwithstanding the principal's lack of consent, to the exercise of such authority. The reason for this is that the principal, by his conduct, has allowed the agent to appear to have authority greater in fact than that which was given to him by the principal.

Example

The plaintiffs, timber merchants, employed *C* as a clerk. They informed the Surrey Commercial Dock Co. that he had authority to sign delivery orders in respect of any of their timber stored at the docks. *C* opened an account in the Dock Company's books in a fictitious name. Some of the plaintiffs' timber was transferred by *C* under this fictitious name and sold in this name to the defendants, who purchased in good faith. The plaintiffs claimed return of the timber from the defendants, who, in turn, claimed that *C* had been held out by the plaintiffs as having authority to sell the timber.
Held: On the facts the plaintiffs had not held out *C* as having authority to sell the timber and were entitled to its return.

(*Farquharson Bros. & Co. v. King 6 Co.*, 1902)

6:4 FACTORS

A factor or mercantile agent is defined by the Factors Act 1889 and has been dealt with in Chapter 4. Under s. 9 of the Factors Act 1889 'where a person having bought or agreed to buy goods, obtains with the consent of the seller possession of the goods ... the delivery ... of the goods ... under any sale ... to any person receiving the same in good faith and without notice of any lien or other right of the original seller in respect of the goods shall have the same effect as if the person making the delivery were a mercantile agent in possession of the goods.'

Example

On 15 June 1962 the plaintiffs sold a car to *A* who gave them a cheque. On 18 June they learnt this had been dishonoured and they attempted to recover the car. In July 1962 *A* sold the car to *B* in Warren Street, London, an established street market for selling cars. *B* purchased in good faith and sold the car to the defendant; the plaintiffs claimed the car from the defendant. The defendant claimed good title on the ground that *B* had obtained a good title under s. 9 of the Factors Act 1889, for *A* had acted in a way in which he would have been expected to act if he had been a mercantile agent, and must be regarded as having done so as the sale had taken placed in a recognized street market.
Held: *B* had obtained a good title on the grounds he had put forward.

(*Newtons of Wembley Ltd. v. Williams*, 1964)

6:5 BROKERS

A broker is a commercial agent employed to make contracts between his principal and others for a commission usually called a brokerage. A broker is primarily agent for the seller of the goods, but on making a contract with a purchaser he becomes agent for the purchaser also. Brokers are not in general liable to their principals for the failure of the buyer to pay the price. However, in some cases if a broker acts in accordance with the customs and rules of the market in which he normally deals he will be bound by them. In a decided case it was held that a broker, who had been forced to follow the custom of Leeds Stock Exchange by paying differences on the price of shares which had to be resold because of the principal's failure to pay the broker and the broker's consequent inability to pay the vendor of the shares, could recover these differences from the principal.

6:6 AUCTIONEERS

Auctioneers are agents whose ordinary course of business is to sell goods or other property by public auction, that is by open sale.

An auctioneer has implied authority to sign a contract on behalf of both the vendor and the purchaser, but not where there has been a mistake on the part of either party. Nor has he authority to receive payment except in cash; he may not give credit. He does not warrant the goods he sells, but he does warrant his authority to sell them.

Example

An auctioneer sold a car at an auction for an unnamed principal. The buyer discovered the car was still under a hire purchase agreement and so attempted to make the auctioneer liable on the contract of sale.
Held: The auctioneer was not liable as he had not warranted the principal's title to sell.

If the sale is advertised as being subject to a reserve price the auctioneer has no authority to sell at less than the reserve, so that his principal will not be liable on the sale, but the auctioneer will be liable for breach of warranty of authority.

Auctioneers may or may not be given possession of the goods, but it is clear that, when given such possession, auctioneers are 'mercantile agents' within the Factors Act 1889.

A peculiarity of auctioneers is that they are agents for both parties to that sale which they negotiate.

6:7 ESTATE AGENTS ACT 1979

The Estate Agents Act 1979 which regulates the operation of estate agents has three main aims. They are:

(*a*) to allow the Director-General of Fair Trading to prohibit certain estate agents from conducting their work by means of a register of unfit persons;
(*b*) to require estate agents to maintain a separate client account; and
(*c*) to ensure that where the agents receive clients' money this is covered by insurance if the agent fails to account for funds.

The Act only applies to estate agency work done in relation to the sale of land, including the sale of leases. It does not apply to work in connection with planning applications, valuations (other than in relation to sale), management or leasing of land, or negotiations undertaken by an agent who did not introduce the prospective buyer.

The Act gives wide powers to the Secretary of State to specify certain arrangements, such as indemnity insurance, by which loss of clients' money by fault or dishonesty by an estate agent is covered (s. 16 (2)). The Secretary of State is empowered to lay down, in the future, standards of competence prescribed in terms of practical experience, or qualifications a person must have before he can take up estate agency work. This power may be delegated to an 'established body' the Secretary of State may choose (s. 22). The Act is to be administered by the Weights and Measures authorities.

6:8 CONFIRMING HOUSES

When a supplier receives an overseas order from a customer it is usual in the export trade for the order to be confirmed by a person in the supplier's country. This person, the confirmer, assesses the bargain and if the overseas buyer fails to carry out the contract, he is personally liable to the supplier.

Example

Buyers in Turkey placed orders for radio sets with British manufacturers, *C* confirming the order. After part had been received the buyers refused delivery of the balance.
Held: C was liable to the manufacturers in damages for non-acceptance by the buyers.

(*Sobel Industries Ltd. v. Cory Bros. & Co. Ltd.*, 1955)

The seller can claim for the price against the buyer if the confirmer fails to pay.

6:9 DEL CREDERE AGENTS

These are mercantile agents who, in return for an extra commission called a *del credere* commission, promise that they will indemnify the principal if the third party with whom they contract in respect of the goods fails to pay what is due under the contract.

6:10 BREACH OF WARRANTY OF AUTHORITY

Every person professing to act as an agent for another impliedly warrants that he has authority to make binding contracts on behalf of his principal. If, therefore, an agent lacks the authority he professes to have he is liable to an action for damages for breach of warranty of authority brought by the person with whom he has been dealing. The agent will be liable whether he acted innocently or fraudulently; even if he did not know he had no authority to act.

Example

On 21 August a firm of solicitors were instructed by a client to commence proceedings against a third party with regard to a libel.

On 8 October, unknown to the solicitors, the client was certified insane. On 30 September the solicitors began proceedings against the third party; on 5 April they discovered that their client had been certified. The third party brought an action against the solicitors in damages for breach of warranty of authority claiming the costs of defending the libel action.

Held: The third party were entitled to succeed. The fact that the solicitors did not know of their client's insanity was irrelevant.

(*Yonge v. Toynbee*, 1908)

However, if the third party is aware of the agent's lack of authority then the agent is not liable.

An agent is not liable for damages for breach of warranty of authority if the contract which he enters into with a third party contains a term to that effect.

Example

The plaintiffs owned a vessel which they chartered to *R* at a freight rate of 3*s*. 9*d*. [19p] per ton. The defendants, shipbrokers, signed the agreement 'by telegraphic authority of *R*, Smales, Eeles & Co., as agents'. The freight rate offered by *R* was only 3*s*. 4½*d*. [17p] per ton. The defendants had made a mistake in the rate quoted due to an error on the part of the telegraph office who sent the defendants the telegram instructing them to enter the charter party with the plaintiffs. *R* repudiated the charter party and the plaintiffs claimed damages from the shipbrokers for breach of warranty on the ground that they had held themselves out as having an authority they did not possess.

Held: The plaintiffs would not succeed as terms 'telegraphic authority' only warranted that the defendants had received a telegram which, if correct, authorized them to enter the charter party at the stated freight rate.

(*Lilly, Wilson & Co. v. Smales, Eeles & Co.*, 1892)

A third party may sue an agent for damages for breach of warranty of authority where he has relied to his detriment on the agent's representation that the agent has the principal's authority.

Example

S, a stockbroker, produced a power of attorney signed by two joint principals, F. and E. Oliver, to the Bank of England, and instructed the Bank to sell stock standing in their joint names and pay the proceeds solely to F. Oliver. The Bank did so and then found that the signature of E. Oliver had been forged on the power of attorney, with the result that the Bank had to replace the stock sold without his authority. *S* was then sued by the Bank for damages for breach of warranty of authority.

Held: Their action would succeed as the remedy was not confined to cases where the third party had been induced to enter a contract.

(*Starkey v. Governor and Co. of the Bank of England*, 1903)

If a principal gives vague instructions and the agent acts reasonably and in good faith, even if he interprets the instructions wrongly, he will not be liable to an action for breach of warranty of authority.

Example

A telegrammed *B*: 'You authorize fix steamer prompt loading 3,000 tons coal Newport Cagliari Messina or Palermo twenty shillings'. *B* let a ship on charter to *C*. *A* repudiated this on the ground that the authority related to hiring not letting of a vessel.

Held: If the telegram were ambiguous, *B* had interpreted it reasonably and in good faith. *A* would be liable to *C* for the interpretation placed on the instructions by his agents. However, no matter which way the telegram were interpreted, the charter party entered into was beyond the authority given so that *B* was liable to *C* for breach of warranty of authority.

(Weigall & Co. v. Runciman & Co., 1916)

Damages awarded will be awarded on the basis of the actual loss suffered.

6:11   CONTRACTS MADE BY AGENTS

Rights and liabilities of parties depend on the circumstances under which an agent contracts.

(i) WHERE AN AGENT CONTRACTS AS AGENT FOR A DISCLOSED PRINCIPAL

In this situation the agent usually has no rights or liabilities under the contract and drops out as soon as it is made. Exceptions to this general rule are: where the agent agrees to accept personal liability; where the agent signs a deed, except where he has been appointed by power of attorney; if the agent signs a bill of exchange in his own name, and where he is liable under a trade custom. It is now settled that an agent contracting on behalf of a foreign principal is not presumed to be liable personally.

Example

T-E, a company incorporated in Persia, had buying agents in England, *R* Ltd. *R* Ltd. negotiated with *B* for supply of air compressors for 'their clients'. *R* Ltd. did not disclose the name of their principals. *T-E* claimed damages from *B* Ltd. on the ground that the goods did not comply with the contract.

Held: The plaintiffs as undisclosed principals could sue the defendants directly and they were not prevented from this action by any principle of English commercial law.

(Teheran-Europe Co. Ltd. v. S. T. Belton (Tractors) Ltd., 1968)

(ii) WHERE THE AGENT CONTRACTS AS AGENT BUT DOES NOT DISCLOSE THE NAME OF HIS PRINCIPAL

In this case the agent drops out in the normal way, providing he makes it clear when contracting that he merely does so as agent. An undisclosed principal is entitled to enforce a contract made by his agent with a third party, where the agent has made no misrepresentation, and personal qualifications of the agent did not form a material part of the contract.

Example

The plaintiff had been employed by the defendants, auctioneers, engaged in developing a building estate. The plaintiff knew he could not make offers to the defendants directly for the plots of land. *C* acted as his agent for purchasing the plots without disclosing he was acting for the plaintiff. When the auctioneers discovered, after *C* had made the purchase, that *C* was acting as agent for the plaintiff they cancelled the agreement. The plaintiff applied for a decree of specific performance.

Held: A decree would be granted. *C* had made no misrepresentation by non-disclosure of his principal. The contract was not one in which *C*'s personal qualifications made up a material part.

(Dyster v. Randall & Sons, 1926)

Personal liability has been imposed on an agent in a number of recent shipping cases of which the following is an illustration.

Example

Negotiations were being carried on through various intermediaries for the shipment of urea from Venice to Indonesia on a vessel, the *Rab* which had already loaded a part cargo in Albania for Japan. At that time it was understood that the charterer was to be 'Brusse and Sippel, Amsterdam, for account of Indonesian Government'. The negotiations fell through and the owners offered another vessel, the *Primorje*. During the new set of negotiations the statement concerning the Indonesian Government was not repeated. A charter was eventually entered into describing Brusse and Sippel as charterers, but apparently signed by the owners only. Brusse and Sippel, after conducting disputes relating to the charter on their own behalf, later claimed to be acting as agents.

Held: The agents were personally liable having been described as charterers.

(The Primorje, 1980)

A contract cannot be enforced against a third party by an undisclosed principal when his agent makes a false representation as to his principal's name, and the agent knows that no contract would be made if the third party was told the principal's real name.

Example

S owned a leasehold shop; he did not wish to sell it to Mr. *X*, Mrs. *X* or her sister Miss *W*. *A*, acting for Mr. *X*, was asked by *S* if he, *A*, was buying for Mr. *X*, which *A* denied. *S* then agreed to sell the shop for £900 to *A*. The contract was then assigned by *A* to Mrs. *X* and Miss *W*. *S* refused to proceed further on discovering the truth. *A*, Mrs. *X* and Miss *W* claimed specific performance of the contract.

Held: No decree would be given as *A*'s misrepresentation has induced *S* to sell, which he would not have done had he been fully aware of the facts.

(Archer v. Stone, 1898)

(ii) WHERE THE AGENT CONTRACTS AND CONCEALS THE NAME AND
EXISTENCE OF THE PRINCIPAL

Where an agent contracts with a third party on behalf of his principal but does not inform the third party that he is an agent and appears to be a principal himself, then the doctrine of undisclosed principal applies. The parties have the following rights and liabilities:

(*a*) The third party may elect to sue either the principal or the agent. Constructive notice to the third party that he is only dealing with an agent does not prevent him from setting off against the principal a debt due to him from the agent.

Example

The defendant traded as D.S. Co. He sold goods valued at £17 to *G* but was not paid. *G* offered to sell him timber which the defendant agreed to buy provided he only paid the difference between the price of the timber and £17, believing his contract was solely with *G*. An invoice was sent to the defendant with the name 'W. MacGregor Greer'. On enquiry *G* stated he was that person, which the defendant believed. In fact, *G* was Greer's agent, selling timber on commission. When the timber was not paid for Greer claimed the price which the defendant held should be set off against the £17. Greer contended that the invoice was notice which should have revealed on further investigation that *G* was only an agent so no set off was possible.

Held: The defendant was entitled to set off the £17 owed as the doctrine of constructive notice did not apply to commercial transactions.

(*Greer v. Downs Supply Co.*, 1927)

A third party cannot set off against an undisclosed principal a debt due from an agent where he does know whether the person with whom he is dealing is acting as a principal or agent.

Example

L & Co., brokers acting on behalf of an undisclosed principal, sold cotton to *C*. The price was not paid so *E*, trustee in bankruptcy, after the undisclosed principal became bankrupt, claimed it from *C*. *C* claimed to set off against the price the debt owned to him by L & Co. When the cotton was sold *C* did not know whether L & Co. were acting on their own behalf or as agents.

Held: *C* was not entitled to set off as when the cotton was sold he did not believe L & Co. were selling on their own behalf.

(*Cooke v. Eshelby*, 1886)

(*b*) An election between principal and agent must be made within a reasonable time, otherwise only the agent may be sued. If the third party elects to sue the principal on discovering his existence he cannot then hold the agent liable on the contract. Election is to be judged from the facts.

Example

The plaintiffs booked flights for twelve persons from Athens to London at the request of the defendant acting for undisclosed principals, P & M Ltd., without paying for the flights. On discovering the existence of the company the plaintiffs claimed payment and eventually their solicitors served a writ on P & M Ltd. but did not proceed as the company were going into voluntary liquidation. The plaintiffs sued the defendant who held that the commencement of proceedings against P & M Ltd. was an election to hold them solely liable. *Held:* In the circumstances there had not been an election and the defendant was liable to pay for the flights.

(Clarkson, Booker Ltd. v. Andjel, 1964)

Once election has been made and the third party has obtained an unsatisfied judgement, he cannot sue the other party.

(c) The third party may be stopped from suing the principal if he allows the principal to believe that the agent has settled matters satisfactorily by payment.

(d) A principal is liable for the frauds and wrongs the agent commits in the course of his employment.

Example

The plaintiff owned cottages and money lent on mortgage. She consulted a firm of solicitors and was fraudulently induced by their managing clerk, *S*, to sign deeds which transferred the mortgage and the cottages to him, which he sold and assigned, disappearing with the proceeds.
Held: The firm were liable for *S*'s fraud.

(Lloyd v. Grace, Smith & Co., 1912)

6:12 RIGHTS AND DUTIES BETWEEN PRINCIPAL AND AGENT

(i) If the agency is contractual, the agent must perform what he has undertaken. Apart from carrying out his job competently, the agent must exercise any special skill he claims to possess. If an estate agent, for instance, receives a better offer than the one he has notified to his principal, unless a binding contact to sell already exists, this new offer must be communicated to the principal.

Example

K instructed *W*, an estate agent, to find a purchaser for a block of flats. On 29 May a prospective purchaser offered £6,150, which *K* accepted 'subject to contract'. On 3 June another offer was made from a different party of £6,750 which *W* did not pass on to *K*.
Held: *W* was liable in damages for a breach of duty to show proper skill and care.

(Keppel v. Wheeler, 1927)

The position of an estate agent when receiving a money deposit from a client has recently been resolved by the House of Lords.

Example

The appellant instructed an estate agent to find a purchaser for his house. The estate agent, unknown to the appellant, was an undischarged bankrupt. The house was offered for sale with nothing said concerning a deposit or payment of commission on the introduction of a willing purchaser. Five prospective purchasers, including the respondents, paid deposits. The estate agent gave signed receipts to the respondents with no definition of the capacity in which they were received and both containing the words 'subject to contract'. The agent then disappeared and the seller was sued by the respondents. The county court and the Court of Appeal judgement was given against the seller on the basis that the deposit was money had and received by the seller, or alternatively as damages for fraudulent misrepresentation and conversion.

Held: On appeal to the House of Lords they found for the seller, reversing the decision of the Court of Appeal. The estate agent was not authorized to receive a pre-contract deposit on the seller's behalf in the absence of express or implied authority to do so, which had not been given here. The seller's knowledge that such a deposit had been received obliged him to repay it. As the estate agent had no authority from the seller to receive the deposit as his agent, nothing the estate agent said to induce such a payment could implicate the seller.

(*Sorrell v. Finch*, 1976, overruling *Ryan v. Pilkington*, 1959, *Burt v. Claude Cousins & Co. Ltd.*, 1971 and *Barrington v. Lee*, 1972)

(ii) An agent must not disclose confidential information entrusted to him by his principal.

Example

After a fire had broken out in the defendants' warehouse they instructed the plaintiffs to prepare a claim under the fire insurance policy on their behalf. Confidential information was given to the director of the plaintiffs' company regarding the policy and he was permitted by the defendants to visit one of their customers whose books were destroyed in the fire. Although expressly forbidden to give confidential information concerning the defendants' policy the director did so. The defendants ended the contract and claimed damages.

Held: They were entitled to do so and the plaintiffs were liable in damages.

(*L. S. Harris Trustees Ltd. v. Power Packing Services* (*Hermit Road*) *Ltd.*, 1970)

(iii) An agent must not delegate the performance of his duties. This is not applied strictly, and the agent may usually delegate performance where this is required by commercial usage, necessity, or if authorized expressly by the principal.

(iv) An agent must not become a principal as against his employer. It follows from this rule that an agent must not let his interest conflict with his duty.

Example

A client instructed a stockbroker to buy shares in a company. The stockbroker did not purchase in the open market but sold shares he already owned himself.

Held: The sale would be set aside as the broker had allowed his interest to conflict with his duty by selling his own shares to his client.

(*Armstrong v. Jackson*, 1916)

(v) An agent must not make a secret profit. This has been defined as any financial advantage which the agent receives over and above the remuneration he is entitled to from his principal. An agent is accountable to his principal for any profit made without his consent from a position of authority to which the agent has been appointed, from any property entrusted to him by the principal, or from any information or knowledge that he has been employed to gather. An agent will not be liable to account for information which is not of a special or secret nature as he cannot be prevented from earning money through his position, provided he does not break his contract or use the principal's property in doing so. The principal may take the following action if the agent does make a secret profit:

(*a*) Refuse to pay the agent his commission.

Example

A client instructed auctioneers to sell property for him. A purchaser was found by them who paid over a secret commission. When the client discovered this he demanded repayment of the auctioneers' ordinary commission of £50 and claimed the sale be set aside.
Held: The £50 must be repaid and the sale set aside.
(*Andrews v. Ramsay & Co. Ltd.*, 1903)

(*b*) Recover the secret profit from the agent.

Example

An army sergeant in the Suez Canal received large bribes from another person for his assistance in leading convoys of lorries carrying black-market whisky in wartime and ensuring, by virtue of his rank, that the vehicles were not checked. The sergeant sued for recovery of this money taken from him by the Crown.
Held: The Crown, as his employer, was entitled to the money as the sergeant had obtained it through the misuse of his rank and uniform.
(*Reading v. Attorney General*, 1951)

The secret commission can be recovered by the principal without his having to show that it was paid with a corrupt motive.

Example

The defendant employed *V* to make arrangements with the plaintiffs for the discovery of a person who would lend the defendant £45,000 for purchase of property. The plaintiffs agreed to pay *V* half the procuration fee they would charge the defendant, both parties keeping this a secret from the defendant. The plaintiffs did not intend to cause *V* to persuade the defendant to accept the fee or to act to his disadvantage. When the plaintiffs claimed the commission the defendant on his part claimed the amount paid to *V* as a bribe.
Held: The defendant would succeed as the mere fact that the bribe had been given was enough to entitle the defendant to claim the amount of the bribe.
(*Industries & General Mortgage Co. v. Lewis*, 1949)

(*c*) The principal may sue the third party for damages.

Example

L paid *H*, manager of gasworks owned by a borough corporation, a secret commission of 1*s*. per ton if he arranged for the acceptance of *L*'s tenders for coal by the borough. *L* put in the tender a price of 1*s*. per ton above the current market prices, in order to cover the commission promised to *H*. After the tender had been accepted by the borough its officers discovered the position, recovered the bribe from *H* and in addition sued *L* for damages of 1*s*. per ton.

Held: They would succeed in their action; the recovery of the bribe from *H* was immaterial as the borough's right against *L* were quite separate.

(*Salford Corporation v. Lever*, 1891)

(*d*) The principal can repudiate the contract even though the bribe did not influence the agent.

Example

B wished to buy horses and asked *P*, a vet, to keep an eye open for some. *P* introduced *B* to *S* and it was agreed that if *P* certified the horses supplied by *S* as sound he, *B*, would buy them. *B* later found they were not sound and that *S* had given a bribe to *P*. *B* refused to pay *S*.

Held: In view of the bribe *B* could repudiate the contract, the effect of the bribe on *P* being irrelevant.

(*Shipway v. Broadwood*, 1899)

A recent case before the Privy Council dealt with the issue of election by the principal between the twin remedies of recovery of a bribe or claim for fraud in respect of loss.

Example

A director and employee of a government housing society in Malaysia arranged with *M* for the latter to purchase of land in Penang and its resale to the society. Before *M* purchased the land the director inspected it and found it suitable for the society's purposes and knew it was available for purchase at $456,000. Nevertheless the director arranged that *M* should purchase at that price and resell it to the society for $944,000. Between purchase and resale *M* incurred $45,000 costs in evicting squatters from the land. He made a resulting gross profit from the sale to the society of $488,000 and a net profit of $443,000. *M* passed a quarter of his gross profit ($122,000) to the director. The society brought civil proceedings against the director who had been convicted under the Prevention of Corruption Act 1961. The civil proceedings claimed relief under two headings:

(i) recovery of the amount of the bribe ($122,000); and (ii) damages of $488,000—being the difference between the price it had paid for the land and the price *M* had paid for it, in respect of the loss the society had sustained as a result of the director's fraudulent breach of duty.

Held: (On appeal by the director from the Federal Court of Malaysia to the Privy Council.) At common law the principal of a bribed agent had, as against the bribed agent and the briber, alternative remedies of (a) claiming the amount of the bribe as money had and received, or (b) claiming damages for fraud in the amount of the actual loss sustained in entering into the transaction in respect of which the bribe had been given. The principal in such a case could not recover both and had to choose between the two remedies once judgement had been entered in his favour on one or other of the alternative remedies. The society, therefore, was bound to choose between the claim to recover the bribe and the claim for damages for fraud. Since the society would have clearly chosen in favour of damages for fraud the director's appeal would be allowed to the extent that judgement would be given to the society for $443,000.

(*Mahesan v. Malaysia Government Officers' Co-operative House Society Ltd*, 1978)

(*e*) The principal can ask the Attorney-General to prosecute the agent and the third party under the Prevention of Corruption Act 1906.

(vi) The agent must keep proper accounts of all transactions connected with the agency and render them to the principal on request.

(vii) The agent must hand over all profits resulting directly or indirectly from the agency.

6:13   DUTIES OF THE PRINCIPAL

The principal is under a duty to pay any agreed commission and remuneration and not to prevent or hinder the agent from earning it. When commission becomes payable depends on the contract between the principal and agent; for example it may be payable on introduction of a client or only on a successful completion of a sale. In order to earn a commission an agent must prove that he was the effective cause of the transaction concluded.

Example
A firm of estate agents were instructed by their client to find a purchaser for his hotel. *C*, who was looking for land for erection of a hall and sports ground, commenced negotiations with agents but these did not result in a sale. *C* had been acting for the War Office which later acquired the land under a compulsory purchase order for £7,000–£8,000. The agents claimed commission from their client.
Held: They were not entitled to commission as they were not the effective cause of the sale.
(*G. T. Hodges & Sons v. Hackbridge Park Residential Hotel Ltd*, 1939)

In the case of estate agents payment of commission depends on the terms of the contract. If a commission is payable on completion of sale it will not be earned if the agent merely finds a purchaser who either refuses to complete or does not pay the purchase money. If the vendor, however, refuses to complete, the agent will be entitled to his commission. If his task is to find a 'prospective purchaser', the agent will be entitled to commission if a purchaser is found who makes an offer but does not, eventually, purchase. An estate agent does not have duty to discover a purchaser for property; the principal is liable to pay commission only if the agent renders the service promised. The vendor is not prevented from finding a purchaser on his own behalf, or from using other agents to sell, unless the agent is employed as 'sole agent', when no other agent can be employed.

Example

A client appointed estate agents 'sole agents' in respect of property he owned. While they were seeking a purchaser, he sold to a third party himself.
Held: The client could do so without being liable in damages for breach of contract to the agents. There was no implied term in the contract that he would not sell the property himself.

(Bentall, Horsley and Baldry v. Vicary, 1930)

Entitlement to commission on introduction of a person 'ready, able and willing to purchase' was considered recently by the Court of Appeal.

Example

An estate agent was entitled to commission on introduction of a person 'ready, able and willing to purchase'. The agent introduced such a person, but by the time of the introduction the vendor had already exchanged contracts with another buyer.
Held: In the absence of other indications there was an implied term that commission was not due on the basis of these words if the property had already been sold before the introduction.

(A. A. Dickinson & Co. v. O'Leary, 1980)

If an agency does not include service and acknowledgement of the principal's authority, the agent being able to act for other principals, the principal is not obliged to supply the agent with the means of earning his commission. If a service contract is in existence then commission is a substitute for a salary and the agent is entitled to compensation if the contract is terminated.

Example

T was employed by *G* as a traveller for five years selling shirts and other goods manufactured or sold by *G*. Two years after the date of the contract, *G*'s factory was burnt down and he went out of business. *T* sued for breach of contract and damages for loss of commission.
Held: The agreement was not dependant on the continued existence of the factory, as *G* could have continued his business. *T*'s contract related to all goods sold by *G* and not just manufactured by him.

(Turner v. Goldsmith, 1891)

Commission may be payable on exceptional grounds after the agency has been terminated. An agreement to pay on repeat orders may come under this heading, depending on the circumstances.

Example

The plaintiffs, sales representatives of the defendants, a clothing manufacturing firm, received a letter from that firm which stated: 'We confirm the arrangement that you represent us for the London area for the wholesale trade. Commission will be 5 per cent on all orders, whether received direct or indirect, and on all repeats. Payable on the 20th of each month on all goods actually dispatched and invoiced.' The contract ran for six months, subject to renewal for three years if business reached £1,000 by the end of the six-month period. This was attained by the plaintiffs; the agreement was ended shortly before the three-year period. The plaintiffs claimed commission on all repeat orders received after the agency was ended.
Held: Their claim would fail as the word 'repeats' meant repeat orders received during the period of agency and *not* afterwards.
(Crocker Horlock Ltd. v. B. Lang & Co. Ltd., 1949)

The principal will be liable if he deprives the agent of his opportunity to earn his commission.

Example

Agents introduced sellers to buyers, and their agreement provided for commission to be paid by the sellers. The sellers in breach of agreement failed to deliver to the buyers.
Held: The agents' entitlement to commission, which was to come out of the price, had not arisen. However, the sellers were liable for depriving the agents of their opportunity to earn commission.
(Alpha Trading Ltd v. Dunnshaw-Patten Ltd, 1980)

The other main duty of the principal is to indemnify the agent against liabilities properly incurred in the discharge of his duties.

Example

A employed *B*, a broker, to purchase cotton for him on a speculative basis and due to falling market prices became deeply in debt to *B*. *B*, as he was entitled, closed the account by selling the cotton purchased for *A*. *B* was personally liable on the contracts and the sale resulted in a loss.
Held: B was entitled to an indemnity from *A*.
(Christoforides v. Terry, 1924)

However, if the agent goes beyond his authority or carries out his duties negligently his right to an indemnity will be lost.

6:14   TERMINATION OF AGENCY

Agency may be terminated:

(i) by mutual agreement on terms acceptable to both parties;
(ii) by complete performance of the contract, e.g. an agent appointed to sell a house ends the agency on selling it;

(iii) by expiration of time in cases where the agency is entered into for a definite period;

(iv) by frustration due to impossibility or illegality after the creation of the agency;

(v) by death or insanity of either the principal or agent;

(vi) by bankruptcy of the principal;

(vii) by either party becoming an enemy alien in time of war;

(viii) by revocation of the agent's authority by the principal. Revocation is not possible where there is an agency 'coupled with an interest' where the agent was appointed to enable him to secure some benefit already owed to him by the principal (e.g. collection of debts). Revocation is not possible either where it would involve the agent in personal loss, or by breaking contracts already made with innocent third parties by the agent. If the principal has allowed the agent to assume authority, revocation of the agency in relation to third parties will be effective only if they are informed of the revocation.

6:15 COMMERCIAL AGENCY AND THE E.E.C.

Each member state of the E.E.C. has its own national law governing agency and there is no common code or move towards harmonization as in the case of company law, for example (*see* Chapter 10). Only the main aspects of the law relating to the commercial agent will be considered here.

In English law the principal is under an implied duty to pay any lawful expenses legally incurred by the agent. This is not the case in other E.E.C. countries where the expenses will only be paid either as part of an existing agreement or custom. Under German law an agent who is appointed area or special customer group dealer can claim commission on contracts that they make without his aid provided they concern his area or group.

In France a distinction is made between a commercial agent (who has to outline his work clearly and expressly state he is an 'agent commercial') and an agent termed a '*voyageur representant placier*' (V.R.P.) who is classed as an employee. The V.R.P. can be paid by commission or salary, is entitled to notice of termination of his contract and an indemnity based on his trade connections (unlike the commercial agent in both respects, although notice is given in practice). No firm or company can be a V.R.P. and commercial agents have to be entered in a special register.

E.E.C. legal systems outside the U.K. permit an undisclosed principal to ratify a contract entered into by an agent acting as a principal himself. This is not allowed in English law under the principle of *Keighley, Maxted & Co. v. Durant*, 1901 (*see above*).

An agent, no matter if he is a national of another E.E.C. member state, can be employed under a U.K. contract which will be enforced in other E.E.C. courts of law. The law chosen by the principal or parties will govern subject to the public policy of the E.E.C. country whose court deals with the agreement in question.

QUESTIONS

1. (*a*) What duties does an agent owe to his principal?
   (*b*) A dealer in second-hand cars was instructed by the owner to sell a Mercedes Benz. The dealer received an offer of £1,500 from *X* and communicated this offer to the owner, who instructed him to accept it. Before accepting it the dealer received a higher offer of £1,650 from *Y*, but did not communicate this higher offer to the owner. The dealer then accepted *X*'s offer.
   What rights, if any, has the owner of the car against the dealer?
   (Diploma in Marketing II, November 1970)

2. (*a*) What are the rights and duties of agents?
   (*b*) A contract between Sarto and Timon provided that Timon would receive commission at an agreed rate, for each litre of Sarto's paint that he managed to sell to customers. At a party Timon told Ungar, who wanted to buy a large quantity of paint, that ample stocks were available at Sarto's shop. Next morning Ungar calls at Sarto's shop and orders one thousand litres of paint. Ungar informed Sarto that Timon had mentioned Sarto's shop as a source from which to buy the paint. When Timon learned what had happened he unsuccessfully asked Sarto for the commission arising from the sale of the paint. Is Timon entitled to the commission?
   (Certificate in Marketing, Part II, June 1979)

3. (*a*) What conditions must be fulfilled before a principal can ratify a contract made for him by an agent acting outside his authority?
   (*b*) Clarke and a number of friends are in the process of forming a company to run a catering business. While registration is pending, Clarke, purporting to act for the Company, agreed to buy the existing catering business of Ellis. After registration, the company wrote to Ellis confirming the arrangement, but subsequently withdrew. Examine Ellis' position in relation (i) to the company and (ii) to Clarke.
   (Diploma in Marketing II, May 1970)

4. Is a principal responsible for liabilities incurred by his agent who acts outside the express terms of his authority? Give two specific examples to illustrate your answer.
   (I.P.S., December 1971)

5. Salem, who is an agent for Exporters Ltd. in an overseas territory, signs a contract with the local Ministry of Supply for £50,000 for the supply of goods by Exporters Ltd. The customer requires the goods urgently, and to get the order, Salem accepts a penalty clause of 1 per cent of the contract price per week of delay. This is contrary to express instructions which he had received from Exporters Ltd. As the legal advisers to Exporters Ltd., indicate whether they are legally bound to supply in accordance with the terms of the contract which Salem signed.
   (I.P.S., May 1969)

6. A clerk in the buying office writes out orders on his firm's official order forms for goods to be delivered to a company which is owned by a friend of his. By the time the fraud is discovered the goods have been disposed of

and cannot be traced. The supplier invoices the firm for the value of the goods which amounts to £5,000. Advise the firm as to whether or not they are liable to pay.

(I.P.S., December 1970)

7. Brown is appointed sole selling agent for Smith in territory X and entitled to a 5 per cent commission on all sales arising in that territory. The National Food Corporation insist on dealing direct with Smith's Head Office which is located within territory X and conclude a contract worth £100,000. Is Brown entitled to commission on this order?

(I.P.S., May 1971)

8. (*a*) (i) Explain how the principal stands in relation to third parties when he revokes the authority of his agent.

(ii) What limitations are imposed by law on the principal's power to revoke his agent's authority?

(*b*) S, a shirt manufacturer, agreed to employ T as a full-time sales representative for a period of five years on a commission basis to sell goods 'manufactured or sold' by G. After two years, G's factory was burnt down and G went out of business. T thereupon sued G for breach of contract and claimed damages for loss of commission. In defence, G claimed that the contract had been discharged by impossibility. What is the legal position?

(Diploma in Marketing II, May 1969)

9. (*a*) How is an agency (i) created and (ii) terminated?

(*b*) Simon runs a one-man greengrocer's business. During his absence on holidays, perishable goods arrive at the local railway station. After several unsuccessful attempts to deliver the goods at Simon's business premises, the stationmaster decided to sell the goods and hold the money in a separate account. Before going away on holiday, Simon left his temporary address with his neighbour. The lorry-driver who called to deliver the goods did not make any inquiries as to Simon's whereabouts. Discuss the legal position.

(Certificate in Marketing, Part II, November 1978)

10. (*a*) Describe FIVE exceptions to the *nemo dat quod non habet* rule.

(*b*) On Friday 16 November 1979, Quentin agreed to buy a luxury car on hire purchase from Rodney, who undertook to renew the car's gearbox before delivery. As a concession Rodney agreed to accept a cheque for the car provided that delivery of it was postponed for seven days in order to allow the cheque to be cleared through the banks. The following Monday, 19 November 1979, Quentin began trading as a seller of cheap second-hand cars. At the date on which he agreed to buy Rodney's car, Quentin was unaware that Rodney was himself buying the car on hire purchase. Outstanding instalments owed by Rodney under the hire purchase agreement were settled by him on Tuesday 20 November 1979. The next day Quentin sold the car to Simon. Indicate whether Simon has acquired a good title to the car.

(Certificate in Marketing, Part II, November 1979)

7. Carriage of Goods

The main methods of carriage of goods are by land, sea, and air—and include canals and pipelines.

7:1 CARRIAGE ON LAND

In common law heavy obligations were placed on carriers, with the result that carriers adopted the practice of contracting out of their common law obligations. In the last 150 years Parliament has passed legislation to hold the balance between the carrier's interests and those who have dealings with him.

TYPES OF CARRIERS AT COMMON LAW

Common law distinguishes between two types of carriers—common and private; heavier duties are laid on common carriers than on private carriers.

(i) COMMON CARRIERS

A common carrier is one who publicly holds himself out to carry goods of another person by way of business. He may or may not restrict his business to the carriage of goods of a particular kind but must carry for anyone who wishes to contract with him. He is bound to carry all goods offered unless:

(a) he has no room in his vehicle, or
(b) the goods offered are not of the kind he normally carries, or
(c) the destination is not one to which he usually goes.

Example

A motor engineer and contractor regularly carried sugar from Liverpool to Manchester for the Tate Company. On the return journey he regularly carried goods for anyone who asked him, but he had no regular tariff and sometimes refused goods when the terms were unsuitable to him. Hemp carried by him for a customer was lost in a fire without negligence on the part of the carrier. The customer sued the carrier as a common carrier.
Held: As the carrying was done on a casual basis he was not a common carrier and therefore not liable in the absence of negligence.
(*Belfast Ropework Ltd. v. Bushell*, 1918)

A common carrier must not deviate from his customary route (which need not be direct) without justification. His charges must be reasonable; he has a lien on goods carried for his charges. He can refuse goods for carriage that are not properly packed.

He is liable for damage to goods carried even when it is not due to his negligence; that is, he is an 'insurer of the goods he carries'. There are exceptions to this rule of absolute liability.

(*a*) Act of God—an event 'due to natural causes directly and exclusively without human intervention and that could not have been prevented by any amount of foresight and pains and care reasonably to be expected of him'.

Example

A common carrier by sea carried a mare from Aberdeen to London. During rough weather on the voyage, the mare died from injuries she received due to her struggles in the rough weather.
Held: The carrier was not liable as the direct cause of loss was an act of nature plus a defect in the thing carried.

(*Nugent v. Smith*, 1876)

(*b*) Acts done by the Queen's enemies—damage caused by the act of a hostile foreign government. Acts of rioters or robbers are not covered.

(*c*) Inherent vice in the goods carried—e.g. explosives, corrosive materials, or dangerous animals.

Example

A bullock was delivered to a railway company for carriage. During transit due to its struggles it escaped and was killed.
Held: The railway company were not liable.

(*Blower v. Great Western Railway*, 1872)

(*d*) Bad packing—if damage is caused by goods being improperly packed, the carrier is not liable, even if he knew on receipt that the packing was defective.

Example

A glass show-case was consigned by rail. The railway company knew when it was received that the case was not properly packed. It was damaged in transit.
Held: The company were not liable.

(*Gould v. South Eastern & Chatham Railway*, 1920)

The liability of the carrier begins when he accepts the goods for carriage and in general ends when he delivers the goods to their destination, or has offered delivery which the consignee has refused.

(ii) PRIVATE CARRIERS

A private carrier is a carrier who is not a common carrier. He is only liable for loss caused by his negligence. If the goods carried are dangerous and the danger is not known to the carrier the consignor may be liable for the damage caused.

Example

Ferro silicon was delivered to a private carrier for carriage described as 'general cargo'. The consignor did not know that the chemical was likely to give off dangerous fumes. During the journey poison gases were given off by the chemical and the carrier died as a result. The consignor was sued by the widow for damages.

Held: The consignor was liable as being in breach of warranty that the goods could be safely carried.

(*Bamfield v. Goole and Sheffield Transport Co.*, 1910)

Note: Common carriers today are rare. The Transport Act 1962 expressly states that British Railways are no longer common carriers. The Transport Act 1968 makes a similar provision with regard to the National Freight Corporation, and the Transport (London) Act 1969 also states that the London Transport Executive is not a common carrier.

(iii) CARRIAGE BY ROAD

The Carriers Act 1830 attempted to give protection to the public against common carriers who tried to exempt themselves from their liability. It provided that notices exhibited at the office of the carrier aimed at modifying his common law liability would be void, but that liability could be modified by express agreement, e.g. as in a consignment note. The Act gives protection from liability in respect of certain enumerated valuables, covering precious stones, coins, jewellery, watches, negotiable securities, writings, title deeds, pictures, china, silk, and glass. The consignor should declare the value of any enumerated valuables worth more than £10 and the carrier is entitled to extra payment for carriage. If the consignor fails to declare the excess value, the carrier is only liable for loss and damage due to a criminal act (e.g. theft). These rules still apply to passengers' luggage carried by public service road vehicles.

Most carriers by road exempt liability under the standard Conditions of Carriage of the Road Haulage Association (1967 edition). Under the Carriage of Goods by Road Act 1965, incorporating the Convention on the Contract for the International Carriage of Goods by Road, standard conditions are laid down for carriage of goods by road between countries party to the Convention, from which the carrier cannot contract out.

Private carriers are liable for negligence at common law and under any relevant statute. As a private carrier does not warrant the fitness of his vehicle, if goods are destroyed due to its dangerous condition the carrier will incur liability with regard to the goods only where he has been negligent as far as the vehicle is concerned, apart from criminal liability under the Road Traffic Act 1960.

Note: A contract for the carriage of passengers in a road public service vehicle containing any provision restricting the carrier's liability for claims arising from death or injury to passengers is void in respect of that provision under s. 151 Road Traffic Act 1960.

(iv) CARRIAGE BY RAIL

The British Railways Board is no longer a private or a common carrier and there is no limit to the power of the Board to restrict or exclude liability for negligence in the delivery or carriage of goods. Carriage is governed by the Railway Board's Conditions of Carriage, which fall into four groups:

(*a*) general conditions for the carriage of goods (other than goods covered by special conditions);
(*b*) conditions for the carriage of livestock (other than wild animals);
(*c*) conditions for the carriage of coal, coke, and patent fuel;
(*d*) conditions of carriage by water.

Special contracts made with traders generally incorporate the relevant Standard Conditions, amended or unamended.

The Board is liable for loss, mis-delivery or damage to goods unless it can prove this has resulted from:

1. act of God;
2. war, invasion, act of a foreign enemy, hostilities, civil war, rebellion;
3. legal seizure;
4. act of omission of the trader;
5. inherent liability to wastage in bulk or weight, latent defect or inherent defect, vice or natural deterioration of the goods;
6. insufficient or improper labelling or addressing;
7. insufficient paper packing;
8. riot, civil commotion, strikes, lockouts, stoppage or restraint of labour;
9. the consignee not accepting or taking delivery within a reasonable time.

Note: The liability of the Board is limited to:

(*a*) £800 per ton on the gross weight of the consignment where the whole consignment is lost.
(*b*) A proportion of the above sum per ton where part only of the consignment is lost, the amount depending on the value which the part of the consignment lost bears to the value of the whole consignment.

The Board is not exempt from liability under Owner's Risk Conditions for non-delivery of the whole or a separate package which is part of the consignment if wilful misconduct by the Board or its servants can be proved. With regard to goods carried at Owner's Risk the Board's only liability for loss or damage is where wilful misconduct by the Board or its servants can be proved, except where there has been a mis-delivery of the whole consignment or a separate package forming part of it, in which case the Board are liable without proof of misconduct.

In the case of damageable goods not properly packed the Board are liable only (i) for wilful misconduct or (ii) if it can be proved that the damage would still have been suffered if the goods had been properly packed.

Claims must be made within seven days of the end of transit (when the goods are delivered or the sender exercises his right of stoppage in transitu) and notice of claims given within three days, both in writing.

Note: Under s. 43 (7) of the Transport Act 1962, the Board cannot limit or exclude its liability with regard to death or bodily injury to any passenger or set time limits for enforcing such liability.

The Transport Act 1962 (Amendment) Act 1981 which came into force on 2 August 1981 makes provision with respect to the experimental reopening of lines for railway passenger services (amending s. 56 of the Transport Act 1962 s. 56).

Transport Act 1981

The Transport Act 1981 amends the law relating transport, road traffic and highways in a number of important ways. Those sections concerning the British Railways Board, the British Transport Docks Board and the National Ports Council are considered here although the Act also deals with road safety and miscellaneous matters. The Act allows for the introduction of private capital into subsidiaries of the British Railways Board (and also into a reconstituted British Transport Docks Board). The Board is allowed to sell shares in its subsidiaries or any of its property with the consent of the Secretary of State (s. 1). The Board is required to secure that its subsidiary, Sealink, put forward a scheme for the Secretary of State's approval to transfer Sealink's harbour undertaking to a new subsidiary harbour company, Associated British Ports (s. 2). The Secretary of State is given power to give directions to the Railways Board (s. 3). British Transport Docks Board is reconstitued as Associated British Ports which is given a financial structure (ss. 5 and 6). The constitution and powers of Associated British Ports are defined (ss. 7, 8 and Schedules 2, 3). That body is under a general duty to provide port facilities to the extent it may consider expedient (s. 9). The National Ports Council is abolished (s. 15 and Part I, Schedule 5). The Secretary of State is required to levy contributions from harbour authorities to be undertaken by charging schemes (ss. 16, 17 and Part II of Schedule 5). The Harbours Act 1964 is also amended (s. 18 and Schedule 6).

The Act makes provision for grants to and the provision of facilities for inland waterway freight haulage (s. 36).

The United Kingdom is a party to two major multilateral treaties on international carriage by rail and to an additional supplementary treaty. The two treaties are the revised International Convention dealing with the Carriage of Goods by Rail (CIM) and the revised International Convention dealing with the Carriage of Passengers and Luggage by Rail (CIV) both signed at Berne on 7 February 1970. An Additional Convention to the 1961 CIV in the form of a supplementary treaty was signed at Berne on 26 February 1961.

Although all three Conventions are in force in the United Kingdom only the Additional Convention has been expressly made part of English law by enactment, the text of the Convention being a schedule to the Carriage by Railway Act 1972. However, the Act provides that where passengers and goods are carried in accordance with the 'Railway Passenger Convention' (CIV) or the 'Railway Freight Convention' (CIM) all rights of action will be governed by the appropriate Convention. The terms of the CIM and CIV Conventions have been incorporated in passenger tickets, consignment notes and luggage registration vouchers issued by British Railways since 1965.

CIM

The Convention, which came into force on 1 January 1975, governs carriage of goods consigned under a through consignment note for carriage over territories of at least two contracting states, including regular road and shipping services complementing rail services (Art. 1). The Convention determines the form and conditions of the contract of carriage, performance, modification, liability for loss, damage and delay, enforcement of claims and the rights and liabilities between the railway authorities dealing with a through consignment. The railway is liable for total or partial loss of goods and for damage and delay and for acts and omissions of its own servants and others it employs in carrying out the contract of carriage. Liability for loss or damage is subject to two types of excepted perils, the first similar to the General Conditions of the Railway Board (Conditions of Carriage of Passengers and their Luggage; s. 1), the second is different.

The second type covers situations where loss or damage arises from special risks inherent in (*a*) carriage in open wagons when this has been agreed; (*b*) lack or inadequacy of packing; (*c*) loading by a sender or unloading by the consignee; (*d*) failure to comply with custom's requirements; (*e*) the nature of goods that specially expose them to loss and damage; (*f*) irregular, incorrect or incomplete description of articles accepted only under certain conditions; (*g*) the carriage of livestock; (*h*) the carriage of consignments which have to be accompanied by an attendant (Arts. 27, 28).

The liability of the railway for total or partial loss is limited to 50 francs per kilogram of gross weight short unless a special declaration of interest in delivery is made in the consignment note by the sender and he pays an increased charge. In this case a claim can be made up to the total amount of interest declared (Art. 31).

CIV

The CIV Convention applies to the carriage of passengers and registered luggage under international transport documents over territories of two or more contracting states where carriage is solely over listed railway lines (Art. 1). The railway is under a general obligation to carry luggage (and passengers) if they comply with the Convention's provisions and carriage can be taken by ordinary transport facilities and carriage is not prevented by unavoidable circumstances. The railway is liable for damage or total or partial loss of any articles a passenger had as hand luggage who has sustained an accident unless the cause of the accident was not connected with the operation of the railway, or which it could not avoid or prevent the consequences. The railway will not be liable either if the accident was the result of the passenger's wrongful act or omission or abnormal conduct as a passenger, or if caused by the action of a third party the consequences which the railway could not avoid or prevent (Art. 2).

Note: The Carriage by Air and Road Act 1979 replaces references to gold francs in the Carriage of Goods by Road Act 1965 and the Carriage of Passengers by Road Act 1974 with references to special drawing rights (s. 4).

(v) PIPELINES

The Pipelines Act 1962 gives a non-owner of a pipeline the right to have things conveyed in it. This does not apply to pipelines belonging to the Central

Electricity Generating Board, area gas and electricity boards, or the United Kingdom Atomic Energy Authority.

A cross-country pipeline (ten miles or more in length) can only be built under a pipeline construction authorization of the Minister of Power. The intended construction of a pipeline of under ten miles (a local pipeline) need only be notified to the Minister, but he can make local pipelines of a particular type or in a particular area conform to the cross-country pipeline regulations, subject to approval of both Houses of Parliament.

7:2   CARRIAGE BY SEA

A carrier by sea may be a common carrier but usually ceases to be so by making a special contract. A contract for the carriage of goods by sea is called a contract of affreightment and the charge for the carriage is known as the freight. There are two forms of a contract of affreightment—a charter party and a bill of lading.

(i) CHARTER PARTY AND BILL OF LADING

A charter party is entered into by a shipper hiring from the shipowner a ship to carry goods. The shipper may hire the ship for a particular journey or series of journeys, the captain being answerable to the owner, or the entire ship with captain and crew may be hired to sail under the hirer's instructions. Where the ship is hired under the charter party the shipper will often carry goods belonging to others on board. These goods will be carried under a bill of lading, a document signed by the ship's master stating that the goods listed have been shipped and serving as a receipt for the goods. Both the charter party and the bill of lading must be in writing.

(a) Charter party

The most important terms are:

1. *Tonnage of the vessel.* This does not have to be exact as long as there is no material variation. If this is the case it will be a breach of condition and entitle the charterer to rescind the charter party.
2. *Position of the ship at the date of availability or charter.* This is a condition.
3. *The port of loading and discharge where the charter party is for a particular voyage.* This is called a voyage charter as distinct from a time charter, where a ship is chartered for a particular period of time.
4. *The ship is stated to be 'tight, staunch, strong, and in every way fitted for the voyage'.* Apart from any *express* undertaking, there is an *implied* undertaking that the ship will be seaworthy when the voyage beings. This means that she is reasonably fit (i) to make the voyage contemplated, and (ii) to receive the type of cargo to be carried. An excessively long delay in getting the ship seaworthy related to the length of the charter party may constitute frustration of the contract.
    (*Hong Kong Fir Shipping Co. Ltd. v. Kawasaki Kisen Kaisha*, 1962)

5. *A 'full and complete cargo' is required.* This does not include deck cargo unless expressly provided for, or the custom of the trade or port of loading covers it. The charterer has to pay 'dead freight' for all cargo space not taken. The owner of the

ship exempts himself in the charter party in the case of certain events—e.g. 'restraint of princes, Acts of God, fire and all other dangers and accidents of the seas, rivers, and navigation'. The Merchant Shipping Acts 1894–1958 detail the extent of exclusion in the case of goods lost or damaged on board ship.

6. *Charterer's liability ceases when cargo is loaded, the masters and owners having a lien on cargo for freight and demurrage.* The charterer's liability ceases when goods are loaded and when a lien for freight and demurrage arises. The liability of the charterer continues if no lien arises.

7. *The Hague Rules of Bills of Lading may be incorporated.* These limit liability of the shipowner to the charterer in the same way as a shipowner's liability is limited in a bill of lading.

(b) The bill of lading

This is a document, signed by the shipowner or his agent or the ship's master, which states that the goods referred to in the bill have been shipped on a particular vessel and sets out the terms of carriage. When goods are delivered to ship, a mate's receipt is given possession of which entitles the holder to a bill of lading. A clean receipt is one on which no note of damaged goods is made. When a shipper's goods are loaded he is entitled to a 'shipped' bill.

The bill of lading has three functions:

1. as a document of title to the goods referred to in the bill;
2. as a statement of the terms of the contract of carriage;
3. as a receipt for goods shipped.

A holder of a bill of lading is entitled to possession of the goods from the vessel. The goods on board may be sold to a third party and cash handed over against the bill by the buyer, which he then presents to the captain at the destination port and obtains the goods. A transferee of a bill of lading gets no better title than the transferor as it is not a negotiable instrument (but *see* ss. 2 and 9 of Factors Act 1889 and *Cahn v. Pockett's Bristol Channel Co.*). The bill is conclusive evidence against the captain or other person signing it that the goods were actually shipped, but only *prima facie* evidence against the carrier.

(ii) CARRIAGE OF GOODS BY SEA ACT 1971 (SUPERSEDING THE ACT OF 1924)

This Act applies to carriage of goods under bill of lading or similar documents of title from any port in Great Britain or Northern Ireland and if the bill of lading is issued in a contracting state or shipment is made from the port of a contracting state. The Act will also apply to the coasting trade, if carried out under bills of lading.

(a) Where the Act applies no absolute warranty of sea-worthiness is given.

(b) Every bill of lading to which the Act applies must contain express reference to the fact that it is subject to the rules in the schedule which adopts the Hague Rules on bills of lading. Under these Rules a shipper can demand a bill of lading showing the following particulars, including:

1. Number of packages or pieces or weight of the goods.
2. Chief identification marks of the goods.
3. Apparent condition and order of the goods. If the goods arrive damaged the shipowner is liable if it can be proved that:
(i) the goods were shipped in good internal condition, or
(ii) the damage resulted from an external cause under control of the shipowner.

(*c*) The following provisions are implied in every bill of lading:

1. The carrier will exercise due diligence before and at the commencement of the voyage to make the ship seaworthy, to properly equip, man, and supply the ship and make the holds, refrigeration, and other parts of the ship where goods are carried fit for their reception, carriage, and preservation.
2. The carrier will not be liable for certain excepted perils, including: Acts of God, war, riot, civil commotion, act, neglect or default of the captain or other servant of the carrier in the management or navigation of the ship, perils, dangers, and accidents of the sea, or other navigable waters.
3. If there is loss or damage to the goods notice in writing must be given to the carrier before or at the time of removal. Where such loss or damage is not apparent, written notice must be given within three days of delivery. Actions must be brought within one year of delivery or when delivery was due.
4. The carrier will carefully load, stow, care for, and discharge the goods.

(*d*) The carrier's liability for loss or damage is limited to £238 (10,000 gold francs) per unit or package or 30 gold francs per kilo of gross weight, whichever is higher. By agreement British shipowners and insurers accept liability limited to £200. A person who is not a party to the contract cannot rely on a limitation or exclusion clause.

(*e*) Where packages or units forming the contents of a container are separately numbered in the bill of lading they are reckoned to be packages or units for the purposes of the Hague Rules; otherwise the container is the unit or package under the Rules.

(*f*) The carrier is not liable for loss or damage caused by a deviation to save life or property or other reasonable cause, bearing in mind the contract terms and parties with interests in the voyage.

(*g*) Where dangerous goods are shipped without their nature being disclosed, the carrier, without liability for paying compensations, may destroy or discharge them. Even if their dangerous nature is disclosed, where they become an actual danger to the ship or cargo they can still be destroyed or discharged. The shipper may have a right to general average in this case.

(*h*) A servant or agent of the carrier (not an independent contractor) can use the same defences and limits of liability as the carrier.

(iii) DEMURRAGE

This is the sum payable by a charterer to a shipowner by way of agreed damages for delay beyond an agreed or reasonable time, caused by loading or unloading of the ship. Dispatch money, on the other hand, is the sum payable by the shipowner to the charterer for time saved in loading or unloading. 'Laydays' are days fixed by charter for loading and unloading.

(iv) LIEN

The carrier has a lien for freight payable on delivery. This lien may be provided for specifically in the bill of lading or charter party. It attaches to all goods of the same consignee on the same voyage.

(v) GENERAL AVERAGE

Loss may be caused to the ship, cargo, or freight and this will be borne by the interest affected. This is the *particular average loss*. A loss caused deliberately to prevent a wider loss is termed *general average loss*. The interest adversely affected can recover contribution from other interests—e.g. a ship scuttled to prevent the spread of fire to save the cargo. Here the shipowners could claim contributions from the owners of the cargo to cover the cost of refloating the ship. Liability to contribution is enforced by the shipowner exercising a lien over the cargo on behalf of all interests. Average adjusters settle the exact amount of contribution each interest bears rateably.

Contribution can be claimed where:

(*a*) there was a common danger;
(*b*) there was a necessity to incur some sacrifice to avoid danger;
(*c*) the sacrifice was reasonable and voluntary;
(*d*) some interest was either partly or wholly saved;
(*e*) the danger arising was not due to the fault of the party claiming a general average contribution.

(vi) LIABILITY OF SEA CARRIERS

Under the Merchant Shipping Acts 1894–1958, carriers by sea in a British ship are not liable for damage occurring without negligence on their part in certain cases; this extends to servants of sea carriers where they are acting as servants in relation to the act or omission on which a claim is made. There will be no liability where:

(*a*) loss or damage is caused by fire on board ship,
(*b*) gold and other valuables are lost or damaged by robbery unless their value and nature had been declared in writing to the master or shipowner at the time of shipment.

If the event has occurred without his fault in the case of a British or foreign vessel liability is limited in the following cases:

(*a*) loss of life or personal injury to any person carried in the ship;
(*b*) damage or loss to goods on board ship;
(*c*) loss of life, personal injury, loss of goods, damage to goods on board ship caused through the act or omission of any person in navigation or management of the ship, or any other person on board in loading, carrying or discharging cargo, or in the embarking, carrying or disembarkation of passengers.

Liability is limited to:

(*a*) loss of life or personal injury—£75 (equal to 3,100 gold francs) per ton of the ship's tonnage;
(*b*) damage or loss to goods—£25 (equal to 1,000 gold francs) per ton of the ship's tonnage.

Note: The Merchant Shipping Act 1981 replaces the amounts in gold francs specified in certain provisions limiting the liability of shipowners and others, by amounts equivalent to special drawing rights of the International Monetary Fund (S.D.R.).

7:3 CARRIAGE BY AIR

The Civil Aviation (Licensing) Act 1960 ended the air corporations' monopoly under the 1946 Civil Aviation Act (applying to B.O.A.C., B.E.A., and British South America Airways). The 1960 Act enabled private airline operators to run scheduled flights as well as charter flights under a licensing system now controlled by the Civil Aviation Authority. No aircraft can be used on any flight for reward, or in connection with any trade or business, except in accordance with an air service licence granted by the Authority authorizing the operator to operate aircraft on such flights as are approved. This applies generally to any flight in any part of the world by an aircraft registered in the United Kingdom, and to any flight beginning or ending in the United Kingdom by an aircraft registered in such other country or territory as the Minister may prescribe. No aircraft may fly in the United Kingdom under the 1949 Civil Aviation Act (without special exemption) unless it is registered in:

(i) a state which is party to the Chicago Convention on International Civil Aviation of 1944, or
(ii) some part of the Commonwealth, or
(iii) a country with which a special convention relating to air navigation is in force for the time being.

Since April 1972 the Civil Aviation Authority has been the authority for aircraft registration in the U.K. and as a general rule an aircraft cannot be registered in the U.K. unless it is wholly owned by:

(i) British subjects or persons under British protection,
(ii) a body corporate established in some part of the Commonwealth and having its principal place of business there.

The constitution and functions of the British Airways Board are set out in the British Airways Board Act 1977. These functions include the provision of air transport services and aerial work anywhere in the world and promotion of the formation of undertakings for air services.

The Civil Aviation Act 1980

The Civil Aviation Act 1980, which came into force on 13 November 1980, amongst other effects abolished the British Airways Board and reduced the public dividend capital of the British Airways Board by £160 million (s. 1). The financial limits of the Board are set out (s. 2) and the vesting of the Board's property is in a company nominated by the Secretary of State (s. 3). Initial government shareholding in this successor company is detailed as is that company's (and its subsidiaries') financial structure (ss. 4–6). The Act additionally outlines the Secretary of State's powers over British air transport business in the case of an emergency (s. 11). The Civil Aviation Act 1971 is amended and the general objectives of the Civil Aviation Authority are set out (s. 12).

Section 4 of the Civil (Eurocontrol) Act 1961 concerning air navigation service charges is also amended (s. 19).

LIABILITY OF AIR CARRIERS TO PASSENGERS AND GOODS

The Carriage by Air Act 1961 and the Warsaw Convention of 1929 (amended at the Hague in 1955) provide rules relating to international carriage by air common to all countries, including Britain, who have acceded to the Convention. The rules, in practice, are applied to internal as well as international flights.

The provisions of the amended Convention include:

1. *Passenger ticket*—the carrier must deliver to the passenger a ticket containing prescribed particulars. It is *prima facie* evidence of the contract of carriage.
2. *Baggage check*—a baggage check is *prima facie* evidence of the conditions of the contract of carriage.
3. *Air waybill*—every carrier of cargo has a right to require the consignor to make out and hand over to him an air waybill (air consignment note) and the consignor has the right to require the carrier to accept this document.

The Carriage by Air Act 1961 exempts the carrier from liability in certain circumstances:

1. if he can prove that his servants or agents have taken all necessary precautions to avoid damage or it was impossible for them to do so;
2. if the damage was caused by or contributed by the negligence of the injured person, the court may, in accordance with the law, clear the carrier in whole or in part from liability;
3. where cargo or baggage are damaged, a complaint in writing must be made to the carrier at latest in the case of baggage within seven days and fourteen days of receipt in the case of cargo;
4. if the action is not brought within two years from the date when the aircraft arrived or ought to have arrived at its destination or from the date on which carriage was stopped, right to recover damages is lost.

The liability of the carrier is limited to 250 francs per kilogram unless the consignee makes a special declaration and pays the required supplement (Art. 22). This limit will not apply if the carrier is guilty of wilful misconduct, or if he fails to issue a proper consignment note for the goods.

The Guadalajara Convention of 1961 covers the situation where an air carrier sub-contracts to another, as occurs in hire and charter. Where the contracting carrier makes an agreement with a passenger or consignor for carriage governed by the Warsaw Convention (with or without the Hague amendment) which is performed by another carrier entirely or partly the contracting carrier and the other carrier are subject to the Warsaw Convention (and the Hague amendment, if applicable)—the contracting carrier for the whole carriage and the other carrier for the part he actually performs (Art. 2). The plaintiff can sue either the contracting carrier or the sub-contractor (Art. 7).

7:4 MULTIMODAL TRANSPORT

Integrated transportation of goods has been developing in the commercial world for some time. Its advent has been noticeably accelerated in recent years by the introduction of containerization which has enabled goods to be shipped by road, air and sea without the load being broken up for transmission.

The IATA standard air waybill covers multimodal transport and the standard form contract of the International Chamber of Commerce (I.C.C.) has been widely accepted on a voluntary basis, both by multimodal transport operators and consignors.

The UN Conference on Trade and Development (UNCTAD) in 1981 adopted a Convention on multimodal transport. The new Convention creates a new regime of liability. Even where it can be shown on which mode of transport damage occurred the Convention provisions apply. However, as in the case of the Warsaw Convention where air carriage is involved, that Convention provides a higher limit of liability than the multimodal Convention and therefore the Warsaw Convention would be applied. The proposed multimodal regime needs more complex documentation than under the Warsaw Convention. The provisions of the UN Convention will apply only to international carriage by more than one mode of transport. However, pick-up and delivery in carrying out a single mode transport contract will not be regarded as multimodal transport (Article 1 (1)). For example, a pick up by van from a freight terminal at Heathrow for delivery to a British Rail terminal for forward shipment to the consignee. A consignor may continue to choose between multimodal and segmented (i.e. broken stage) transport (Article 3 (2)).

The Convention provides that it should affect the application of any international Convention or national law relating to the regulation and control of transport operations. The Conventional states that carriage of goods governed by Conventions such as CMR (international carriage by road) and CIM (international carriage by rail) (see above) is not to be regarded as multimodal transport so far as the provisions of those conventions apply (Article 30 (4)). This meets, particularly, the IATA's wish that carriage by air should be wholly excluded from the UN Convention (see also Art. 38). The UN Convention is applied whenever the place of taking up the goods by a multimodal transport operator or the place for delivery is in the territory of a Contracting State (adherent to the Convention). The States of departure or destination which become parties to the new Convention will therefore impose the regime of the Convention even though it has not been accepted by the other State concerned.

It is likely, due to the complexity of the UN Convention that it will be some time before it comes into force, particularly as thirty States are needed to become parties to the Convention before it comes into force.

QUESTIONS

1. What are the liabilities of a carrier under a bill of lading?
2. Outline the usual terms of a charter party and indicate the exemptions it normally contains.
3. What are the main liabilities of the British Railways Board as a carrier and how far are these liabilities restricted?
4. (a) What is a common carrier and what defences can he seek to rely upon in legal actions brought against him?

   (b) Sam, a self-employed carrier of goods, parks his lorry near a river bank for the night. Sam knows, from past experience, that very heavy rainfall gives rise to floods which are likely to reach this particular bank of the river which meanders considerably at this point of its course. Heavy rain is falling when Sam decides to make an overnight stop at this site. Sam, who goes to collect the lorry next morning, finds that the force of the flood water from several days of heavy rain has caused the river bank to collapse and his lorry is partly submerged in the swollen river. Goods which Sam is carrying for Tom have been damaged in the water. Tom unsuccessfully asks Sam to settle for the ensuing loss. Tom chooses to sue Sam. What defence(s) would you advise Sam to put up when the case finally comes on for hearing in court?

   (Diploma in Marketing, Part II, November 1974)

8. *Patents, Copyright, Trade Marks, and Passing Off*

INTRODUCTION

There are special rights in industrial property protected by law. Patents, designs, and trade marks come under this heading and are controlled respectively by the provisions of the Patents Acts 1949 and 1977, the Registered Designs Act 1949, and the Trade Marks Act 1938 (together with common law rules relating to unregistered trade marks). There are additionally legally enforceable rights in artistic property, termed copyright, which are governed by the Copyright Act 1956. The Design Copyright Act 1968 covers, somewhat obviously, copyright and design.

8:1 PATENTS

The Patents Act 1977 has reformed the existing law relating to national patents by introducing certain recommendations of the 1970 Banks Report on the Patent System (Cmnd. 4407) (Part 1 of the Act) and adapting present law to bring it into line with European and Community patents (Part II of the Act) (*see* 8:5). Its principal aim, however, is to enable the United Kingdom to take part in the various International and European patenting agreements, so that when all the conventions covered by the 1977 Act are in operation patent protection for the United Kingdom may be arranged by either a British or Community patent. The 1977 Act partly repeals the Patents Act 1949 but provisions are made in Schedule 1 of the 1977 Act for the application of the 1949 Act to existing patents and applications.

(i) OBJECTS OF THE PATENT SYSTEM

The main objective of the patent system is (according to the 1970 Report on the Patent System) 'the encouragement of new industries in the country'. As noted legal specialist writers have put it:

'The basic theory of the patent system is simple and reasonable. It is desirable in the public interest that industrial techniques should be improved. In order to encourage improvement, and to encourage also the disclosure of improvements in preference to their use in secret, any person devising an improvement in a manufactured article, or in machinery or methods of making it, may upon disclosure of his improvements at the Patent Office demand to be given monopoly in the use of it for a period of sixteen years. After that period it passes into the public domain and the temporary monopoly is not objectionable, for if it had not been for the inventor who devised and disclosed the improvement nobody would have been able to use it at that or any other time, since nobody would have known about it. Furthermore, the giving of the monopoly encourages the putting into practice of the invention, for the only way the inventor can make a profit from it (or even recover the fees for his patent) is by putting it into practice either by using it himself, and deriving an advantage over his competitors by its use, or by allowing others to use it in return for royalties.'

(T. A. Blanco White, Q.C., and R. Jacob in *Patents for Invention* (Stevens, 1962))

(ii) PATENTABILITY

A patent may be granted under s. 1 of the 1977 Act for an invention only where the following three conditions are satisfied:

(*a*) the invention is new;
(*b*) it involves an inventive step;
(*c*) it is capable of industrial application.

The following (among other things) are not inventions for the purposes of the Act; anything which consists of:

(*a*) a discovery, scientific theory or mathematical method;
(*b*) a literary, dramatic, musical or artistic work or any other aesthetic creation;
(*c*) a scheme, rule or method for performing a mental act, playing a game or doing business, or a programme for a computer;
(*d*) the presentation of information.

These provisions prevent anything from being treated as an invention for the purposes of the Act only to the extent that a patent or an application for a patent relates to that thing as such.

A patent will not be granted:

(*a*) for an invention the publication or exploitation of which would be generally expected to encourage offensive, immoral or anti-social behaviour;
(*b*) for any variety of animal or plant or any essentially biological process for the production of animals or plants, not being a micro-biological process or the product of such a process.

The Secretary of State is empowered to make orders to vary provisions (*a*) and (*b*) above to keep them in line with developments in science and technology.

An invention is taken to be new if it does not form part of the state of the art. This is defined in the case of an invention as including all matter (whether a product, a process, information about either or anything else) which has at any time before the priority date (i.e. the date of filing the application for grant) of that invention been made available to the public within or outside the United Kingdom by written or oral description, by use or in any other way (s. 2 (2)). The state of the art also includes matter contained in an application for another patent which was published on or after the priority date of the invention if

(*a*) that matter was contained in the application for that patent both as filed and published; and
(*b*) the priority date of that matter is earlier than that of the invention.

An invention will not be taken to involve an inventive step if it is not obvious to a person skilled in the art with reference to s. 2 (2). An invention is taken to be capable of industrial application if it can be made or used in any kind of industry, including agriculture (s. 4). An invention of a method of treatment of the human or animal body by surgery, therapy or diagnosis is not included as capable of industrial application. However, this does not prevent a product consisting of a substance or composition being so treated merely because it is invented for use in any such method of treatment.

(iii) APPLICATIONS

An application for a patent is made to the Patent Office. If the invention has been made by an employee in his job (as are most of them) the employer owns the invention, subject to qualification, dealt with later, and may apply for a patent with the inventor's consent. Alternatively, a joint application may be made, or the employee may apply, when the grant will be subject to the employer's interest.

A document is filed at the Patent Office called the Complete Specification containing a description of the article, process or machine, including working instructions, and statements known as 'claims' defining in complex legal terms what degree of monopoly is given by the patent. In practice an earlier application is made known as a Provisional Specification containing a very generalized statement about the invention; twelve months after this is filed the Complete Specification must be filed.

The job of negotiating with the Patent Office is normally done by professional patent agents, who also draw up the specifications, since the complicated nature of the work does not encourage faith in a 'do-it-yourself' approach.

An examiner at the Patents Office checks the specification, not the practical operation of the process or machine. In 1924, for instance, the Office was held to accept an application for a perpetual motion machine as long as it was clearly described. This would now be thrown out under the Patents Act as 'so obviously contrary to well established natural laws that the application is frivolous'. If the examiner feels that the specification describes nothing that can be patented it will not be passed. A scheme or idea alone is not enough, it must be a process, a substance, an article. In *W*'s *Application*, 1914, a special navigation marking *system* was rejected although a new method of *constructing* buoys would have been patentable. The problem is particularly difficult with discoveries involving the preparation of substances already existing or discovering new properties of old substances (e.g. penicillin and D.D.T. respectively). In the field of drug invention, if a new chemical has been discovered it is patentable, but if it is simply a new drug the inventor will have the problem that if he includes a useless constituent in the drug it will make the patent invalid.

The main task of the examiner is to see that the claims of the specification describe things that are not only new, but also inventive; the monopoly of making or doing anything that is obvious cannot be given. If the validity of a patent is tested in a court of law the court will consider, amongst other matters, whether the Complete Specification describes anything approximating to an obvious development. The examiner has only to decide at the application stage whether the specification under his consideration is claiming what has been earlier described in a publication, e.g. a 'bonded razor blade', so that if a patent were granted the use or manufacture could be prevented. If an examiner sees anything too close to an earlier specification in the field of the application, the applicants will either have to disprove the examiner's contention, or alter the claims, or even abandon the application.

Once the examiner is satisfied the specification is published and for three months afterwards any interested party can object by notice to the Patent Office. The case will then be heard by a senior official of the Patent Office. In practice this may give the inventor an opportunity to alter part of the specification.

In the event of no opposition or of the failure of objections, the 'Letters Patent' will be sealed and the patentee can sue in the High Court for any infringement since the publication of the Complete Specification. For a year after sealing of the 'Letters Patent' proceedings are available, after which the only way to get the patent revoked is by an expensive court action to obtain invalidation.

The patent, once granted, covers the U.K. and is in force for four years from the date when the Complete Specification was sealed, or can be renewed annually for twenty years (s. 25) (sixteen years in the case of patents existing before the 1977 Act), after which it can be extended by the High Court on application for five years, or exceptionally ten. In practice the invention will not be profitable within the four-year period so that this will have little value.

Since the majority of inventions are made by employees of a firm, the usual practice is that the company buys out their inventions or the service agreement states it is company property (*British Syphon Co. v. Homewood*). The patent can be sold by anyone registered as owner even though other parties have an interest in it. Therefore it is usual for a company and the inventor to register as part owners.

The 1977 Act regulates the right to employees' inventions and compensation of employees for certain inventions. Notwithstanding any rule of law, an invention made by an employee shall, as between him and his employer, be taken to belong to his employer if

(*a*) it was made in the course of the normal duties of the employee or in the course of duties falling outside normal duties, but specifically assigned to him, and the circumstances in either case were such that an invention might reasonably be expected to result from the carrying out of his duties; or
(*b*) the invention was made in the course of the duties of the employee and, at the time of making the invention, because of the nature of his duties and the particular responsibilities arising from the nature of the duties he had a special obligation to further the interest of the employer's undertaking.

Any other invention made by an employee shall, as between him and his employer, be taken for those purposes to belong to the employee (s. 39).

Where it appears to the court or the controller of patents on application by an employee that the latter has made an invention which belongs to the employer for which a patent has been granted, that the patent is of outstanding benefit (having regard, not exclusively, to the size and nature of the employer's undertaking) then, it is just on these facts to award compensation to the employee, the court or comptrollers may do so on the basis of securing for the employee a fair share of the benefit which the employer has derived or might be reasonably expected to derive from the patent or from its exploitation (ss. 40, 41).

(iv) LICENSING

Licensing is a common method of developing a patent. In this case the patentee gives permission for the manufacture, sale, importation or use of the patented article, normally subject to express limits or conditions. A purchaser of an article under licence will be liable to an action for infringement if he does not abide by the limitations.

(v) EVASION OF PATENTS

About half the patents challenged in the law courts, according to an authority, are found to be invalid. In practice those that go unscathed may be equally invalid, but the business community is not prepared to risk infringement. Few actions for infringement are successful and no doubt the costs involved are a serious deterrent to all but the dedicated opponent, who will normally level his legal armoury only at the most important patents.

A competitor may 'design round' and thus avoid infringement. The patents that have been in use for some years are particularly vulnerable. It is vital for the patent agent to foresee in his 'claims' drafting not only existing works but also future developments. If his assessment is wrong his client's patent will be invalid for obviousness because it will be only triflingly different from an earlier patent specification or because he has limited the patent to an inessential feature which means the competitors have only to leave this out to avoid an infringement. Most patents are imitation-proof unless again a determined outflanking is attempted by lawyers and designers advising a rival.

Alternatively, a competitor may produce something differing little from the earlier inventions. The Schick razor, for example, was protected by a valid U.S. patent. Imitative makes were marketed later and the Schick manufacturers successfully sued for infringement as the competitor had used a patent predating the Schick razor but altered it too much. Competition based on earlier designs can be very worrying; in practice the patentee has to rely on goodwill and hope that, as in most cases, the other competitors will steer clear of this method unless the commercial stakes are high. Again, the more important the process or article, the greater the temptation will be.

(vi) ACTION FOR INFRINGEMENT

The circumstances in which an action for infringement may be brought have been touched on already. If a patentee succeeds his patent is likely to be respected in future; if he loses, the patent is either invalidated and the grant revoked or the claims in the specification are found not wide enough to cover the articles or process of the defendant competitor. If a patentee wins he is given a 'certificate of contested validity' which entitles him to considerably larger costs in a future infringement action. In practice it may be wiser to persuade a prospective competitor to license rather than to bring an action against him, or where the patent is fairly certainly valid it may pay to await its expiry and demand damages in an infringement action. Care should be taken to avoid a notification to a competitor that a patent is being infringed reading as a threat of proceedings, as the competitor might be able to obtain an injunction to prevent further threats being made unless the patentee can prove that the acts complained of amount to an infringement.

For the first time a statutory definition of infringement is provided by s. 60 of the 1977 Patents Act. A person infringes a patent for an invention if the following are done in the United Kingdom while the patent is in force without the consent of the proprietor of the patent

(*a*) where the invention being a product, he makes, disposes of, offer to dispose of, uses or imports the product or keeps it for disposal or otherwise;
(*b*) where the invention being a process, he uses or offers it for use in the United Kingdom knowing, or where it would be obvious to a reasonable person in the circumstances, that its use there without the proprietor's consent would be an infringement;
(*c*) where the invention is a process, he disposes or offers to do so, uses or imports any product obtained directly by means of that process or keeps it for disposal or otherwise (s. 60(1)).

It will also constitute infringement where a person (other than the proprietor), while the patent is in force and without the proprietor's consent, supplies or offers to supply in the United Kingdom any of the means, relating to an essential element of the invention, for putting it into effect, to a person other than a licensee or other entitled person when he knows or should reasonably know that those means are suitable, and intended, for putting the invention into effect in the United Kingdom.

The above will not apply to the supply or offer of a staple commercial product unless made to induce the person concerned to do an act amounting to infringement for the purposes of s. 60(1). Among other matters it will not constitute an infringement in the case of an act which is done privately and for non-commercial purposes (s. 60(5)) (*see also* 8:5 regarding the Community Patent Convention).

(vii) MONOPOLY REFERENCES ON PATENTS AND AGRICULTURAL SCHEMES

The Patents Act, s. 51(2), is amended by the Competition Act 1980, s. 14, in respect of application by the Crown in cases of monopoly or'merger. Section 51(2) applies the anti-competitive reference provisions of ss. 5 and 11 of the Competition Act (*see* 2:3) to patented products. The Comptroller of Patents is given power to cancel or modify a condition imposed in relation to patented products or processes where the practice concerned operated or might be expected to operate against the public interest. The Comptroller may, as an alternative to cancellation or modification of such a condition, make an entry in the register to the effect that licences under the patent are to be available as of right.

Section 15 of the Competition Act amends s. 19A(1) of the Agricultural Marketing Act 1958 under which the Minister is given power to make an order under that Act where a report of Commission on a monopoly reference contains certain conclusions. This simply incorporates reference to s. 8 of the Competition Act (conclusions and reports of the Commission).

8:2 DESIGN COPYRIGHT

Prior to 1968 industrial design was protected by registration. Under the Design Copyright Act of 1968 (operational from 25.10.68) the owner of an industrial design can enforce his own copyright against those who infringe it within fifteen years from the date he first marketed the designed articles; after that period the design can be used without infringement.

In order to bring an action for infringement the following prerequisites are necessary:

(i) an example of the copyright article, in model or drawn form,
(ii) an article that has been either directly or indirectly copied from the copyright work,
(iii) a person must have copied it, or possess, or have possessed the copy,
(iv) the copy must have been made within fifteen years after the article was first marketed.

8:3 COPYRIGHT

The Copyright Act 1956 (as amended by the Copyright Amendment Act 1971) defines copyright and how it is infringed. Part 1 deals with copyright in original works. Part 2 deals with copyright in sound recordings, films, television and sound broadcasts. Part 3 deals with remedies for infringement of copyright. Parts 4 and 5 deal with the Performing Rights Tribunal and the extent or limits of the Act, respectively. Part 6 includes provisions for assignment and licensing of copyright, broadcasting and use of copyright material for education.

Copyright law exists primarily to protect the fruits of a person's work from exploitation by others. It is unlawful as an infringement of copyright to reproduce or copy any literary, dramatic, musical or artistic work.

Copyright extends to practically everything published or unpublished that can be called a work if produced in the United Kingdom or in any other country to which the Act extends (s. 1 (1)). The Act includes as subjects of copyright: novels or other 'literary works' (which includes tables and compilations); lecturers' addresses, speeches, sermons; plays, film scripts, ballets and 'entertainments in dumb show' (the last two included as 'dramatic works'); artistic works which include paintings, drawings, engravings, photographs, sculpture, works of 'artistic craftsmanship' not covered under any other heading and works of architecture; music; records, tapes, perforated rolls and other devices for producing sounds (e.g. pianola rolls), sound and television broadcasts; book typography.

Copyright comes into existence without the need for formalities. Thus the question of ownership of copyright may never arise unless and until the copyright is disputed. Copyright belongs initially to the author of the work, that is the person who provides the work, knowledge or skill by which the work is copyright. Exceptionally where the author is not the first owner of the copyright and the work is commissioned by another who agrees to pay for it then the copyright belongs to the person giving the commission. The second example would be when the author of the work is employed by another under a contract of service and the work is made in the course of employment. In such cases the copyright belongs to the employer.

Copyright in a work will be infringed if the work is copied, without the consent of the owner of the copyright. The Act uses the term reproducing the work, or a substantial part, in a material form. However, copying is essential to this type of infringement. It is enough to show for an infringement that the work complained of derives, in some way from the original. Copying need not be direct nor conscious or deliberate. It will usually be difficult to prove infringement as it is rare to be able to prove directly that copying has taken place. The reproduction has to be a substantial part of the original work.

Of particular importance is commercial dealing in works which infringe copyright. Case examples are given subsequently.

The periods of copyright for each category under the 1956 Act are as follows:

(a) literary, dramatic and musical works—fifty years from the death of the author or publication, whichever is later;
(b) artistic works—fifty years from publication for a photograph, fifty years from the death of the author or publication (whichever is later) for an engraving; fifty years from the death of the author for other artistic works.
(c) films (this includes a recorded television programme)—fifty years from registration in the case of a British film under the Cinematograph Films Act registration provisions, otherwise fifty years from publication, that is release of copies of the film.
(d) sound recordings—fifty years from publication, i.e. issue to the public records (or tapes).
(e) broadcasts—both the BBC and the ITA have a special copyright in their own broadcasts, which lasts for fifty years from the first broadcast.

Books generally carry the year of first publication (as this one does) and records are required to under the Act. As a general rule it is not easy to discover when copyright expires. There are still a number, if diminishing proportion, of works in existence that have copyright pre-dating the 1956 Act; to an extent the old law is applicable.

These cases are not sufficient to be of practical importance and it is enough to assume the 1956 Act operated retrospectively.

The House of Lords recently considered a case involving infringement of copyright in a fabric design.

Example

Infabrics made printed fabrics for use in manufacturing shirts and owned the copyright in a fabric design known as 'the P design'. In March 1974 Infabrics' representative visited Jaytex, who were shirt wholesalers, and showed a director of Jaytex a portfolio of designs, including the P design. In July 1974 the director of Jaytex while in Hong Kong was shown about two thousand fabric designs including the P design by a Hong Kong textile company. The Jaytex director did not recall that Infabrics had shown him the design and he selected it and others from the Hong Kong company for the manufacture of shirts for export to the United Kingdom. Infabrics discovered shirts bearing the P design on offer for sale in London. Infabrics wrote to Jaytex in February 1975 claiming to be the owners of the copyright in the design. Jaytex responded that they had purchased the fabric in good faith in Hong Kong without knowledge that any copyright was being infringed. In May Infabrics issued a writ against Jaytex claiming damages under ss. 17 and 18 of the Copyright Act 1956 for infringement of copyright and conversion. Infabrics relied, in part, on the 'publication' of the design when the shirts were offered for sale in London as constituting an infringement of copyright under s. 3 (5) of the Copyright Act. If proved, such an infringement being a primary infringement, Jaytex could not use the defense of lack of knowledge of copyright. After the court of first instance had held that sale and distribution of the shirts by Jaytex did not amount to infringement by publishing the design, the Court of Appeal held that publishing was not restricted to the first publication of a previously unpublished work. Therefore Jaytex had published the design and were consequently liable in conversion for the infringement under s. 18 (1) to pay for the value of all the shirts with the P design on, sold by them. Jaytex appealed to the House of Lords.

Held: The appeal would be allowed for the following reasons: (i) As the long established distinction in copyright law between published and unpublished works had not been changed by the 1956 Act on the true construction of s. 3 (5) (*b*) of the Act, infringement by 'publishing the work' meant making available to the public a work previously unpublished. This excluded sales or the issue of reproductions to the public unless such sale or issue was the first publication of the work. As Infabrics had already made public the P design in the United Kingdom it followed that Jaytex had not 'published' the design within s. 3 (5) (*b*) and had not committed a primary infringement of the design when they sold the shirts manufactured in Hong Kong.

(ii) The remedy for conversion under s. 18 (1) of the 1956 Act was in addition, or alternative, to the remedy of damages and depended on proof of infringement. If a plaintiff failed to establish infringement he had no independent cause of action in infringement. Infabrics having failed to establish infringement they were not entitled to damages for conversion.

(iii) The measure of damages in conversion under s. 18 (1) is the value of the 'infringing copies' within s. 18 (3) on the basis that the plaintiff is entitled to damages as if he were the owner of the articles.

(*Infabrics Ltd. v. Jaytex Ltd.*, 1981)

Infringement has recently been considered in relation to public performance of a record.

Example

The Performing Rights Society (the Society) exploited the performing rights in musical works by taking assignments in the performing rights of composers' works who became members of the Society. The Society had sole right under its articles to authorize, permit or forbid the exercise of the performing rights assigned to it. The Society exploited the performing rights in the recordings of composers' works by granting licenses in return for fees to persons who habitually played the recordings in public. The licence fees were divided amongst the members of the Society. After 1976, by a change of policy, the Society sought to recover fees from the owners of record shops for playing records of works assigned to the Society over loudspeakers in the shops. The defendants, record shop owners, did not obtain a licence from, or pay a fee to the Society for playing records over loudspeakers. They argued that playing records in this way promoted record sales generally and as a result increased the royalties payable to the composers of the works. The Society claimed that playing the records without a licence or payment of a fee to the Society infringed its performing rights in the works and sought an injunction restraining the defendants' alleged infringement. The defendants denied infringement and counter-claimed for a declaration that the playing of records did not constitute performance 'in public' within s. 2 (5) (*a*) of the Copyright Act 1956. As an alternative the defandants claimed a declaration that the exclusive right of public performance of the works, granted by the assignments of the performing rights, was subject to an implied reservation to the composers (assigners) of the right to licence record shops to play records of their works to promote sales of the records.

Held: The Society was granted the injunction sought for the following reasons: (i) the playing of records in each shop constituted a performance in public with s. 2 (5) (a) of the 1956 Act as a performance given to an audience consisting of members of the public present in shops which the public at large was permitted and encouraged to enter with a view to purchasing records and increasing the shop owner's profit could only be described as a performance in public; (ii) since the evidence showed that a prudent record shop owner would pay a fee to the Society rather than cease playing records in his shop, it had not been shown that restraining performance in the record shops would reduce record sales and thereby injure the composers. Additionally, if the composers took the view that the Society should charge a fee for performance of the records to potential purchasers such an audience would form part of the 'composer's public' in that the composers would expect to receive a fee for the performances and unauthorized performances would constitute an infringement of the composer's rights; (iii) no term could be implied in the assignment to the Society of the performing rights that the composers reserved the right to licence performances of recordings of their works in record shops.

(*Performing Rights Society Ltd. v. Harlequin Record Shops Ltd.*, 1979)

Infringement of copyright in resale records was recently at issue in the case of a person having a limited interest in the copyright.

Example

The defendant purchased in the U.S.A. for resale in England records made by CBS Inc., an American company, which as owner or exclusive licensee of the copyright in records it made had granted exclusive rights to an English subsidiary, CBS Ltd., to manufacture and market the same records in the United Kingdom. The records purchased and resold by the defendant included new releases from CBS Inc. which CBS Ltd. intended to release on the United Kingdom market at a later date. CBS Ltd. brought an action for infringement of copyright against the defendant, claiming that its actions adversely affected the sales of CBS Ltd. in the United Kingdom, and seeking an interlocutory injunction restraining the defendant from importing, selling or distributing in the United Kingdom without CBS Ltd.'s licence records made by CBS Inc. in respect of which CBS Ltd. was exclusive licensee. CBS Ltd. argued that the defendant had infringed CBS Ltd.'s copyright under s. 16 (2) and (3) (a) of the Copyright Act as it had, without the licence of the owner, imported an article into the United Kingdom and sold it when the defendant knew the making of that article would have constituted an infringement of copyright if the article had been made in the United Kingdom. CBS Ltd. further argued that it was entitled to bring the action against the defendant because CBS Ltd. as the exclusive licensee was to be treated as the owner of the copyright and thus manufacture by someone else, including CBS Inc., in the United Kingdom would have constituted infringement.

Alternatively, for the purposes of s. 16 (2) and (3) it was to be assumed that the maker of the records was not CBS Inc. but the importer (the defendant) or any other person not specifically authorized to make the records in the United Kingdom, therefore manufacture by the defendant or any other unauthorized person in the United Kingdom would have constituted infringement. CBS Ltd. submitted that even if CBS Inc. were assumed to be the 'maker' of the records for the purposes of s. 16 (2) and (3) there had nevertheless been an infringement of copyright at the suit of CBS Ltd. since by virtue of being the exclusive licensee of the United Kingdom recording rights it was to be treated as 'owner' of those rights for the purposes of s. 16. Therefore any manufacture by CBS Inc. in England would infringe CBS Ltd.'s rights.

Held: The defendant had not infringed copyright at the suit of CBS Ltd. for primarily the following reasons: (i) CBS Ltd. could not claim to be treated as 'owner' of the copyright for the purposes of s. 16 (2) and (3) because the Act kept the normal distinction between an assignee and a licensee and so treated a licensee of copyright (as CBS Ltd. was) as merely having contractual rather than proprietary rights. If it was assumed that the hypothetical maker of the records in the United Kingdom was the actual maker (i.e. CBS Inc.), there would have been no infringement of copyright since as owner of the copyright CBS Inc. was protected by s. 1 (2) of the Act. CBS Inc. could not claim to be treated as owner of the copyright under s. 49 (5) of the Act as the words 'or otherwise' in the section merely applied to rights in a copyright conferred on different persons without any assignment or licence and did not cover an exclusive licensee. It followed that an exclusive licensee (e.g. CBS Ltd.) was not a person entitled to the copyright and was not the owner of the copyright under s. 49 (5); (ii) CBS Ltd. was also unable to claim that for the purposes of s. 16 (2); and (iii) the hypothetical maker of the records in the United Kingdom was the importer or any unauthorized person who might have made the records there because s. 16 (2) and (3) assumed the 'maker' to be the person who actually made the article abroad (e.g. CBS Inc.). This followed from the fact that the person assumed to be the 'maker' of an imported article had to be the same for purposes of s. 16 (2) and (3) and s. 5 (2) and (3) which related to the importation of literary, dramatic and other works. There was no obvious reason why in each of these subsections the assumed maker should be the importer, having regard to the fact that very often the original maker would be known or readily ascertainable whereas the identity of the importer would not.

(*CBS United Kingdom Ltd. v. Charmdale Record Distributors Ltd.*, 1980)

The House of Lords recently considered the effectiveness of an assignment of copyright in songs some of which had been assigned before the 1911 Copyright Act and others before the 1956 Act.

Example

Music publishers, the appellants, acquired in the course of their business numerous copyrights from songwriters and exploited and promoted the songs on payment of royalties to the songwriters and their successors in title. In some cases the words of a song had been written by one person and the music by another. Under the 1911 Copyright Act copyright in a work by its first owner reverted to the author's legal personal representatives as part of his estate twenty-five years after his death except where the work was a 'collective work' within s. 35 (1) of the 1911 Act. The respondent company was the assignee from persons claiming under the estates of deceased songwriters of copyrights in the words and music of many songs exploited by the appellant publishers. The respondent company claimed to be entitled to the copyright in many of the songs on the ground that the works were not collective works under s. 35 (1) of the 1911 Act.

In 1934 the author of the words of one of the songs and the composer of the music assigned their copyright to New York publisher and transferred to them copyright including world copyright. By an agreement made in 1948 in New York the administratrix of the composer of the music of that song sold U.S. renewal copyright in the music to the publishers for a further twenty-eight years. A clause in that agreement provided that the publisher should pay 50 per cent of all receipts from sales until the expiration of the copyrights in all countries outside the U.S. and Canada. In another case the songwriter had written and assigned them before the 1911 Copyright Act. The appellant music publisher claimed that the assignments constituted an 'express agreement' under the 1911 Act (s. 24 (1)) so as to vest the extended term of copyright under the Act in them which but for that agreement would have passed to the songwriter's personal representatives. The respondent company denied that the assignments had this effect.

Held: The House of Lords dismissed the appeal on the grounds that (i) "copyright in a collective work" meant one which existed in addition and separate from any copyright which might exist in its constituent parts. Although the words of a song and its music each had copyright those copyrights did not merge to form a third and separate copyright in each song. Therefore the songs themselves were not collective works and the exception in s. 35 (1) of the 1911 Act did not apply. The copyright in the songs therefore reverted to the author's personal representative; (ii) the terms of the 1948 agreement were not wide enough to cover the reversionary rights of the copyright. The clause in agreement relating to 50% payment by the publisher of all receipts from sales did not, on its true construction, involve such an assignment; and (iii) 'express agreement' in the 1911 Act meant an agreement which referred to the substitution right in terms clearly identifying the right by naming it. A general expression was not sufficient. The assignments of copyrights made under the agreements made *before* the 1911 Act did not vest in the appellants the extended terms of copyright given by the Act, which therefore passed to the personal representatives of the authors of the works.

(Chappell & Co. Ltd. v. Redwood Music Ltd., 1980)

The problem of 'pirating' dates back to Shakespeare and before. A current example of the legal problems confronting owners of copyright is exemplified in an illustrative case concerning the selling of unauthorized video cassettes.

Example

The appellants, film companies owning copyright in films which they produced, believed that certain unauthorized persons were pirating copies of their films and recording and selling unauthorized video cassettes of them. Writs were issued by the film companies against suspected unauthorized persons seeking an injunction restraining them from infringing the appellants' copyright. The appellants sought and were granted orders which, amongst other matters, required the respondents to disclose (i) the names and addresses of persons who supplied the cassettes and the customers who bought them; (ii) the whereabouts of all pirate cassettes and master copies known to the respondents; (iii) all invoices, letters and other documents relating to the cassettes. The respondents argued that if they were compelled to disclose the information they would incriminate themselves by providing evidence on which they could be prosecuted and convicted of breach of s. 21 of the Copyright Act 1956, breach of s. 18 of the Theft Act 1968 and conspiracy to defraud at common law. A person associated with the respondents in the pirating of films was in the course of being prosecuted on charges of conspiracy to defraud. At first instance the judge dismissed the respondents application but the Court of Appeal held the orders requiring disclosure should be struck out as they were contrary to the principle against self-incrimination. The appellant film companies appealed to the House of Lords for reinstatement of the order.

Held: Since a charge of conspiracy against the respondents to defraud was not a remote possibility but exactly described what the respondents and others involved had done, disclosure by the respondents of the information sought would tend to expose them to such a charge which, if proved, attracted heavy penalties. It followed that the claim of privilege against self-incrimination would be upheld. There was no way in which the court could compel disclosure while simultaneously protecting the respondents from the consequences of self-incrimination. This was so because an express restriction imposed by the court on the use of information disclosed would be binding only on the appellants and not on anyone else who bought a criminal prosecution.

The court noted that in cases involving large-scale and systematic infringements of copyright (such as in the case before it), offences against s. 21 of the 1956 Act are probably too trivial, with regards to the £50 fine, to be taken into account when considering whether a claim for privilege against self-incrimination should succeed. The risk of successful prosecution under s. 18 of the Theft Act 1968, which applies to theft of property, was too remote to be considered because copyright is not 'property' for the purposes of s. 18. Per Lord Russell: Because the privilege against incrimination could largely deprive the owner of copyright of his just rights to the protection of his property, legislation similar to s. 31 of the 1968 Act would be welcome. The aim of such legislation should be to remove the privilege while at the same time preventing the use in criminal proceedings of statements that would otherwise be privilege.

(*Rank Film v. Video Information Centre*, 1981)

Under the 1956 Copyright Act a design in the form of drawings will be copyright if they were made after June 1957 when the Act came into force. Copyright will cover a sculpture and possibly most moulded articles; 'a work of artistic craftsmanship' will come under copyright, presumably as it is more than ordinary assembly or machine finishing; much may turn on the complexity and arresting design qualities of the article.

In *George Hensher Ltd. v. Restawile*, 1974, the House of Lords decided that furniture designers had no artistic copyright under Act in a three-piece suite of furniture, indicating in their speeches that any attempt to lay down general guidance on the question of artistic craftsmanship should not be part of their function. Lord Morris gave his opinion that 'the thing produced must be assessed without giving decisive weight to the author's scheme of things'.

Under s. 9 (8) of the Copyright Act there will be no infringement with regard to drawings if the article complained of is not regarded by non-experts as a reproduction. In *Dorling v. Honnor Marine Ltd.*, 1964, the court held that a boat did reproduce the general arrangement drawing of the plans from which it was constructed.

If an article is infringing a copyright design or an imported article comes under this heading, the owner of the copyright can demand its surrender and damages if it is sold. Even if an importer or manufacturer pleads ignorance, a copyright owner will usually obtain an injunction against repetition.

If a design is registered the court has to decide if the registered design and the defendant's are basically similar. Rather like a patent, a design, to be valid, must be new in relation to existing designs, which means registration before marketing. A design registration is valid for five years and can be renewed for two additional periods of five years.

The Whitford Committee on Copyright and Design Law (Cmnd. 6732) reported in March 1977 with recommendations for the reform of the existing law. Their main conclusion was that an attempt should be made to recover a copyright fee or royalty by means of blanket licensing (in a manner akin to that applying to public performance of music in copyright). The recommendation was for the division amongst owners of pooled copyright of the product of an annual fee for permission to make reprographic copies for purposes other than for public distribution (such as teaching and research). Fair dealing exemptions under existing copyright law would be withdrawn once such a blanket licensing scheme was in operation. This main proposal of the Whitford Committee has come under attack, largely from educational circles, and, despite its merits, will require further elaboration before legislation is enacted.

THE PUBLIC LENDING RIGHT ACT 1979

The Public Lending Right Act 1979 establishes a public lending right. This gives authors the right to receive payments from a central fund in respect of such of the books as are lent out to the public by local library authorities in the United Kingdom. The Registrar of Public Lending Rights has the duty of establishing and maintaining a register which shows books which are affected by the right and listing persons entitled to that right in respect of any registered book. The public lending right attached to a book runs from the date of the book's first publication (or, if later, the beginning of the year in which application is made for it to be registered) until fifty years from the end of the year in which the author died.

8:4   TRADE MARKS

(i) NATURE OF TRADE MARKS

A trade mark has been described in an official publication as 'a symbol (whether word, device or a combination of the two) which a person uses in the course of trade in order that his goods may be readily distinguished by the purchasing public from similar goods of traders'. Registration is not compulsory and many commonly used trade marks are unregistered either because their proprietors are content with this situation or because the marks do not qualify for registration. Statutory provision for trade mark registration is limited to marks either used or proposed to be used in relations to goods.

Registration confers a statutory monopoly in the use of that mark regarding goods for which it is registered and a registered owner may sue for infringement. Section 9(1) of the Trade Marks Act 1938 lays down the criteria for deciding whether a trade mark is sufficiently distinctive for registration in Part A of the register; one of the following particulars must be present:

(*a*) the name of the company, individual or firm represented in a special or particular manner;
(*b*) the signature of the applicant for registration or some predecessor in business;
(*c*) an invented word or words;
(*d*) a word or words having no direct reference to the character or quality of the goods, and not being according to its ordinary signification a geographical name or surname;
(*e*) any other distinctive mark.

Registration of a trade mark on Part B of the register gives less protection than those registered on Part A, but less distinctiveness is required. In an infringement action a Part B trade mark owner may be met with the defence of a defendant that the use of the mark was not done in a way likely to mislead the public.

(ii) REGISTRATION

In order to be registered a trade mark must be distinctive, in that it distinguishes the owner's goods from those of others. Marks whose distinctiveness must be proved are a large group that may become registrable when use has made them familiar. In *Dunlop*'s *Application*, 1942, 'Trakgrip' was registered for tyres by Dunlop, proving that only they used it and others in the trade did not do so or did not wish to. Some marks can never be distinctive. These are marks that anyone might wish to use. In *Yorkshire Copper Works' Application*, 1954, registration was refused for the mark 'Yorkshire' on pipe fittings although the applicants showed that the whole trade understood it to refer only to their product. Other marks are deemed to be distinctive due to either imaginative, made-up words or designs. Refusal of registration will only occur where it can be shown to be in common use in the trade or too similar to existing marks.

A mark must also show a trade connection, however small, between the mark owner and his goods. Unless this connection is present the mark is not used as a trade mark. In practice a mark used widely for a long period is not likely to be used by competitors. Even if the mark is unregistrable in trading terms this may be unimportant, although it may be inadvisable to attempt registration of such a mark as the chances of failure are high.

In one case, a firm began to manufacture vacuum cleaners under the 'Electrix' mark in 1936; a vacuum cleaner under the 'Electrolux' mark had been marketed since 1928. The makers of 'Electrix' debated registering under 'Electrux' but did not use this until 1947. In an action against the use of 'Electrix' by the 'Electrolux' firm in 1953 the court decided it was an infringement but refused to grant an injunction. The makers of 'Electrix' were unable to register this mark on the grounds it was similar to 'Electrics' and so was totally unregistrable (*Electrix Ltd.'s Application*, 1959).

(iii) APPLICATION

Application to register is made to the Register of Trade Marks at the Patents Office, which is part of the Department of Trade. The firm, company or person intending to use the trade mark applies; there may be instances where two or more apply, for example the overseas manufacturer and the sole importer of his goods.

The Registrar may object that a mark is not distinctive, or too like those in use, or illegal, indecent or misleading. A case may be argued before the Registrar by a trade mark agent or by counsel. Appeal may be made to the High Court or to the Department of Trade. If the Registrar does not object the intention to register will be advertised in *The Trade Marks Journal*. Opposition may be brought on grounds of similarity and misleading the public. In one case the Registrar allowed an application to register a triangular mark for beer on condition it was a white one. One appeal to the House of Lords they forbade its use on bottled beer (*Bass Ratcliff Gretton Ltd. v. Nicholson & Sons Ltd.*, 1932).

(iv) INFRINGEMENT

If a trade mark is used on goods not belonging to the registered trade mark owner, or another mark is used very similar to his, then an action for infringement can be brought. The following rulings have been made: 'Watermatic' infringed 'Aquamatic' (toy pistols), 'Pem Books' infringed 'Pan Books'—but 'Gala' did *not* infringe 'Goya' (cosmetics) nor 'Kidax' infringe

'Daks' (clothing). However, if goods are honestly described with little likelihood of the public being misled this will not amount to infringement—e.g. 'Yale', 'Vaseline', 'Biro', and 'Thermos'.

Infringement of registered trade marks is rare. When it does happen an action can be brought against the person using the mark on his goods or the importer (in the case of goods marked overseas) or any person who trades in them. It is an implied condition under the Sale of Goods Act 1893 (s. 12) that the seller has title to pass to the buyer; this will not be the case where goods are sold with an infringing mark.

(v) REFORM

The Mathys Committee on British Trade Mark Law and Practice Report of 1974 (Cmnd. 5601) found no basic defects in the present trade-mark system in this country. With reference to the E.E.C. moves towards a community trade-mark system (which has now taken shape as the Memorandum on the Creation of an E.E.C. Trade-Mark (Sec. (76) 2462 SEC)) the Report generally welcomes this but urges retention of a strong examination of applications and a well-controlled register. The Report recommended the abandonment of the B register and the substitution of its lower standards of distinctiveness for all registrations.

(vi) EEC PROPOSALS ON TRADE MARKS

The Commission of the European Communities has recently published two major proposals which have potentially far-reaching effects on trade mark law and practice with the EEC.

The proposals are the 'Proposal for a First Council Directive to Approximate the Laws of the Member States relating to Trade Marks' (the Draft Directive) and 'Proposal for a Council Regulation on Community Trade Marks' (the Draft Regulation). Their full implications cannot be considered here; only an outline is given.

(a) *Draft Directive*

The purpose of the Draft Directive is to require Member States to legislate so far as it is necessary for their trade marks to conform to the terms laid down. Article 2 (3) provides essentially that a trade mark will be invalidated where goods for which it is registered in the Member State concerned have been marketed in another Member State under another trade mark by the proprietor or with his consent. This has been criticised on the grounds that the Article is based on the false assumption that if a trader uses different marks for the same goods in different States, he does so in order to maintain separate markets. The requirement for surrender could encourage pirating in that a formerly used mark could become free for use by a competitor with resultant deception of the public. Article 3 provides that the exclusive right given to a domestic proprietor will entitle him to prevent use of a sign identical or similar to the trade mark where such use creates a serious likelihood of confusion on the part of the public. This provision appears to exclude from consideration possible confusion in the trade which is an important factor in whether protection to proprietors under the 1938 Trade Marks Act is reduced. There is concern that the trade mark rights could be diluted. Article 10 provides that where a proprietor of a trade mark or other exclusive right has acquiesced in the use in one Member State of a later trade mark likely to create confusion with his mark or right, that proprietor shall not be entitled to apply for invalidation of the later trade marks or prohibit its use. This is unless the application for the later trade mark was made in bad faith. The criticism here is that a trader in one State may be prevented from asserting his right there because he has known of use for three years, in another State by another person of a conflicting mark but has no right to prevent the use of the mark in that State. Also a trader in one State may be prevented from asserting his right there because he took no action in another State where he has registration of the same mark registered in his home State. This would be so where under the laws of the second State there was no likelihood of confusion.

(b) The Draft Regulation

The purpose of this proposal is to provide a unitary trade mark, registrable on a single application covering the whole of the Community. The rights of national trade mark owners are likely to be affected by the proposal. In proceedings opposing the granting of a registration the opponent, relying on his prior national registration, has to establish a serious likelihood of confusion of the public in the territory in which the earlier trade mark had effect (Article 7). This provision can be criticised on the same grounds as Article 3 of the draft directive—that confusion in the trade is excluded from consideration.

If traders in the United Kingdom are not permitted to rely on common law rights (as may be the case under the preamble to the Directive) in opposing applications for the Community trade marks these traders will be put at a considerable disadvantage in addition to those already outlined. It may be that a greater degree of flexibility would encourage registration. This could be done by allowing registration of a Community mark with a disclaimer to protect local descriptive use.

8:5 PASSING OFF

In law no trader may by his conduct lead customers to mistake his business, services or goods for another's. To do so basically constitutes the tort (civil wrong) of passing off. This can take many forms which range from near infringement of trade marks to misleading packaging or misuse of business and trading names.

These are the chief methods of passing off:

(i) MARKETING A PRODUCT AS THAT OF THE PLAINTIFF

Example

A firm acquired car windscreen wipers direct from sub-contractors of the plaintiff manufacturing company and passed them off as their own.

Held: The manufacturers could obtain damages against the defendants. As the manufacturing company normally checked the wipers the defendants were held to represent that this had been done.

(*Vokes Ltd. v. F. J. Evans and Marble Arch Motor Supplies*, 1931)

(ii) USING THE PLAINTIFF'S TRADE MARK

If registration cannot be proved, or it does not cover the goods in point, or the mark is invalid, no infringement action is possible, but a passing-off action will be a valid alternative (s. 2 Trade Marks Act 1938).

(iii) USING THE PLAINTIFF'S TRADE NAME

Example

When broadcasting with his band the plaintiff used the name 'Dr. Crock and his Crack-pots'. After leaving the programme the defendant gave the same title to a replacement band.
Held: An injunction would be granted to restrain the defendant from doing this.

(Hines v. Winnick, 1947)

Protection will be given to a business which enjoys goodwill in England even if it is situated abroad.

Example

In December 1975 the defendants opened a restaurant in Norwich under the name 'Maxims' and furnished it in such a style to give it a French atmosphere. Maxims Ltd., an English company brought an action against the defendants. It claimed that since 1907 it had owned a famous restaurant in Paris known as Maxims which enjoyed fame and goodwill in England and that the English public understood the name Maxims to refer to the plaintiff's restaurant. The plaintiff contended that the defendant's restraurant was run at a much lower standard than Maxims in Paris and that the defendant's conduct was calculated to injure the plaintiff's goodwill and reputation. The plaintiff never had any business in England. The plaintiff claimed injunctions to restrain the defendant from operating a restaurant under the name Maxims and from passing off or attempting to pass off in any other manner her business as the plaintiff's business.
Held: The existence and extent of a plaintiff's reputation and goodwill in his business was in every case a question of fact. A plaintiff could therefore establish that he had goodwill in England in respect of a foreign business which the courts would protect without it having to be shown that he carried on business in England. Relief would be granted as it has to be assumed that the plaintiff had proved it had a reputation and goodwill in England derived from its restaurant business in Paris.

(Maxims Ltd. v. Dye, 1977)

The courts are more prone to protect a fanciful name such as 'Apollinaris' or ones associated with places—e.g. 'Chartreuse' liqueurs. Even if the argument is raised that the word as used describes only a type not a trade name it is unlikely to succeed.

Example

The defendants described cigars as 'Corona' and when sued by the original manufacturers argued the word only described a cigar of a particular size. *Held:* The defendants were liable.

(*Havana Cigar and Tobacco Factories Ltd. v. Oddenino*, 1924)

(iv) USING THE PLAINTIFF'S NAME

A person may honestly trade under his own name or one he has used for some time without doing so unlawfully. But if the goods in his name are described in a confusing manner, good faith is no defence.

Example

The plaintiff published a best-selling unexpurgated edition of *My Life and Loves* by Frank Harris. The defendant purchased the rights and published an abridged and expurgated edition under the same title.
Held: The defendant had committed the tort of 'passing off'.

(*W. H. Allen & Co. Ltd. v. Brown Watson Ltd.*, 1965)

Unfair competition as a concept was applied in a case involving the marketing of fictitious names. This is known as 'character merchandising' and in America merchandising is protected by an independent tort of unfair competition.

Example

The plaintiffs, which were assignees of the author of numerous 'Womble' books and television programmes, sought to prevent the defendant company, named 'Wombles Skip', who were contractors, from trading on the Wombles reputation for cleanliness. There had been no breach of copyright and there had been no attempt to register the name 'Wombles' as a trademark.
Held: The plaintiff's application would be refused as the defendants were not engaged in 'a common field of activity'. Therefore the plaintiffs had failed to establish the tort of passing off.

(*Wombles v. Wombles Skip*, 1977)

(see also *Traverner Rutledge v. Trexaplan*, 1977—the Kojak lollipop case)

The issue of passing off and unfair competition was raised in a case concerning the fictitious adventures of an Australian amorist.

Example

A television series was made by the defendants, the Australian Broadcasting Commission (ABC), based on the amorous adventures of 'Alvin Purple' who had starred in two similar films made and distributed by the plaintiffs. The ABC had obtained the services of a number of those involved in the original screenplay, including the scriptwriter and 'Alvin Purple'. The plaintiffs claimed against the ABC, chiefly on grounds of passing off and unfair competition.
Held: The court found there was a prima facie case on both of those grounds. However injunctive relief was refused on the basis that the plaintiffs had acquiesced in the ABC making the television series. 'The cases seem to be to assert that unfair competition is an extension of the doctrine of passing off or possibly a new and independent tort. It consists of misappropriation of what equitably belongs to a competitor,' (per Needham J.)

(*Hexagon Property v. Australian Broadcasting Commission*, 1976)

(v) IMITATING THE APPEARANCE OF THE PLAINTIFF'S GOODS

If the handling, processing or operation of goods requires a particular appearance this will not amount to passing off, nor if all types of a manufactured product have a common shape or size, etc. But what is known in trading circles as 'get-up' will often come under passing off. In one case a manufacturer of laundry blue who marketed with a knobbed stick in the middle of the container was able to prevent a competitor from imitating it, by proving the appearance was not simply functional.

The decision of the Court of Appeal in *Hoffman La Roche v. D.D.S.A. Pharmaceuticals*, 1972, shows that if the colour combination given to a drug is sufficiently striking this characteristic may be successfully protected in a passing-off action.

The Privy Council recently decided a case which involved imitation of an advertising campaign and get-up of goods marketed in Australia.

Example

In 1974 the appellants began marketing in Australia a lemon-flavoured drink called 'Solo'. The drink was sold mainly in cans similar to those used for beer and had a distinctive colour and a medallion device also akin to those commonly found on beer cans. The marketing of Solo was accompanied by an intensive national television and radio advertising campaign emphasizing Solo as a drink associated with rugged masculine endeavour and evoking memories of the sort of squash drink hotels and bars used to make in the past. The campaign which ran, with a brief break, until 1977 was remarkably successful and by 1977 Solo was selling well.

In 1975 the respondents launched a similar product called 'Pub Squash'. This was sold in cans of the same type, colour and medallion device as Solo accompanied by a similar (if lower key) television campaign emphasizing mateship and masculinity. In 1976 the appellants noted a 15 per cent drop in sales of Solo which they attributed to the introduction of Pub Squash and the way in which the respondents had deliberately copied the appellants' advertising campaign for Solo. The appellants brought an action against the respondents claiming, amongst other matters, damages on account of profits and an injunction in respect of the passing off of Pub Squash as Solo. The claim was dismissed by the New South Wales Supreme Court on the basis that the promoters of Pub Squash had sufficiently distinguished their product from Solo and although the respondents had deliberately taken advantage of the Solo campaign they had not represented Pub Squash as Solo. The appellants then appealed to Privy Council. *Held:* The tort of passing off was not linked to the name or trade mark of a product or business but was wide enough to cover other descriptive material which was part of the goodwill of the plaintiffs product, such as slogans or visual images associated with a plaintiffs product by means of an advertising campaign. The test of this attachment of goodwill to the material was whether the plaintiff had acquired an intangible property right in his product by virtue of the product deriving from the advertising a distinctive character recognized by the market. In applying that test the court had to bear in mind the balance to be struck between protecting the plaintiffs' investment in his product and the protection of free competition.

The two themes used by the appellants in their radio and television advertising campaign to promote Solo, although descriptive of the type of product advertised, had never become a distinguishing feature of the product or generally associated with it. Although the promoters of Pub Squash had deliberately taken advantage of the appellants' advertising campaign for Solo the consuming public were not deceived or misled by either the get up, the formula or the advertising of Pub Squash into thinking that it was Solo. The appellants had not established a cause of action for passing off against the respondents and the appeal would be dismissed.

(*Cadbury Schweppes Pty. Ltd. v. Pub Squash Co. Pty. Ltd.*, 1981)

(vi) MISLEADING PURCHASERS BY SELLING LOW-GRADE GOODS OF THE PLAINTIFF

If goods are sold of a quality inferior to those currently marketed by the plaintiff the result may be that prospective buyers are misled into believing these lower-grade goods are a typical sample. Gillette, for example, were able to obtain an injunction to restrain a dealer from selling used Gillette razor blades as 'genuine'. Wilts United Dairies similarly succeeded in an action against a firm who sold old tins of their canned milk.

(vii) FALSE ADVERTISING

Only exceptionally will this ever amount to passing off.

Example

The defendants deliberately copied the plaintiff's catalogue so that the public would believe their products were those of the plaintiff; this was done by using similar ordering key-words in the catalogue; the defendants' goods were inferior to the plaintiff's.
Held: The defendants had passed off their goods as those of the plaintiff.

(*Masson Seeley & Co. Ltd. v. Embossotype Manufacturing Co.*, 1924)

In all cases of passing off it must be shown that the parties to an action are competing in some business or trading field.

Example

A Spanish wine was marketed by the defendants as 'Spanish Champagne'. An action was brought against them by champagne manufacturers in Champagne, France, on the grounds that the public were mistakenly purchasing the defendants' product believing they were buying champagne from its traditional manufacturing area.
Held: The defendants had passed off their product as the plaintiff's.

(*J. Bollinger v. Costa Brava Wine Co.*, 1961)

Note: It had been held that the intention behind the use by producers of the terms 'champagne cider' and 'champagne perry' was to transfer the glamour of champagne to their products, which potentially led to confusion and deception, intended or not, and an injunction to restrain such usage was granted.

(Bulmer (H.P.) Ltd. v. J. Bollinger S.A., 1974)

An Australian 'champagne case' was recently decided in the Federal Court.

Example

The plaintiffs, a professional body of French wine producers, sought interlocutory injunctions to restrain the use, amongst other matters, of the word 'champagne' in advertisements for wine imported other than from France, by Australian producers as being misleading or deceptive conduct (under s. 52 of the Commonwealth Trade Practices Act).

Held: In dismissing the appeal the Federal Court of Australia held that the descriptive nature of the words 'champagne' and 'imported champagne' suggested that they were not distinctive of wine from any particular locality and that their application to wine produced by the 'methods champenoise' elsewhere than in France would not ordinarily have misled the relevant purchaser in Australia. Although some consumers might have been misled, until the point of purchase, by unrestrained use of the words complained of, the balance of convenience was against the grant of injunctions. Confusion amongst consumers had long existed but traders were unlikely to be misled. Champagne imported from countries other than France had, to some extent, been sold in Australia by the respondents and others. The applicants did not challenge Australian-made champagne. Refusal of the injunctions would not have resulted in significant or particular harm to the applicants.

(Comite Interprofessionel du Vin de Champagne v. N. L. Burton Pty. Ltd., 1981)

The reputation of a product gained under particular name distinguishable from other products will be protected against deceptive use.

Example

The plaintiffs manufactured and distributed an alcoholic drink known as 'advocaat' made out of a mixture of eggs and spirits. Advocaat was a distinct and recognizable drink made almost exclusively in Holland by a number of manufacturers as well as the plaintiffs. It had been sold in England for over fifty years and become a popular drink through advertising there where the name 'advocaat' had acquired a substantial reputation and goodwill. The plaintiffs had 75 per cent of the English market, the rest being held by other Dutch manufacturers. The defendants manufactured an alcoholic drink in England out of dried eggs and Cyprus sherry, properly called an egg flip, which they marketed as 'Old English Advocaat'. Since it contained sherry rather than spirits less excise duty was payable on it and it could therefore be sold at a lower price than Dutch advocaat. Although an expert drinker could tell the difference between the two drinks this was not so marked that a casual and inexperienced drinker would notice. The defendants had not passed off their product as that of the plaintiffs and it was unlikely that any purchaser would suppose the defendant's drink to be the plaintiff's product. However, the plaintiffs applied for an injunction restraining the defendants from selling or distributing under the name 'advocaat' any product which was not made out of eggs and spirits without the addition of wine. The basis of the plaintiff's argument was that, although they did not have an exclusive right to use the particular trade name 'advocaat' they were members of a class consisting of all those who had a right to use the name and as such were entitled to protect the name by a passing off action. At first instance the plaintiffs were granted an injunction. On appeal to the Court of Appeal the injunction was discharged and the action dismissed on the ground that the name 'advocaat' was purely descriptive and not distinctive.

Held: The House of Lords allowed the appeal on the following grounds: (i) If a product of a particular character or composition was marketed in England under a descriptive name and gained a reputation there under that name which distinguished it from competing products of different composition, the goodwill in the name of those entitled to make use of it there was protected against deceptive use there of the name by competitors. This was so whether the name denoted a product made from ingredients from a particular place or the goodwill associated with the name was the result of the product being made from particular ingredients. It was the reputation the product had gained in the market because of its recognizable and distinctive qualities which had generated the goodwill; and (ii) advocaat was the name of a spirit-based product defined by reference to the nature of its ingredients. The defendants were seeking to take advantage of the product's name by misrepresenting that their wine-based product was of the same type as advocaat. As the plaintiffs were within that class of traders whose right to describe their products as advocaat formed part of their goodwill and who were being injured by the defendants' mistrepresentation they were entitled to the injunction sought.

(*Erven Warnink BV v. J. Townend & Sons (Hull) Ltd.*, 1979)

Remedies granted in this action are an injunction with or without damages, an injunction being the most important. The injunction may be given without a sale occurring if the actions of the defendants are likely to take away the plaintiff's customers. Damages will be a measure of profit lost by the plaintiff where he can prove loss of customers; loss of goodwill and reputation can also be taken into account.

8:6 PATENT LAW AND THE E.E.C.

Patent laws differ amongst member states of the E.E.C., but steps have been taken within the last four years to provide a means of increased co-operation in this field. There are two Conventions to be considered: first, the European Patent Convention; and secondly, the Community Patent Convention. The aim of both Conventions is to provide an alternative, but not a substitute, system for national patents secured through national patent offices.

(i) EUROPEAN PATENT CONVENTION

The European Patent Convention which was signed at Luxembourg in December 1975 initially arose from the meetings of the original six member countries of the E.E.C. It has three main aims:

(*a*) To aid free movement of goods by long-term abolition of national patents within the E.E.C. since these are basically a restriction on trade. However, a dual system of protection to both a national and an E.E.C. patent will operate for an interim period which, under the terms of the Convention, will eventually disappear.

(*b*) To aim for a greater degree of common ground, short of uniformity amongst the national patent laws of E.E.C. member states.

(*c*) To develop supranational alongside national patent legislation.

The European Patent Convention provides for the granting of a patent for any inventions which have an industrial (including an agricultural) application, which are new and involve an inventive step. The term of patents granted is twenty years from the date of filing the application, the extent of protection being determined by the terms of the claims; the terms to be used as guidelines as to what the patentee contemplated. The inventor or his successor in title has the right to apply for a patent; where the inventor is an employee his right to the patent is to be determined by national law. As to applications, the examination by the European Patent Office covers all the requirements of the Convention and once the application is passed the patent is granted. However, third parties are given nine months to institute proceedings before the European Patent Office. The application can give national patents for individual E.E.C. member countries under an arrangement which runs for ten years.

(ii) COMMUNITY PATENT CONVENTION

The Community patent is, under the Convention, a European patent for E.E.C. member countries. Therefore the validity of the Community patent is judged by the principles of the European Patent Convention and will be dealt with in the application and opposition stages like any other European application by the European Patent Office. In cases of infringement, countries, such as Britain, who use a combined approach are allowed to reserve power to their national courts in dealing with infringements relating to a Community patent to decide, with the parties' agreement, on the effect of that patent. Proceedings for infringement should be brought in the E.E.C. country where the defendant resides, or his business place, failing this, in the E.E.C. country where the plaintiff resides or his place of business; if none of these apply, then in the Federal Republic of Germany. Procedures and remedies are matters of local law under the Community Patent Convention. Infringement under the Convention was previously more widely defined than under English law, and this has required alterations of our domestic legislation (see Patents Act 1977). The Convention provides for exhaustion of patent rights on a Community-wide basis for both Community and national patents. For example, an owner of a national or Community patent in the U.K. who markets goods in France will not by his patent prevent their entry into the U.K. unless there are grounds under E.E.C. law which justify the extension to such acts of the patent rights. This applies where the goods are marketed with the patentee's express consent. Although the Convention does not expressly refer to goods first marketed outside the E.E.C. their entry into the E.E.C. may be stopped by Community or national patent rights whether they are the products of the patentee or an unrelated third person.

The Community Patent Convention allows the grant of compulsory licences of Community patents by a state as for its national patents, but only with a territorial effect. The patentee will be able to prevent the entry of the compulsory licensee's goods into parts of the market for which there is no compulsory licence. Compulsory licences under Community and national patents may not be granted for lack or insufficiency of exploitation if sufficient production under the patent is taking place in another E.E.C. country to meet the needs in the state where the licence is sought. However, countries wishing to preserve existing arrangements are given a transitional period of fifteen years.

The European Patent Convention has settled the location of the European Patent Office in Munich, with the International Patent Institute at the Hague as part of the Office. The European Patent is expected to come into operation over a three-year period. During this time examination by national offices, such as the London Patent Office, will continue. Ultimate appeal on grounds of procedural infringement may be taken to the European Court of Justice.

If the European Patent and the Community Patent offer both cheaper and more effective protection than existing national patents they may become popular. It seems likely that the European Patent will be preferred and that the Community Patent will develop more slowly. Much will depend on the fees for both in relation to a series of national fees and whether a Community Patent becomes necessary to protect against imports by a third party.

(iii) PATENTS ACT 1977

Part II of the Patents Act, as noted earlier (8:1), brings present law into line with European and Community patents and enables, once all the conventions are operating, patent protection for the United Kingdom to be arranged by either a British or Community patent. Provisions concerning European patents and applications and implementation of the Community Patent Convention are dealt with in ss. 77–85 and ss. 86–88 respectively. The provisions of s. 60(1) and (2) (*see* 8:1) concerning infringement are expressly excluded from applying to any act which under any provision of the European Patent Convention relating to the exhaustion of the rights of a proprietor of a patent cannot be prevented by him.

(iv) LICENCE AND DISTRIBUTION AGREEMENTS

Patents are particularly affected by Article 85(1) of the Rome Treaty, whose provisions have already been noted in Chapter 2 with regard to restrictive trade practices. Even where the E.E.C. Commission decides that Article 85(1) applies to any agreements, practices or decisions, which can include patents and related exploitation, they can still grant exemption (negative clearance).

Patents are commonly developed by the granting of licence agreements for royalty payment. These, according to a 1962 statement by the E.E.C. Commissioners, do not come within Article 85(1) and provided no further restrictions are put on the licencee the agreement is exempt from notification. In practice restrictive agreements normally included with patent licences may fall foul of Article 85(1), for example in the case of an exclusive licence. The following cases give only a general framework of the views taken by the Commission of exclusive licences and their relation to restriction of the market.

In the case of a licencee with a minor share of the French market and unrestricted right to sell throughout the E.C.M. under the licensing agreement, the Commission was prepared to grant negative clearance, setting out the following observations:

'A patent confers on its holder the exclusive rights to manufacture the products which are the subject of the invention. The holder may cede by licences for a given territory the use of rights derived from its patent. However, if it undertakes to limit the exploitation of its exclusive right to a single undertaking the right to exploit the invention and to prevent other undertakings from using it, it thus loses the power to contract with other applicants for a licence. In certain cases such exclusive character of a manufacturing licence may restrict competition and be covered by the prohibition set out in Article 85(1).'

(Burroughs A. G. and Gehon-Werke GmBh's Agreement (1972)— Common Market Law Reports D. 72)

A different view was taken where a patented process was the most important of its kind and a large share of the E.E.C. market was held by prospective licencees. Here restriction would result, in the view of the Commission, if exclusive licences were granted, and Art. 85 (1) be infringed (Re *Davidson Rubber Company's Agreement* (1972)—Common Market Law Reports D.45).

Where agreements between associated companies in the same group are concerned the Commission has distinguished between 'legally' and 'economically' separate bodies, the test being that if the companies concerned are legally but not economically separate the agreements are not agreements between enterprises under Art. 85(1). A particularly important decision involved the Deutsche Grammophon company and the French Polydor company, both part of the Philips group. A licence agreement, not covering West Germany, was in existence between Polydor (nearly 100 per cent owned by Deutsche Grammophon) and the German firm. Polydor exported records to Germany which Metro Gross Market (a German company) sold below the price controlled by Deutsche Grammophon. On reference to the Commission by Deutsche Grammophon the court stated:

'It is contrary to the provisions on free movement goods that a manufacturer of recordings should exercise an exclusive right granted by a member state to market protected articles in order to prohibit sale in that member state of products sold by him or with his consent in another member state solely because that sale had not occurred in the territory of the first member state.'

(Deutsche Grammophon v. Metro Gross Market (1971)— Common Market Law Reports 631)

In a recent case the defendant imported into Holland a urinary drug from Britain marketed in both countries as *Negram* by different subsidiaries of

Sterling Drug Inc. The British price for the drug was much lower than the price in Holland. Sterling held patents in both countries for the Drug. The Dutch Court of Appeal held the defendants action was an infringement under Dutch patent law. The European Court of Justice ruled, however, that 'the exercise by a patentee of the right given him by the laws of a Member State to prohibit the marketing in another Member State by such patentee or with his consent would be incompatible with the rules of the E.E.C. Treaty relating to the free movement of goods in the Common Market' (*Centrafarm BV v. Sterling Drug Inc.*, 1974 2 C.M.L.R. 480); (the same principle was applied to trade marks in *Centrafarm BV v. Winthrop BV*, 1974 C.M.L.R. 480).

Know-how agreements have been considered by the Commission and in Re *Harbison-Walker and B.A.S.R.E.F.* a territorial restriction was permitted. In this case Harbison-Walker (an American firm) agreed to make know-how available to B.A.S.R.E.F. (a Dutch company) on the basis that a fixed percentage of royalties were paid, technical data were kept secret and not used after the licence ended, plus an obligation by Harbison-Walker not to make the know-how available to any other Dutch firm. The Commission did not apply Art. 85(1) so that it seems that territorial restrictions on know-how agreements are valid whether supported by a patent or not.

QUESTIONS

1. On what grounds can the validity of a patent be challenged?
   (I.P.S., May 1969)
2. It has been stated that 90 per cent of British patents are to some extent invalid. If this statement is correct, of what significance is this to purchasing officers?
   (I.P.S., December 1967)
3. What defences may be open to a manufacturer who is sued for infringement of a patent?
   (I.P.S., May 1967)
4. Do you consider it necessary to include in a set of standard purchase conditions a clause under which the supplier indemnifies the purchaser against any patent infringement in the manufacture or use of goods being supplied? If a supplier refused to accept such a clause what action would you take as the purchaser?
   (I.P.S., December 1970)
5. You wish to purchase 1,000 of article *X*, which is patented only in the U.K. The U.K. patentee will only sell it for £100. You can buy the same article from Italy for £60. As chief buyer of your company what action would you take?
   (I.P.S., May 1968)
6. What is the object of the patent system? How does it affect the purchasing officer?
   (I.P.S., December 1971)
7. (a) What is meant by 'passing off'? Give two examples and state what protection is afforded by the law against the practice.

(*b*) For a number of years Smith & Jones had carried on business as blacking manufacturers in East London under the name of Day & Night. Two other persons named John Day and William Knight formed a partnership to manufacture blacking and marketed their product under the name of Day & Knight, their true names, but using their own distinctive type of container. Smith & Jones applied for an injunction to restrain them from carrying on the business under the name of Day & Knight. State, with reasons, whether the application would or would not be granted.

(Diploma in Marketing II, May 1970)

9. *Trade Descriptions and Advertising*

9:1 INTRODUCTION

The Trade Descriptions Act 1968 which is based on the recommendations of the Molony Committee on Consumer Protection (1962) replaces the Merchandise Marks Acts (1887–1953) which dealt generally with the incorrect description of goods.

The Trade Descriptions Act covers oral and written statements and is enforced by Weights and Measures inspectors. The Act does not require traders and manufacturers to give information about their goods, but only deals with the legal position when they do so. The Trade Descriptions Act provides no civil remedies for the consumer, it is a branch of the criminal law.

The main sections of the Act are as follows:

(i) PROHIBITION OF FALSE TRADE DESCRIPTIONS

It is an offence for anyone in the course of trade or business to apply a false trade description to any goods or to supply or offer to supply any goods to which a false trade description is applied (s. 1).

A trade description is a wide definition, it covers:

(*a*) quantity, size or gauge (e.g. size 7, 30 denier)—quantity includes capacity, weight, number, volume, area, height, width, and length;

(*b*) method of manufacture, production, processing or reconditioning (e.g. drop-forged, hand-made);

(*c*) composition (e.g. nylon, 3-ply, solid steel);

(*d*) fitness for purpose, strength, performance, behaviour or accuracy (e.g. 'shockproof', 'suitable for children');

(*e*) any other physical characteristics (e.g. shape and quality);

(*f*) testing by any person and the results (e.g. passed M.O.T. test);

(*g*) approval by any person or conformity with a type approved by any person (e.g. recommended by the A.A.);

(*h*) place or date of manufacture, production, processing or reconditioning (e.g. brand new, Nuits St. George 1953, Made in Scotland);

(*i*) person by whom it has been manufactured, produced, processed or reconditioned (e.g. Heinz Baked Beans, Austin Mini);

(*j*) other history, including previous ownership or use (e.g. one owner, ex-R.A.F. officers, salvage stock, discontinued line);

(*k*) in the case of animals—sex, breed, cross, fertility, and soundness (e.g. Hereford, Jersey cow, warranted unserved);

(*l*) in relation to semen—identity of donor animal and degree of dilution.

(ii) POWERS TO DEFINE TERMS AND REQUIRE DISPLAY OF
INFORMATION

The Department of Trade under s. 7 may make orders defining terms when used as part of a trade description (e.g. rust-proof, shower-proof) and require that information be given on or with goods or in advertisements for goods (ss. 8–10).

(iii) MIS-STATEMENTS OTHER THAN FALSE TRADE DESCRIPTIONS

False indications concerning the price of any goods and false comparisons with an earlier price are prohibited under s. 11. Similarly, false representations regarding royal approval or award and supply of goods or services to any person are illegal (ss. 12 and 13 respectively). Section 14 covers misleading or false statements as to services, accommodation or facilities.

(iv) PROHIBITION OF IMPORTATION OF CERTAIN GOODS

The importation of goods bearing a false indication or origin is prohibited (s. 16) and the importation of goods bearing infringing trade marks is restricted (s. 17).

(v) DEFENCES

These fall under mistake, accident, innocent publication, and fault of another person (ss. 23–25).

(vi) ENFORCEMENT

This is carried out by the Weights and Measures Inspectorate who have power to make test purchases (s. 27) and enter premises and inspect and seize goods and documents (s. 28).

(vii) PENALTIES

Traders or manufacturers giving materially false information about their goods, prices or services can be summarily fined up to £400, with a fine or a maximum of two years' imprisonment or both if convicted on indictment.

Falsity to a 'material degree' can be best explained in the terms of the Molony Committee that the prosecution must prove that the description would be fairly regarded as inducing a purchase. Supply of goods and services in the course of trade or business includes manufacturing, sales promotions, advertising, distribution of samples, and exchange of goods for trading stamps. Market research experiments, however, are specifically exempted (s. 37). At this point it would be useful to consider some of the topics listed in greater depth.

Sale or supply of goods

Section 1 has been so interpreted by the courts that an offence is only committed if the application of the false trade description was linked with the sale or supply of goods.

Example

Forty days after a car had been sold to a purchaser he complained to sellers

about it with special reference to its steering and was told 'There is nothing wrong with the car'. The car was proved to be unroadworthy when sold.
Held: No offence was committed under s. 1 as the false description after the sale was not associated with that sale.

(*Wickens Motors (Gloucester) Ltd. v. Hall*, 1972)

The section applies to a buyer:

Example

A car dealer negotiating the purchase of a car told the seller it was beyond repair and only fit for scrap; he purchased it for £2, repaired it and sold it for £136.
Held: Buyers came within the terms 'any person in the course of trade or business' and the dealer was liable under s. 1.

(*Fletcher v. Budgen*, 1974)

The section has been considered in relation to honest but careless misdescription by a trade.

Example

An old rusted car sold by *M* had been partly repaired by him with plastic filler before sale to car dealers. They disguised this with preparation and painting and sold it to another dealer who was unaware of the defect and who also sold it.
Held: The latter dealer did not breach s. 1 as he was not aware at the time of supply or offer to supply that the trade description was applied to the goods.

(*Cottee v. Douglas Seaton (Used Cars) Ltd.*, 1972)

In the case of false odometer readings, which have provided the grounds for a number of prosecutions under s. 1, the dealer who requires protection can either blank out the reading or put on the vehicle in question a notice which has to be as bold, precise and compelling as the mileage reading and effectively brought to the notice of any person to whom the goods might be supplied; such a disclaimer can be applied in the case of any trade description of goods (*Norman v. Bennett*, 1974). In a recent case a disclaimer of liability for odometer readings in a document headed 'specific guarantee' was held not to be sufficiently bold, precise or compelling to displace the inference of the reading.

(*R. v. Hammertons Cars Ltd.*, 1976)

A recent case considered the situation where the trader was unaware of the true mileage of the car.

Example

A car dealer bought a car registered in 1973. Its odometer recorded that the car had done 716 miles but it had in fact done 73,000 miles. A prospective buyer, on enquiring what the car's true mileage was, had been told truthfully by the dealer he did not know. On selling the car to the purchaser the dealer asked the purchaser his own estimate which the latter refused or was unable to give. The dealer than gave his own estimate and wrote on the sales invoice 'recorded mileage indicator reading is 716 estimated 45,000', a mileage accepted by the purchaser. The dealer then gave a warranty document (issued by an insurance company) to the purchaser which only applied to cars with a mileage of less than 60,000 miles. The dealer was charged with a breach of s. 1 (1) (b) in that he supplied a car, in the cause of his trade or business, with a false trade description. The dealer appealed from the magistrate's decision that the dealer's estimate of the car's mileage amounted to a false trade description under s. 3 (3) as it was likely to be taken as an indication of the history of the car.

Held: Even if the dealer's estimate had not been false trade description under s. 2 his estimate was likely to be taken as an indication of the history of the car. This was so since there would have been no point in the purchaser asking for the dealer's opinion unless the purchaser wanted an indication of the actual mileage. The description was thus false to a material degree and a false trade description under s. 3 (3). The conviction of the dealer therefore stood and the appeal was dismissed.

(Holloway v. Cross, 1981)

Prices

A person commits an offence in relation to s. 11 by offering to supply goods of any description and giving a false indication that the price of the goods is less or equal to a recommended price or the price of similar goods previously offered.

Example

Proprietors of a self-service store displayed Ribena priced at 5s. 9d. [29p] with manufacturer's labels worded 'The deposit on this bottle is 4d. [1½p] refundable on return'. There was a notice exhibited some distance away at the check-out point which stated 'In the interests of hygiene we do not accept the return of any empty bottles. No deposit is charged by us at the time of purchase.' Two purchasers were refused a refund. The firm were prosecuted under s. 11 (2) for offering to supply goods for sale and giving an indication that the goods were being offered at a price less than that at their Woolwich and Eltham branches. *Held:* The offence was committed when the Ribena was placed on the stack with the indication that the price was 5s. 9d. [29p] and 4d. [1½p] would be returned. The defence that the check-out point notice was a correction failed. (*Note:* The question was left open as to whether the firm could have avoided prosecution by placing a notice immediately above the stack.)

(Doble v. David Greig Ltd., 1972)

All that is required under the Act is that there is an 'offer to supply' which will be done by what s. 6 terms 'exposing goods for supply'. This provision makes no difference to the contractual position of a supplier who is under no duty to a customer to sell goods displayed.

(Fisher v. Bell, 1961)

It is a defence under s. 24 (1) for any person prosecuted to prove that:

(*a*) the commission of the offence was due to a mistake or reliance on information supplied to him or to the act or default of another person, an accident or some other cause beyond his control and

(*b*) that he took all reasonable precautions and exercised all due diligence to avoid the commission of such an offence by himself or any person under his control.

Example

Posters in a supermarket advertised a brand of washing powder normally sold at 3*s*. 11*d*. [20p] a pack at 2*s*. 11*d*. [15p]. A shopper could only find packs marked 3*s*. 11*d*. [20p] and was told by the check-out cashier that there were none in stock for sale at 2*s*. 11*d*. [15p]. A supermarket employee whose duty it was to replenish stock had not told the manager that specially marked packs had run out and displayed packs with the ordinary price. The manager had similarly failed in his duty to see the proper packs were on sale.

Held: The company would succeed in their defence under s. 24(1). The manager came under the term 'another person' and his default was not that of the supermarket company itself.

(Tesco Supermarkets Ltd. v. Nattras, 1971)

Both elements of the defence must be proved.

Example

A dealer sold a car with an incorrect odometer reading which he had not checked with the previous owner nor checked the vehicle to discover if its condition conformed with the reading.

Held: The dealer succeeded in proving reliance on information supplied to him but failed to prove that he had taken all reasonable precautions; the defence therefore failed.

(Richmond-upon-Thames London Borough Council v. Motor Sales (Hounslow) Ltd., 1971)

Mistake can be used as a defence only when it is the defendant's own mistake.

Example

A trader pleaded mistake as a defence, it being that of a shop assistant who accidentally put the wrong label on meat displayed for sale.

Held: This was no defence for the defendants who should have relied on the defence of act or default of another person.

(Birkenhead & District Co-op Society v. Roberts, 1970)

If a retailer claims he has reduced the price of goods from £5 to £1 he must have had the goods on sale for a continuous period of at least 28 days in the last six months.

(viii) SERVICES

It is an offence under the Act to make a deliberately false statement about services, or to make a reckless statement which turns out to be false (s. 14).

'Services' covers accommodation, garages, travel facilities, dry-cleaners, repairs. The nature of the services are dealt with, as is the time for which they are to be provided (24-hour service), and any approval alleged to be given to them (R.A.C. approved).

Reckless statements are those made by a person who did not care whether they were true or false and who could have discovered the truth had he wanted to. This must be proved in the same way that it must be shown that the false statement was made deliberately. In one case an insurance company advertised its intention to settle claims quickly but failed to do so in a certain instance. It was not convicted under s. 11 as it could not be shown that the statement was made recklessly at the time it was made (*Midland Northern and Scottish Assurance Company Ltd.*, 1969). In another prosecution a travel agency offered accommodation which was not in fact provided. The court decided that at the time when the offer was made in the brochure it was accurate and the firm had no means of knowing that the accommodation (a hotel) would not be available at a later date (*Sunair Holidays Ltd. v. Dodd*, 1970). In another travel case a prosecution succeeded where an old couple were put in accommodation some distance from the hotel pictured in the brochure and had to travel to it daily for meals.

A key travel case included the issue of conviction of a defendant for the same offence.

Example

A firm organized and sold 'package holidays'. In August and September 1970 they printed, published and distributed to travel agencies and the general public two copies of a holiday brochure offering particulars of holidays on offer for the season. Mr and Mrs *B* read the brochure, were attracted by an advertisement for a holiday at a Greek hotel and booked for that holiday. On arrival they found that the hotel did not have certain of the amenities that had been advertised in the brochure. The firm were subsequently charged, after the couple's official complaint, with recklessly making a false statement in the course of their trade or business as to an amenity of accommodation at the hotel, in breach of s. 14 (1) (6). Another holidaymaker, *X*, who had also read the brochure and stayed at the same Greek hotel as Mr and Mrs *B*, also complained on finding similar deficiencies there as experienced by the couple.

The firm pleaded guilty and were convicted under s. 14 (1) (6) on *X's* complaint in July 1972 and fined £450. The trial in respect of Mr and Mrs *B* commenced in March 1973. The firm entered a plea of autrefois convict, that is that they could not be prosecuted twice of the same offence. The firm was convicted and fined £1,000 and ordered to pay £50 compensation to Mr and Mrs *B*. The firm appealed on the grounds that only one offence had been committed, alternatively a second prosecution was oppressive, or it was unjust that penalties should be imposed.

Held: In dismissing the appeal the court held that a false statement within s. 14 (1) (6) was made when communicated to someone and each time a false statement was communicated to a reader, a fresh offence was committed. Therefore the firm could not plead autrefois convict (*Sunair Holidays Ltd. v. Dodd* 1970 applied). Under the Act more than one prosecution could be brought against accused persons in respect of the same course of conduct. Two prosecutions in respect of false statements in the same brochure was not oppressive. The penalty imposed was neither wrong in principle nor too severe for a second prosecution.

(*R. v. Thompson Holidays Ltd.*, 1974)

Although s. 14 is primarily concerned with the quality of services provided, some cases have been concerned with prices. A radio and television relay firm were successfully prosecuted when they advertised their service at a weekly rental figure but omitted to state that the service was not available unless customers paid extra for the wired relay service.

Under s. 14 defences available are those already discussed in relation to prices, but the burden of proof is higher regarding false or reckless statements about services, accommodation, and facilities. It should lastly be noted that s. 14 does not apply to houses or land.

Judicial decisions have notably limited the operation of s. 14, to the concern of the Weights and Measures Inspectorate and consumer bodies. Both cases to be discussed here are High Court rulings and relate to the question of what is meant by 'reckless' and the offer of future services.

Example

A company issued an advertisement which made reference to louvre doors and contained the words 'folding door gear (carriage free)' and offered a folding door gear set on fourteen days' free approval. Two purchasers believed the gear sets could be purchased without doors, another discovered carriage had to be paid on the gear set before delivery and it could not be obtained on fourteen days' approval. The company's chairman who had studied the advertisement for only a few minutes before approval did not realize that the gear set was being offered as a separate item. The company were prosecuted under s. 14(1).

Held: The word 'recklessly' in the section did not involve dishonesty. It did not have to be proved that the statement had been made without regard as to whether it was true or false. All that had to be shown was that the advertiser did not have regard to the truth or falsity of the advertisement, even though it could not be proved he was deliberately ignoring the truth or was being dishonest. The company were not liable.

(*M.F.I. Warehouses Ltd. v. Nattras*, 1972)

Example

A builder agreed to construct a garage for a customer 'within ten days' and identical to that of the customer's neighbour. The garage was not built within the stipulated time and it was not like the other garage. The builder was prosecuted under s. 14(1)(b).

Held: The section did not apply to statements made in regard to the future, which, when they were made, could be neither true nor false. The court stated that Parliament had not intended the Act to be used in making what was essentially a breach of warranty a criminal offence.

(*Beckett v. Cohen*, 1972)

A promise in regard to the future, specifically in relation to airline policy of overbooking flights, was examined by the House of Lords. Their Lordships distinguished between a statement of fact and a promise of future conduct.

Example

BOAC wrote on 14 August 1973 to a customer stating 'I have pleasure in confirming the following reservations for you: London/Bermuda flight B.A. 679—Economy Class—29 August Dep. 1525 hours Arr. 1750 hours.' It was BOAC's policy to overbook whereby they made reservations for more passengers than there were seats available on a particular flight. Although on 14 August there were sufficient seats available for the customer to travel on flight B.A. 679 by 29 August, as a result of BOAC overbooking, there were more reservations than there were seats available. On 29 August, the day of the flight in question, the customer was informed at the airport that his flight was overbooked; as a result he had to travel the next day. On 1 April 1974 BOAC's property, rights and liabilities became those of the British Airways Board under the Air Corporations (Dissolution) Order 1973. On 26 June information was laid against the Board alleging the letter of 14 August to the customer breached s. 14 (1) (6) in that it recklessly made a statement about the provision of services, transport of a person by air, which was false as to the time at which the service was to be provided. A magistrates' court convicted the Board. The Divisional Court, on appeal, quashed the conviction on the ground that the letter from BOAC contained merely a promise as to future conduct as distinct from a statement of fact. As a result s. 14 (1) did not apply. The prosecution appealed to the House of Lords.

Held: The magistrates were entitled to find the letter of 14 August to be a statement of fact to *E* that he had a definite and certain booking on a particular flight. The statement was false within s. 14 (1) since, in view of the airline's overbooking policy *E's* booking was exposed to the risk that he would not get a seat on the aircraft.

However, in the circumstances, the Board could not be held liable for the criminal acts of BOAC as there had been no delegation of duty by the Board to BOAC. Further the 1973 order had no provision that on dissolution of BOAC; offences by BOAC were to be treated as offences by the Board.

(*British Airways Board v. Taylor*, 1976)

9:2 POWERS OF THE DEPARTMENT OF TRADE

The Act empowers the D.O.T. to make orders defining trade terms and labelling, and to require display and provision of information. Before any order can be made under these powers (ss. 7–10) the D.O.T. is required to consult with organizations representing any interests that may be affected by the order.

The object of definition orders is to give a fixed legal meaning to certain terms used in relation to goods. This could be useful where trade terms are understood by business men within that trade but not by the public in general—e.g. 'stainless', 'creaseproof', and 'waterproof'. Services are also covered by this provision.

Marking orders allow the D.O.T. to instruct that certain kinds of goods will be marked with or accompanied by certain information. Health and safety are likely areas of Government action (e.g. electrical appliances, safety belts); at present voluntary schemes are being used in this respect. With regard to advertising, the D.O.T. may require certain information to be provided in advertisements and lay down the form and manner in which this is to be done. Initially the D.O.T. attempts to obtain this by voluntary means without resort to the powers under the Act.

9:3   ENFORCEMENT AND PENALTIES

Enforcement lies with local Weights and Measures officers under the supervision of the Department of Trade. If it is intended to prosecute in a local area notice must be given to the D.O.T. The Weights and Measures officers have discretion to prosecute and much of their work involves giving information and, in particular instances, warning to the trading community.

9:4   REMEDIES

It is open to a private person to initiate a prosecution, but, if he wishes to recover his losses from a supplier or advertiser, his only remedy until recently has been to go to the courts and obtain damages in a court action. Since the Criminal Justice Act 1973 provisions have come into operation and the criminal courts are now empowered to order persons convicted under the 1968 Trade Descriptions Act (besides other offences) to pay compensation for personal injuries, loss or damage. The compensation order made by magistrates is additional to a fine and subject to a maximum of £400 which can be ordered even if not requested by the prosecution. A successful prosecution under the Act will provide an adequate basis for a separate civil action for damages or rescission of the contract. The Act provides that a contract will not become void or unenforceable because its terms involve a mis-statement amounting to an offence under the Act. The purchaser can insist on the goods being delivered or the services carried out and claim a reduction in the price as damages. Alternatively, the purchaser can reject the goods or services and claim damages. This aspect of the buyer's position in law has been dealt with earlier in Chapter 4.

9:5   TRADE DESCRIPTIONS ACT 1972

This Act came into operation on 29 December 1972 and makes the following provisions:

If any person, in the course of trade or business, supplies or offers to supply goods manufactured or produced outside the U.K. with a name or mark which is:

(i) a U.K. name or mark; or

(ii) is likely to be taken for a U.K. name or mark (whether or not such a U.K. name or mark actually exists);

the person or persons offering to supply or supplying such goods will be guilty of an offence unless:

(i) the name or mark is accompanied by a conspicuous indication of the country in which the goods were manufactured or produced; or
(ii) the name or mark is neither visible in the state in which the goods were supplied nor likely to become visible on such inspection as may reasonably be expected to be made of the goods by a person to whom they are to be supplied (s. 1).

Note: The above do not apply where the goods are second-hand or where the goods are used or will be used as containers or labels for other goods offered for supply in the course of trade or business. Additionally, the Secretary of State (D.O.T.) may grant exemption from this section of the Act on application by interested parties if it seems reasonable for him to do so.

A person charged with an offence under the 1972 Act has the following defences:

(i) that the name or mark had not been applied by him and that he did not know, and could not, with reasonable diligence, have ascertained, that the goods were manufactured or produced outside the U.K.; or
(ii) that he did not know, and had no reason to believe, that the name or mark was, or was likely to be, taken for a U.K. name or mark (s. 2).

Note: A U.K. name or mark is defined under the Act as:

(i) the name of any person carrying on trade or business in the U.K.;
(ii) the name of any part of, or area, place, or geographical feature in the U.K.;
(iii) a trade mark of which the person carrying on the trade or business in the U.K. is the proprietor or registered user; and
(iv) a certification mark of which a person in the U.K. is the proprietor.

9:6   REVIEW OF THE TRADE DESCRIPTIONS ACT 1968

In 1976 the Director-General's report, *Review of the Trade Descriptions Act 1968*, was published (Cmnd. 6628). It made a number of suggestions, details of which can be obtained directly from the report. The report recommended, amongst other matters, that the Act should apply to trade descriptions used, indications of price given, and statements made in the course of trade or business at all levels of trade. The Act should be amended to make it clear that persons engaged in the professions were engaged in business. The report recommended that a new offence should be created relating to false statements made in the course of a trade or business about the condition of goods or property or about the services applied in the past by others to goods or property or about the availability of spare parts. Such an offence would be limited to cases where the goods or property belonged to a person other than the one making the statement, the statement was made either knowing it to be false or recklessly, or made to induce a person to enter into a transaction with the trader making the statement or one in which he had an interest. The report also recommended the widening of s. 14 of the principal Act to cover statements about the standing, capabilities and professional or technical qualifications of the person providing the services, statements about the duration of the services, or the place where they are provided and misleading (as distinct from false) statements or other indications about the provision of services.

To date no legislative action has been taken on these and other recommendations in the report.

9:7 PRICE MARKING (BARGAIN OFFERS) ORDER 1979

The Price Marking (Bargain Offers) Order 1979 (effective 2 July 1979) prohibits indications by retailers that their price is lower than another price for goods of the same description unless:

1. that other price has actually been charged by the retailer (or by some other identified person); or
2. the retailer proposes to charge that price in future (perhaps after an initial 'bargain offer'); or
3. the other price applies in different circumstances (e.g. when goods are bought singly rather than in multiple units) and the retailer is comparing the prices in each of the circumstances; or
4. the other price relates to the price charged to the public generally and the retailer is comparing that price with a special offer to a limited group (e.g. students); or
5. the other price is one which has been recommended by another person who does not sell by retail (e.g. 'manufacturers' recommended price').

9:8 WEIGHTS AND MEASURES ACT 1979

The Weights and Measures Act 1979 includes duties laid on packers and importers of packages. It is the duty of a person who is a packer or importer of packages of a prescribed quantity to ensure that when a group of packages marked with the same nominal quantity is selected by a local weights and measures inspector for prescribed tests that:

(*a*) the total quantity of the goods shown by the test to be included in the packages tested divided by the number of those packages is not less than the nominal quantity on those packages; and
(*b*) the number of non-standard packages among those tested is not greater than the number prescribed as acceptable in relation to the number tested.

9:9 ADVERTISING

The field of advertising is subject to over sixty separate relevant statutes and various voluntary codes laid down by bodies such as the Institute of Practitioners in Advertising, the Institute of Marketing and the Independent

Broadcasting Authority. To deal with every legislative provision would be counter-productive, so only one vital aspect of advertising is mentioned here, that of promotion, with particular reference to competitions.

The law ruling consumer competitions is contained in the Betting, Gaming and Lotteries Act 1963 (ss. 41–47) as amended by the Lotteries Act 1975. Under the 1963 Act any consumer promotion which appears to be competition must be legal as all lotteries which do not constitute gaming are unlawful. This covers games such as bingo which would otherwise be illegal and exempts from prosecution those who run small lotteries as part of entertainments (as at a dance) or conduct them for charitable or private purposes.

The definition that the courts have accepted for a lottery is 'a scheme for the distribution of prizes by lot or chance'. The key factor would appear to be that in order for a competition not to constitute a lottery it must contain a marked element of skill that influences the result. This is equally so where there is a two-part competition; in this case the determination of the first round and the final result must both depend on skill. If the first round is determined solely by chance and the final result by skill such a competition will be in breach of the Act.

However, where free gifts are awarded or where the apparent lottery is a 'free' one, benefits can legally be awarded, without skill, based on chance and not be regarded as lotteries. If the number of gifts or their types or value vary and the purchaser cannot determine which gift he will get the scheme *will* be a lottery; essentially the benefit must be a gift and not a prize. This does not affect a presentation by way of promotion to the millionth purchaser of a new model car as the purchaser has no knowledge of this; such a promotion is perfectly legal. The status of the free lottery or 'personality' promotion needs comment. A washing powder which contains a cut-off entry form for a lottery may fall foul of the Act as the courts may regard the promotion as a way of increasing purchases (which it is). The awarding of prizes for correct replies to a television for film star's question may be similarly faulted as the essence of such a promotion is the chance meeting in the supermarket or shopping centre of consumer and superstar; the element of skill is lacking. In the case of this type of promotion no prosecution has yet been taken under the Act. It is illegal under s. 47 (1) to conduct through any newspaper, or in connection with any trade or business or the sale of any article to the public:

(*a*) any competition in which prizes are offered for the forecasting of either a future event or a part event not yet known or ascertained,
(*b*) any competition in which success does not depend on a substantial degree of skill.

Example

The News of the World conducted a 'spot-the-ball' competition. Competitors had to apply their skill and judgement to decide where the ball was likely to be on the photograph and mark a cross upon it. The merits of the entries were judged by a panel of experts and the winning entry was that which coincided closest to their view as most accurately representing the most logical position of the ball in all the circumstances, which might not be the actual position in the original photograph. The newspaper proprietors were charged with an offence under s. 47 (1)(a).

Held: On appeal to the House of Lords it was decided that competitors were not being asked to forecast the decision of the panel of experts but to use their skill and judgement to arrive at the most logical result. As there was no forecast of a future event there was no offence committed.

(*News of the World Ltd. v. Friend*, 1973)

A degree of skill involved to significantly effect the competition result must exist if a promotion is not to be in breach of the Act.

Example

Imperial Tobacco, manufacturers of 'Players' cigarettes, launched a sales promotion campaign, known as 'Spot Cash', for this brand. In every packet of cigarettes there was a ticket with six spaces covered with silver foil. When the spaces were rubbed with a coin possible prizes were disclosed and if three of the prizes corresponded the ticket holder was entitled to collect that prize. The prizes ranged from a free packet of cigarettes to £5,000. The scheme was advertised as being free, and packets containing the cards were sold at the normal retail price. Imperial Tobacco and their directors were charged by the Director of Public Prosecutions with (*a*) distributing tickets in an unlawful lottery contrary to s. 2(1)(b) of the Lottery and Amusements Act 1976, and (*b*) conducting an unlawful competition contrary to s. 14(1)(b) of the same Act.

The trial judge held the scheme to be an unlawful lottery because the purchaser was buying both the cigarettes and the ticket. It was also an unlawful competition because the purchaser competed with others for the limited number of prizes available. Imperial Tobacco appealed and the Court of Appeal held the scheme to be lawful, since the participants in the scheme did not pay for their opportunity to take part nor competed against one another for the prizes. The Crown then appealed to the House of Lords.

Held: Allowing the appeal—(i) To establish an unlawful lottery it was not necessary to prove that money paid by the participants in return for obtaining a chance of winning was used to provide prizes or was paid into a fund out of which the prizes were provided. What was essential was that there was a distribution of prizes by lot or chance and that the chance of winning was secured by a payment, contribution or consideration by those taking part. Where, to get a prize, a customer had to pay for an article, even at the normal price, that amounted to a payment, contribution or consideration for the chance of a prize. On that basis the purchase of a pack of cigarettes in Imperial Tobacco's scheme was the consideration in return for which the card containing the chance of a prize changed hands. That made the scheme a lottery contrary to s. 2(1)(b) of the 1976 Act, even though it was impossible to ascribe any part of the purchase price to the value of the chance obtained.

(ii) The scheme in question was not a competition since for the purposes of s. 14(1)(b) of the 1976 Act a competition involved the exercise of some degree of skill. In the Imperial Tobacco scheme no effort or striving or dexterity was required of those taking part. Therefore Imperial Tobacco had not breached s. 14 (1) (b). (*Whitbread & Co. Ltd. v. Bell*, 1970, was overruled on this point.)

(*Imperial Tobacco Ltd. v. Attorney-General*, 1980)

A large-scale sales promotion was recently judicially considered:

Example
The Reader's Digest set up a sales promotion which involved the distribution of £30,000 in prize money in a draw of over 200 out of 4,700,000 numbers each allocated to individuals selected as winning numbers. Those circulated were invited to make purchases of the promoter's goods; some did and some did not. The question arose as to whether the promoters were running an illegal lottery contrary to s. 42 (1) of the Betting, Gaming and Lotteries Act 1963.
Held: As eligibility for the draw did not depend on the making of a purchase and therefore the participants did not have to pay for their chance the promotion did not breach the Act and was not a lottery.

(*Reader's Digest Association Ltd. v. Williams*, 1976)

An offence committed before the Lotteries Act 1975 commenced, where successfully prosecuted, is punishable on a first offence by a fine of up to £100 or £500 (depending on summary conviction or on indictment), and for subsequent offences there can be a fine of £200 and/or three months' imprisonment or a £750 fine and one year's imprisonment. If the offence was committed after the 1975 Act commenced, whether for the first time or subsequently, there is a fine of £400 on summary conviction or an unlimited fine and a maximum of two years' imprisonment on indictment or both.

QUESTIONS

1. (*a*) Outline the main provisions of the Trade Descriptions Act 1968.
   (*b*) In his window, *R*, a dealer in electrical goods, exhibited a television receiver on which was displayed a price tag bearing the deleted price £95 and the substituted price £78.
   (i) What conditions is the deleted price required to satisfy under the 1968 Act?
   (ii) If these conditions are not satisfied, what is the legal position of the dealer?

(Diploma in Marketing II, May 1969)

2. (*a*) What is the position under the Trade Descriptions Act 1968 of an employee, and his employer, where a false or misleading representation by the former induces the customer to make a purchase?
   (*b*) *E*, an importer, bought a consignment of watches from a dealer in Switzerland, knowing them to have been made in Russia. *R*, his sales representative, knew that the watches were Russian, but in offering them to a customer, *C*, described them as 'watches from Switzerland' and did not mention that they were Russian made. Examine *R*'s position under the Trade Descriptions Act.

(Diploma in Marketing II, November 1970)

10. *Commercial Associations*

INTRODUCTION

For the purpose of commercial practice and law, only two types of commercial associations are to be considered in this chapter, namely the registered company and the partnership. A registered company has the legal status of a corporation and thus a separate legal existence from its shareholders. Thus, a company can own property and sue in the courts in its own name. Its actions can be made only through living agents, the directors and officers. Each member of a registered company may freely transfer his shares according to the rules of the company. Registered companies are governed by the Companies Acts 1948 1967, 1980 and 1981. Consolidation of these acts is likely in the near future.

A partnership is an association of persons carrying on business in common with a view to profit, existing for a commercial or professional purpose—e.g. market research, accounting, or a solicitor's practice.

10:1 REGISTERED COMPANIES

(a) Nature

Because a registered company is a corporation this has important legal effects:

1. Members of a registered company have limited liability; the debts and contracts of such a company are not those of the members but of the company, and the members can only be made liable for amounts unpaid on their shares.
2. The company has perpetual succession, it never 'dies' (except in the sense of being wound up—*see* p. 280 so that it survives its members and officers.
3. The property of a registered company is vested in the company and remains unaffected by changes in share ownership.
4. A registered company can contract with its members (e.g. directors) and sue and be sued in its own right.
5. Members of a registered company are not agents of that organization. Directors act under the limitation of articles of association on behalf of the company.
6. Subject to provisions in the articles of association, shares are freely transferable.

The number of members of a private company is limited by the Companies Act 1948 to a maximum of fifty (exclusive of employees and ex-employees), with a lower limit of two, and those of a public company must not fall below seven but there is no upward limit.

(b) Formation

Registration

Companies are formed by registration with the Registrar of Companies, an official of the Department of Trade, and registration itself is governed by the provisions of the 1948 Act. The following documents have to be delivered to the Registrar:

1. A memorandum of association, which includes the objects of the company, the amount of share capital with which the company is to be registered, and its division into shares.
2. Articles of association governing transfer of shares, the holding of meetings, directors' powers, and rules governing dividends.
3. A list of persons who have agreed to be directors of the company (not required if the company is a private one or has no share capital).
4. A statement of nominal share capital.
5. A statutory declaration by a solicitor involved in the company's formation or by the company secretary or a director that the registration requirements of the Act have been adhered to.

In addition the following documents are sent:

1. Notice of the address of the company's registered office.
2. A form containing particulars of the directors and the secretary.

In the case of directors of a public company who are appointed under the articles, the written consents of such persons to act as directors and their written agreement to take up qualification shares are required unless they have done so in the memorandum.

Once the Registrar is satisfied that all the requirements of the Act have been fulfilled he will issue the certificate of incorporation; the company can then commence business once the minimum subscription has been satisfied and certain other requirements have been complied with. Provisions concerning simplifications of arrangements for approval of company names are covered by the Companies Act 1981.

(i) PROMOTERS

Contracts made before the incorporation of a company are governed by special rules which have been affected by recent legislation. The legal position of pre-incorporation contracts has been that as a company had no existence it lacked capacity to contract, it could not sue on or enforce such an agreement nor ratify it. In practice the promoters of companies prepare a draft agreement before incorporation which describes the company as being a party, and for this agreement to be carried out by the promoters after incorporation under a clause in the memorandum of the company effecting this. Normally the promoter's business is acquired by the company on formation.

The situation is clarified by s. 9 (2) of the European Communities Act 1972 which lays down a simple rule that pre-incorporation contracts shall have effect as contracts entered into by the persons purporting to act for the company or as agents for it. These persons would then be able to sue or be sued in their own names.

A distinction must be drawn between pre-incorporation contracts and provisional contracts. Provisional contracts are those entered into after the company has been formed but before it is entitled to commence business. Such contracts are not binding on the company until it is entitled to commence business, when they automatically becoming binding (s. 109 (4), Companies Act 1948).

(ii) PROSPECTUSES

(*a*) *Definition*

A prospectus is defined as:

'Any prospectus, notice, circular, advertisement or any other invitation, offering to the public for subscription or purchase any shares or debentures of a company' (s. 455, Companies Act 1948).

(*b*) *Contents*

The statutory requirements regarding information to be made available to a prospective investor include:

1. the names, addresses, description, and payment of directors;
2. the past record of the company's finances, including the auditor's report on profits, losses, assets, liabilities, and dividends during the last five years;
3. voting and dividend rights of each class of shares;
4. details of material contracts entered into by the company in the last two years—i.e. not made in the ordinary course of business;
5. minimum subscription, amount payable on application and on allotment;
6. duties of the company under contracts entered into, together with preliminary expenses.

(*c*) *Misrepresentation*

A person who has been induced to subscribe for shares or debentures in a company by a misrepresentation may be able to obtain a remedy against the company, or the directors, or expert responsible, or both.

1. *Remedies against the company*

(*a*) *Rescission*

Rescission of the contract of allotment will be given where the injured party can prove that the misrepresentation was a material false statement of fact which induced him to subscribe. Statements of fact must be distinguished from statements of opinion (*see Bisset v. Wilkinson*, p. 34). Where a prospectus contains statements made by a company based on a report about which the company makes no reservation, it will be liable if the facts turn out to be inaccurate.

Example

A prospectus inviting subscriptions for the purchase of a Peruvian rubber estate contained a false report from an expert there concerning the state and number of trees.

Held: Rescission would be granted as the false statement was *prima facie* the basis of the contract.

(Re Pacaya Rubber and Produce Co. Ltd., 1914)

(b) Interest

This will be granted on the purchase price at the rate of 4 per cent.

(c) Damages

If the misrepresentation was fraudulent, damages for fraud will additionally be given.

2. Remedies against the directors and promoters

(a) Damages for fraud

If it can be shown that the directors, promoters or others making an offer for sale signed or authorized the issue of a prospectus containing a false statement that they did not believe in good faith to be true, then they will be liable to pay damages for fraud. The measure of damages is *prima facie* the difference between actual value of the shares on allotment and the price paid.

(b) Under s. 43

A promoter or director then acting or any other person authorizing the issue of a prospectus is liable to pay compensation to those subscribers who suffer loss as a result of any untrue statement in the prospectus. The directors and others authorizing the issue of the prospectus have the following defences in such an action:

(i) that consent to act as a director was withdrawn before the prospectus was issued and it was issued without his consent or authority; or

(ii) that the prospectus was issued without his consent or knowledge and reasonable notice was given to the public on his becoming aware of its issue; or

(iii) that consent was withdrawn after issue of the prospectus and before allotment and public notice of withdrawal and the reason for it were given; or

(iv) that up to the time of allotment he had reasonable ground to believe that the statement was true; or

(v) that the statement was contained in a correct copy of, or extract from, an expert's report or valuation, or was a fair representation of an expert's statement and he had reasonable ground to believe up to the issue of the prospectus and did believe that the expert was competent to make the statement. Additionally, that the expert had not withdrawn consent before a copy of the prospectus was registered, or before allotment; or

(vi) that the statement was a correct copy of or extract from an official document, or a correct and fair copy of an official statement.

An expert has the following defences:

(i) that consent to the issue of the prospectus was withdrawn in writing before a copy had been delivered for registration; or

(ii) that before allotment and after delivery of the prospectus for registration he withdrew his consent in writing, giving reasonable public notice of this and the reason for his action; or

(iii) that he believed the statement to be true up to the time of allotment and that he was competent to make the statement.

(c) *Under s. 44*
Any person authorizing the issue of a prospectus containing an untrue statement is liable under s. 44 to a fine of £500 or imprisonment for two years or both unless he can prove:

(i) that the statement was immaterial;
(ii) that up to the time of the issue of the prospectus he had reasonable ground to believe and did believe that the statement was true.

(iii) MEMORANDUM OF ASSOCIATION

(a) *Contents*

1. *Name clause*
Any name may be chosen for a company except one regarded by the Department of Trade as 'undesirable'; this is covered in D.O.T. Practice Note C. 186 and includes:

(i) a name too like that of an existing company;
(ii) a name that is misleading;
(iii) names including words which might be trade marks—e.g. 'sterling';
(iv) names suggesting royal patronage or connection with a government or municipal undertaking;
(v) names including 'Bank', 'Banking', 'Bankers', 'Investment Trust' will only be allowed if justified by the business of the company concerned;
(vi) 'British' will not normally be allowed unless the company in question is sizeable and almost entirely British-owned (but now see Part 2 of the Companies Act 1981).

2. *Limitation clause*
This states that the company is one limited by shares and thus the liability of the shareholders is limited to the nominal amount of shares.

3. *Registered office clause*
This must state that the registered office of the company is in England and Wales or Scotland. This fixes the company's nationality and is the address to which all official documents should be sent.

4. *Objects clause*
These clauses are widely drawn as they set out the business that the company intends to pursue. Any contract entered into by the company outside the scope of its objects clause may be declared *ultra vires* and void by the courts.

Example
A company engaged in a dressmaking business used its assets to develop veneered panelling, an activity not covered by its objects clause. On liquidation the creditors of the company claimed their debts.
Held: As the veneered panel business was *ultra vires* the company contracts with it were void.

(Re *Jon Beauforte* (*London*) *Ltd.*, 1953)

Now, under s. 1 of the European Communities Act, any third party who deals with a company in good faith will be able to enforce an *ultra vires* contract against the company. It is up to the company to prove that a third party has not acted in good faith. Therefore, the creditors in the case above would now be able to recover against the company.

However, a company itself is still bound by the doctrine of *ultra vires* and cannot enforce such a contract *against* third parties.

5. *Capital clause*
This states the total nominal capital of the company and the manner of division into shares—e.g. 'The capital of the company shall be £250,000 divided into one million shares of 25p each'.

6. *Association and subscription clause*
This sets down the names, addresses, and descriptions of the subscribers to the memorandum together with the number of shares they have agreed to take.

(b) *Alterations*
An objects clause may be altered subject to the following statutory provisos:

1. that the alteration is to enable the company to carry on business more efficiently; or
2. to carry out the main purpose of the company by new and improved methods; or
3. to carry on some activity which under present circumstances may be usefully combined with its existing business; or
4. to enlarge or change its local area of operations; or
5. to sell or otherwise dispose of the whole or part of its business; or
6. to amalgamate with another company or organization; or
7. to restrict or abandon any of its present objects.

The objects clause is altered by a special resolution but shareholders of at least 15 per cent of the nominal value of issued shares who do not vote in favour of the resolution can apply to the court within twenty-one days in order to object to the alteration. The court has power to confirm the alteration, impose conditions, or arrange for the purchase of the shares of the dissentient minority.

(iv) ARTICLES OF ASSOCIATION

(a) *Contents*
The articles of association spell out the internal rules of a company. Model articles known as 'Table A' are contained in the appendix to the Companies Act 1948. Articles usually have provisions for the following:

1. calls on shares;
2. transfer of shares;
3. alteration of capital;
4. share capital and variation of class rights;
5. meetings;
6. directors;
7. dividends;

8. accounts;
9. borrowing powers;
10. accounts;
11. notices;
12. winding up.

(b) Alteration

As with objects, articles of association may be altered by special resolution, subject to the following common law limitations:

1. The alteration must not give powers to the company beyond the scope of its objects clause.
2. The alteration must be legal.
3. The effect must not be to increase the liability of a shareholder.
4. The alteration must be for the benefit (bona fide) of the company as a whole.

(v) SHARES

(a) Definition

A share is the interest a shareholder has in a company, 'measured by a sum of money, for the purpose of liability in the first place, and of interest in the second, but also consisting of a series of initial covenants entered into by all the shareholders' (s. 20, Companies Act 1948).

The rights of shareholders are set out in the company's articles of association. As soon as a person's name is entered on the company's register of members he becomes a shareholder for legal purposes.

(b) Types of share

There are two main types of share:

1. *Preference shares*
These entitle the holder to preferential payment of dividends at a set rate (e.g. 5 per cent) prior to payment of the ordinary shareholders. They do not usually include voting rights.

2. *Ordinary shares*
These usually only give a right to receive the dividend when it is declared but provide full voting rights.

(c) Transfer of shares

Every shareholder has the right to transfer his shares freely, subject to contrary provision in the company's articles.

In the instance of a private company, articles restrict the right to transfer shares. If a stock exchange quotation is to be obtained for a public company then their shares must usually be freely transferable.

The normal method of transferring shares that are fully paid is by a stock transfer under hand in the form laid down by the Stock Transfer Act 1963.

(d) Transmission of shares

A transmission of shares will result from the death or bankruptcy of a member, the shares vesting in the executor or administrator or in the trustee in bankruptcy if he wishes to be registered as a member.

(e) Mortgage of shares

Mortgage of shares may be either legal or equitable.

1. *Legal mortgage*

This will be done by the shareholder as security for a loan. The shares will be transferred to the lender on the register of shareholders. On repayment the shares are transferred back to the borrower.

2. *Equitable mortgage*

This may arise where the legal formalities of a mortgage have been omitted but the intention can be proved. Usually the borrower deposits his share certificate with the lender together with a blank transfer, i.e. a transfer form with the name of the transferee left out. On default by the borrower, the lender can protect his interest by becoming registered as the owner. An equitable mortgage, however, is likely to be defeated by a legal mortgage created later.

(f) Forfeiture

Only where authorized by the articles, and then only on non-payment of calls, may shares be compulsorily surrendered (forfeited) to the company. Such shares may be reissued subject to the requirement that the new purchaser is under the duty to pay calls.

(g) Surrender

Directors may be empowered under the articles to accept the voluntary surrender of shares. Articles sometimes permit a member to surrender fully paid-up shares in return for other shares of the same nominal value.

(h) Lien

Articles give a company the right to restrict dealings in shares (lien). A lien is allowed on paid-up shares where the transferee owes money to the company, or in the case of partly paid-up shares where the directors disapprove of the proposed transferee (Table A, Article 11).

(vi) DIVIDENDS

(a) Definition

A dividend is the share of the company's profits that is legally available for division amongst the members. Dividend can only be paid out of profits and normally payment is covered by provision in the articles.

(b) Profits

It should be noted that company practice and company law are at variance when it comes to calculation of profits; the standards required by the law are lower than would be accepted in sound financial practice.

1. Legally a company can pay dividend out of profits without making up losses on fixed capital. This would not be done in practice.
2. Dividend can be paid from accretions to capital as long as there is an overall increase in the value of company assets. Such a course of action would be financially dangerous as it would leave little margin for the purchase of new facilities and plant.
3. Dividends can be paid from current year's profits without making up previous losses—again, an unwise method of running a business.
4. Before payment of a dividend losses on circulating capital must be made up.

(c) Capitalization

Articles normally empower a company to declare at a general meeting that its profits will be treated as capital and distribute the sum capitalized as bonus shares to existing shareholders. Such an issue is looked upon in law not as income from the shares but as an accretion to capital.

(vii) DEBENTURES

(a) Definition

A debenture is a document that is evidence of a loan to a company, providing for payment of interest and security for the loan.

(b) Types

There are two main types of debenture:

1. Fixed charge

This is a mortgage of defined assets of the company (e.g. a warehouse) and the company cannot dispose of the property free from the charge without consent of the debenture holders. It can be either a legal or an equitable mortgage.

2. Floating charge

This is an equitable charge on assets of the company for the present and future. Thus it 'floats' over property which changes—e.g. stock-in-trade. Such property could not be secured by a fixed charge. The company is free to deal with property under a floating charge. A floating charge becomes fixed ('crystallizes') when:

(i) the company ceases trading;
(ii) a receiver is appointed;
(iii) the company goes into liquidation;
(iv) the conditions in the debenture deed giving rise to crystallization occur.

A floating charge is ranked below fixed charges for payment purposes on liquidation of a company. A charge fixed or floating should be registered within twenty-one days of its creation with the Registrar, otherwise it will be void, in the event of the liquidation of the company, against the liquidator and other creditors, although the holder will be able to qualify as an ordinary creditor (*see* p. 280).

(c) Remedies of a debenture holder

The remedies of a debenture holder when there has been default on payment of principal or interest are:

1. either to sue for principal and interest and levy execution against the company after judgement, or to petition for the winding-up of the company where the debenture holder has no charge on company assets and is therefore an unsecured creditor;
2. where there is a charge on the company's assets to sue for the principal and interest, to petition for winding-up, or exercise any powers in the debenture deed, including the appointment of a receiver;
3. in the case of a number of debenture holders in the same class one of these may bring a debenture holder's action on behalf of the others.

(viii) DIRECTORS

(a) Appointment

Every public company is statutorily required to have a minimum of two directors. The articles usually name the first directors or they are appointed by the subscribers to the memorandum or by the company in a general meeting. Matters such as co-option of a maximum number of directors, the filling of casual vacancies, and retirement of directors by rotation are normally dealt with in the company's articles.

(b) Position

A director is classified as an officer of the company although he may not be termed a 'director' (s. 455 (i), Companies Act 1948). He has to act in the interests of the company and must disclose any conflict between those of the company and his private affairs. Directors are not given onerous duties in law; for instance, they do not have to pay continuous attention to the company's management and will not be liable for wrongful acts of company officials unless there are clear grounds of culpability.

There are certain similarities between directors, who are not servants but managers of the company, and agents and trustees. Directors are not true trustees as the company's money and property which they must apply for its purposes are not vested in them but in the company. As agents, directors are liable for breach of warranty of authority if they exceed the powers given to them by the memorandum and articles. However, a general meeting of the company may ratify directors' actions if they act outside the powers given them in the articles but within the powers in the memorandum. Directors are under a general duty to act honestly and without negligence; they cannot be exempted from breaches of duty, trust or negligence under their company's articles. However, the courts are empowered to grant relief where a director has acted reasonably and in good faith and should be excused in all the circumstances. In addition, a majority of members at a general meeting may waive a breach of fiduciary duty by a director after a full disclosure of all the material facts.

(c) Responsibilities

The chief duties of directors are as follows:

1. presenting an annual report to members;
2. calling the Annual General Meeting;

3. ensuring that proper accounts are kept;
4. keeping a register of charges;
5. dispatching copies of extraordinary and special resolutions to the Registrar;
6. submitting a statement of affairs on the winding-up of the company.

(d) Powers

The powers of directors are determined by the company's articles of association. Business can only be validly carried out at a meeting of the company of which due notice has been given and attended by a quorum. Action carried out by the directors beyond their authority, but within the limits of the objects clause of the company's memorandum, can be ratified by a general meeting of the company.

Where a director acts for the company without authority, the person he is dealing with will be able to hold the company bound by the director's actions under the rule in *Royal British Bank v. Turquand*, 1856. This rule states that although a person dealing with a company has notice of the memorandum and other public document, where officers responsible for running the company are doing so in a way which accords with those documents, then that person's rights are not hindered by shortcomings in the internal management and affairs of the company.

Example

Under the articles of a company formed to buy and sell an estate, the directors were authorized to appoint a managing director from amongst themselves. One director, with full knowledge of the board, acted as managing director although never actually appointed as such. Architects were instructed, by this director, to carry out work on the estate. The architects sued for their fees.
Held: The company were bound to pay as the director in question had apparent authority as he was held out by the board as its managing director with all the powers of that position.
(*Freeman & Lockyer v. Buckhurst Park Properties (Mangal) Ltd.*, 1964)

The rule in Turquand's case does not apply where:

1. the person dealing with the company knows of its agent's lack of authority;
2. where a director privately contracts with his own company through another director;
3. where the public documents of a company do not include a copy of the special resolution authorizing the relevant transaction;
4. where the person dealing with the company should have been put on enquiry by suspicious circumstances;
5. where a document is forged, unless vouched for by a company officer acting within his authority.

(e) Payment of directors

As managers of the company's affairs, directors have no claim to payment for their services. In practice, this is provided for in the articles (Table A, Article 76), and remuneration voted to directors under those provisions stands as a debt due to them from the company. On liquidation of the company, directors do not rate for preferential payment of their fees as they are not servants. Compensation for loss of office may only be made to directors if this is fully disclosed to the members and approved by the company.

Managing directors are in a different position. They are appointed by the board under powers in the articles and are bound under service agreement to the company. If this contract is breached, the company will be liable to pay damages to them, usually of a considerable amount.

(*f*) *Termination of office*
This may happen in three ways:

1. *Disqualification*
A director may be disqualified for instance where he becomes bankrupt, or insane, or loses control of any qualification shares he is required to have under the company's articles, or resigns (Table A, Article 88).

2. *Removal*
A general meeting of the company may pass an ordinary resolution to remove a director from office. Intention to remove the director must be given by twenty-eight days' special notice to the company. The company must allow the director the right of being heard at the meeting in his own defence and of making written representation to members. Articles normally provide that a director shall vacate his office if he is absent from board meetings for a specified time unless this is due to illness.

3. *Resignation and retirement*
A director may resign; if he does so his office is automatically vacated and the resignation cannot be withdrawn without the company's consent. A director has to retire after reaching the age of 70 unless the articles provide otherwise, or he was appointed or approved by the company in general meeting by ordinary resolution of which special notice, stating his age, was given; or where the company is a private company not subsidiary to a public company (s. 185).

(ix) SECRETARIES

(*a*) *Appointment*
All companies must have a secretary who is normally professionally qualified (although there is no statutory requirement to this effect). The secretary is either appointed in the articles, or, more usually, by the directors.

(*b*) *Function*
It can no longer be said of the secretary today as it was in 1887 that he is a 'mere servant'. In *Panorama Developments (Guildford) Ltd. v. Fidelis Furnishing Fabrics*, 1971, the company secretary was held to have the apparent authority to hire cars for his company thus making them liable. The judges took the opportunity of noting that the secretary is the company's chief administrative officer, involved in daily company operations, including the signature of contracts and employment of staff by the company.

The secretary has to be present at all directors' and company meetings and minute their proceedings, and has the responsibility for issuing notices of meetings (*see below*). He is primarily responsible for the company's books and returns to the Registrar. He cannot be relieved of liability under the articles, but the court may give relief in appropriate circumstances.

(x) AUDITORS

(a) Appointment

Directors may appoint the first auditors; if they do not then a general meeting of the company can appoint them. At each annual general meeting, the company must appoint an auditor or auditors. A retiring auditor is automatically re-appointed without a resolution of the meeting unless he has written a letter declining re-appointment to the company, or he is unqualified, or a resolution is passed appointing another or stating that he should not be re-appointed. If the A.G.M. of a company does not appoint an auditor the D.O.T. may do so.

An auditor to be appointed must be a member of an accountancy body in the U.K. recognized by the D.O.T. or authorized by the D.O.T. as holding recognized qualification from overseas.

(b) Function

An auditor is treated as an officer of the company in so far as he acts as its agent and under those sections of the Companies Act that relate to auditors.

His main duty is to prepare the auditor's report, which must be read to the general meeting of the company and open to inspection by any member (s. 14 (2), Companies Act 1967). He has right of access to books and accounts and receipts and can investigate the actions of any officer. He is under a general duty to the company to act honestly, with reasonable care and skill. Additionally an auditor owes a duty of care to third persons who rely on his skill and judgement although he is in no contractual or fiduciary relationship to them (*see Hedley Byrne & Co. Ltd. v. Heller & Partners*, 1964).

(xi) MEETINGS AND RESOLUTIONS

(a) Types of meetings

Meetings of a company fall into two main types: annual general meetings and extraordinary general meetings.

1. Annual general meetings

An annual general meeting must be held by every company in each calendar year not more than fifteen months apart. However, a company can hold its first annual general meeting after incorporation within eighteen mobnths. If the annual general meeting is not called by the directors any member may apply to the D.O.T. for it to be convened.

Twenty-one days' notice of the annual general meeting must be given and it must indicate any special business to be discussed; shorter notice may be given if it is agreed by all members who are entitled to attend and vote. All business is special business at an annual general meeting with the exception of:

(i) reports of auditors and directors;
(ii) consideration of accounts;
(iii) election of directors;
(iv) declaration of dividend;
(v) appointment and payment of auditors.

2. *Extraordinary general meetings*

An extraordinary general meeting may be called either by the directors or by written requirement of members holding not less than 10 per cent of the company's paid-up capital which carries voting rights. In the case of such a demand the directors have to convene such a meeting; if they do not the members concerned can convene it within three months of the date on which it was required.

All business at an extraordinary general meeting is termed special business and must be set out in the notice convening the meeting. Fourteen days' notice is given but, where a numerical majority of shareholders with not less than 5 per cent of the voting shares consent, shorter notice may be given.

(*b*) *Chairman*

The Articles normally provide that the chairman of company meetings is the chairman of the board. Where there is no provision in the Articles, the chairman can be elected by the meeting.

A chairman is under a duty to present issues clearly to members, to allow minority views to be heard, to preserve order at meetings, and not to adjourn it without consent of the members present, except where there is disorder. The common law, the Companies Act, and the Articles of the company all determine the limits and manner in which a chairman should act.

(*c*) *Resolutions*

There are three types of resolution:

1. *Ordinary resolution*

This is passed by a simple majority voting at a general meeting (in person or by proxy).

2. *Extraordinary resolution*

This is passed by a three-quarters majority vote of the members (in person or by proxy) at a general meeting, notice of which contained the intention of proposing the resolution.

3. *Special resolution*

This is passed by a three-quarters majority vote of the members (in person or by proxy) at a general meeting of which twenty-one days' notice has been given particularizing the intention to propose the special resolution. Such a resolution is required for important matters, including:

(i) alteration of objects;
(ii) alteration of Articles;
(iii) alteration of the name of the company;
(iv) winding-up under a court order.

(xii) RECONSTRUCTION AND AMALGAMATION

A company is reconstructed when a company transfers its assets to a new company of which the shareholders are basically those of the old one. Amalgamation is the merger of two or more companies into one where, for instance, a company acquires the shares of another.

The Companies Act 1948 provides for amalgamation under s. 287 and ss. 206–208.

(a) Under s. 287

A company in a members' voluntary winding-up can sell all or part of its property or business to another company and authorize the liquidator by special resolution to receive cash or shares, policies or other interests to distribute among members of the transferor company. Shares may also be given directly to the members of the transferor company.

Such an arrangement or sale binds all members of the transferor company. However, a dissentient member who did not vote for the special resolution and puts this disagreement in writing to the liquidator through the registered office within seven days after the passing of the resolution may require the liquidator not to carry it out or purchase his shares by agreement.

(b) Under s. 206

This provides for a compromise or arrangement with creditors by a company before, or in the course of, winding-up.

Such compromise or arrangement will be binding on the creditors, members or classes of them, and the company if:

1. the court sanctions it;
2. the compromise or arrangement is agreed to by a majority in number representing three-quarters in value of those present and voting at the meeting (either in person or by proxy);
3. the court orders a meeting of the creditors, members, or classes of them on the application of the company or any member or creditor.

(xiii) WINDING-UP

A company comes to an end as a business entity by winding-up (or liquidation). There are two types of winding-up:

(a) Winding-up by the court

Any creditor or group of creditors whose debt or debts exceed £50 may petition the court for the company to be wound up. The company itself, the Official Receiver or a contributory (anyone liable to contribute to the assets on winding-up) may also petition. The grounds on which such a petition can be presented are:

1. failure by the company to commence business within a year of incorporation or suspension of business for one year;
2. the number of members falls below the statutory minimum of seven (or two in the case of a private company);
3. the company is unable to pay its debts;

4. special resolution by the court to be wound up;
5. where it is just and equitable for the company to be wound up in the view of the court.

On presentation of the petition to the court, application can be made for a provisional liquidator to be appointed where the assets are endangered. If a provisional liquidator is appointed, he immediately takes charge of company property and, unless the court allows, no legal action can be taken against the company. On hearing the petition, the court has various courses open to it, including dismissal of the petition or making a compulsory winding-up order. This order has the following effect:

1. actions against the company can only be brought with the leave of the court;
2. no court judgements can be carried out against the company's property;
3. all dispositions made after the commencement of winding-up are void unless the court orders otherwise;
4. all the powers of the board of directors end and the company's servants are dismissed.

If it is felt desirable that the company's business should be carried on during liquidation, the court may appoint a manager on application.

The first meeting of Creditors and Contributors is summoned by the Receiver after he has made his report on the statement of affairs made by the company secretary and a director. A liquidator is appointed by the court after the meeting has looked at the Receiver's report on the statement of affairs and recommended a liquidator, deciding whether or not such a person should be subject to a Committee of Inspection (which the contributories and creditors appoint). The liquidator then collects in all the property of the company for distribution. If the company is insolvent the distribution of assets is in the following order:

1. costs of the winding-up, including charges of the liquidator;
2. preferential creditors, including rates and taxes for twelve months and wages of a servant for four months not in excess of £200;
3. unsecured creditors;
4. referred creditors, for example those whose debts bear interest varying with the business profits.

After distribution of the company's property the liquidator applies for a court order dissolving the company, this order he then reports to the Registrar who enters the dissolution of the company on the register, thus ending the company's legal existence.

(b) Voluntary winding-up

This is done by the company and the creditors settling the company's matters without going to the court. This type of winding-up may be done on three grounds:

1. on the passing of a special resolution to wind up the company;

2. on the expiry of the time fixed for the company's existence or the achievement of the purpose for which it was created and the passing of an ordinary resolution for liquidation;

3. an extraordinary resolution being passed by the company that it cannot carry on business due to its liabilities and that the company should be wound up.

If a company is solvent it follows the procedure known as Members' Voluntary Winding-Up, involving the directors filing a declaration of solvency which states that they have examined the affairs of the company and believe it will be in a position to pay its debts in full within twelve months.

The other method involves a Creditors' Voluntary Winding-Up where no declaration of solvency has been made and a liquidator and Committee of Inspection are appointed.

(xiv) INVESTIGATION OF COMPANY AFFAIRS BY THE DEPARTMENT OF TRADE

The Department of Trade is given authority by the Companies Acts 1948 and 1967 to investigate company affairs and related matters such as company share ownership and share and debenture dealings. This is mainly done by appointment of an inspector who is normally either a Q.C., a D.O.T. official, or a chartered accountant. (*See now* Companies Act 1980, p. 287.)

(a) Company affairs

The D.O.T. *must* appoint an inspector when a court order declares that a company's affairs ought to be inspected (*see* Companies Act 1981).

The D.O.T. *may* appoint an inspector:

1. where it appears to the D.O.T. that the circumstances suggest that the business of the company either is, or has been, conducted with the intent to defraud its own or another's creditors, or has been conducted for fraudulent or other unlawful purposes, or in an oppressive manner;

2. on the application of two hundred or more members, or of members holding not less than 10 per cent of the issued share capital;

3. where it appears to the D.O.T. that the company was formed for a fraudulent or unlawful purpose;

4. where it appears that the members of the company have not been given all the information regarding the company affairs which they might reasonably expect. This would include its goodwill, profits or losses, contracts, assets and shareholding, and control of a subsidiary;

5. where the promoters or officers of the company have been guilty of a breach of duty to the company or its members.

(xvii) COMPANIES ACT 1981

The Companies Act 1981 received the royal assent on October 30, 1981. Part 1 deals with company accounting and disclosures, Part 2 with company names and business names, Part 3 deals with share capital (including relief from s. 56 of the 1948 Act dealing with the share premium account), Part 4 deals with disclosure of interests in shares. Part 5, finally, deals with miscellaneous and supplemental matters. The Act can now be briefly outlined.

Part 1 aims at giving effect to the Fourth E.E.C. Directive on Company Law Harmonization. The contents of Part 1 were foreshadowed in the Department of Trade consultative document *Company Accounts and Disclosure* (Cmnd. 7654 (1979)). Under the Fourth Directive member States are required to introduce legislation which should apply to the accounts of companies from February 1982 onwards. Together with the Seventh Directive on Group Accounts these measures make company accounts comparable throughout the Community.

For the purposes of accounting and disclosure companies are divided into three classes; small medium, and other companies.

The 1948 Act rules relating to the form and content of the accounts of companies and group accounts are replaced and a new form of accounts set down in Schedule 1 to the 1981 Act (s. 1, renumbering s. 149 Companies Act 1948 as s. 149A and introducing a new s. 149). Small and medium-sized companies are relieved from many of the strict requirements relating to balance sheets and profit and loss accounts under the 1948 Act.

Small and medium sized companies are defined (by s. 8) as:

Small companies—one which satisfies two or more of the following criteria; up to £1.4 million turnover; total balance sheet not exceeding £700,000; average number of persons employed by the company in the financial year in question not to exceed fifty. Small companies are permitted to file only an abridged balance sheet and will therefore not be required to file a profit and loss account or a directors' report.

Medium sized companies—one which satisfies two or more of the following criteria; turnover not exceeding £5.75 million; total balance sheet not exceeding £2.8m; not more than two hundred and fifty employees. Medium sized companies are allowed not to include in their accounts details of their turnover and gross profit margin.

Other companies—the following regardless of their size have to give full disclosure: public companies, banking companies, insurance companies, certain shipping companies, members of groups containing public, banking, insurance or shipping companies (s. 5). This applies to both holding and subsidiary companies in the above categories. Banking, shipping and insurance companies are permitted to continue to prepare accounts broadly on the basis of the statutory requirements under the 1948 Act.

A company publishing full individual accounts has to publish the relevant auditors' report with those accounts. A company required to prepare group accounts (under s. 1 of the 1976 Act, with s. 150 of the 1948 Act) which also publishes full individual accounts is required to publish the group accounts prepared or modified accordingly. 'Full individual accounts', 'full group accounts' and 'the relevant auditors' report' are defined in s. 11.

Dormant companies are specially dealt with in the 1981 Act. These are companies eligible to be treated as small companies and in respect of which no significant accounting transaction has taken place in the period in question. Such companies do not have to have their accounts audited (s. 12).

Part 2 provides for simplification of the arrangements governing approval of company names (s. 25 (3)). Restrictions, however, are maintained on the use of certain words and phrases (s. 22). Persons wishing to form a company are enabled to form their own judgement about whether a name will be acceptable by comparing it with those in a statutory index of the names of existing companies kept by the Registrar of Companies. Under the previous system the Registrar was required to check on the desirability of every proposed name prior to registration. Under the new provisions, in the majority of cases, there will be no need to obtain the approval of the Department of Trade and documents can be immediately submitted for registration.

The Register of Business Names is abolished by s. 119 and Schedule 4. The public disclosure provisions contained in the Registration of Business Names Act 1916 (which used a central registry) is now replaced by a self-regulating system involving individual disclosure to customers of the proprietors' names and addresses for service of writs. This is done firstly on business documents, secondly by a notice displayed at business premises, thirdly on a written request to do so by a business contact (s. 29). The abolition of the central registry and the introduction of the new system for reasons of government economy have been criticised both inside and outside Parliament. The effectiveness of the new system will depend on the degree of compliance by the business community and how rigorously it is enforced by local officials.

Part 3 deals with exceptions to s. 56 of the 1948 Act. This provides that a share premium account has to be set up in all cases in which on the issue of shares the consideration received by the company exceeds the nominal amount of the newly issued shares and that assets representing the share premium account cannot be distributed by way of dividend.

Part or complete exceptions are (a) merger by the formation of a new holding company (s. 37). This has the effect of abolishing the rule in *Henry Head Ltd. v. Ropner Holdings Ltd.* 1952 and *Shearer v. Bercain* 1980 that on acquisition of shares in a subsidiary on a share for share basis any excess in value of the acquired shares over the nominal value of the issued shares must be regarded as premium and transferred to the share premium account. Section 37 goes beyond the simple merger or take over situation. It applies to the acquisition of any shares by an issuing company on such a basis that gives that company a 90 per cent holding in the subsidiary; (b) take over by a new holding company (s. 37); (c) group reconstructions (s. 38); and (d) shares for share acquisitions before February 4, 1981 (ss. 37–39).

Part 3 also contains radical revision of the law relating to the giving of financial assistance by a company for the purchase of its own shares or those of its holding company (ss. 42–44). The prohibition under s. 54 of the 1948 Act is re-enacted by s. 42 of the 1981 Act in a modified form and applies to all companies. However, private companies are now permitted to give such financial assistance except for shares in any public holding company, subject to safeguards for creditors and minority shareholders (ss. 43, 44). These provisions, applying to private companies stem from the proposals of the Jenkins Committee Report 1962 (paras 170–187). The general prohibition against public companies was required in the 1981 Act for the reason of Article 23 of the Second E.E.C. Directive on Company Law (see p. 291) which applies only to public companies.

Part 4 strengthens the law on disclosure of interests in shares. Any person who acquires a 5 per cent interest in the voting shares of a public company or who disposes of such an interest is required to inform the company of that and also of any significant change in the number of shares in which he is interested above the 5 per cent level (s. 63). This provision applies to all public companies. A person interested in shares will be criminally liable only if he knows he has an interest which requires notification to the company and he fails in that obligation. The prosecution have to prove that the defendant knew he had interests of the relevant amounts and failed to report them. It will be enough to prove he knew enough to be aware that he possesses a substantial interest, since once he knows that and fails to notify it, he is in breach of his obligation. He will not be liable in respects of interests which he has or had but does not know about. This could arise where a person is interested in shares under a trust or by way of a concert party, that is an agreement not necessarily legally binding, to acquire interests in shares. No reporting obligation will arise where a company increases its share capital. This is because a person's interest percentage will remain unchanged unless he makes a significant acquisition.

Sections 63, 68 and 69 deal with concert parties (see above). The aim of provisions of the sections is to prevent avoidance of the existing disclosure provisions through the use of companies where interests are held on trust or for family purposes (ss. 66 and 70). Each member of the 'concert party' has the interest of other members attributed to him, even though some of the interests may not have been acquired under the concert party agreement (s. 61 (1)–(6)). Not every agreement concerning shares will be a notifiable concert party. There has to be an agreement (whether or not legally binding) by which at least one party either will retain an interest in the company's shares acquired by agreement or will acquire an interest in shares as distinct, for example, from an agreement as to have rights attached to interests in shares already held might be exercised. The latter will not be the concern of s. 63. Before an agreement becomes an effective concert party there must be an actual acquisition in accordance with it.

Under s. 71 certain interests are to be disregarded for the purposes of ss. 63–65. These include any interests in shares which are part of property held in trust in England, Wales or Scotland, a life interest in a settlement which consists of, or includes, shares, an exempt interest held by a jobber (who is a member of the Stock Exchange), or an exempt security interest, that is one held by a bank, a trustee savings bank, a Stock Exchange stockbroker, by the Bank of England or by the Post Office.

All public companies are required to keep a register for the purposes of ss. 63–65 (s. 73).

Part 5 deals with miscellaneous and supplemental matters. It includes provisions for strengthening investigations and inquiries by Department of Trade Inspectors. A company may now apply to have its affairs investigated instead of, under the 1948 Act, requiring the Secretary of State to appoint inspectors if the company so resolves by special resolution (s. 85). The Department of Trade is now forced to act only when a court order declares that a company's affairs ought to be investigated. The maximum amount for security for costs the

Department of Trade may require from an applicant or applicants is increased from £100 to £5,000.

The classes of persons required to give evidence during an investigation are extended and inspectors are given power to examine directors' bank accounts which may have been used in connection with certain offences under the Companies Acts. Inspectors no longer have to seek a court order compelling persons, other than officers and agents of the company, to come before them. Persons notified now are required to comply with an inspectors request. Such persons may be compelled to produce any books and documents relating to the company or any related company (s. 87). The Secretary of State is now only duty bound to supply a copy of an investigation to the company concerned where inspectors have been appointed by the court. In all other instances it is at the discretion of the Secretary of State to furnish such a copy (s. 88).

Where it has been alleged that the affairs of the company have been carried on in a manner oppressive to some members—i.e. in a burdensome, harsh, and wrongful way with a lack of honesty or fair dealing—then a petition under s. 210 of the Companies Act 1948 may be presented.

(b) Company membership

The D.O.T. is empowered to investigate and report on the membership of a company to determine the true persons who are able either to control or materially influence company policy or who have had, or still have, a financial interest in the success or failure of the company.

The D.O.T. does not need to appoint an inspector in such a case as under s. 173(1) of the Companies Act 1948 they can require anyone to give information, giving names and addresses, whom they reasonably believe to be or to have been interested in the shares and debentures or is, or has acted as, an agent or solicitor for another in relation to them.

In the event of difficulty in obtaining the information during investigation the D.O.T. can:

1. take away voting rights from the shares;
2. forbid the related issue of bonus shares;
3. forbid payments in relation to shares (unless the company is in liquidation);
4. forbid transfer of shares.

(c) Dealings in shares and debentures

The D.O.T. may appoint inspectors with wide powers of investigation where express provisions of the Companies Act 1967 have been reached in relation to:

1. disclosure of the interests of directors, their spouses or children in their own or an associated company's shares or debentures (ss. 27 and 31);
2. option to buy or sell quoted shares or debentures of the company or associated companies.

(d) Unit trust affairs

Under the Prevention of Fraud (Investment) Act 1958, the D.O.T. may appoint inspectors to investigate the affairs of a unit trust where the D.O.T. feels the matter is of public concern, or the interests of the unit trust holders require them to do so.

(xv) COMPANIES ACT 1976

The Companies Act 1976 makes minor changes in the law, pending legislation on the recommendations of the Bullock Committee Report 1977 (Cmnd. 6706) on employee participation.

These changes include the requirement that prior to registration the documents required must be accompanied by a form specifying the first directors and secretary of the company and the intended location of its registered office. A new structure is set up for the preparation, laying before the general meeting, and filing of annual accounts. Each company is required to specify a particular accounting reference date on which its accounting reference period is to end each year. The Act also lays down what internal accounting records must be kept by companies; these must be preserved for three years by a private company and six years by any other company. An auditor's period of office is to last from one meeting before which accounts are laid until the next such meeting and there is no automatic reappointment. The general meeting also is given power to remove an auditor in mid-term. If an auditor resigns in mid-term he must make a statement to be circulated to the shareholders and filed with the Registrar that there are no circumstances relating to his resignation which should be notified to the shareholders or creditors, or else a statement of such circumstances.

A director must notify the company of his interest within five days (previously fourteen), and if the shares or debentures of the company are listed, the company must notify the Stock Exchange of its director's interests. Substantial interests in listed voting shares requiring disclosure are re-defined as 5 per cent (or such percentage as the Secretary of State may fix by statutory instrument). Notification of acquisition, or a change in such interest must be given within five days (previously fourteen) only if the change amounts to 1 per cent or more of the company's capital. Listed companies are given the power to demand information as to any interest, substantial or not, in, and any voting agreement affecting, its voting shares. Such information must be recorded on a register.

The Insolvency Act 1976 increased financial limits relating to company liquidation. The Stock Exchange (Completion of Bargains) Act 1976 allows a computerized accounting and stock transfer to operate fully on the Stock Exchange which dispenses with the need for companies to issue certificates in respect of shares or stock held by a Stock Exchange nominee company (SEPON).

(xvi) COMPANIES ACT 1980

The Companies Act 1980, which received the royal assent on 1 May, makes important changes in company law. It implements the Second Council Directive of the E.E.C. on the formation of public limited companies and the maintenance and alteration of their capital. The Act also makes insider dealing a criminal offence. Only a brief outline is given.

Part I of the Act establishes a new classification for public and private companies. Public companies are defined by the Act to qualify for registration or re-registration as a 'public limited company'. Requirements are laid down as to the allotted or issued share capital of the company. Only public companies are now allowed to make offers allotment with a view to offer of shares and debentures to the public. It is a criminal offence for such offers or allotments to be made by private companies (s. 15). Existing public companies have fifteen months from the date when the Act comes into force to change their status to the new classification. The final part of the name of a public company will now be 'public limited company'. Private companies are not affected unless they wish to become public. In that case the Registrar of Companies now needs to be satisfied that the company's share capital meets the requirements of the Act.

Part 2 of the Act deals with the share capital of public and, in certain cases, private companies. Where the net assets of a public company fall below half of the amount of the company's called up share capital, the directors are required to call an extraordinary general meeting of the company to consider what action should be taken (s. 34). Part 2 also contains important provisions about the payment of the share capital of public companies and restates the rules in this respect concerning private companies. If the consideration for the shares is not cash, safeguards are laid down concerning the time within which the assets must be transferred to the company. Valuation must be undertaken by an independent expert. In general, the shares of public companies must be paid up or allotment to at least 25 per cent of their nominal value and the whole of any premium, whether in cash or otherwise.

Part 3 governs the distribution of profits to shareholders. The Act defines distributable profits as the aggregate of realized profits less realized losses. This carries out a requirement of the Fourth Directive that unrealized profits may not be distributed and follows the lines for clarifying the law suggested by the Jenkins Committee. Public companies under Part 3 will have to comply with an additional test whereby dividends may be paid only if the net assets of the company are, after payment of dividends, at least equal to the capital of the company plus those reserves not available for distribution. Thus public companies have to cover net losses, realized or unrealized, from realized profits before paying a dividend. An alternative method is provided for investment companies that comply with certain specified conditions.

Part 4 deals broadly with the duties of directors. A duty is imposed on directors to have regard to the interests of company employees, which is expressed clearly as a mandatory duty (s. 46). This new duty is part of the directors' general fiduciary duties towards their company. The duty is enforceable, as with such duties, by the company or, in certain circumstances, the members. This provision should encourage companies to work out means of ensuring that the interests of their employees are properly considered. The decision in *Parke v. Daily News* is expressly reversed by s. 74 which enables a company to provide for its employees if it ceases or transfers its business (including in a liquidation). This is subject to either approval by the shareholders or authorization in the memorandum and articles. Payments can only be made out of sums available for distribution in order to safeguard company creditors.

In addition certain types of transactions are regulated involving a director and persons connected with him which could lead to a conflict between the director's personal interests and his duty to his company (ss. 47–67). A general meeting of a company, and where necessary, its holding company, is required to affirm any agreement which gives a director the right to be employed for more than five years (s. 47). This provision also applies to any property transactions over £50,000 between a company and a director (s. 48). The existing prohibition on loans to directors by any company for directors of a 'relevant' company (that is, one which is itself, or is in the same group as, a public company) is now extended to include members of the director's immediate family and companies with which he is associated (s. 49). Relevant companies are also prohibited from making quasi-loans to, or other credit transactions with, directors and connected persons. Quasi-loans are defined as including payments, or agreements to do so, made by a company to a third party on a director's behalf where he is liable to repay the company. These provisions in no way affect payments or advances made for the purposes of paying expenses incurred by the directors acting as agents for the company.

Money-lending companies are permitted to have outstanding loans and quasi-loans of up to a total of £50,000 to each director and persons connected with him (s. 50). Recognized banks are allowed to lend directors without any limit (save their own) provided the lending is in the ordinary course of business and the director is in no other way connected with the bank concerned. Directors have to make proper disclosure of credit transactions and all other arrangements in which they or connected persons are interested; criminal penalties for breach are provided (ss. 54–61).

Part 5 contains provisions that make insider dealing a criminal offence. The Act stipulates that a person who has been knowingly connected with a company in the previous six months cannot deal in that company's securities if he has unpublished price-sensitive information in relation to them (s. 65). A connected person is defined as a director or an officer or an employee of the company concerned or somebody who is in a professional or business relationship with the company, such as a banker, auditor, solicitor or a consultant. This relationship must be reasonably expected to give such a person access to information which is unpublished and price-sensitive and which ought not to be disclosed to third parties (s. 69(1)). Also included is a person who obtains insider knowledge in his official capacity, such as a Crown servant or inspector appointed by the Department of Trade.

Unpublished price-sensitive information is defined as information which consists of specific matters relating to the company and which is not generally known to those persons who are accustomed or would be likely to deal in those securities but which if it were generally known to them would be likely to affect materially the price of the securities (s. 69(2)).

Exemptions are provided mainly for those acting in the ordinary course of business, such as jobbers. Their legitimate transactions are protected. Specifically trustees or personal representatives and liquidators, receivers or trustees in bankruptcy acting in good faith do not fall within the definition of an insider.

Penalties for breach of the insider provisions are a fine and up to two years' imprisonment (s. 68). Any transaction entered into in breach of the insider provisions is expressly stated to be not void or voidable as a result. No civil remedy is provided for the company or an outsider who has suffered loss. The insider provisions have received substantial criticism from business and legal circles and clearly this part of the Act will cause considerable interpretative difficulties.

The whole of 1980 Companies Act is now in operation (by virtue of the Companies Act 1980 (Commencement) Order 1980 (S.I. 1980 No. 4) and the Companies Act 1980 (Commencement No. 2) Order 1980 (S. I. 1980 1785). The exceptions to this are ss. 82 (f), 88 (2) and Schedule 4, which deal with the repeal of s. 438 and Schedule 15 to the Companies Act 1948 (penalty for false statement) and s. 65 (i); in respect of definition of 'relevant company' for the purposes of Part IV of the Companies Act 1980.

(xvii) EUROPEAN COMMUNITIES ACT 1972

The effects of the European Communities Act 1972 have already been noted with regard to the changes brought about in the *ultra vires* rule and pre-incorporation contracts.

The main aim of this part of the Act is to prepare the way for further adjustment so that a 'harmonization' of company law in the E.E.C. becomes possible (*see below*). This does not mean a unified system but the removal of important differences between member states. The Act puts into effect the Council of Ministers' directive of 9 March 1968 (s. 9). Apart from matters already dealt with, the Act provides for much more stringent publicity regulations. In future the Registrar of Companies must publish a notice of the receipt or issue by him of certain documents in the *London Gazette*. This is to bring the U.K. into line with the E.E.C. countries, where publication in the respective *Gazettes* is automatic. The E.E.C. method of compelling publication of certain documents in the *Gazette* is to make access to certain information easier.

The Act also tries to ensure that companies will officially notify certain prescribed events at the proper time. This is done by making it a rule that the company will not be able to rely on the facts, as against other persons, if the event has not been officially notified. An exception is if the company can show that the other person knew of the event at the material time. These 'events' are:

1. the making of a winding-up order in respect of the company or the appointment of a liquidator in a voluntary winding-up of the company;
2. any alteration to the company's memorandum or articles of association;
3. any change among the company's directors;
4. (as regards service of any document on the company) any change in the situation of the company's registered office (s. 9 (3), E.C.A. 1972).

The remaining sub-sections cover alterations to the articles of association and memorandum, company particulars and unregistered companies:

(a) Alterations to articles of association and memorandum (s. 9 (6))

Alterations in a company's memorandum or articles made in the past which have not been notified to the Registrar must now be so notified within one month of s-s. 6 coming into operation (31.1.73). The notification must be in the form of a printed copy of the memorandum or articles.

This is a far-reaching provision since many private and public companies will have made changes in their memorandum or articles and will not have delivered a copy of the altered articles or memorandum to the Registrar (unless they are already required to do so, e.g. s. 5 (7), Companies Act 1948).

Failure to comply with the requirements of s-s. 6 will result in default fines for both the company and the officers concerned.

(b) Company particulars (s. 9 (7))

Every company shall have the following particulars mentioned in legible characters on all business letters and order forms of the company:

1. the place of registration of the company, and the number with which it is registered;
2. the address of its registered office;
3. in the case of companies having a share capital, where there is a reference on the letter-headings or order forms to share capital, the reference shall be to paid-up share capital;
4. where limited companies are permitted to dispense with the word 'limited', a statement that the company is limited.

(c) Unregistered companies (s. 9 (8))

Under the Companies Act 1948, an unregistered company includes any trustee savings bank (certified under the Trustee Savings Bank Act 1863), any partnership, limited or not, any association and any company, with the following exceptions:

1. a partnership or association with less than eight members, not being a foreign partnership or association;
2. a limited partnership registered in England or in Northern Ireland (s. 398, Companies Act 1948).

The effect of s-s. 8 is to bring unregistered companies broadly under the provisions which are required to be filed in the case of registered companies. (*Note:* s-s. 8 should be read with s. 435 and the 14th schedule of the Companies Act 1948 in this context.)

(xviii) THE E.E.C. AND COMPANY LAW

(a) Harmonization

The E.E.C. Commission has laid down a series of proposals for the harmonization of company law in the form of Directives which will, no doubt, even with modification and amendment, have considerable effect on our own system.

There are important differences between the company law and practice of other E.E.C. member states and our own. For instance, continental equivalents of our public companies (the German A.G. and the French S.A.) are governed by legislation that is separate from that which regulates their 'private' companies (the German GmbH and the French SARL); in the U.K. all companies are dealt with under one Act. Additionally the continental members of E.E.C. have not such well-developed Stock Exchanges as we have with similarly stringent company formation, dealing and quotation requirements.

Again, although E.E.C. company law strongly emphasizes creditor protection, financial disclosure provisions are not as wide or as sophisticated as those demanded by U.K. law.

(b) Methods

The first Directive has already been incorporated into English Company Law in the form of s. 9 of the European Communities Act 1972. The remaining four Directives deal with the following matters:

1. share issue and the maintenance of capital;
2. national mergers;
3. form and content of annual accounts;
4. company structure and management.

1. *Share issue and maintenance of capital*

This Directive requires companies to have a minimum share capital of £10,000. Clearly such a provision would mean that, unless exempted, private companies in the U.K. would no longer be able to operate with token share capital. This is an area which obviously will need compromise and amendment.

The Directive also provides that there will be no distribution of dividend if net assets fall below subscribed capital. Dividends should only be paid out of 'clear profits'.

Where capital is increased by shares issued for cash the existing shares must be fully paid.Any reduction of capital must be approved by a general meeting and class meetings if the reduction is detrimental to the class. Creditors must be satisfied or given security unless the assets of the company are sufficient to make this unnecessary.

2. *National mergers*

This topic has been discussed under Restrictive Trade Practices (Chapter 2). This Directive deals with internal mergers of public limited companies and foreshadows an E.E.C. convention on mergers across frontiers under Article 220 of the E.E.C. Treaty, but yet to be formulated. The governments of the E.E.C. have until 9 October 1981 to give effect to the Directive.

3. *Form and content of the annual accounts*

This Directive is firstly concerned with the layout and content of the annual accounts. This contains precise accounting rules which are absent from British legislation and the proposals, as they stand, would apply to all companies except insurance and credit companies. The other proposals contain extensive requirements for the full publication in the *Gazette* of the accounts and the auditor's report of all quoted public companies and large private companies. Member states have two years to amend their national laws in order to conform to the Directive's requirements (the Directive was published on 14 August 1978). However, member states may stipulate that national legislation shall not apply for a further eighteen months; in certain circumstances this period of time is extended to five years. This is the case of unregistered companies in the U.K. and Ireland, and the situation in which other forms of layout of balance sheets and profit and loss accounts other than those prescribed in the Directive have been brought into force by national legislation not more than three years before notification of the Directive.

Note: The Eighth Directive deals with qualification of auditors. These must have satisfactory qualifications in order to be approved by the governments of member states as persons fit to be company auditors.

4. *Company structure and management*

This last Directive will only apply to the continental equivalent of our large public companies (A.G. and S.A.), so that it is unlikely to have any effect on the smaller companies. The proposals are aimed at all major multi-national companies based in one or more of the E.E.C. countries.

The Directive includes machinery for joint decision-making within companies which although novel to British practice has been part of the industrial scene in other E.E.C. countries for some years, notably West Germany where it is termed 'co-determination'. The aim of the Directive is to provide a common legal framework for each of the member states of the E.E.C. Three levels of the proposed 'European Company' are laid down:

(i) the general meeting of shareholders;
(ii) the supervisory board (appointed by the shareholders);
(iii) the management board (appointed by the supervisory board).

In a company of over five hundred employees one-third of the supervisory board is elected by the employees. A member of the supervisory board cannot serve on the management board or on more than ten supervisory boards.

10:2 PARTNERSHIPS

(i) DEFINITION

A partnership is 'a relationship which subsists between persons carrying on a business in common with a view to profit' (s. 1 (1), Partnership Act 1890).

(ii) CREATION

A partnership can be created by conduct, in writing, orally, or under seal; normally a partnership deed will be drawn up which provides for the internal management of the business. The law of contract governs capacity to enter into a partnership. An alien may enter into partnership with a British subject, but this would be dissolved on the alien becoming an enemy. A minor is bound by a contract of partnership unless he repudiates it within a reasonable time of reaching the age of 18 (about one year).

(iii) PARTNERSHIP NAME

A partnership with a place of business in the U.K. must have its name registered under the Registration of Business Names Act 1916 (unless the true names of the partners are used without any addition except the initials or christian names). Change of partners also requires registration.

A firm that does not register in this way cannot sue on any contract entered into during the period of non-compliance, but it can defend an action on such a contract if sued.

(iv) NUMBERS

The general limit on partnership membership is a maximum of twenty. If this figure is exceeded then the partnership has to register as a company under the Companies Act 1948. Normally, banking partnerships must not exceed ten but they may rise to twenty with the permission of the D.O.T. under the 1967 Companies Act. The Act also permits partnerships of solicitors, accountants or members of the Stock Exchange of over twenty members.

(v) RELATIONS OF PARTNERS TO THIRD PARTIES

For the purpose of carrying on the firm's business every partner is looked on as the agent of the other partners and of the business. The acts of a partner bind the firm if these are carried on in the way of business normally transacted by the firm, unless the partner was unauthorized to act in this manner or the person with whom he was dealing knew of his lack of authority or did not believe he was a partner. Apart from this the partners of a firm have an authority implied by law to:

(*a*) purchase goods usually used in the firm's business on its behalf;
(*b*) take on employees for the carrying out of business;
(*c*) sell the firm's goods;
(*d*) take payment of debts due to the firm and give receipts for these.

Partners in a trading firm in addition may:

(*a*) borrow money on the credit of the business and charge the firm's goods for this purpose;
(*b*) take, make, and issue negotiable instruments in the name of the firm;
(*c*) instruct a solicitor to sue on behalf of the firm for a trade debt.

If the credit of the firm is pledged by a partner for a purpose not apparently connected with the firm's usual business, unless he is specially authorized to do this by his fellow partners, the firm is not bound. However, although the partner incurs personal liability in this case, his act may be ratified by the other partners. Where, under the partnership agreement, restrictions are placed on the power of any of the firm's partners, any act in breach of these does not bind the firm, nor can a third party enforce any agreement outside the limitations if they had notice of them. Where a third party has no notice and the act is within the usual business of the firm then the partnership will be bound.

The partnership is liable for wrongs committed by any of its partners where these have been authorized by the others or done in the ordinary course of the firm's business. For example, if a partner acting within the apparent scope of his authority misapplies the property of a third party he has received or which is in the firm's care, then the partnership will have to compensate the third party in the event of loss. Liability for the firm's wrongs is several (individual) and joint, while their liability for the firm's contracts is joint only. Where liability is *joint*, a judgement obtained against some but not all of the partners frees the others from liability, so that a creditor cannot obtain judgement against these others if the earlier judgement is not satisfied. But where liability is *joint and several*, a judgement against one partner is no bar to a subsequent legal action against the others.

In respect of unsatisfied debts the estate of a deceased partner is liable jointly and severally for debts incurred while he was a partner, subject to his own private debts being given priority. However, where a partnership continues to use the name of a partner who has died this does not make the estate liable for partnership debts contracted after his death.

(vi) RIGHTS AND DUTIES BETWEEN PARTNERS

The articles of partnership govern the relations between the individual partners. Most partnerships are governed by Articles; in their absence the following rules are laid down by the Partnership Act 1890:

(a) Rights

1. All partners are entitled to share equally in the profits and capital and must contribute equally to losses (except where one of the partners is a limited partner under the Limited Partnership Act 1907, and is therefore not liable for the debts of the firm beyond the amount he has contributed).
2. Before profits have been determined no partner is entitled to interest on capital.
3. No partner is entitled to remuneration for acting in the partnership (however, 'drawings' are allowed, which in practice amounts to the same thing).
4. Unless the partners all agree no new person can be introduced without the agreement of all the existing partners. (Most Articles provide for the introduction of new partners.)
5. The majority of partners acting in good faith and considering minority views must decide any differences over ordinary partnership matters. All must consent if there is to be a change in the nature of the partnership business.
6. A partner cannot be expelled by a majority of the partners unless they are empowered to do so under the Articles (which is frequently the case).
7. Any partner advancing money for the purpose of the business over the amount of capital he has agreed to subscribe is entitled to receive interest on the advance at the rate of 5 per cent.
8. Partners have the right of access to books, which must be kept at the place of business.
9. The firm must indemnify a partner for payments and liabilities resulting from the ordinary course of partnership business, or arising from the need to preserve the firm's business or property.

(b) Duties

Each partner is under the following duties to the other to:

1. Disclose any benefit he has obtained from a deal or use of the property of the partnership, or involving its name, or business connections. This includes

disclosure of, and accounting for, any secret profit made in the course of the firm's dealings.
2. Render full information and true accounts in relation to all matters affecting the partnership.
3. Avoid competition with the firm. If a partner does compete with the firm he must account to the partnership for all profits accrued. A business that does not involve utilization of the firm's property and is of a non-competitive nature is perfectly valid.

(vii) CHANGE OF PARTNERS

A partner who retires from a partnership must give notice of his retirement and, to be safe, advertise this fact in the *London Gazette* to avoid liability for debts incurred by the firm after his retirement. He continues to be liable for debts incurred during his membership of the firm unless there is an agreement, express or implied between the new partnership, the creditors, and himself. A new partner has no liability for debts incurred before he became a partner unless he agrees to take over the liability of the retiring partners.

The firm can be reconstituted when a partner either dies or retires and the partnership is continued by the remaining partners. The partner who retires has the following rights:

(*a*) Any sums owing to him are deemed to be a debt accruing at the date of his retirement unless the articles provide otherwise.
(*b*) An account may be taken on his request of the partnership assets, on retirement.
(*c*) He is entitled (subject to a contrary intention in the articles) to:

1. either interest at 5 per cent on the value of his share of the assets, or
2. a share of the partnership's profits attributable to the use of his share of the assets (allowing for management by the remaining partners) where the partners who stay to carry on the business are using the retired partner's share.

(viii) PARTNERSHIP PROPERTY

In accordance with the partnership agreement, partnership property must be used solely for the partnership. Such property is:

(*a*) property acquired on account of the firm or for the purpose of, and in the course of, the partnership business;
(*b*) unless the contrary appears, property purchased with the firm's money;
(*c*) property brought into the partnership stock on the firm's formation.

Unless a judgement is entered against the firm, partnership property cannot be taken in execution of a debt.

(ix) DISSOLUTION OF PARTNERSHIP

(a) Grounds

1. Withdrawal of one partner from the partnership may dissolve the partnership (unless the articles provide otherwise).
2. If the partnership is of a limited duration or for a specific purpose, it ends when time has elapsed or the purpose has been achieved.
3. Transfer by a partner of his share will dissolve the partnership (unless the articles provide otherwise) by:
(i) a partner permitting his share to be charged by the court for his separate debt; here the partner may either dissolve the partnership or pay off the debt;
(ii) death or bankruptcy of the partner.
4. The partnership ends if it becomes illegal.
5. If the partnership has been fraudulently created it may be dissolved.
6. The partnership may be dissolved by the court on application by a partner:
(i) if the conduct of one of the partners makes it impracticable for the others to continue with him as a member;
(ii) if the partner becomes permanently incapable of performing his part of the partnership agreement;
(iii) if the business can only be carried on at a loss;
(iv) where the court thinks it just and equitable to dissolve the partnership (for instance if the partnership is permanently locked in hostile disagreement and its management is greatly impaired as a result);
(v) where the court feels dissolution necessary because of the mental incapacity of a partner. The partner concerned may obtain relief from the court under the Mental Health Act 1959, ss. 101 and 103.

(b) Distribution of property

On dissolution property is distributed as follows:

1. in satisfying the claims of partnership creditors;
2. in repaying to partners rateably amounts they have paid to partnership funds as distinct from capital;
3. in paying each partner on a rateable basis what is due to him in respect of capital;
4. in distributing any surplus to the partners in the same proportion as profits are divided (unless the articles provided otherwise, this will be equally).

Under the partnership agreement rules (2) and (4) may be varied but creditors' claims have to be satisfied first.

Example A

A partnership goes into dissolution. Total assets are £6,200. Creditors' claims total £2,500. There are three partners, *A*, *B*, *C*, each of whom has contributed £1,000 on the formation of the partnership. *A* has special technical knowledge so they agree that profits shall be distributed 40 per cent to *A* and 30 per cent each to *B* and *C*. Two years earlier the partnership got into difficulties and *B* advanced a further £500.

On dissolution:

The creditors take	£2,500
B takes his advance (5% interest)	550
A, B, and C take their original capital	3,000
A takes 40% of the surplus	60
B takes 30% of the surplus	45
C takes 30% of the surplus	45
	£6,200

If partnership assets are not sufficient to meet the claims of creditors and leave a surplus for the partners the debts are met from:

(*a*) any partnership profits,
(*b*) from partnership capital,
(*c*) from the separate estates of the individual partners in proportion to the distribution of profits if there had been any.

Example B

Taking the facts of the previous example, but assuming partnership assets totalling only £2,100, there would be a deficit of £400 with regard to creditors. This would be met by the partners out of their separate estates as follows:

A	£160
B	£120
C	£120
	£400

A's advance would then be repaid.

If after payment of the firm's creditors' and partners' advances the assets are insufficient to repay each partner his capital in full, this deficiency must be borne by the partners in the same proportion as the profits would have been divided.

But if one of the partners is insolvent and cannot pay in his share of the deficiency, the other partners must make good the insolvent partner's portion of the deficiency in proportion to their respective capitals, and not in proportion to their share of profits and losses.

(*Garner v. Murray*, 1904)

Example C

A, B, and C are partners with agreed capitals of:

A	£6,000
B	4,000
C	700
	£10,700

and they share profits and losses equally.

After creditors' and partners' advances had been paid off the assets left over amounted to £8,000, leaving a deficiency of £2,700 on capital. Each partner is therefore liable to contribute £900. If *C* is insolvent and can pay nothing he will lose his right to repayment of his capital of £700, and leave the fund with £200 short. This shortage must be borne by *A* and *B* in proportion to their capitals, as follows:

$$A: \tfrac{3}{5} \text{ (£6,000 capital)} = £120$$
$$B: \tfrac{2}{5} \text{ (£4,000 capital)} = £80$$

Note: Accountants differ as to the practical interpretations of the rule in *Garner v. Murray*.

QUESTIONS

1. (*a*) What is meant by the memorandum of association of a company? How, and for what reasons, may it be changed?
   (*b*) A company has been formed to carry on the business of selling fish and chips together with half-a-dozen other objects. The fish and chip business collapses after six years and the directors now propose to rely on another object set out in the memorandum of association, namely: 'To borrow money and to use it profitably in furtherance of the company's objects'. The memorandum of association makes it clear that this object is to be construed as a main object of the company. Is the proposal of the directors free from legal problems?

   (Diploma in Marketing, Part II, November 1974)
2. (*a*) How does a partnership differ from a company?
   (*b*) Business associates, Victor and Walter, bought in equal shares, with fees received from profits made in the business, additional property for use as a warehouse. The business between Victor and Walter is run as a limited partnership, in which they enjoy limited liability. A sleeping partner, Xan, has unlimited liability. The partnership runs into difficulties and the creditors wish to sell the warehouse to meet the debt owed to them. Advise the creditors.

   (Certificate in Marketing, Part II, June 1979)
3. (*a*) What is meant by *ultra vires*?
   (*b*) What is the basic legal position of a company that has entered into an *ultra vires* agreement with a third party?
4. Distinguish the memorandum of a company from its articles of association. How, and for what reasons, may they be changed?

   (Certificate in Marketing, Part II, June 1979)
5. What are the rights of a person who applies for shares or debentures in a company where there has been fraud or misrepresentation in the prospectus? What defences are open to a director or an expert named in the prospectus?
6. Distinguish a floating charge from a fixed charge and briefly summarize the advantages and disadvantages of each.
7. Outline the position, powers, and duties of directors.
8. What are the different classes of resolution that may be passed by a company and give examples of the type of business for which each is required.

9. Outline the statutory powers given to the Department of Trade to carry out an investigation into the affairs of a company?
10. (*a*) What is meant by the reconstruction of a company?
    (*b*) How may this be carried out?
11. Under what circumstances may a company be wound up and by what means can this be done?
12. Describe the liabilities of partners to third parties with whom they deal.
13. How are partnership assets distributed on dissolution?

11. *Insurance*

DESCRIPTION

A contract of insurance is one where the insurer agrees to indemnify the insured on the occurrence of a specified happening. The insured person pays a premium under the insurance policy, which insures him against the particular risk.

11:1   INSURABLE INTEREST

A person must have an insurable interest in the property he is insuring—i.e. the likelihood of loss if the property is destroyed or damaged. In the case of marine insurance the Marine Insurance Act 1906 states that a person has an insurable interest in a maritime transaction when he will 'benefit by the safety or due arrival of insurable property, or may be prejudiced by its loss, or by damage thereto, or by detention thereof, or may incur liability in respect thereof'. In c.i.f. contracts (Chapter 4) the seller insures on the buyer's behalf and the goods insured are at the risk of the buyer, who can claim under the policy. With contracts of life assurance the insurable interest must exist when the policy is taken out but does not have to exist at the time when a claim is made.

Example

An insurance company issued to *B* a life policy on the life of *A*, who was *B*'s creditor. *A* died and the company refused to pay out the policy on the basis that the beneficiary had no insurable interest.
Held: The sum stated in the policy was payable on death or any other agreed date of maturity and no insurable interest at the date of payment was required.
(*Dalby v. India and London Life Assurance Co.*, 1854)

A company can insure its employees' lives including those of its executives; similarly, a person has an insurable interest in his own life, and in that of his wife, but not in the lives of his children unless he is dependent on them. A shareholder does not own the company's property in law and so he has no insurable interest in its activities.

Example

The chief asset of a company was insured by its majority shareholder. When the asset was destroyed by fire he sued the insurance company on the policy.
Held: He would not succeed as he had no insurable interest in the company's property as the company was a separate legal person.
(*Macaura v. Northern Assurance Co.*, 1925)

Under the Life Assurance Act 1774, s. 2, a person assuring the life of another must insert the name of the beneficiary in the policy or it will be void. The sum insured must not exceed the interest in the life insured.

11:2 UBERRIMAE FIDEI

An insurance contract is one of utmost good faith (*uberrimae fidei*) which is owed to the insurer. The person seeking insurance must disclose what are legally termed all 'material facts'. In practice it will be a term of the proposal form that the facts stated there are the basis of the contract. So if any of the statement in the proposal form are untrue even in a minor sense the insurers may avoid the policy.

Example

A insured his lorry with an insurer. The policy stated that the proposal form would be the basis of the contract. In answer to a question as to the place where the lorry was usually garaged, *A* put down his Glasgow address although the vehicle was in fact garaged outside the city.
Held: The insurer could avoid the policy as the mis-statement was a breach of the conditions under which the policy was issued.

(*Dawsons Ltd. v. Bonnin*, 1922)

A person is under a duty to an insurer to reveal all facts that are material to the risk and likely to affect the insurer's judgement, even if no questions are put on that particular point.

Example

On a proposal form *A* answered the question 'Has a proposal ever been made on your life at any other office or offices?' by stating the names of two offices. He did not mention that other offices had refused to insure his life.
Held: He was under a duty to disclose this and as there had been a material concealment the company could set aside the policy.

(*London Assurance v. Mansel*, 1879)

11:3 TYPES OF INSURANCE

(i) LIFE ASSURANCE

Under this type of insurance an insurer undertakes to pay a certain sum of money at the end of a definite period or on the death of the insured if it occurs at an earlier date. A life-only policy will provide a man's widow with the insurance monies due. Alternatively, a life endowment policy provides for regular payment of premium over a period of years at the end of which, or at the date of death (if earlier), the specified sum becomes payable; this is basically a form of saving.

(ii) MARINE INSURANCE

A contract of marine insurance is defined as one under which the insurer agreed to indemnify the assured against marine losses. The policy is usually negotiated through Lloyd's or one of the large insurance companies. A Lloyd's policy will be underwritten by a number of other underwriters each of whom is only liable for his share under the underwriting agreement. Under a company policy the company remains liable for the full amount even if it has re-insured part of the risk.

Marine policies fall into five main categories:

(a) Floating policies

Where the insurance is described in general terms. The name of the ship, goods to be shipped, and their value are defined by subsequent declaration to the insurer. If the value is not stated until after notice of loss or arrival, the goods are treated as unvalued for the purposes of the policy. After completion of the voyage the amount is written off the policy.

(b) Time policies

These are insurance contracts for a specific period of time. A 'continuation clause' is usually added which provides that if the ship is still at sea at the end of the period, cover will continue until the ship's arrival in port or for a reasonable time afterwards.

(c) Voyage policies

Under this type of contract the subject-matter is insured for only a specified voyage.

(d) Valued policies

Under these the value of the subject-matter is agreed in advance and specified in the policy.

(e) Unvalued policies

Here the value of the subject-matter is left to be assessed subsequently subject to the limit of the sum insured.

(iii) THIRD PARTY

This type of insurance has various forms; for example, under the Occupier's Liability Act 1957, occupiers of property can insure against liability. Car insurance provides a key illustration of how third-party insurance operates. The 1930 Road Traffic Act gives an injured third party the rights of the insured motorist against the insurance company. The insurer's duty to indemnify the motorist is dependent on the motorist's duty to compensate the injured third party being proved either by judgement of a court or by arbitration award, or by agreement between the parties and the insurers.

All drivers have to be insured against liability for death or injury caused to anyone as a result of the use of the vehicle on the road. The insurer cannot limit the insurance in relation to the condition of the vehicle, weight of goods, or number of passengers carried, or the age or condition of the driver. The majority of passengers carried in motor vehicles from 1 December 1972 are now compulsorily insured. Thus the common use of 'all passengers travel at their own risk' stickers will generally cease to have any legal effect (Road Traffic Act 1971, s. 145 (1)).

Note: A third party who is injured by an uninsured driver (in relation to third party risks) can bring an action against the Motor Insurers' Bureau.

(iv) FIRE INSURANCE

Like all the types of insurance mentioned so far, fire insurance is a contract of indemnity. Under this agreement an insurer agrees to indemnify the insured against loss or injury by fire with regard to certain property for a specified period. The insured must have an insurable interest in the property insured and if he suffers no loss he will not be entitled to recover any money under the agreement.

Example

A took out a fire insurance policy on his house. He agreed to sell the house to *B*, but before the sale was completed fire damaged the house. The insurance company paid the agreed compensation to *A* and then sought to recover it after *B* had completed the sale on the ground that *A* had suffered no loss.
Held: The company could recover from *A*, otherwise *A* would have made a profit on the insurance.

(Castellain v. Preston, 1883)

To avoid this type of situation the insurer can stand in the shoes of the insured and enforce any remedy to which the insured was entitled against any third party. This is known as the principle of subrogation.

Example

A insured her property with an insurance company, and while the policy was in force Plymouth Corporation gave her notice for the compulsory purchase of the premises. Before the Corporation had proceeded further, fire destroyed the property and the insurers paid out £925 to *A* under the policy. *A* later agreed with the Corporation to reduce the purchase price they were to pay by the amount of compensation received from the insurers.
Held: The insurers could recover the £925 as the contract was one of indemnity and from the date of the compulsory purchase notice the buildings were at the Corporation's risk, *A* being entitled to the full amount of the purchase money in spite of the fire.

(Phoenix Assurance Co. v. Spooner, 1905)

Similarly a person who under-insures must bear any loss proportionately with the insurers. This is the principle of average. In practice it is included in fire insurance policies.

Example

A purchases a house for £10,000 which insures for £10,000. After two years it is worth £15,000 but the policy is renewed for £10,000. The house is damaged by fire to the extent £3,000. The policy contains an average clause under which *A* can only recover two-thirds of the loss:

i.e.
$$\frac{£10,000}{£15,000} \times \frac{£3,000}{1} = £2,000$$

Where there is total loss and the property is over-insured, the insured cannot recover the sum under the policy; if the over-insurance was done in good faith the insured may recover a proportionate part of the premium.

11:4 CONSEQUENTIAL LOSS

Consequential damages are those arising from some form of loss which has occurred as a direct consequence of an earlier event, a fire, an accident, negligence, or some other insurable risk. Consequential loss has already been considered in connection with exemption clauses (*see* Chapter 2); here only the insurance aspect will be considered.

A businessman has to learn to live with certain risks inherent in trade, such as change in import and export controls, devaluation of the currency, strikes, and international crises. Some risks can be insured against, including actual destruction of goods and property, and additionally loss of profits that may result. A well-recognized insurable risk is that of a supplier, who may suffer fire damage with a consequential loss of profits to the firm. This type of insurance emerged from fire insurance. A standard fire insurance policy would cover only the value of the property destroyed and not profits likely to be lost due to rebuilding of premises. Most businesses today regard insurance limited to the value of the property as inadequate, and consequential or loss of profit insurance has developed as a result. Insurance can also be obtained to cover losses due to interruption of gas, water, or electricity supplies. Cover for loss of profits must be specified and it is not insured against in ordinary fire or other policies.

Example

An inn was insured against fire by *A*. After a fire had taken place and damaged the property, *A* included in his claim the rent he had to pay to his landlord, the cost of hiring other accommodation while the premises were being repaired, and the loss sustained due to his customers not being able to use the inn while under repair.
Held: None of these was recoverable.

(Re *Wright and Pole*, 1834)

Where a policy allows recovery for consequential loss, a line is drawn between events that are a direct consequence of the original risk occurring and those that are not. The degree of remoteness tested is that the consequential event must have been foreseeable. This point has already been considered in Chapter 1 in relation to remoteness of damage arising from a breach of contract (*Hadley v. Baxendale, Victoria Laundry v. Newman Industries*). In the context of fire insurance on a business, loss of profits and personal injuries are foreseeable and would be specified under the policy.

11:5   CONTROL OF INSURANCE

In the last four years Parliament has legislated for closer control of insurance businesses.

The Insurance Companies Amendment Act 1973, following on the difficulties of Nation Life, gave power to the then Department of Trade and Industry to make regulations on solvency, asset valuation, and on the types of investment which insurance companies might make. The Insurance Companies Act 1974 which came into operation on January 1, 1981, consolidated earlier enactments and protects the public against small companies which fail to meet their liabilities. The Act includes provisions relating to minimum paid-up capital and the Secretary of State is empowered to petition for winding-up. Regulations made under the Act lay down forms of revenue account, and statements of business to be prepared by insurance companies in respect of their industrial assurance business (see Insurance (Accounts and Forms) Regulations 1980, S.I. 1980 No. 6). The Policyholders' Protection Act 1975 set up a Policyholders' Protection Board of five members appointed by the Secretary of State. When an insurance company goes into liquidation the Board has to ensure that certain liabilites are met. These must be met in full where particular statutes apply—e.g. the Road Traffic Act 1972, the Employers' Liability (Compulsory Insurance) Act 1969, the Nuclear Installations Act 1965 and the Riding Establishments Act 1964. In other cases where the Policyholders' Act applies these liabilities must be met up to 90 per cent; such cases include private policies with th exception of marine, aviation, transport insurance and reinsurance. The Insurance Companies Act 1981 amends the 1974 Act. The Act includes provisions restricting the carrying on of insurance business (as distinct from industrial assurance business) in the United Kingdom to those bodies authorized by the Secretary of State. This will not apply to insurance business carried on by a member of Lloyds, a registered friendly society or a trade union or employers' association.

QUESTIONS

1. (a) With the aid of illustrations, show what is meant by a contract *uberrimae fidei* (utmost good faith).
   (b) Fido fills in proposal forms for a policy on his own life and for a fire insurance policy. On the proposal form for the life assurance policy, he answers a question about his health as follows: 'No illness to report. Please contact my doctor for confirmation and further particulars.' Lower down the form, there is a space for the doctor's name and address. Fido had consulted his doctor about a year previously about a chest pain but the doctor had assured him that there was nothing wrong with his health.
   As to the fire insurance policy, Fido does not declare:
   (i) that he claimed on a policy with another insurance company for jewellery lost when his wife emptied the contents of a handbag into the dustbin without checking carefully whether it contained any valuables; and,
   (ii) that his neighbour in the semi-detached house next door has had two outbreaks of fire within the last five years.

Three months later, after taking out these policies, Fido becomes seriously ill with lung cancer, although his death follows an outbreak of fire at his home when his lighted cigarette end sets the bed clothes on fire. Is the insurance company entitled to refuse to pay up on either or both of the policies when Fido's widow lodges a claim?

(Diploma in Marketing, Part II, May 1975)

2. *A* purchases a house for £8,000 in 1968 which he insures for £8,000. In 1970 when the house is valued at £12,000 fire breaks out and does damage to the extent of £8,000. *A*'s insurance policy contains an average clause. What will *A* receive from his insurers?

3. (*a*) What is meant by subrogation?
    (*b*) *X* insures property against fire risk. Shortly before the buildings are damaged by fire, negotiations are begun with a prospective purchaser and *X* receives £1,000 from the insurance company. On completion of the sale the company seek to recover the sum from *X*. Advise *X*.

12. *Negotiable Instruments*

12:1 TYPES OF NEGOTIABLE INSTRUMENTS

The most commonly used negotiable instruments are cheques, bills of exchange, and promissory notes, and it is with these first two that this chapter is primarily concerned. The other types of negotiable instrument should be noted:

(a) Banknotes

These are issued only by the Bank of England and are promissory notes payable on demand but inconvertible. They are legal tender.

(b) Bearer bonds

These are negotiable where issued by an English company and payable to bearer. Foreign government bonds are negotiable if they are customarily negotiable in this country and the country of origin.

(c) Treasury bills

These are bills issued by the British government under statutory provision.

(d) Dividend and share warrants

Share warrants are negotiable only if they are made out to bearer.

The chief characteristics of a negotiable instrument are:

(a) Delivery of the instrument to another party also transfers rights it represents.
(b) A holder in due course (*see* Cheques) is not affected by previous defects of title to the instrument.
(c) The holder in due course is bound to be paid by the acceptor of a bill of exchange.
(d) A holder of a bill of exchange can sue on it in his own name.
(e) Any person liable on a negotiable instrument does not need to be given notice of assignment.

The following documents, although similar in some ways to the examples of negotiable instruments listed above, are *not* negotiable:

(a) bills of lading;
(b) dock warrants;
(c) share certificates;
(d) postal orders.

12:2 BILLS OF EXCHANGE

(i) DEFINITION

A bill of exchange is an unconditional order in writing, addressed by one person to another, signed by the person giving it, requiring the person to whom it is addressed to pay on demand or at a fixed and determinable future time a sum certain in money to or to the order of a specified person, or to bearer (s. 3 (1), Bills of Exchange Act 1882).

Much of the law that applies to bills of exchange also applies to cheques so that the common rules will be explained in later reference to cheques.

(ii) PARTIES TO A BILL OF EXCHANGE

(*a*) the drawer—the person giving the order to pay;
(*b*) the drawee—the person who is ordered to pay;
(*c*) the payee—the person in whose favour the payment is made.

Capacity with regard to liability of a party on a bill of exchange is co-extensive with contractual capacity. The holder of a bill can enforce payment against other parties to it where a minor or corporation have drawn or endorsed a bill without the capacity to do so.

(iii) ACCEPTANCE

Acceptance of a bill indicates the agreement of the drawee to the drawer's order. Acceptance, to be valid, must be written on the bill and signed by the drawee (his signature sufficing), who thereby undertakes to make a payment of the money indicated.

Acceptance can be either general or qualified:

(*a*) *General acceptance*

This amounts to unqualified agreement by the drawee to carry out completely the order of the drawer.

(*b*) *Qualified acceptance*

By this the drawee shows that his acceptance will not extend to all the terms in the bill. There are five types of qualified acceptance:

1. *Local*
'Accepted payable at Barclays Bank, High Street, Colchester' indicates that the bill will only be accepted for payment at that particular place.

2. *Qualified in time*
Where a bill is drawn payable twenty days after the date but accepted payable thirty days after that date.

3. *Conditional*
'Accepted, payable on delivery of bill of lading for 1,000 tons bright bar steel'—payment is dependent on this condition being carried out.

4. *Acceptance by some, but not all, drawees*

5. *Partial*
Where the acceptance is to pay only part of the amount for which the bill is drawn—e.g. a bill drawn for £300, accepted for £100.

The holder may refuse a qualified acceptance and decide to treat the bill as dishonoured.

(iv) INLAND AND FOREIGN BILLS

(*a*) An inland bill is one drawn and payable in the British Isles or drawn in the British Isles on a person resident in them (this includes the Channel Islands).

(*b*) A foreign bill is any other bill.

(v) NOTICE OF DISHONOUR

If a bill is dishonoured for non-payment the holder can act against the drawer and endorsers of the bill (*see under* Cheques) by giving notice of dishonour to the drawer and each endorser (if this is not done they are not liable).

Noting and protesting are legal formalities that must be complied with when a foreign bill is dishonoured so as to provide clear evidence to international businessmen that they have been so dishonoured. Noting is a preliminary to the more formal procedure of protesting, but neither is necessary in the case of an inland bill.

(*a*) *Noting*

In the case of a dishonoured bill this is taken to a notary public who notes on it the date, a register reference, noting charges and initials it, with an attached ticket giving the answer received on presentment for payment.

(*b*) *Protest*

A certificate formally confirming that the bill has been dishonoured is obtained from a notary public with a copy of the bill.

In cases where a notary public is unavailable, any householder can give a certificate attesting dishonour. The certificate must be witnessed and signed by two other persons.

(vi) DISCHARGE

A bill may be discharged by:

(*a*) cancellation;
(*b*) negotiation on the bill maturing to the acceptor;
(*c*) renunciation or express waiver;
(*d*) payment to a holder in due course either by the drawee or by someone on his behalf;
(*e*) material alteration (exclusive of one that is accidental or unintentional). If such an alteration has been made on purpose all the drawers must make confirmation of this.

12:3 CHEQUES

(i) DEFINITION

A cheque is a bill of exchange drawn on a banker and payable on demand (s. 73, Bills of Exchange Act 1882). Cheques are additionally governed by the Cheques Act 1957.

(ii) NATURE

(*a*) A cheque must be payable to or to the order of a specified person (or exceptionally to bearer).

(*b*) A cheque must be for a sum certain in money signed either by the drawer or on his behalf.

A customer owes a duty to his bank to use reasonable care in the way he draws and signs his cheques to avoid their easy alteration or addition. In one decided case a customer who had drawn a cheque so that the words and figures '£50' could be easily changed to '£150' was held liable to reimburse the full amount paid by his bank. If the alteration is an obvious one, forged or otherwise, the bank will be judged to have been negligent and must bear the loss itself (*see under* Banker's position). A cheque may be justifiably refused if there are grounds for suspicion; as where cheques have been drawn in an unusual or ambiguous way or there is evidence that they have been tampered with.

(*c*) A cheque must be unconditional; a document requiring payment on demand of a sum of money subject to the completion of a receipt form is a 'conditional order to pay' and not a cheque.

(*d*) A cheque can be post-dated or pre-dated.

(*e*) A cheque must be drawn on a bank. A bank draft (any document drawn by a branch bank on another branch or head office) is not a cheque.

(*f*) A cheque may be crossed or uncrossed. Where it is crossed this may be a general or special crossing.

1. *General crossing*

The following are examples of general crossings:

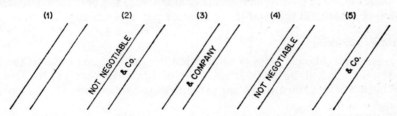

(4) takes away its character as a negotiable instrument so that a transferee does not take free of defects in the title of the transferor.

2. *Special crossings*

The following are examples of special crossings; here the bank must pay into the account of the named bank.

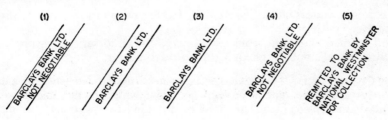

Additions such as 'A/C John Jones' or 'A/C Payee' have no statutory authority although often made on cheques. For duties and protection of bankers regarding crossed cheques *see* (vii)(b)2 and (viii).

(iii) NEGOTIATION

Like any bill of exchange a cheque is negotiated by transfer from one person to another so that the transferee becomes the holder. A cheque is negotiated by mere delivery where the last or only endorsement is in blank. It is also negotiated by mere delivery when the person named as payee is not intended to take the benefit of the bill (i.e. fictitious or non-existent payee). If 'not negotiable' is written across the face of a cheque it may still be negotiated, but the transferee takes it 'subject to equities'. Nor does a crossing with the addition of 'Pay J. Smith only' prevent further negotiation of the cheque, but the transferee runs the risk that a banker may be unwilling to receive it for collection.

(iv) HOLDERS

A holder is a person who is the payee or endorsee of a cheque and who is in possession of it. There are two types of holder:

(a) Holder in due course

This is a person who has taken the cheque, complete and regular on the face of it, in good faith and for value without knowing any defect in title at the time of negotiation; he also became holder of it before it was overdue and he had no knowledge of its having been dishonoured previously.

A holder will not be a holder in due course where the cheque is undated or overdue or where the name of the drawer or payee is missing.

(b) Holder for value

This is a holder who provides consideration for the cheque or claims through a person who has done so (s. 27 (2), Bills of Exchange Act 1882). This will apply even where a third party has provided the consideration.

(v) ENDORSEMENT

An endorsement is the signature of the endorser who is either the payee or the person to whom the cheque was endorsed by the payee. There are three main types of endorsement:

(a) special endorsement—stating the specific person or persons to whose order the cheque is payable;
(b) restrictive endorsement—preventing further negotiation on directing payment, 'Pay Smith only';
(c) endorsement in blank—consisting only of the endorser's signature without any further addition; the cheque is payable to bearer.

The Cheques Act, s. 1 (1), gives special protection to banks whereby a banker who pays a cheque, either crossed or open, which is not endorsed or is irregularly endorsed, incurs no liability provided the payment was made in good faith and in the ordinary course of business. This effectively renders redundant the provisions regarding the endorsement of cheques.

(vi) LIABILITY OF PARTIES

Principal liability is on the drawee once he has accepted the cheque; he then becomes the acceptor. When the acceptor has been applied to for payment or where the cheque has not been accepted by the drawee the other parties to it are liable. Their liability is solely in their capacity as either drawer, acceptor or endorser.

(a) The endorser

The endorser is unable to deny his title to the cheque or its validity when he endorsed it with regard to those who later endorse the cheque. Additionally, he cannot deny to a holder in due course that the previous endorsements and drawer's signature are invalid. If a cheque is dishonoured the endorser undertakes that he will compensate the holder or any later endorser who is forced to pay on the cheque, as the endorser warrants that it will be accepted on presentation.

(b) The drawer

The drawer undertakes to compensate any holder or endorser who has to pay on the cheque (provided the statutory proceedings on dishonour are taken—*see* p. 310), as he warrants acceptance of the cheque on presentation. The payee's existence and his capacity to endorse the cheque at that time cannot be denied by the drawer to the holder in due course.

(c) The acceptor

The acceptor cannot deny to the holder in due course the existence, signature or capacity of the drawer to draw the cheque, nor the drawer's capacity to endorse a cheque drawn to his order. In cases where the cheque is payable to a person other than the drawer or drawee, the acceptor similarly cannot deny the existence and capacity of the payee to endorse the cheque. An acceptor cannot be asked to pay on a cheque earlier than the date on which it was accepted by him.

(vii) POSITION OF A BANKER

(a) General

The banker is an agent for the customer for collecting payment of cheques drawn on other banks and paid in by the customer to his own account. The banker must honour cheques where the customer has sufficient funds to meet them and the cheque is valid on its face and presented within six months of being drawn (s. 36, Cheques Act 1957). If a banker dishonours a cheque in error he may be liable to pay damages. In one case a cheque drawn by a bookmaker was returned by mistake marked 'Not sufficient'. The court in a subsequent libel action awarded exemplary damages for defamation against the bank (*Davidson v. Barclays Bank*, 1940). One eminent legal authority suggests that where a cheque is refused for payment the best terms to be used by the bank to avoid litigation would be 'Irregularly drawn—requires confirmation' (*see Sheldon's Practice and Law of Banking*, 10th edition, p. 30). The banker must also give reasonable notice of the closure of the customer's account.

The banker's authority to pay cheques is ended by:

1. notice of the customer's death or lunacy;
2. notice of a bankruptcy petition being presented against the drawer (Bankruptcy Act 1914, ss. 45 and 46);
3. notice of a receiving order being made against the drawer (e.g. publication of the order in the *London Gazette* amounts to constructive notice and would be sufficient);
4. actual receipt by the banker of notice countermanding payment, either oral or written, but a banker who acts on an unauthenticated oral, or telegraphic, countermand exposes himself to risk. He must make certain that the countermand comes from the person entitled to give it.

(b) Statutory protection

Special protection has been given to bankers in view of the ease with which cheques can be forged. That provided by the Cheques Act 1957, ss. 1 and 4, is the most important.

1. Defences available to a collecting banker

The banker's main defence against the true owner of a cheque is under s. 4 of the Cheques Act 1957 which states:

'(1) Where a banker, in good faith and without negligence,
   (a) receives payment for a customer of an instrument to which this section applies; or
   (b) having credited a customer's account with the amount of such an instrument, receives payment thereof for himself; and the customer has no title or a defective title, to the instrument, the banker does not incur any liability to the true owner of the instrument by reason only of having received payment thereof.'

This section includes cheques (but not other bills of exchange) as well as other documents intended by the customer of a bank to enable another person to obtain payment of the sum stated in the document from the bank, and, additionally, it applies to banker's drafts—that is a draft payable on demand drawn by a banker on himself.

2. Defences available to a paying banker

(i) A banker who pays a cheque in accordance with the crossing, acting in good faith and without negligence, is in the same position and has the same rights as if payment of the cheque had been made to the true owner (s. 80, Bills of Exchange Act 1882).

(ii) Where a cheque payable to order bears a forged endorsement and the banker pays out in good faith and in the ordinary course of business the banker is deemed to have paid out the cheque in due course. This applies whether the payee's or subsequent payee's endorsement was forged or was made without authority (s. 60, Bills of Exchange Act 1882). Section 1 of the Cheques Act 1957 has already been noted in relation to forged or irregular endorsements where the banker incurs no liability provided payment was in good faith and in the ordinary course of business.

If, for example, a cheque issued by John Smith was drawn 'Pay Ralph Bradley or order' and was stolen by Bill Evans who endorsed the cheque 'Pay Charles Scott' and signed the name of Bradley. On Scott's presenting the cheque to the bank for payment which they credit to his account the bank would be able to debit Smith's account and be protected by s. 60.

However, if the bank could show that Smith was not the true owner they could defend an action against them for civil wrong of conversion. Apart from his criminal liability, Evans would be liable to Smith (if he were the true owner) for conversion and the court would then order him to pay damages.

If a banker pays out a cheque on which the *drawer's signature* is forged he is not given statutory protection as the cheque in this case is treated as a nullity.

(c) Negligence by a banker

A recent case (*Marfani v. Midland Bank*, 1967) laid down the principles by which the courts should judge whether or not there has been negligence on the part of a banker. These are:

1. The standard of care required of bankers is that to be derived from the ordinary practice of careful bankers; as an earlier judge has put it, 'the test of negligence is whether the transaction of paying in any given cheque was so out of the ordinary course of business that it ought to have aroused doubts in the banker's mind, and cause them to make inquiry'.

(Lord Dunedin in *Taxation Commissioners v. English, Scottish, and Australian Bank Ltd.*, 1920)

2. The standard of care required of bankers does not include the duty to subject an account to microscopic examination; 'it is not to be expected that the officials of banks should also be amateur detectives'.

(Sankey, L.J., in *Lloyds Bank Ltd. v. Chartered Bank of India, Australia, and China*, 1928)

3. In considering whether a bank has been negligent in receiving a cheque and collecting the money for it, it is permissible to scrutinize the circumstances in which a bank accepts a new customer and opens a new account. This is the point raised in *Marfani's* case.

Example

Mr. Marfani, a Pakistani running an import–export firm in Manchester, instructed his company's office manager to draw a cheque to pay *E* for company work. His manager drew a crossed cheque for £3,000 on the Bank of India which Marfani signed. His manager then went to the Midland Bank pretending to be *E* and opened an account after *A*, a restaurant owner who had known him for one month, vouched for his standing (believing him to be *E*). Midland Bank were sued for conversion by Marfani. They set up s. 4 of the Cheques Act 1957 as a defence, alleging that they had received the proceeds of the cheque in good faith and without negligence.

Held: On the facts the bank had acted in accordance with the practice of careful bankers and as they had shown themselves not to be negligent were protected by s. 4 of the Cheques Act 1957.

(*Marfani v. Midland Bank*, 1967)

4. The onus is on the defendant banker to show that he acted without negligence.

The following actions have been held in decided cases to constitute negligence:

(i) Failure to note the state of a customer's account and discover anything amiss.
(ii) Receiving a cheque drawn on a customer's employer for payment into the customer's account without checking his title to the cheque.
(iii) Failure to check the identity and status of a customer who wishes to open an account.
(iv) Failure to validate the title of a customer to a cheque where it is drawn by him as an agent for another for himself, or is drawn on his employer for a thirty party or the bearer.
(v) Where a customer alters the magnetic ink coding on a cheque to that of another branch, using ordinary ink which will not be picked up by the computer, and the bank pays the cheque after the customer has stopped it, then the bank may be liable. However, the bank may give valid notice to a customer that cheques issued may only be used for his account.

(*Burnett v. Westminster Bank*, 1966)

With regard to crossed cheques (*see* p. 311) where a cheque has been crossed 'A/c Payee' and a banker fails to take reasonable precautions on this restriction this may constitute negligence and the banker will not have the benefit of statutory protection (*see above*).

(viii) POSITION OF THE CUSTOMER

A customer is someone whose money the bank has accepted on the basis that cheques will be honoured by the bank up to the credit of the account, subject to overdraft and loan arrangements between the parties.

The customer has a duty to the bank to take reasonable care in drawing cheques to avoid forgery.

Example

An employer's clerk made out a cheque for £20 in figures leaving the space for words blank. After his employer had signed the cheque the clerk put a '1' in front of the '2' and wrote 'one hundred and twenty' in the space for words, making the cheque payable to 'ourselves' which he then cashed.

Held: The customer had been negligent in making out the cheque and made forgery easier so that the bank were entitled to debit his account with the amount.

(*London Joint Stock Bank Ltd. v. MacMillan and Arthur*, 1918)

The customer is also under a duty to indemnify his banker with respect to payments made on his behalf.

12:4 PROMISSORY NOTES

A promissory note is 'an unconditional promise in writing made by one person to another signed by the maker engaging to pay on demand or at a fixed and determinable future time a sum certain in money to or to the order of a specified person or bearer' (s. 83 (1), Bills of Exchange Act 1882).

The most common type of promissory note is a bank note. A new type of instrument treated as a promissory note is the certificate of deposit, a bearer document which, since its innovation in 1966, is a negotiable instrument. These certificates are evidence that a sum of money has been deposited with the issuing bank and undertake repayment of this sum with a fixed rate of interest on a specific day to the holder of the certificate. Under s. 55 of the Finance Act 1958 certificates of deposit were given the status of 'securities', enabling the Bank of England to approve their issue (s. 42 (1), Exchange Control Act 1947).

12:5 CREDIT CARDS AND CHEQUE CARDS

Banks such as Barclays have issued credit cards (administered by Barclaycard Ltd.) to applicants to enable them to obtain credit without resorting to the use of cheques. Retailers and other commercial organizations indicate by an authorized sign which cards they will accept. The issuing bank pays the retailer or firm the customer's purchase price less a discount and sends monthly invoices to the card holder charging interest on the unpaid balance.

Cheque cards and bankers' cards (which must be distinguished from credit cards) are issued by most main banks to guarantee payments by cheque of up to £50. These cards can also be used by the holder to obtain cash withdrawals from any branch of the leading British and Irish banks. Credit cards, cheque cards, and bankers' cards may also be used by the holders to make cash withdrawals from Continental banks participating in the Eurocheque scheme (*see also* Chapter 5). The House of Lords have differentiated between a credit card and a cheque card.

Example

The defendant used a credit card to obtain goods beyond her limit. She had been asked to return the card to the bank but did not do so. She was charged with 'obtaining a pecuniary advantage by deception' contrary to the Theft Act 1968. On conviction she appealed to the Court of Appeal (Criminal Division) which allowed her appeal. The Crown appealed to the House of Lords.

Held: The defendant's presentation of the credit card to the shop (constituting the offence) was regarded as a representation that the bank would honour the relevant voucher that the defendant signed when receiving the goods (on which the signature was compared with that on the credit card). In the case of a cheque card, where the bank undertakes to pay cheques issued in accordance with the conditions on the card, the holder represents that he has the bank's authority to enter into a contract resulting from the use of the card. Therefore a similar offence is committed as the result of such use of a cheque card as in the case of a credit card.

(*R. v. Lambie*, 1981)

12:6 BILLS IN SETS

Bills in sets are bills of exchange drawn in two or three separate parts, similarly worded. These are drawn in this country on foreign traders who also draw them on traders in the U.K. The first part of such a bill, the 'first of exchange', is sent to a banker or agent in the overseas country who presents it to the drawee for acceptance; the banker then keeps the first part until claimed by the holder of the other part or parts. On the second and third parts is written the name of the holding part 'Imperial Metals Co. Ltd.' The holder then obtains the first part from 'Imperial Metals' and together all the parts make up a bill of exchange. The system facilitates earlier acceptance of the bill than would otherwise be the case.

BANKING ACT 1979

The Banking Act 1979, parts of which came into operation on 1 October 1979, makes it an offence to take deposits unless authorized to do so by the Bank of England. Applicants who wish to obtain recognition or licensing would have had to make their claims by 1 April 1980. Guidance as to application has been issued by the Bank of England.

Under the Act only recognized banks will be allowed to use banking names, describe themselves as banks or carry on a banking business. There are exceptions in the case of overseas institutions, municipal and savings banks, as long as their exact status is made clear.

A Deposit Protection Scheme, to protect bank depositors, commenced operation on 1 April 1980. The Scheme is expected to produce initial cash resources of around £6 million.

One important change made in the position of a collecting banker is provided by s. 47 of the Act. Under this, such a banker can raise contributory negligence as a defence to an action in conversion (this removes the barrier previously imposed by s. 11 of the Torts (Interference with Goods) Act 1977; *see* 4:13). This action can be brought by the true owner of a cheque where a banker collects a cheque for a customer who has no title to it. This will only apply where a banker has been negligent himself and is not protected by s. 4 of the Cheques Act 1957 (*see* p. 314).

12:7 CONFLICT OF LAWS

Problems sometimes arise over the question of which country's law is to govern internationally transacted bills of exchange. With certain exceptions the general rules are as follows:

(i) The validity of a bill with regard to form is governed by the law of the place of *issue*.
(ii) The validity with regard to protest, endorsement, and acceptance is governed by the place where the *contract was made*.
(iii) The duties of the holder regarding presentment, protest, and notice of dishonour are governed by the law of the place where the bill is dishonoured or the act is done. It should be noted that a bill issued outside the U.K. is not

invalidated because it has not been stamped as required by the place of issue. Providing a bill adheres to the form required by the Bills of Exchange Act 1882, it may be enforced for payment and is valid between the parties to it and all holders and negotiators (s. 72 (i) (b)).

12:8 DOCUMENTARY CREDITS

(i) USE

Documentary credits are mainly used between U.K. importers and exporters and overseas firms or dealers and for covering the financing of international shipments. A banker may issue such a credit on behalf of an importer which, subject to the accompaniment of particular documents (bills of lading, certificate of insurance, etc.), will result in payment or acceptance of bills to a specific amount drawn by the export. U.K. banks are governed in their dealings with documentary credits by the Uniform Customs and Practice for Documentary Credits (1974 revision).

(ii) FUNCTION ILLUSTRATED

A buyer in Bristol wishes to purchase palm oil from Ghana for £10,000. The terms f.o.b. contract state that payment is to be confirmed by an irrevocable letter of credit against the shipping documents of the cargo—bills of lading, etc. The terms lay down that the buyer must open a credit in favour of the supplier one month prior to date of shipment. A Bristol bank then obtains completion and signature by the buyer of a request form which sets out the terms of the credit and states that it is governed by the Uniform Customs, giving the bank a charge over the goods, shipping documents, and, if required, a power of sale, since the bank is liable to the seller once the credit has been opened. A letter of credit is sent by the bank to its Ghanaian counterpart asking it to confirm the credit and notify the seller, who will be paid by his local bank if the shipping documents are presented within the period set down in the contract. The buyer does not have to pay for the consignment until the issuing bank (in this case, in Bristol) receives the shipping documents from its Ghanaian counterpart and passes them to the buyer, either against payment of the accompanying draft bill of exchange (D/P terms), or against his acceptance (D/A terms).

(iii) TYPES

There are two types of documentary credit:

(*a*) revocable, and
(*b*) irrevocable.

Of these two, only revocable credit needs further explanation as in the example we have dealt with where the U.K. bank has confirmed the buyer's credit. In such a case the bank is bound to pay, no matter what the parties may decide.

Example

Purchasers in Jordan of steel rods from British sellers were to take these in two instalments, payment being under separate confirmed credits with a London bank. After the first instalment had arrived, but before the second, the buyers sought a court injunction to stop the U.K. sellers from taking the benefit of the second credit, having already instructed the bank to issue it. *Held:* The bank was strictly bound to pay the second credit once the shipping documents had been presented and the injunction would not be allowed.

(*Hamzeh Malas & Sons v. British Imex Industries Ltd.*, 1958)

But if the credit is revocable the bank's authority to make payment, or to pay or accept bills of exchange in return for the shipping documents, may be modified or even cancelled by the buyer without notice to the export. Unless the seller tenders the exact documents required by its instructions, a correspondent bank will not accept them against payment.

Example

S, an Italian company, purchased South American fish meal from A. Co., a New York firm, under a *c.f.* contract, the buyers undertaking to open a documentary credit with a New York bank. The bills of lading were to be in order and an analysis document was required verifying the meal protein content was 70 per cent minimum protein. The bills of lading were not made out properly when submitted and the analysis document showed the protein content to be 67 per cent minimum. The bank rejected the documents and the buyers later rejected a second, but correct, offer of documents. *Held:* The bank was correct in rejecting the first offer and the second offer did not count.

(*Soprama SpA v. Marine & Animal By-Products Corporation*, 1966)

The courts will be guided by commercial custom in deciding on the positions of a banker and a seller where a banker's confirmed irrevocable credit is involved and instructions are possibly ambiguous.

Example

Buyers opened a confirmed irrevocable credit at a Sydney bank in favour of the seller covering a consignment of battery-operated light decorations. The terms of credit included presentation by the sellers of a 'Certificate of Inspection', showing that the goods and packaging had been inspected by qualified supervisors and were correct as to quantity. On arrival, the lights were discovered to be defective in quality and the bulk unmarketable. The buyers held that the bank should not have accepted the certificate of inspection as the ordinary commercial meaning of the document was that it certified that the condition and quality of the goods were commensurate with the contract requirements and of a commercially acceptable standard. *Held:* (On appeal to the Judicial Committee of the Privy Council.) The bank was not to blame for putting its own reasonable interpretation on a vague term and accepting the certificate in question as coming within the general meaning of a 'certificate of inspection'. The bank was under a contractual liability to the buyer and the seller in a transaction of this kind and owed a duty to indemnify the correspondent bank for accepting the seller's drafts. Delay by the bank might have led to a breach of these obligations, so in the circumstances the bank had carried out their instructions in a way that was reasonable on the facts of the case and the court would not put a different construction upon them.

(*Commercial Banking Company of Sydney Ltd. v. Jalsard Pty, Ltd.*, 1972)

Prevention by a foreign court of payment of an irrevocable credit does not absolve the bank paying against the documents if these are in order and the terms of the credit are satisfied.

Example

The plaintiffs exported goods from the United States to be paid by a documentary credit issued by the National Bank of Kuwait. The credit was irrevocable and the correspondent bank was the North Carolina National Bank. The Kuwait bank wished to honour the credit but a court in Kuwait had made an order of provisional attachment, preventing further payment under the credit. The question arose in the English courts as to whether the prohibition by the Kuwait court prevented the London branch of the National Bank of Kuwait from making payment.

Held: It had long been established that, when a documentary credit was issued and confirmed by a bank, the bank must pay if the documents were in order and the terms of credit satisfactory. Any disputes between the buyers and the sellers must be settled between themselves. The question in the case at issue was where the debt arising from the documentary credit was situated. If it was in Kuwait then the Kuwait prohibition applied. If it was outside such a prohibition had no effect. The provisional attachment order of the Kuwaiti court did not prevent the London branch of the National Bank of Kuwait from making payment under the documentary credit.

(*Power Curber International Ltd. v. National Bank of Kuwait*, 1981)

A number of recent cases have illustrated the position where fraud affects documentary credits.

Example

Glass Fibres, a British company, sold a glass fibre forming plant to a Peruvian company (Vitro) in Lima. Payment was under an irrevocable documentary credit issued by the Banco Continental S. A. and confirmed by the Royal Bank of Canada. The directors of Vitro requested the doubling of the purchase price of the installation in the documents and transfer of the excess amount to a 'draw down' account in favour of an American company in Miami closely associated with Vitro. The reason for this transaction was to withdraw money from Peru, in breach of the Peruvian exchange control regulations, and to transfer it to the United States. The shipment was to be made from London to Callao on or before 15 December 1976 and the credit, after amendment as opened until 31 December was $784,503.20. The only amount paid, $66,208.60, was paid to the American company. Glass Fibres assigned their rights, entitlements and benefits due under the documentary credit, notice of the assignment being given to the Royal Bank of Canada. Shipment was made on 16 December and not, as provided in the amended credit, 15 December. The bills of lading were altered to read 15 December fraudently by an employee of the loading brokers and without the knowledge of the sellers or the Royal Bank of Canada. The documents were rejected by the bank and new bills of lading were tendered bearing a signed and dated notation that the goods were shipped on 15 December. The second tender of the bills of lading were rejected by the Royal Bank of Canada because they were fraudulent, and they also refused to pay the credit on the grounds that, in their view, the transactions was unenforceable in English law.

Held: Although the bills of lading, to the knowledge of the bank, were fraudulent the bank was obliged to accept them because the fraud was not committed either by or with the knowledge of the sellers, assignees or an employee of them but, without their knowledge or approval, by a third person. In respect of unenforceability both Peru and the United Kingdom were members of the Bretton Woods Agreements. The contract was an exchange contract because, although it was for the sale of goods, in the present case the transaction was a monetary transaction in disguise and was thus unenforceable under the Bretton Woods Agreements Order (United Kingdom). The court found for the bank on this ground.

(*United City Merchants (Investments) Ltd v. Royal Bank of Canada*, 1981)

(The Court of Appeal subsequently affirmed this decision on appeal).

In a case which involved forgery of a bill of lading and shipment of cement to Nigeria the Court of Appeal considered the position of the bankers.

Example

A European bank paid out a substantial part of the amount of the credit against a set of documents including a forged bill of lading and a certificate of origin which contained fraudulent misstatements. The ships, on which the goods were supposed to have been loaded, had not called on the port in question in order to take shipment of cement, the subject matter of the contract. The bank refused payment and on being sued by the seller applied for security for costs.

Held: The bank was entitled to the remedy. Lord Denning observed, in respect of fraud, that 'documents ought to be correct and valid in respect of each parcel. If that condition is broken by forged or fraudulent documents being presented— in respect of any one parcel—[the bankers] have a defence in point of law against being liable in respect of that parcel.'

(*Establissement Esefka International Anstalt v. Central Bank of Nigeria*, 1978)

Note: It is suggested by observations of Lord Denning in this case that, if the buyer had applied for an injunction to restrain the bankers from paying, the court would probably have granted it on the basis of the evidence available.

In a recent complex case concerning a refusal to honour a letter of credit by an overseas bank, subsequent assignments of a right of action proved profitable to a third party.

Example

A transaction for the purchase and resale of cement to Nigeria was financed by a Swiss bank which was the main creditor of the purchaser, Trendtex. The Central Bank of Nigeria refused to honour the letters of credit opened in favour of Trendtex for the payment of the cement. The Swiss bank then undertook to finance proceedings against the Central Bank of Nigeria in the English courts in consideration of the assignment of Trendtex's claim against the Nigerian bank. The Court of Appeal rejected the defence raised by the Nigerian bank of sovereign immunity. Before judgement was given Trendtex and the Swiss bank made an agreement on 4 Janaury 1978, in Switzerland which stated that an offer had been received from a third party to buy Trendtex's rights against the Nigerian bank, these having been assigned to the Swiss bank in 1976. The agreement confirmed that assignment against the Swiss bank undertaking to pay $800,000 sufficient to cover all Trendtex's·creditors; 90 per cent of Trendtex's shares were to be, and were, transferred to a legal representative of the Swiss bank. The agreement gave exclusive jurisdiction to the courts of Geneva. On 8, January 1978, the Swiss bank assigned the rights of action against the Nigerian bank to a third party for $1,100,000—a profit of $300,000. Subsequently on 12 February the legal representative of the Swiss bank visited Nigeria and negotiated a settlement with the Nigerian authorities under which they paid $8,000,000. The second assignment of the right of action netted the third party, whose identity was not disclosed in the English proceedings, $6,900,000. Trendtex then commenced action against the Swiss bank. The latter applied for an order that proceedings in the English courts be stayed. Trendtex chiefly argued that the assignment of a bare right of action in the English courts was illegal and void on the ground that it constituted maintainance. This has been defined as 'improperly stirring up litigation and strife by giving aid to one party to bring or defend a claim without just cause or excuse'. Trendtex further argued that if the January 4 agreement was void the clause in favour of exclusive jurisdiction of the courts of Geneva was similarly void.

Held: Since the Swiss bank had financed the action in England it had a legitimate, genuine and sufficient interest in the suit. Accordingly, the assignment of the cause of action to the Swiss bank did not constitute maintainance and was valid.

(Trendtex Corporation v. Credit Suisse, 1980)

Note: on the facts of the above case it would appear to be an unfortunate result if rights of action in the English courts could be traded in the world markets like transferable securities.

12:9 COLLECTION ARRANGEMENTS

The law relating to the collection of overseas bills and other credit documents is covered by the code for the collection of 'commercial paper' (as these instruments are commonly known) drawn by the International Chamber of Commerce and accepted by the British Bankers' Association and the Accepting Houses Committee. The Uniform Rules for the Collection of Commercial

Paper, as the code is entitled, has been adopted by many foreign banks and has gained wide international acceptance.

The Rules are binding on the bank's customers and other parties if all have agreed, either expressly or impliedly, to be bound by them. The practice is for a bank accepting commercial paper for collection to sign and complete a letter of instructions containing the following undertaking: 'Collections are handled subject to Uniform Rules for the Collection of Commercial Paper (1967 revision) International Chamber of Commerce Brochure No: 254, on countries that conform.'

When the commercial paper is sent on it has to be accompanied by a remittance letter which states that its sending on is subject to the terms of the Uniform Rules together with instructions for collection. Banks in the U.K. accepting commercial paper for collection from foreign banks on terms similar to those of the Rules will be treated as collecting banks for that purpose.

QUESTIONS

1. (*a*) What is a negotiable instrument? What are the main characteristics of a negotiable instrument? Define the term, *bill of exchange*, and comment upon its main features.

   (*b*) Thomas signed a bill of exchange and asked Ulick, the drawee, to insert Victor's name as payee. Ulick took the bill of exchange, inserted the words, 'Pay bearer' on it, and then handed it to his brother, Walter. A thief stole the bill of exchange from Walter's house and handed it to Xerxes in payment for a car. Xerxes was aware of the thief's criminal record until he was converted to a respectable mode of life fifteen years earlier under the influence of a priest. Xerxes did not suspect that the bill of exchange was stolen property when he handed it to Yoland as a gift. What title, if any, did Ulick, Victor, Walter, Xerxes and Yoland have to the instrument?

   (Certificate in Marketing, Part II, November 1978)

2. (*a*) 'Guidelines exist which clearly indicate to the banker the precise moment at which he ceases to have authority to debit a customer's account.' Discuss.

   (*b*) Reginald is a customer at the Hellfire Bank, Ltd. He discovers that he has lost his wallet in which he carried his credit card bearing his signature and cheque book. Immediately, he writes a letter to inform the bank of the loss. The letter is not opened immediately as it was temporarily mislaid until mid-morning; by that time, a rogue has come into the bank and presented a cheque on which Reginald's signature has been forged so cleverly that it is virtually indistinguishable from the genuine signature unless the signature is scrutinized very carefully. Is the bank liable to Reginald whose account has been debited by the amount for which the cheque was drawn?

   (Diploma in Marketing, Part II, November 1975)

3. (*a*) What is a 'holder in due course' and in what circumstances does his title become defective?

   (*b*) *A* owed *D* £200 and accepted a bill drawn on him by *D* for this amount.

D skilfully altered the amount to £250 and endorsed the bill to *X* who took it in good faith and in turn endorsed it to *Y* in payment for goods supplied by *Y*. What is *Y*'s position in relation (i) to *A* and (ii) to *D* and *X*?

(Institute of Marketing, May 1970)

4. Discuss the nature of the duty owed by a banker to his customer in relation to cheques.

C and *D* were partners: *R* was their clerk. *R* forged a bearer cheque for £100 in *C*'s name. *D* saw the cheque on *R*'s desk and asked him when *C* signed the cheque. *R* replied that *C* had signed it 'yesterday'. In fact *C* had been absent from the office all that day and had *D* given the matter a moment's thought he would have realized it.

R has now cashed the cheque and absconded with the £100. Advise the Bank as to its liability.

(Chartered Institute of Secretaries, December 1970)

5. (*a*) What significant difference between the two documents is to be under stood from the statement that 'a bill of lading may be negotiated, but a cheque is negotiable'? Illustrate your explanation with examples.

(*b*) A cheque drawn payable to 'P. Palmer or Order' was received by Palmer and endorsed by him preparatory to presentation to the bank for payment. On his way to the bank, Palmer lost the cheque which was found by F. Farley, who passed it to T. Thomas, a house furnisher, in exchange for goods to the value of the cheque. Upon learning that the cheque had been passed to Thomas, Palmer sought to recover it from him, or its equivalent in value. Examine Palmer's position.

(Diploma in Marketing, May 1969)

6. Consider the following:

22 July—Exporter consigns goods to importer in Durban and sends him bill of lading together with a bill of exchange for his acceptance and return.

27 July—The importer is insolvent and fails to accept and return the bill of exchange. He nevertheless sells the bill of lading to *X*, who paid him the price for the goods.

15 August—Not having received the importer's acceptance, the exporter endorsed the copy of the bill of lading he had retained and sent it to *Y*, a buyer whom he knew and could trust, with authority to claim the goods upon arrival.

28 August—The ship arrived at Durban and *Y* obtained delivery of the goods.

X now demands the goods from *Y*, but *Y* refuses to part with them, contending that he stood in the exporter's shoes and had exercised the exporter's right to stop the goods in transitu.

To whom do the goods belong—to *X* who has paid the original buyer, or to *Y*, to whom the exporter now wishes to sell them? Give the reasons for your answer.

(Diploma in Marketing, November 1971)

7. Explain the purpose and value of a documentary letter of credit:
    (*a*) to the buyer who arranges for it to be issued; and
    (*b*) to the seller in whose favour it is issued.

(Institute of Bankers (Part II), September 1968)

Further Reading

1 CONTRACT

Charlesworth, J. *Mercantile Law*, 13th edition (Stevens, 1977), Part 1.
Powell-Smith, V. *Law Students' Companion: Contract*, 5th edition (Butterworth, 1977).
Yates, D. *Exclusion Clauses*, 2nd edition (Stevens, 1982).
The Law Commission and the Scottish Law Commission: *Second Report on Exemption Clauses* (H.C. 605) (published 5.8.75). H.M.S.O.
Lawson, R. G. *Exclusion Clauses after the Unfair Contract Terms Act* (Oyez, 1978).
Thompson, P. J. K. *The Unfair Contract Terms Act 1977* (Butterworth, 1978).

2 RESTRICTIVE TRADE PRACTICES

Charlesworth, J. *Mercantile Law*, 13th edition (Stevens, 1977), Part 4.
Korah, V. *Competition Law of Britain and the Common Market* (Elek/Matthew Bender, 1975).
Bellamy, C. and Child, G. D. *Common Market Law of Competition*, 2nd edition (Sweet & Maxwell/Matthew Bender, 1978).
Cunningham, J. P. *The Fair Trading Act 1973* (Sweet & Maxwell, 1974, with 1978 supplement).

3 CONTRACTS OF EMPLOYMENT

Charlesworth, J. *Mercantile Law*, 13th edition (Stevens, 1977), Chapter 12.
Rideout, R. W. *Labour Law*, 3rd edition (Sweet & Maxwell, 1979).
Hepple, B. A. and O'Higgins, P. *Employment Law*, 3rd edition (Sweet & Maxwell, 1979).

4 SALE OF GOODS

Charlesworth, J. *Mercantile Law*, 13th edition (Stevens, 1977), Chapter 15.
Atiyah, P. S. *Sale of Goods*, 5th edition (Pitman, 1975).
Lowe, R. *Commercial Law*, 5th edition (Sweet & Maxwell, 1976), Chapter 3.
The Law Commission and the Scottish Law Commission: *Liability for Defective Products* (Cmnd. 6831) (published June 1977).
Royal Commission on Civil Liability and Compensation for Personal Injury (Cmnd. 1754) (The Pearson Report) (published March 1977). H.M.S.O.

Association Européene d'Etudes Juridiques et Fiscales, *Product Liability in Europe* (Kluwer Harrap, 1975).
Miller, C. J. and Lovell, P. A. *Product Liability* (Butterworth, 1978).
Munro, C. and Teff, H. *Thalidomide: the legal aftermath* (Saxon House, 1976).
Benjamin, *Sale of Goods* (Sweet & Maxwell, 1981).
The Law Commission and Scottish Law Commission, *Sale and Supply of Goods*, Working Paper No 85 (published October 1983).

5 CONSUMER CREDIT

Charlesworth, J. *Mercantile Law*, 13th edition (Stevens, 1977), Chapter 17.
Goode, R. M. *Consumer Credit Act 1974* (Butterworth, 1974).
Dobson, A. P. *Sale of Goods and Consumer Credit*, 2nd edition (Sweet & Maxwell, 1979).

6 AGENCY

Charlesworth, J. *Mercantile Law*, 13th edition (Stevens, 1977), Chapter 13.
Fridman, G. H. L. *The Law of Agency*, 4th edition (Butterworth, 1976).

7 CARRIAGE

Charlesworth, J. *Mercantile Law*, 13th edition (Stevens, 1977), Part 8.
Ridley, J. *Law of the Carriage of Goods by Land, Sea and Air*, 5th edition (Shaw, 1978).
Palmer, N. E. (Livermore, J.) *Bailment* (Law Book Co., 1979, Chapters 15, 17, 18.
Hill, D. J. *Freight Forwarders* (Stevens, 1972).
Payne, W. and Ivamy, E. R. H. *Carriage of Goods by Sea* (Butterworth, 1976).

8 PATENTS, COPYRIGHT, TRADE MARKS, AND PASSING OFF

White, T. A. B. and Jacob Robin, *Patents, Trade Marks, Copyright and Industrial Designs*, 2nd edition (Sweet & Maxwell, 1978).
White, T. A. B. *Patents for Inventions and the Protection of Industrial Designs*, 4th edition (Stevens, 1974).
Walton, A. M. and Laddie H. I. *Patent Law of Europe and the United Kingdom* (Butterworth, 1978, supplement service).
Flint, M. F. *A User's Guide to Copyright* (Butterworth, 1979).
Cawthra, B. I. *Industrial Property Rights in the E.E.C.* (Gower Press Ltd., 1973).
Cornish, W. R. *Intellectual Property, Patents, Copyright, Trade Marks and Allied Rights* (Sweet & Maxwell, 1982).
Whitford Committee Report on Copyright and Design Law (Cmnd. 6732). H.M.S.O.

9 TRADE DESCRIPTIONS AND ADVERTISING

O'Keefe, J. A. *Trade Descriptions Act 1968* (Butterworth, 1968 (supplement service)).
Woolley, D. *Advertising Law Handbook*, 2nd edition (Business Books, 1976).
Lawson, R. G. *Advertising and Labelling Laws in the Common Market* (Jordan, 1975).

10 COMMERCIAL ASSOCIATIONS

Pennington, R. R. *Company Law*, 4th edition (Butterworth, 1979).
Gower, L. C. B. *Modern Company Law*, 4th edition (Stevens, 1979 with 1981 supplement).
Arden, M. and Eccles, G. W. *Tolley's Companies Act 1980* (Tolley Publishing Co., 1980).
Ryan, C. and Morris, R. *The Companies Act 1981* (Sweet & Maxwell, 1982).
Smith, F. E. *Cracknell's Law Students' Companion: Company Law*, 2nd edition (Butterworth, 1976).

11 INSURANCE

Charlesworth, J. *Mercantile Law*, 13th edition (Stevens, 1977), part 7.
Ivamy, E. R. H. *Casebook on Insurance Law*, 3rd edition (Butterworth, 1977).
Birds, J. *Modern Insurance Law* (Sweet & Maxwell, 1982).

12 NEGOTIABLE INSTRUMENTS

Charlesworth, J. *Mercantile Law*, 13th edition (Stevens, 1977), Part 5.
Reeday, T. G. *Law Relating to Banking*, 3rd edition (Butterworth, 1976).
Richardson, D. *A Guide to Negotiable Instruments*, 5th edition (Butterworth, 1976).
Mcgrath, M. and Ryder, F. R. *Byles on Bills of Exchange* (Sweet & Maxwell, 1979).

E.E.C. LAW

The literature on the Common Market is extensive; only basic references are given:
European Community Treaties, 2nd edition (Sweet & Maxwell/Matthew Bender, 1975).
Simmonds, K. R. (editor) *Encyclopedia of European Community Law* (Sweet & Maxwell, 1973 (supplement service)).
E.E.C. Information Unit: *E.E.C. Your Questions Answered* (*A Businessman's Guide*) obtainable from the Department of Industry, 1 Victoria Street, London SW1H 0ET.

The European Commission also issues annual reports obtainable from H.M.S.O.

Table of Cases

Table of Statutes

Index